METAMORPHOSES

A. D. MELVILLE was a scholar of King's College, Cambridge, where he gained a double First in Classics and won a Craven Studentship. His love of the Classics was kindled at Charterhouse and he discovered the seductive charms of Ovid at King's. After a long career as a solicitor in London, interrupted by distinguished service in the Second World War, he returned to Ovid, and his translations of the *Metamorphoses*, the *Love Poems*, and *Sorrows of an Exile (Tristia)* are all available in World's Classics.

E. J. KENNEY is a Fellow of Peterhouse and Emeritus Kennedy Professor of Latin in the University of Cambridge. His previous publications include a critical edition of Ovid's amatory poems (Oxford Classical Texts, 1961), an edition with commentary of Lucretius, *De Rerum Natura III* (1971), *The Classical Text. Aspects of editing in the age of the printed book* (1974), *The Ploughman's Lunch. Moretum: a poem ascribed to Virgil* (1984); and he is Editor of and a contributor to *The Cambridge History of Classical Literature*, Vol. II, *Latin Literature* (1982).

'This ought to become the standard modern complete verse translation.'
Greece & Rome

'Melville's new translation enables us to understand this unique and witty poetic narrative with a fresh approach. His use of modern idiom and of occasional rhyming couplets for added special effect are a great bonus and a delight to readers. The text . . . is highly recommended to both students and readers who have a special interest in the subject.'
Greek Review

'Melville has produced a fluent and readable version which conveys a sense both of Ovid's wit and of his elegance.' *Classical Review*

'Melville has chosen blank verse, pleasantly varied by rhymed couplets to round off each sequence. His narrative is taut, his vocabulary vivid and flexible, his speeches pungent or powerful, and his command of wit a delight.' *Classical World*

OXFORD WORLD'S CLASSICS

OVID

Metamorphoses

Translated by
A. D. MELVILLE

With an Introduction and Notes by
E. J. KENNEY

OXFORD
UNIVERSITY PRESS

Great Clarendon Street, Oxford OX2 6DP

Oxford University Press is a department of the University of Oxford.
It furthers the University's objective of excellence in research, scholarship,
and education by publishing worldwide in

Oxford New York

Athens Auckland Bangkok Bogotá Buenos Aires Calcutta
Cape Town Chennai Dar es Salaam Delhi Florence Hong Kong Istanbul
Karachi Kuala Lumpur Madrid Melbourne Mexico City Mumbai
Nairobi Paris São Paulo Shanghai Singapore Taipei Tokyo Toronto Warsaw

with associated companies in Berlin Ibadan

Oxford is a registered trade mark of Oxford University Press
in the UK and in certain other countries

Published in the United States
by Oxford University Press Inc., New York

Translation, Translator's Note, Glossary, and Index of names
© A. D. Melville 1986
Introduction, Historical Sketch, and Explanatory Notes
© E. J. Kenney 1986

First published 1986 by Oxford University Press
First issued as a World's Classics paperback 1987
Reissued as an Oxford World's Classics paperback 1998

British Library Cataloguing in Publication Data

Data available

Library of Congress Cataloging in Publication Data

Ovid, 43–17 or 18 B.C.
Metamorphoses.
Bibliography: p.
Includes index.
I. Title.
PA6522.M2M45 1986 873'.01 85–15479
ISBN 0–19–283472–X

5 7 9 10 8 6

Printed in Great Britain by
Cox & Wyman Ltd.
Reading, Berkshire

UXORI NATISQUE CARISSIMIS

ACKNOWLEDGEMENT

Dr S. E. Hinds has kindly read the Introduction and the Explanatory Notes in draft, and I am indebted to him for many helpful criticisms and acute suggestions, the majority of which I have gratefully adopted.

E.J.K.

CONTENTS

METAMORPHOSES

HISTORICAL SKETCH

OVID (Publius Ovidius Naso) was born on 20 March 43 BC at Sulmo (now Sulmona) in the Abruzzi. The year of his birth was long remembered as that in which both consuls fell fighting Antony at Mutina, leaving Octavian (the future Augustus) in a position of strength which he exploited to become Triumvir and eventually sole ruler of the Roman world. In view of Ovid's fate at his hands it is not surprising that in the poem which is our chief source for his life (*Tristia* iv. 10) he lays some stress on these circumstances—more especially as there was a contemporary report that the deaths of both consuls had in fact been compassed by Octavian (Tacitus, *Annals* i. 10. 2, Suetonius, *Augustus* 11). By the time that Ovid came to manhood the combined forces of Antony and Cleopatra had been routed at Actium (31 BC) and the Roman Republic had been transformed into an (ostensibly) benevolent despotism.

Ovid's family was prosperous, and he was sent to Rome to study under the leading teachers of the day. For Roman boys education then and for centuries to come was verbal, literary and rhetorical, its principal aim the production of fluent and convincing extempore speakers. The reminiscences of the elder Seneca (*Controversies* ii. 2. 8–12, ix. 5. 17) illustrate vividly the effects of this kind of training on Ovid, in whom it encouraged and developed an obviously innate delight in words, their metrical arrangement and artistic manipulation. Possibly the encouragement went too far: Quintilian thought that he would have been a better poet 'if he had controlled his genius rather than letting it control him' (*Institutio Oratoria* x. 1. 98). His education was rounded off in the manner usual for the governing class, by the then equivalent of the Grand Tour through Greek lands. There followed on his return to Rome some minor judicial posts, but he soon decided (in spite of his father's discouragement) that his true vocation was poetry and abandoned his official career to dedicate himself to literature.

His earliest work, the *Amores* (Loves) appeared in its original (five-book) form when he was a very young man, perhaps as early as *c.*25 BC. There followed a second edition in three books; the *Heroides* (Letters of Heroines); the *Ars Amatoria* (Art of

Love) i–ii and (later) iii; the *Remedia Amoris* (Remedies of Love), all extant; and the lost tragedy *Medea*. There is great uncertainty as to the chronology and sequence of these works, but even supposing a more even spread of activity than has been generally assumed, extending possibly from *c.*15 BC to AD 2, the *terminus post quem non* of the *Remedia*, this is an extraordinary feat of literary productivity.

From about AD 1 onwards Ovid was simultaneously working on the *Metamorphoses* and the *Fasti* (Calendar), a long elegiac poem in twelve books on Roman festivals and cults, an aetiological work inspired by Callimachus' *Aetia* (see Introduction, p. xxii). This was half completed and the *Metamorphoses* (so, in spite of Ovid's disclaimers, we must believe) substantially ready for publication, when disaster struck. In AD 8 Ovid, who was by then, since the deaths of Virgil and Horace, indisputably the premier poet of Rome, was suddenly sent into exile at Tomis (now Constanța in Romania) on the Black Sea. The sentence was decided and pronounced personally by Augustus, the two causes of offence being *carmen*, a poem, the *Ars Amatoria*, and *error*, an unspecified indiscretion. The mystery surrounding this episode has never been cleared up; though Ovid in his exile poetry is sometimes surprisingly bold in pleading his case, and many of his contemporaries must have been in the secret, he nowhere allows a clear inference as to the nature of the *error*. The picture that emerges from such hints as he does give is that of involuntary complicity in some scandal, in which politics and morals were interlocked, affecting the Imperial house and Augustus in particular.

Of the poetry written by Ovid at Tomis the five books of *Tristia* (Sorrows) and the four of *Epistulae ex Ponto* (Letters from Pontus) were devoted to pleading his case, ostensibly before the Emperor, really before the bar of public opinion, to which he can be seen repeatedly appealing over Augustus' head. Tone and theme are constantly varied, but central to the whole campaign is Ovid's consciousness of his poetic vocation and his confidence in his identity as a poet. The second book of the *Tristia*, a single long elegy, is a witty and at times astonishingly outspoken defence of himself and his poetry. Standing apart from these works is the *Ibis*, a curse invoking many dire fates culled from Greek myth on an unidentified (and probably fictitious) enemy; its purpose was in all likelihood to uphold his reputation as a learned poet and so his claims to special consideration by the public and by posterity. Public and private pleading alike proved powerless to appease Augustus or Tiberius, who succeeded him in AD 14, and Ovid spent the rest of his life at Tomis, dying there in AD 17.

He was three times married, and had one daughter.

INTRODUCTION

The elation of comedy is saying hooray for life in its own terms, however incongruous and absurd. *Donald Davie*

I

WHEN the present writer was at school, the proposition that Ovid was a better poet than Virgil, or even that the *Metamorphoses* was fit to stand alongside the *Aeneid*, would not have been generally entertained. It had not always been so. In 1873 James Henry, the great commentator, who devoted his life (to say nothing of the life of his daughter Katharine) to the explication of the *Aeneid*, could write of Ovid that he was 'a more natural, more genial, more cordial, more imaginative, more playful poet . . . than [Virgil] or any other Latin poet'. Few more comprehensive tributes have come his way. In 1799 Gilbert Wakefield, writing to Charles James Fox from Dorchester gaol (where he was undergoing imprisonment for seditious libel), called Ovid 'to my fancy, the first Poet of all Antiquity'; and half a century earlier than that the young Edward Gibbon had 'derived more pleasure from Ovid's Metamorphoses' than from the *Aeneid*. The word 'pleasure', of course, gives the game away: in Gibbon's day and for long afterwards English boys were not sent to school to enjoy themselves, and the *Metamorphoses* is not in any obvious sense edifying literature. It is only in recent years that critics, having conceded that the poem is, after all, entertaining, have also turned to enquire seriously what, if anything, it is about. Some of the obstacles encountered by such an enquiry are of Ovid's making, for his love of teasing is almost Nabokovian.

The quality in which Wakefield thought that 'no poet of antiquity seems capable of supporting the contest with Ovid' was *invention*. This is a technical term of classical rhetoric meaning, not the faculty of making things up, but that of finding them: the art of discovering and combining the materials from which an argument could most effectively be constructed. This faculty Wakefield bracketed with 'copiousness of thought' as the 'first endowment' of a poet, in which he judged Ovid preeminent. The resources of material at Ovid's disposal for this undertaking were immense—the whole field of Greek and (what there was of it) Roman myth and legend, so far as it was available in written form—and he exploited them with a combination, truly professional, of profusion and economy. Economy is apparent from the beginning in the apportionment of material, where it might suit either poem, between the *Metamorphoses* and the *Fasti;*[1] profusion in the repeated 'throw-away' references to stories or variant versions which for one reason or another he did not choose to include or to tell in full.[2] A hint of how much Ovid must have read only to discard for the purposes immediately in hand is offered by his *Ibis*. This poem, his swan-song as a learned poet, was written in the early years of his exile, we may guess in order to demonstrate to his enemies and detractors that his powers were not exhausted. Tomis had no libraries, and Ovid had brought few books with him into exile. The mythological learning of *Ibis*, as extensive as it is obscure, is a sample of what was surplus in his reading to the requirements of the two long poems, material which at the time of his sudden banishment was in his notebooks or his head. A lesser artist might have been overwhelmed by this *embarras de richesses*. Ovid's 'copiousness of thought' was equal to the copiousness of his materials and to the scale of his undertaking. The *Metamorphoses* is without doubt the most witty and ingenious book that has come down to us from the ancient world.

II

In one sense there is no mystery as to what the *Metamorphoses* is 'about', because the author tells us: it is about metamorphosis, transformation, change. So much emerges from the brief Proem (i. 1–4). Yet the very brevity and allusiveness of that introduction should put us on our guard. There is one striking ambiguity in Ovid's Latin with which no translator can be expected to cope. The first four words of the poem, *In noua fert animus*, can and indeed must be read as an autonomous statement as well as part of the whole sentence: 'My inspiration carries (me) on to new things'. The fourth verse underlines this pronouncement by

---

[1] Occasionally a story figures in both poems, e.g. Callisto (ii. 401–530, *Fasti* ii. 155–92), Proserpine (v. 332–571, *Fasti* iv. 417–620); see on the latter the Explanatory Notes, v. 341–571. Subsequent references to the Explanatory Notes are in the form 'v. 341–571 n.'

[2] See, e.g., ii. 589–90 n., iv. 55–168 n., 276 n., vii. 362 n., 465 n., viii. 261 n., x. 65–71 n., 729 n., xiii. 715 n., 717 n.

declaring a paradox: *ad mea perpetuum deducite tempora carmen*, 'Bring down to my own times a continuous song'. This is to be a 'continuous' poem in the innocuous chronological sense, but *perpetuum*, in this context, must also be read in the technical literary sense as connoting orthodox epic.[3] That, however, contradicts the further implication of *deducite*, that the poem, when 'brought down', that is finished, will be a *deductum carmen* in another sense, the 'fine-spun', unpretending—in a word, *unepic* —kind of poetry written by Callimachus, the Alexandrian scholar-poet to whom Catullus and subsequent Latin poets had, with varying degrees of explicitness, pledged allegiance. What sort of a poem is this which thus, obliquely and by way of verbal paradox, apparently subscribes to two incompatible poetics, will remain to be seen. At least the lines serve as a warning not to take the poet too literally;[4] and after all it was Callimachus himself who had remarked that it is the poet's *métier* to deceive.

There was nothing new in the idea that the universe was in a state of continual flux. This was the teaching of Heraclitus, and Ovid's admired Lucretius, following in the steps of his master Epicurus, had proclaimed that change was inseparable from mortality:

> nam quodcumque suis mutatum finibus exit,
> continuo hoc mors est illius quod fuit ante.

'For if anything is so transformed as to overstep its own limits, this means the immediate death of what it was before.'[5]

Where Ovid parted company from Lucretius was in the application of this doctrine to the human soul. This, it may be suggested, is the point of a passage of the *Metamorphoses* that has puzzled some critics and bored others, but which delighted Dryden and C. J. Fox, who 'always considered it as the finest part of the whole poem', the great speech of Pythagoras (xv. 75–478). What is formally a long digression is accommodated to the argument of the poem with great skill, prophetically bridging the long interval

[3] For this sense of *perpetuus* compare Horace, *Odes* i. 7. 6 and the parallel passages quoted by Nisbet and Hubbard in their commentary (Oxford, 1970).

[4] Or rather not according to the obvious literal sense of his words; what he is really getting at may emerge, as here, by taking him very literally indeed. The same is true of Lucretius, as Ovid cannot fail to have noticed.

[5] Lucretius, *De Rerum Natura* i. 670–1; the lines recur at i. 792–3, ii. 753–4, iii. 519–20. Compare iii. 756 *quod mutatur enim dissoluitur, interit ergo*, 'whatever changes is disintegrated and therefore destroyed'.

between Numa and Augustus and achieving a climax (ll. 448–9) on a theme that informs and dominates the whole book: apotheosis, divinization, the supreme change to which human beings can aspire. The speech turns on the premiss that in all the constantly changing universe one thing remains unchanged, *anima*, the soul:

> our souls
> Are still the same for ever, but adopt
> In their migrations ever-varying forms ...
> We too ourselves, who of this world are part,
> Not only flesh and blood, but pilgrim souls ...
>
> (xv. 171–2, 456–7)

All else must eventually yield to the assaults of time:

> Time, the devourer, and the jealous years
> With long corruption ruin all the world
> And waste all things in slow mortality.
>
> (xv. 234–6)

At the very end of the poem, using words clearly meant to recall these lines,[6] Ovid exempts his own work from this general law:

> Now stands my task accomplished, such a work
> As not the wrath of Jove, nor fire nor sword
> Nor the devouring ages can destroy.
>
> (xv. 871–2)

Horace (*Odes* iii. 30. 6–9) and Virgil (*Aeneid* ix. 446–9) expected to be read as long as the power of Rome endured. By making Pythagoras lead up to Rome as the last of a series of great powers that have in their turn declined and fallen (xv. 420 ff.), Ovid allows the reader to infer that in the end Rome too must bow to the inexorable law of change. Only his poetry, identified with his soul, the 'better part' of himself, will live on to eternity, *per omnia saecula*:

> Let, when it will, that day, that has no claim
> But to my mortal body, end the span
> Of my uncertain years. Yet I'll be borne,
> The finer part of me, above the stars,
> Immortal, and my name shall never die.

---

[6] xv. 234 *tempus edax rerum tuque inuidiosa uetustas*; cf. 872 *nec poterit ferrum nec edax abolere uetustas*.

Wherever through the lands beneath her sway
The might of Rome extends, my words shall be
Upon the lips of men. If truth at all
Is stablished by poetic prophecy,
My fame shall live to all eternity.

(xv. 873-9)

The lines are richly ambiguous. In the words 'I'll be borne . . .
above the stars, / Immortal' we may discern a hint of the
Pythagorean doctrine that a soul 'might ultimately shake off the
body altogether . . . and attain the final bliss of losing itself in
the universal, eternal and divine soul to which by its own nature
it belonged'.[7] The last word of the poem, however, is *uiuam*, 'I
shall live', suggesting a more personal mode of survival through
poetry. It is idle to ask what Ovid 'believed'. He was neither a
devotee nor a philosopher, but a poet who, when it suited him to
do so, used the language and the ideas of religion or philosophy
to lend authority to his fixed convictions. These flowed from his
instinctive understanding of his own nature and his own gifts.
He was a poet because that was what he was called to be. In
his famous 'autobiography' he records how his father had tried
to cure him of his obsession with poetry and what came of it:

motus eram dictis totoque Helicone relicto
    scribere temptabam uerba soluta modis.
sponte sua carmen numeros ueniebat ad aptos,
    et quod temptabam scribere uersus erat.

'Obediently I threw Helicon over and tried to write prose. Each
time a poem would come willy-nilly in correct metre, and all my
attempts at prose were verse.'   (*Tristia* iv. 10. 23-6)

Poetry was his life, till death—and after.

III

The *Metamorphoses* conforms to the conventional pattern of
classical epic in so far as it is a long poem in hexameters of high
literary pretensions. That is as far as conformity extends. Aristotle
did not so much lay it down as take it for granted that epic, like

---

[7] W. K. C. Guthrie, *A History of Greek Philosophy*, i (Cambridge 1962),
202-3.

tragedy, should be serious; the *Metamorphoses*, if it is anything, is high comedy. Unity too he took as read; the *Metamorphoses* is *ex hypothesi* and of set purpose episodic. More fundamentally still, it is of its nature anti-generic. At i. 452 the theme of love makes the first of its many appearances, and in introducing it Ovid makes a pointed reference to his own poetic début as a love-elegist: Apollo's rebuke to Cupid for not minding his own business echoes the poet's own reproach on the same grounds in the opening elegy of the *Amores*.[8] This is an implicit assertion of the poet's freedom (in defiance, if need be, of the normal demarcations set forth in the *Remedia Amoris* 371 ff.) to handle each theme in the style which it seemed to him to demand: elegiac, pastoral, tragic—or indeed, as in the battles of Books V and XII, epic itself. The *perpetuum carmen* turns out to be, among other things, an anthology of genres.

In time and space the scope of the *Metamorphoses* is comprehensive, being nothing less than universal history from the Creation to the present. That at least is its ostensible scope; its real subject is the microcosm of human psychology. People, and how they react under stress, were what interested Ovid. That had been the theme of his earlier poetry, especially of the lost tragedy *Medea* and the *Heroides* (Letters of Heroines). The *Metamorphoses* does not, like the *Aeneid* or the *Pharsalia* or the *Thebaid* (in their different ways), state a case; rather it asks questions, exploring and analysing for the most part without comment or commitment. Ovid depicts a universe in which human beings, and more often than not the gods who are supposed to be in charge, are at the mercy of blind or arbitrary or cruel, and always irresistible, forces. E. M. Forster might have had the *Metamorphoses* in mind when he wrote to Siegfried Sassoon that 'the devil who rules this planet has contrived that those who are powerless shall suffer'. In this dangerous and uncertain world the happy ending is the exception (iv. 575 n.). Repeatedly the emphasis is on deception and violence; the reader soon comes to realize that the description of an idyllic landscape is a prelude to rape or bloodshed (iii. 407 n., etc.). Nothing is ever quite what it seems; nobody's identity is ever wholly secure.

---

[8] i. 456; cf. *Amores* i. 1. 5. I am obliged to Dr S. E. Hinds for pointing out to me the implications of this and other parallels between the two passages. For Ovid's penchant for 'self-reference' in the *Metamorphoses* see below, pp. xxvii–xxviii.

IV

The true Midas is the poet, the true golden touch his trans-
forming art. Ovid's achievement in the *Metamorphoses* is to
transmute what ought to be a profoundly depressing vision of
existence into a cosmic comedy of manners. To read him is to be
perpetually reminded of Horace Walpole's favourite saying, that
life is a comedy to those that think, a tragedy to those that feel.
One attitude is as philosophical as the other, and neither calls
for apology. This Ovidian parody or burlesque of the actual world
indeed exploits the incredible and the absurd to a degree that
some have found inordinate. Ovid himself had no doubt about
poet's licence:

> exit in immensum fecunda licentia uatum,
>   obligat historica nec sua uerba fide.

'The poet's fruitful freedom knows no bounds and takes no oath
to tell it as it happened.'   (*Amores* iii. 12. 41–2)

Yet under the wild fantasy and the vast exaggerations, the black
humour and the occasional cruelty, Ovid's is a serious way of
looking at the world, or at least a way that can be taken seriously.
The delicate interplay of humour and pathos in stories such as
those of Io or Callisto or Ceyx and Alcyone; the ambivalent treat-
ment of Hercules; the even-handedness with which the balance
of sympathy is held between Ajax and Ulysses: these and many
other ambiguities reflect the detachment of a mind fascinated
by the vicissitudes, paradoxes, and contrarieties of existence.
These are visible and comprehensible phenomena, explicable on
the hypothesis of an endless and inexorable flux (having much in
common, though the point emerges only by implication, with
Epicurean atomism) in created things. The quest for a deeper
underlying meaning, if it exists, Ovid left to others. It was enough
for him to illustrate and explore the reflection on the psycho-
logical plane of that universal physical turbulence. This may help
to account for the length and elaboration of Pythagoras' speech.
The immense and unpredictable variety of human (and divine)
behaviour so entertainingly reviewed in the first fourteen books
of the poem is finally accounted for and justified only after the
evidence has been produced. Pythagoras' exposition, that is to say,
may be seen as a kind of theodicy.

V

These behavioural characteristics have their counterpart in the poet's management of language and literary structure. Apart from the tragedy *Medea* all Ovid's earlier work (and the poetry written in exile) was in elegiac couplets: a discontinuous medium, in which each couplet is a semi-autonomous unit. The epic hexameter called for a fundamentally different technique, in which the relationship between the syntactical units (clauses and sentences) and the metrical units (the individual verses) was more flexible, more subtle, and more expressive. Rather as Macaulay invented the English paragraph, so Virgil invented the Latin verse period, by establishing a balance of length and emphasis between the units of epic discourse that satisfied the mind and the ear. To Ovid this balance clearly approved itself, for he did not in essentials alter it. The average length of his periods in the *Metamorphoses* is almost identical with Virgil's in the *Aeneid*, between three and four verses. What differs is the distribution of emphasis, resulting in a more even tempo and a higher overall speed.

This is the index of a fundamental preoccupation, to keep the poem moving. Virgil could afford to pause, to build up atmosphere, and to contrive expectations or uncertainties which would only be resolved some hundreds or thousands of lines later. In the *Aeneid*, plot and structure are completely integrated. The individual books of the poem are members of a complex interlocking composition in which the parts are rigorously subordinated to the whole. Only when Book XII has been read can Book I, and all that has intervened, be seen to make sense, and for the whole to be properly appreciated every part of the poem must be read in the light of the rest. The organization of the *Metamorphoses* is quite different. It is true that Pythagoras' speech, as argued above, can be read as the theoretical premiss of the main argument of the poem; and it is also true that in it is picked up and amplified the account of the Creation in Book I. However, this 'ring-composition' is of purely formal significance. The essential difference from the *Aeneid* is that the structure of the *Metamorphoses* is serial, cutting right across the divisions between the books. These are indeed ingeniously exploited by the poet—for Ovid never misses a technical trick—but in a purely 'local' way, to provide immediate surprise or drama and to whet the reader's expectations. The overriding aim of the poet is to carry the reader effortlessly from episode to episode, his appetite constantly titillated by variety of subject-matter, tone, tempo, linguistic wit, and literary treatment.

In this plan the transitions from one character or episode or cycle of stories to the next take on their true functional importance. Quintilian criticized Ovid for excess of ingenuity in this area, while acknowledging that there were practical reasons on his side:

> It is a tasteless and childish affectation of rhetoricians to make even their transitions the vehicle of an epigram and to court applause for such tricks. Ovid plays the fool in this way in the *Metamorphoses*, though he can plead necessity, having to impart a semblance of unity to such heterogeneous subject-matter.[9]

This as far as it goes is a fair comment, and in this as in other things Ovid sometimes indulged himself (see, e.g., ix. 666–7 n.); but the transitions are integral in another way, as being themselves demonstrations of metamorphosis in action, verbalizations of the continuous flux of events, which in the real world do indeed flow into one another in ways which are now easy and natural, now unexpected or indeed incredible. One of the reasons why the *Metamorphoses* is, as reviewers used to say, 'hard to put down' is precisely that the poet has built into it a continuity that makes it hard. It turns out to be a *perpetuum carmen* in a quite different sense from that first understood. Until the invocation of the Muses when the end is almost in sight (xv. 622 n.) Ovid does not allow the reader to draw breath.

VI

Ovid was a learned poet and the *Metamorphoses* is a learned poem. The terms require further definition. The Latin noun which, in this technical context of poetics, complements the adjective *doctus* (learned) is not *doctrina* (erudition) but *ars*: professional skill, craftsmanship (Greek *techne*). It goes without saying that the learned poet was expected and assumed to be

---

[9] Quintilian, *Institutio Oratoria* iv. 1. 77.

erudite. How many achieved real and solid erudition—were, that is, widely and deeply read, not only in the recognized classics but in the obscurer byways of the literary, scholarly, and indeed the scientific tradition—admits of some doubt. Few could measure up to the standard set by Callimachus. What tended to count in practice was the ability to use what you did know, to set out your wares to the best advantage. The poet's art lay in combining, varying, and embellishing the available materials and in the manner of his doing so—wittily, obliquely, allusively, piquantly, and above all unexpectedly. This was the mode taken over by Catullus and later Roman poets from the scholar-poets of Alexandria, *imprimis* Callimachus; and in this mode Ovid excelled. Genius is, among other things, the ability to transform common artistic property into something original and individual. Ovid's use of his sources in the *Metamorphoses* exemplifies with unusual brilliance the power of the creative intelligence to work this recurrent miracle.

Ovid had read his Roman epic predecessors, especially Lucretius and Virgil, and had learned much from them; but models for a poem such as the *Metamorphoses* had to be sought elsewhere. At the source of this tradition of mythological epos stood not Homer, but Hesiod. His *Theogony*, on the genealogy of the gods, and its continuation, the Catalogue of Women or *Eoeae* (ascribed to him in antiquity, whether or not his), were particularly influential examples of the 'collective' or catalogue poem: assemblages of legendary material rather than unified narratives such as the *Iliad* or the *Odyssey*. The form of discrete episodes strung on a thread of poetical editorializing had been adopted by Callimachus for his *chef d'œuvre*, the *Aetia* (Causes). This was an elegiac poem in four books, totalling some 7,000 verses, expounding the legendary origins of various historical Greek rites and customs. Callimachus seems to have been the first to make systematic poetical capital out of a general interest in local history and aetiology, and his poem, with his views on poetics expressed vigorously in its famous Proem, was extremely influential. Many of the stories in the *Metamorphoses* end with or embody some such explanation or *aition*. Callimachus too offered hints for the management of transitions. In view of the role played in the *Metamorphoses* by the dinner-table as a setting for story-telling, it is interesting to find Callimachus introducing his account of the worship of Peleus in the island of Icos by recalling how he found himself by chance next to a native of the island at dinner.[10]

Ovid's ostensible subject-matter, metamorphosis, was of course a common theme of Greek, as of all, myth, exploited by more than one Hellenistic poet. The *Ornithogonia* of Boios or Boio (date and sex uncertain) dealt with one of the recurrent themes of the *Metamorphoses*, transformations into birds. The *Heteroeumena* (Transformations) of Nicander of Colophon (second century BC) is known from the prose paraphrases of the mythographer Antoninus Liberalis (second century AD)[11] and provides the opportunity for enlightening comparisons. Ovid, as might have been expected, tended to treat his material with some freedom. Thus in Nicander's version Dryope (*Metamorphoses* ix. 326 ff.) was abducted (out of kindness) by the hamadryads, who substituted for her a poplar tree and a spring, while she became a nymph with good grace; and the tale ended with an *aition*, the foundation by her son Amphissus of a sanctuary and a foot-race. This is a far cry from Ovid's tragic treatment, but Nicander is the only other known authority for the story and it seems most probable that he was Ovid's source.[12] Variation sometimes takes the form of refinement, as in the stories of Procris (vii. 687–8 n.) or Iphis (ix. 687 ff. n.) or, mostly notably, Pygmalion (x. 243–97 n.). In all this he keeps well within the poet's traditional licence to innovate on his material; it is perhaps more surprising to find him making free with Homer, as he does in the debate over the arms of Achilles (xiii. 216–17 n., 230 n., 279 n.).

The most characteristic and successful technique applied by Ovid to his sources is that of combination. In Nicander's version of the story of the Pierides the verdict on the songs of the competitors was pronounced by nature: when the girls sang the skies loured, for the Muses rivers stood still and Helicon swelled heavenwards for joy until Pegasus at Poseidon's orders stopped it

[10] Frag. 178 Pfeiffer; compare *Metamorphoses* iv. 765 ff., viii. 571 ff., xii. 155 ff.

[11] Wherever Nicander is mentioned in the Explanatory Notes it can be assumed (unless otherwise indicated) that the source of the information is Antoninus. Those wishing to pursue the matter may be referred to the excellent edition with French translation and copious notes of Antoninus by M. Papathomopoulos (Paris, 1968).

[12] For other examples of Ovid's use of Nicander see ii. 706 n., iv. 415 n., v. 294–678 n., 461 n., vi. 317–81 n., vii. 353 n., 371 n., viii. 543–4 n., ix. 280–323 n., 454–668 n., 669–797 n., xi. 347 n., xiii. 692 n., 715 n., xiv. 525 n.

with a hoofstroke. Ovid had certainly read this part of the
Heteroeumena,[13] but chose not to develop these apparently
promising details.[14] The idea, however, of making Typhoeus
(Typhon) the ill-omened subject of the Pierides' song might well
have been suggested to him by the fact that both myths were
treated in the same book (IV) of Nicander's poem. An example
of this combinatory technique at its happiest is seen in the story
of Acis and Galatea, in which motifs from Homer, Theocritus,
and Virgil (himself dependent on Theocritus) are brilliantly inter-
twined to produce a wholly original serio-comic *tour de force*
without parallel in ancient literature.[15] Occasionally he combined
two stories originally distinct; often, pre-eminently in the case of
Narcissus and Echo, his treatment has become canonical.[16]

VII

In seeking to define the character of the *Metamorphoses* com-
parisons with Virgil are often instructive. Recent work on the
Aeneid has shown that Virgil's use of Homer is crucial to an
understanding of his intentions, that 'to achieve a true sense of
the meaning of the *Aeneid*, the reader must have a sense . . . of
what Homer's *Iliad* meant to the implied reader of the *Aeneid*
and to Virgil himself'. The *Aeneid* emerges from this analysis as
'the most notable instance, probably, in European literature of
"intertextuality" '.[17] Ovid's relationship with his models is not
of this kind. It is, as has been suggested above, always instructive
and often amusing to compare his sources, when we can come at
them, with what he made of them, and more than once he can be
felt jogging the reader's elbow. In Theocritus (*Idylls* xi. 20–1) the
Cyclops addresses Galatea as 'whiter than curd to look on, softer
than the lamb, more skittish than the calf, sleeker than the unripe
grape'. In Virgil this becomes part of a dialogue in which two
shepherds challenge and answer each other alternately (*Eclogues*

[13] Only Nicander and he (v. 669) call the daughters of Pieros *Emathides*.

[14] Pegasus' hoofstroke is otherwise exploited (v. 256 ff.); the reactions of
nature in Nicander's version duplicate the more famous legend of Orpheus
(x. 86 ff.).

[15] xiii. 750–890 n. Compare Cyparissus, x. 106–42 n.

[16] Compare Salmacis and Hermaphroditus, iv. 285–388 n.

[17] K. W. Gransden, *Virgil's Iliad. An Essay on Epic Narrative* (Cambridge,
1984) 1–2, 5. The beginnings of this realization must be dated to the publica-
tion of G. N. Knauer's seminal *Die Aeneis und Homer* (Göttingen, 1964).

vii. 37–44), one addressing Galatea as 'sweeter than thyme of Hybla, whiter than swans, fairer than white ivy', and the other styling himself 'more bitter than Sardinian herbs, rougher than broom, more worthless than cast-up seaweed'. Ovid's Cyclops is made to expand these hints into a prodigious apostrophe to the nymph of nineteen verses (xiii. 789–807), incorporating what must surely be the longest sequence of comparative ablatives in Latin literature, divided into thirteen phrases praising Galatea followed by another thirteen qualifying her praises. This was certainly an in-joke, as is the brief and apparently innocuous *multa querenti*, 'complaining at length', applied to the abandoned Ariadne (viii. 176): for the reason that she does not and cannot develop her complaints is that Ovid has already appropriated them, from Catullus' classic and influential treatment in the *Peleus and Thetis*, to give, along with more material culled from Euripides and Virgil, to Scylla (viii. 108 n.). Of course, Ovid was entitled to expect that his readers at least knew their Virgil. The alert student of Books XIII and XIV was expected to be diverted and impressed by the poet's adroit interweaving of extraneous episodes into a narrative sequence based on the *Aeneid*.[18]

None of this, however, amounts to a true case of intertextuality. (Self-reference, mentioned below, is something different again.) Our understanding and appreciation of the *Metamorphoses* is not materially enhanced by such allusions, when we notice them, or diminished, when they escape us. So far from sending us back to his models, indeed, Ovid has rendered them expendable. No transformation recounted by him is as remarkable as this poetic miracle whereby legend after legend assumed for ever afterwards the form that he had chosen to give it. No doubt the powerful effect exercised by his poem on European writers and artists has been accentuated by the accident that much of the Greek literature which he laid under contribution has disappeared or is accessible only in second-hand or fragmentary form. One may suspect that even if it survived we should admire him all the more and that it would still be in their Ovidian guise that most of these stories would impose themselves on our imagination. 'There is a plastic quality about his work. He catches the significant moment or attitude or gesture and imprints it on our mind.'[19] It is not only the descriptive passages of the *Metamorphoses* to which this perceptive comment applies. Whole characters[20] and episodes have been reshaped and integrated into the grand design in a form which renders them always fresh and always memorable.

VIII

Ars also connotes artfulness. The *Metamorphoses* is among other things an exercise in sheer ingenuity. That in itself would not recommend it: the literature of Hellenistic Greece and her Roman imitators abounded in the ingeniously unreadable. Ovid has often been taxed with being too clever for his own good, and the poet of the *Ars Amatoria* had cause to admit the truth of the charge:

> me mea fata trahebant,
> inque meas poenas ingeniosus eram.

'My fate drew me on, and I was witty to my own undoing.'

(*Tristia* ii. 341–2)

In the *Metamorphoses* artfulness is by and large kept in its place, subordinate to the main purpose of keeping the poem on the move and so continuously engaging the reader's interest. The transitions, as has been said, are essential to that purpose; they also serve to articulate the extremely elaborate structure of the poem, a *tour de force* in its own right. In one sense this structure is simple, being determined by the chronological scheme. Within the framing episodes of the Creation (elemental Chaos to Cosmos) and the Apotheosis of Caesar (political Chaos to Cosmos) we can distinguish three divisions of approximately equal length in which the chief actors are (1) gods (i. 452–vi. 420); (2) heroes (vi. 421–xi. 193); (3) historical figures[21] (xi. 194–xv. 744). Chronology, however, was not and could not be rigidly followed, if only because the mythological tradition enshrined numerous inconsistencies; and such an arrangement would have been both tedious and inartificial. Within this tripartite scheme the stories are grouped

---

[19] L. P. Wilkinson, *Ovid Recalled* (Cambridge, 1955), 172.

[20] Ovid also knows when to refrain. It is worth noting that in the 'Aenean' episodes of Books XIII–XIV Aeneas himself hardly figures. Virgil's Dido had been remodelled elsewhere, in the *Heroides* (vii).

[21] History proper was taken to begin with the Trojan War.

on various principles of similarity and contrast, thematic, geographical, and genealogical. Attempts have been made to show that the structure of the poem is an integral part of its message. This is true in the sense that its fluid and often elusive texture faithfully reflects that of life itself and the ever-changing universe, in which individuals, families, peoples, cities, empires, territories come and go without apparent reason or order. Ovid's use of the enclosing or 'Chinese box' technique in arranging the stories may sometimes leave the reader uncertain of his bearings: who, reading the story of Arethusa (v. 577 ff.), could say offhand who is really speaking?[22] Some of this may simply be meant to tease or impress, but consciously or not it contributes to the overall intended effect.

Epic was traditionally an impersonal genre. In the *Metamorphoses* the reader is continuously aware of the poet. At ii. 219 Haemus is called *nondum Oeagrius*, 'not yet Oeagrian'. Oeagrus was Orpheus' father, and the phrase is modelled on Virgil's *Oeagrius Hebrus* (*Georgics* iv. 524). That was a recherché expression in its own right, the first appearance in Latin of an exotic Greek proper name. By varying it Ovid draws attention to himself: Haemus (and the same indeed applies to Hebrus) cannot at this stage be famous, for Orpheus does not yet exist—because the poet has not yet got to him.[23] Midas' disastrous foray into literary criticism is characterized in the technical language of Augustan and Alexandrian poetics. His wits are 'crass', *pingue ingenium* (xi. 148); Greek *pachys*, Latin *pinguis* epitomized all that the taste of those bred up on Callimachus agreed to reject in poetry and recall the words of Apollo's admonition to the poet of the *Aetia* to 'feed the victim fat as you can, but keep the Muse slender'.[24] That at the end of the contest 'Old Tmolus bade the reed bow to the lyre' (xi. 171) ought to have surprised nobody but Midas, who clearly had never been instructed in the hierarchy of genres, in which bucolic was outranked by lyric. Similarly the Pierid who undertook to challenge the Muses (v. 318 ff.) cannot have been aware, as Ovid's readers were expected

---

[22] As Dr Hinds has pointed out to me, it is the poet telling how an unnamed Muse tells how Calliope tells how Arethusa tells her story—remarkable even for Ovid.   [23] Compare v. 282–3 n., vi. 415 n., vii. 233 n., x. 448–51 n.

[24] Frag. 1. 23–4 Pfeiffer; cf. Virgil, *Eclogues* vi. 4–5 *pastorem, Tityre, pinguis/pascere oportet ouis*, deductum *dicere carmen*.

to be aware, that it did not improve her already exiguous chances to submit a Gigantomachy, which to the Callimachizing poets of Augustan Rome stood for the 'thundering' epic which they spurned.[25] The inclusion of Theseus in the audience of the tale of Baucis and Philemon was a sly reminder that Ovid's model for much of the detail of the episode was Callimachus' epyllion *Hecale*, which told how Theseus, on his way to encounter the Bull of Marathon, took shelter in the cottage of the poor old woman who gave the poem its title. Hence the point of the comment that 'the tale . . . Had moved . . . Theseus especially' (*praecipue*, viii. 726). When the god of poetry begs Cyparissus 'not to yield to grief . . . So ill-proportioned' (x. 133), literally 'to grieve in proportion to the matter', *pro materia*, he is made to seem unaware that the motivation *is* proportioned—to the *poet's* matter (*materia* being in this connection a technical term), the frivolous story (as he tells it) that he has contrived for the sake of the metamorphosis and the *aition*.

Ovid can also be seen mocking the conventions. One story (xi. 751) is put in the mouth of 'His neighbour . . . (Or maybe the same man)', *proximus aut idem si fors tulit*. The speaker's identity is wholly immaterial, but Callimachus himself had proclaimed 'I sing nothing unattested' (Frag. 612 Pfeiffer). Like 'Gertrude' in Randall Jarrell's *Pictures from an Institution*, Ovid perhaps occasionally felt 'the contempt for [his] audience that the real virtuoso so often has': 'Swift once wrote to Pope—or Pope once wrote to Swift, I don't care.' Inconsistencies or variant versions in the tradition might themselves be turned to account. By dismissing the story of Daphnis as too familiar to merit retelling, while at the same time alluding to a little-known version of it (iv. 276–8), Ovid manages to have his cake and eat it. By failing to specify which sister became which bird in the story of Procne and Philomela Ovid showed, without ostentation of pedantry, that he was aware that his predecessors differed on the point (vi. 668–9 n.). This helps to explain his apparent acquiescence in flagrant discrepancies, as with Atlas (ii. 297 n., iv. 772 n.) or Hercules (xi. 213 n.) or Argo (vi. 444–5, 511, 721 n.). In the last case the contradiction was already in evidence in Catullus and before him in Apollonius Rhodius, suggesting that the unacknowledged but unmistakable adoption of a contradictory chronology might itself be a form of learned showing-off.[26]

In general, however, Ovid's wit is not as esoteric as these examples imply and can be appreciated by any alert and appreciative reader. It is unnecessary to document here what is amply illustrated in Mr Melville's sensitive and accurate version, but in conclusion it is proper to draw attention to the descriptions of the metamorphoses themselves. Nowhere is Ovid's infinite versatility and resourcefulness more strikingly in evidence. Certain types of metamorphosis—into trees, into water, into stones, into birds—naturally recur; this was a property of the stories themselves, which in the main the poet could not alter. Making a virtue of this necessity, Ovid rings the changes on the theme of change itself. But

> desinet ante dies et in alto Phoebus anhelos
> aequore tinguet equos quam consequar omnia uerbis
> in species translata nouas.

> 'The day will wane, the Sun beneath the waves
> Will plunge his panting steeds before my tale
> Recounts the sum of things that take new forms.'

> (xv. 418–20)

—including that which now confronts the reader. However, of the metamorphoses that the poem has undergone at the hands of its translators—something even Ovid could not foresee—and of this, its latest, transformation it is for Mr Melville to speak.

E. J. KENNEY

---

[26] See C. Weber, 'Two Chronological Contradictions in Catullus 64', *Transactions of the American Philological Association*, 113 (1983), 263–71.

EVERY translator of the *Metamorphoses* can profit by the examples of his predecessors, guided by their successes, warned by their failures. In the past five hundred years translations have not been numerous. Caxton made a prose version[1] in 1480 taken from the French. I have found most value in the versions of Golding (1567), Sandys (1626), and Watts (1955). The rambling 'fourteeners' of Golding, which Shakespeare knew and Pound over-praised, distort the effect of Ovid's swift and elegant hexameters, but have a clumsy charm of their own. The terse, ingenious couplets of Sandys suffer from the opposite defect; they are compressed to the point of obscurity and the tyranny of the rhyme inhibits a faithful translation. Watts, using heroic couplets three hundred years later, is often admirable and, if Ovid had written the *Metamorphoses* in elegiac couplets (as he wrote almost always), would indeed rank high. But the speed, variety, and music of Ovid's hexameters cannot be conveyed by closed couplets; and the difficulty of finding rhymes requires omissions or additions so that Ovid's meaning is at times not mirrored but veiled.

In 1717 a translation appeared assembled by Sir Samuel Garth from versions 'by the most eminent hands'. This included large portions of the poem by Dryden, one story by Pope, and several by Addison. Dryden is often brilliant, but with the arrogance of his age he did not hesitate to 'improve', so that a substantial part of his version is his own invention. There were attempts in the nineteenth century which had little merit. Miller's version in the Loeb edition of 1916 would not claim literary distinction but has occasional flashes of insight and is not to be disdained. The prose translation of Innes, published in 1955, will have introduced many readers to Ovid's famous stories, but is not to be recommended for stylistic merit. In more recent years translations have appeared in the USA whose main value is as a warning of the difficulty of the task.

If the *Metamorphoses* had been written in elegiac couplets, the right form of an English version would no doubt be heroic

[1] The original, now complete, is in the possession of Magdalene College, Cambridge.

couplets, such as were perfected by Dryden and Pope. But who reads Dryden or Pope for the music of their verse, or thinks as he reads 'what a lovely line!'? Yet in the original the music of Ovid's hexameters is a delight; his swift and limpid narrative is often borne on a stream of gorgeous sound. A worthy translation must try to match this music. We have outgrown the drab, sad decades when Eliot mocked at blank verse and his followers disdained it. It remains an admirable medium for narrative poetry; its versatility matches the variety of Ovid's verse; and when we recall and savour lines of exquisite beauty, are they not very often lines of blank verse? What is needed is not some new-fangled system, more or less metrical, turning its back on past achievements that it is frightened to face. The bolder and better course today is to return to the tried and tested measure of English tradition, and adapt and revive it in a modern mould, with language that speaks directly to a modern reader. To match Ovid's style the verse must be taut, swift, elegant, and sonorous. Given these qualities, the fact that it is also 'blank' need be no blemish. But, in addition, there is much to be gained by an occasional rhyming couplet, for at times Ovid's hexameters seem almost to break into the elegiacs of which he was so fond. This too has the warrant of Elizabethan tradition, and that precedent has been followed in this translation. A rhyming couplet sometimes rounds a paragraph or closes a speech or marks the end of a story, or in some other way makes a special point or effect.

English has one great advantage over Latin—its vocabulary is so much larger. A translator may often have three or four words where Ovid has only one; and these three or four will all be subtly different. Conversely he can often express in one apt word a meaning for which Ovid needs several. And of course the English language, developed and matured over so many centuries, with a literature of incomparable richness, supports the translator with echoes and overtones which he can use to enhance the effect which Ovid intended; though Ovid too had behind him centuries of the glorious literature of the Greeks, familiar to the cultured and sophisticated audience for whom he wrote. Indeed without this Greek literature (and in particular that of the third-century Alexandrians, Theocritus, Callimachus, and many others) there could have been no *Metamorphoses*.

Latin has two great advantages over English—its incomparable sonority and the freedom of its word-order. While both languages share many of the artifices of literary composition, the music of Latin in the hands of a master is supreme. In English the order of words in a sentence is fixed within narrow limits, but the variety of position which Latin allows makes possible effects which English often cannot achieve. Nevertheless the translator must be alert to those effects and do his best to reproduce them. Take, as a single instance out of many, the description of the gift of Polyphemus to Galatea:

> inueni geminos, qui tecum ludere possint,
> inter se similes, uix ut dignoscere possis,
> uillosae catulos in summis montibus ursae.

> 'I found one day among the mountain peaks,
> For you to play with, twins so much alike
> You scarce could tell, cubs of a shaggy bear.'

(xiii. 834–6)

It is not until the very last word that the surprise is revealed. Ovid uses the same cunning artifice in describing the lions into which Atalanta and Hippomenes are changed (x. 704) and the frogs to which the Lycian peasants are transformed (vi. 381) and the weapon with which the ungrateful farmer kills his ox (xv. 126). This word-order, so subtle and striking, is preserved in this translation, but, as far as I am aware, in no other, with the sole exception of Watts, who invents bogs to rhyme with frogs.

Other distinctive characteristics of Ovid's style must be reproduced in a worthy translation. His narrative is always swift, concise, and lucid (he is never obscure unless he means to be); the English must never be slow or verbose or obscure. He is often witty and his wit must not be squandered; he is always elegant and the translation must match his elegance.

Cephalus is telling of his wife's grief and beauty:

> ... tu collige qualis in illa,
> Phoce, decor fuerit, quam sic dolor ipse decebat.

> 'Imagine, Prince, how lovely was her grace,
> When grief itself so graced her loveliness.'

(vii. 732–3)

Narcissus is gazing at his reflection in the pool:

> quid uideat nescit, sed quod uidet urit in illo,
> atque oculos idem, qui decipit, incitat error.

> 'Not knowing what he sees, he adores the sight;
> That false face fools and fuels his delight.'

(iii. 430–1)

In the Golden Age

> uer erat aeternum, placidique tepentibus auris
> mulcebant zephyri natos sine semine flores.

> 'Springtime it was, always, for ever spring;
> The gentle zephyrs with their breathing balm
> Caressed the flowers that sprang without a seed.'

(i. 107–8)

The father of Iphis is a man of humble birth and poor,

> . . . nec census in illo
> nobilitate sua maior . . .

> '. . . nor did his purse
> Surpass his pedigree . . .'

(ix. 671–2)

An artifice of the Latin which a translator must never overlook is what is known as a 'golden line'. This is a line in which the words, usually only five, are arranged in a special symmetrical order:

> candida Dictaei spectans tentoria regis

> '. . . watched
> The white pavilions of the Island king'

(viii. 43)

> decolor extremo qua tinguitur India Gange

> '. . . remotest lands
> Where Ganges waters dusky India'

(iv. 21)

> torua colubriferi superauit lumina monstri

> '. . . availed against
> The ghastly snake-haired Gorgon's glaring eyes'

(v. 241)

Such a line is, by the nature of its structure, infrequent; it has, and is intended to have, a striking effect. This effect can hardly be reproduced in English, but the translator must strive to find words that will be equally striking. Alliteration is another artifice of which Ovid was a master and that artifice should be a feature of the English. He sometimes uses onomatopoeia with great success, which the translator can only admire and admit defeat; and always in translating one must relish the music of the Latin and aim to compose in words of corresponding harmony.

One, more technical, point should be noted. From time to time, following an established literary convention, Ovid turns to address his characters himself—Pyramus and Thisbe, for instance: 'this chink . . . you lovers found . . .'. He does this partly for variety and partly for metrical reasons. But in English there is no corresponding tradition and the effect is strange. Therefore, except in one or two special passages, I have changed the Latin to conform with English practice.

It is sometimes asked how a translator of such a famous poem can avoid reproducing the words of his predecessors. Such a question shows a misunderstanding of the duty of a translator; it implies that he has a duty to be different. His duty is to provide a version in tune with his own time, in an idiom as welcome to his contemporaries as Ovid's was to his audience two thousand years ago. Such a version is bound to be different from those of earlier generations, and the translation here offered to the reader does indeed differ strikingly from earlier versions. But when an earlier expert has found what is clearly the right word or phrase or rhyme, it would be perverse to prefer an alternative for the sake of being different, especially when, as I have often been pleased to find, the same idea has independently occurred to me. Sandys profited from Golding, Dryden from Sandys, Watts from them all; Innes likewise gained much from Miller, and Miller very likely from nineteenth-century prose versions. I gladly acknowledge my debt in general; some particular instances are mentioned in the Explanatory Notes.

The number of lines that rhyme in my translation is, of course, a minute proportion of the whole. For instance, in Book I there are thirteen rhymes; in Book II, which probably has the most, there are thirty-five; in Book XIII, the longest, with more than eleven hundred lines, there are twenty-seven, of which four are shared by one or more of my predecessors. Two of those four I have expanded to triple rhymes (doom, tomb, womb; bay, day, away), the first of which marks an agonized climax of a speech, the second honours a stately 'golden line' that closes an episode. The number of my rhymes is indeed small, but their impact is striking and enhanced by their rarity. Freedom from the constraints of rhyme makes much easier the use of other artifices, notably alliteration, which versions in heroic couplets seldom achieve, and sonority, which they usually lack.

Successive translators often use the same rhymes; indeed some rhymes are so obvious that they are common to all the versions that I have consulted. Some brief examples may be instructive.

The final lines of the story of Narcissus (iii. 509–10):

> nusquam corpus erat; croceum pro corpore florem
> inueniunt foliis medium cingentibus albis.

I translate:

> no body anywhere;
> And in its stead they found a flower—behold,
> White petals clustered round a cup of gold!

Golding has:

> But as for bodie none remained: in stead thereof they found
> A yellow floure with milke-white leaves new sprong upon
>   the ground.

Sandys:

> In stead whereof a yellow flowre was found
> With tufts of white about the button crown'd.

Addison:

> When, looking for his Corps, they only found
> A rising stalk, with yellow Blossoms crown'd.

Watts:

> No body, but a flower, their eyes behold,
> White rays in circle round a heart of gold.

The final lines of the story of Myrrha (x. 501–2):

> est honor et lacrimis stillataque robore murra
> nomen erile tenet nulloque tacebitur aeuo.

> 'Those tears in truth
> Have honour; from the trunk the weeping myrrh
> Keeps on men's lips for aye the name of her.'

Golding:

> The which her tears are had in pryce and honour. And
>   the Myrrh
> That issueth from her gummy bark dooth beare the name
>   of her.

Watts:

> Immortal tears: for aye the oozing myrrh
> Shall bear her name, and men shall speak of her.

Two lines describing the shield of Nileus (v. 187–8):

> . . . clipeo quoque flumina septem
> argento partim, partim caelauerat auro.

> '. . . and bore a shield embossed
> In gold and silver with those seven streams.'

Sandys:

> And bare seven silver Rivers in his shield,
> Distinctly waving through a golden field.

Watts:

> And bore the boastful blazon on his shield,
> Seven streams of silver on a golden field.

Iphis in despair (ix. 762–3):

> pronuba quid Juno, quid ad haec, Hymenaee, uenitis
> sacra, quibus qui ducat abest, ubi nubimus ambae?

> 'Ay me! why should the Wedding-god preside
> Without a groom, with both of us a bride!'

Watts:

> For vainly Juno o'er a rite presides
> Which lacks a bridegroom—where we both are brides.

(In my translation this rhyme has its clinching counterpart in the
last two lines of the story, an effect achieved in no other version:

> their love was sanctified,
> And Iphis gained Ianthe, groom and bride.)

It may be doubted whether any poem has had so great an
influence on the literature and art of Western civilization as the

Metamorphoses. Very many of the stories have been illustrated by famous masterpieces of painting and sculpture, particularly in the Renaissance. Among paintings there is the great series of Rubens, many of Poussin (including *Acis and Galatea*), P. Bruegel's *Fall of Icarus*, and countless others. In sculpture there is Bernini's marble of Apollo and Daphne and Cellini's bronze of Perseus. In English literature from Chaucer to the eighteenth century Ovid's influence was outstanding. Shakespeare drew on every book of the poem; Milton made great use of it in *Paradise Lost*. (It is said that his daughter read to him the story of the Creation so often that she knew it by heart.) For centuries Ovid's vogue was immense. But with the fading of the Renaissance his reputation began to fade. To the nineteenth century his spirit was alien, almost anathema. Now, towards the end of the twentieth century, values have changed again. It is time to enjoy once more the tales of the *Metamorphoses*, not only for the famous stories that they tell, but for the grace and fluency of Ovid's style, the wit, humour, pathos, mischief, and majesty that make this one of the most enjoyable poems ever written.

In making my translation I have received much encouragement and helpful advice from my family and friends; I thank them all. I am especially grateful to Professor Kenney for his vigilance and erudition, which have saved me from so many errors, and for the elegance and ingenuity of his suggestions. Several of these stories were first printed in *Agenda* thanks to the enthusiasm of Mr William Cookson; their publication in this periodical was notable and the welcome they then received proved the success of my style of translation. I have lived with Ovid in the *Metamorphoses* for a number of happy years; it is my hope that my readers will share my happiness.

A.D.M.

SELECT BIBLIOGRAPHY

GENERAL

E. K. Rand, *Ovid and his Influence* (London, 1926)
L. P. Wilkinson, *Ovid Recalled* (Cambridge, 1955)
J. W. Binns (ed.), *Ovid* (London, 1973)
E. J. Kenney, 'Ovid', in *The Cambridge History of Classical Literature*,
   II, *Latin Literature*, ed. E. J. Kenney and W. V. Clausen (Cambridge,
   1982), 420–57 = *The Age of Augustus* (Cambridge, 1983), 136–63

LIFE AND CHRONOLOGY

R. Syme, *History in Ovid* (Oxford, 1978)

THE METAMORPHOSES

Text

F. J. Miller, rev. G. P. Goold (Loeb: Cambridge, Mass., and London,
   1977–84)

Commentaries

F. Bömer (Heidelberg, 1969–   ) (in German)
Book I: A. G. Lee (Cambridge, 1953)
Book III: A. A. R. Henderson (Bristol, 1979)
Books VI–X: W. S. Anderson (Norman, 1972)
Book VIII: A. S. Hollis (Oxford, 1970)
Book XI: G. M. H. Murphy (Oxford, 1972)

Interpretation

B. Otis, *Ovid as an Epic Poet*, 2nd edn. (Cambridge, 1970)
O. S. Due, *Changing Forms. Studies in the Metamorphoses of Ovid*
   (Copenhagen, 1974)
G. K. Galinsky, *Ovid's Metamorphoses. An Introduction to the Basic
   Aspects* (Berkeley and Los Angeles, 1975)

METAMORPHOSES

*

BOOK I

OF bodies changed to other forms I tell;
You Gods, who have yourselves wrought every change,*
Inspire my enterprise and lead my lay
In one continuous song from nature's first
Remote beginnings to our modern times.

THE CREATION

Ere land and sea and the all-covering sky
Were made, in the whole world the countenance
Of nature was the same, all one, well named
Chaos, a raw and undivided mass,
Naught but a lifeless bulk, with warring seeds
Of ill-joined elements compressed together.
No sun as yet poured light upon the world,
No waxing moon her crescent filled anew,
Nor in the ambient air yet hung the earth,
Self-balanced, equipoised, nor Ocean's arms
Embraced the long far margin of the land.
Though there were land and sea and air, the land
No foot could tread, no creature swim the sea,
The air was lightless; nothing kept its form,
All objects were at odds, since in one mass
Cold essence fought with hot, and moist with dry,
And hard with soft and light with things of weight.
   This strife a god, with nature's blessing, solved;
Who severed land from sky and sea from land,
And from the denser vapours set apart
The ethereal sky; and, each from the blind heap
Resolved and freed, he fastened in its place
Appropriate in peace and harmony.
The fiery weightless force of heaven's vault
Flashed up and claimed the topmost citadel;

Next came the air in lightness and in place;
The thicker earth with grosser elements
Sank burdened by its weight; lowest and last
The girdling waters pent the solid globe.
    So into shape whatever god it was
Reduced the primal matter and prescribed
Its several parts. Then first, to make the earth
Even on every side, he rounded it
Into a mighty sphere, then bade the sea
Extend and rise under the rushing winds,
And gird the shores of the encircled earth.
Springs too he made and boundless fens and lakes,
And rivers hemmed in winding banks to flow,
Which, in their diverse journeyings, sometimes
The earth absorbs, sometimes they reach the sea
And in its broad domain, instead of banks,
With new-found freedom beat upon the shores.
He bade the plains spread wide, the valleys sink,
The craggy mountains rise, the forest trees
Don their green leaves; and as the vault of heaven
Has five divisions, two zones on the right,
Two on the left, and hottest burns the fifth,
With that same number Providence divine
Parcelled in zones the solid earth below.
The midmost uninhabitable heat
Claims for its own; two lie clothed deep in snow;
Two, in between, were given a temperate clime
Where warmth and cold combine in harmony.
    The air hangs high above them, weightier
Than the empyrean in the same degree
As earth than water. There he bade the mists
And there the clouds to have their dwelling-place,
And thunder that should shake the hearts of men,
And lightning flashing through the freezing gales.
The world's Creator did not grant the winds
Full freedom of the sky; who, even so,
Though each in separate regions rules his blasts,
Can well nigh tear the world apart, so fierce
Is brothers' strife. The east wind far withdrew
Towards the morning and the rose-red walls

Of royal Petra and the Persian hills,* *doesn't mean the Far East*
Clear in the long bright sunshine of the dawn.
The evening and the shores that glow beside
The setting sun are the west wind's abode.
To Scythia and the wastes beneath the Wain
The blustering north wind marched; far opposite,
Wrapped in continual clouds, the flooded fields
Lie sodden as the south wind brings the rain.
High over these he set the empyrean
Weightless, serene, with naught of earthly dross.
    Scarce had he thus all things in finite bounds
Divided when the stars, in darkness blind
Long buried, over all the spangled sky
Began to gleam; and, that no part or place
Should lack fit forms of life, the firmament
He made the home of gods and goddesses
And the bright constellations; in the sea
He set the shining fish to swim; the land
Received the beasts, the gusty air the birds.
A holier creature, of a loftier mind,
Fit master of the rest, was lacking still.
Then man was made, perhaps from seed divine
Formed by the great Creator, so to found
A better world, perhaps* the new-made earth,
So lately parted from the ethereal heavens,
Kept still some essence of the kindred sky—
Earth that Prometheus moulded, mixed with water,
In likeness of the gods that govern the world—
And while the other creatures on all fours
Look downwards, man was made to hold his head
Erect in majesty and see the sky,
And raise his eyes to the bright stars above.
Thus earth, once crude and featureless, now changed
Put on the unknown form of humankind.

THE AGES OF MANKIND

Golden was that first age which unconstrained,
With heart and soul, obedient to no law,
Gave honour to good faith and righteousness.

No punishment they knew, no fear; they read
No penalties engraved on plates of bronze;
No suppliant throng with dread beheld their judge;
No judges had they then, but lived secure.
No pine had yet, on its high mountain felled,
Descended to the sea to find strange lands
Afar; men knew no shores except their own.
No battlements their cities yet embraced,
No trumpets straight, no horns of sinuous brass,
No sword, no helmet then—no need of arms;
The world untroubled lived in leisured ease.
Earth willingly, untouched, unwounded yet
By hoe or plough, gave all her bounteous store;
Men were content with nature's food unforced,
And gathered strawberries on the mountainside
And cherries and the clutching bramble's fruit,
And acorns fallen from <u>Jove's</u> spreading tree.*

*Jove =
Jupiter =
Zeus)*

Springtime it was, always, for ever spring;
The gentle zephyrs with their breathing balm
Caressed the flowers that sprang without a seed;
Anon the earth untilled brought forth her fruits,
The unfallowed fields lay gold with heavy grain,
And streams of milk and springs of nectar flowed
And yellow honey dripped from boughs of green.

*Saturn =
Cronos*

  When Saturn* fell to the dark Underworld *him being defeated*
And Jove reigned upon earth, the silver race *by zeus*
Replaced the gold, inferior, yet in worth
Above the tawny bronze. Then Jupiter
Curtailed the pristine spring and led the year
Through winter, summer, autumn's varying days
And brief precarious spring in seasons four.
Then first the blazing sky with torrid heat
Sweltered, and ice hung frozen in the gale;
Then men sought shelter—shelter under caves
And thickets and rough hurdles bound with bark;
Then in long furrows first were set the seeds
Of grain and oxen groaned beneath the yoke.
  Third in succession came the race of bronze,
Of fiercer temperament, more readily
Disposed to war, yet free from wickedness.

Last came the race of iron. In that hard age
Of baser vein all evil straight broke out,
And honour fled and truth and loyalty,
Replaced by fraud, deceit and treachery
And violence and wicked greed for gain.
Men sailed the sea—as yet the novice crew
Scarce knew the winds; timbers that long had stood
High on the mountain ranges triumphed now,
Riding in arrogance on waves unknown;
And on the ground, common till then and free
As air and sunlight, far across the fields
By careful survey boundaries were marked.
Nor did earth's rich return of crops and food
Suffice; the bowels of the world were forced
And wealth deep hidden next the gates of Hell
Dug out, the spur of wickedness and sin.
Iron now was in men's hands to bring them bane,
And gold a greater bane, and war marched forth
That fights with both and shook its clashing arms
With hands of blood. Men lived by spoil and plunder;
Friend was not safe from friend, nor father safe
From son-in-law, and kindness rare between
Brother and brother; husbands plotted death
For wives and wives for husbands; stepmothers
With murderous hearts brewed devilish aconite,
And sons, importunate to glut their greed,
Studied the stars to time their fathers' death.
Honour and love lay vanquished, and from earth,
With slaughter soaked, Justice, virgin divine,
The last of the immortals, fled away.
Nor were the heights of heaven more secure:
Giants, it's said, to win the gods' domain,
Mountain on mountain reared and reached the stars.
Then the Almighty Father hurled his bolt
And shattered great Olympus and struck down
High Pelion piled on Ossa. There they lay,
Grim broken bodies crushed in huge collapse,
And Earth, drenched in her children's weltering blood,*
Gave life to that warm gore; and to preserve
Memorial of her sons refashioned it

In human form. But that new stock no less
Despised the gods and relished cruelty,
Bloodshed and outrage—born beyond doubt of blood.
    When Jove from his high tower beheld men's crimes
He groaned and, mindful of that loathsome feast
Lycaon* set (new crime then known to few),
In mighty anger blazed, celestial wrath
Befitting Jupiter, and called the gods
To conclave, urgent summons soon obeyed.
    Across the height of heaven there runs a road,
Clear when the night is bare, the Milky Way,
Famed for its sheen of white. Along this way
Come the immortals to the royal halls
Of the great Thunderer; on either hand
The mansions of the aristocracy
Are thronged, their doors flung wide; the common sort
Live in the scattered suburbs; here reside
The great and famous; this majestic place
(To speak so bold) is heaven's Palatine.*
    So in the marble council-chamber sat
The gods; and Jupiter above them throned,
Leaning upon his ivory sceptre, tossed
From side to side his fearsome locks, and shook
Ocean and earth and all the starry sky,
And thus in wrath and indignation spoke:
'Never felt I more anxious for the world,
My realm, not when the serpent-footed giants
Strove each to grapple in his hundred arms
The captive sky. Fierce was that foe indeed,
Yet war hung on one front, sprang from one source;
But now throughout the whole great orb whose shores
Resound with Ocean's roar the mortal race
Must be destroyed. By that dark stream* I swear,
That glides below the world through glades of Hell,
All has been tried and, when no cure avails,
Rightly the knife is used lest the disease
Spread and infection draw what still is sound.
I have my demigods, my fauns and satyrs,
My nymphs and rustic sprites of wold and wood,
Not worthy yet to win the sky, but sure

The earth, their portion, we must prove secure.
Can you suppose them safe when against me,
Me whom the lightnings, whom yourselves obey,
Lycaon plots his treacherous devilry?'
    An angry murmur rose; the gods, outraged,
For sin demand fit doom. So when the blood
Of Caesar* by mad impious hands was spilt
To expunge the name of Rome, the human race
And all creation shuddered, dazed with fear
Of instant ruin; nor dost thou rejoice,
Augustus,* in thy subjects' loyalty
Less than great Jove in his; whose gesture then
And voice rebuked their noise, and silence fell,
Their clamour hushed by his grave majesty,
And Jove again with speech the silence broke.
    'Lycaon, rest assured, has paid the price
Of sin, but how he sinned and what the price
You now shall learn. A tale of infamy
Came to my ears. I, keen to prove it false,
Descending from Olympus, walked the world
A god in human guise. The tale were long
Of sin found universal; that report
Of infamy the infamous truth surpassed.
Mount Maenalus I crossed, feared for its lairs
Of lurking beasts; I crossed the cold pine-groves
Of high Lycaeus and Cyllene's crest
And reached at last the inhospitable roof
Of that Arcadian king, at evenfall,
As the late lingering dusk led on the night.
    My signs made manifest a god had come,
And all the people knelt in prayer, but he
Scoffed at their worship. "A clear test", he said,
"Shall prove if this be god or mortal man
And certify the truth", and planned for me,
At dead of night, when I was sunk in sleep,
Death unforeseen—so would he test the truth.
Nor was that all. He slew a hostage sent
From far Epirus, slitting his throat, and boiled
Part of the flesh, scarce dead, and roasted part
And bade me eat. At once my avenging flame

Whelmed in just ruin that guilty house and him.
He fled in fear and reached the silent fields
And howled his heart out, trying in vain to speak.
With rabid mouth he turned his lust for slaughter
Against the flocks, delighting still in blood.
His clothes changed to coarse hair, his arms to legs—
He was a wolf, yet kept some human trace,
The same grey hair, the same fierce face, the same
Wild eyes, the same image of savagery.
So one house died; but not one house alone
Deserves to die; in the whole world sin reigns,
Conspiracy of crime! Soon on them all—
My sentence stands—due punishment shall fall.'
    Many are loud in favour of Jove's speech
And spur his anger; many give quiet assent;
But all deplore the loss of humankind,
And ask what would the future world be like
Bereft of mortals? Who would cense their shrines?
Can Jove intend to abandon earth's domain
To the brute beasts to ravage and despoil?
Such were their questions; but the gods' great king
Bade them take heart (his forethought would provide)
And promised a new race of men on earth,
Unlike the first, a race of marvellous birth.
Now he was poised to launch his thunderbolts
Against the whole wide world, but paused for fear
The holy empyrean be set alight
By fires so many and blaze from pole to pole;
And he recalled the Fates foretold a time*
When sea and land and heaven's high palaces
In sweeping flames should burn, and down should fall
The beleaguered bastions of the universe.
He laid aside his lightnings; better seemed
A different punishment—to send the rains
To fall from every region of the sky
And in their deluge drown the human race.

The Flood of Deucalion
and Pyrrha

THE FLOOD

Swiftly within the Wind-god's cave he locked
The north wind and the gales that drive away
The gathered clouds, and sent the south wind forth;
And out on soaking wings the south wind flew,
His ghastly features veiled in deepest gloom.
His beard was sodden with rain, his white hair drenched;
Mists wreathed his brow and streaming water fell
From wings and chest; and when in giant hands
He crushed the hanging clouds, the thunder crashed
And storms of blinding rain poured down from heaven.
Iris,* great Juno's envoy, rainbow-clad,
Gathered the waters and refilled the clouds.
The crops lay flat; the farmer mourned his hopes;
The long year's labour died, vain labour lost.

    Nor was Jove's wrath content with heaven above;
His sea-blue brother* brings his waters' aid,
And summons all the rivers to attend
Their master's palace. 'Now time will not wait
For many words', he says; 'pour out your strength—
The need is great! Unbar your doors! Away
With dykes and dams and give your floods free rein!'
The streams returned and freed their fountains' flow
And rolled in course unbridled to the sea.
Then with his trident Neptune struck the earth,
Which quaked and moved to give the waters way.
In vast expanse across the open plains
The rivers spread and swept away together
Crops, orchards, vineyards, cattle, houses, men,
Temples and shrines with all their holy things.
If any home is left and, undestroyed,
Resists the huge disaster, over its roof,
The waters meet and in their whirling flood
High towers sink from sight; now land and sea
Had no distinction; over the whole earth
All things were sea, a sea without a shore.
Some gained the hilltops, others took to boats
And rowed where late they ploughed; some steered a course
Above the cornfields and the farmhouse roofs,

Neptune
Poseidon

And some caught fishes in the lofty elms.
Perchance in the green meads an anchor dropped
And curving keels brushed through the rows of vines,
And where but now the graceful goats had browsed
Gross clumsy seals hauled their ungainly bulk.
The Nereids see with awe beneath the waves
Cities and homes and groves, and in the woods
The dolphins live and high among the branches
Dash to and fro and shake the oaks in play.
Wolves swim among the sheep, and on the waters
Tigers are borne along and tawny lions.
No more his lightning stroke avails the boar
Nor his swift legs the stag—both borne away.
The wandering birds long seek a resting place
And drop with weary wings into the sea.
The waters' boundless licence overwhelmed
The hills, and strange waves lashed the mountain peaks.
The world was drowned; those few the deluge spared
For dearth of food in lingering famine died.

DEUCALION AND PYRRHA

Between Boeotia and the Oetean hills
The land of Phocis lies, a fertile land
When land it was, but now part of the sea,
A spreading wilderness of sudden waters.
There a great mountain aims towards the stars
Its double peak, Parnassus, soaring high
Above the clouds; and there Deucalion,
Borne on a raft, with his dear wife beside,
Had grounded; all elsewhere the deluge whelmed.
Praise and thanksgiving to the mountain's gods
And nymphs they gave, and to the prophetess,
Themis, then guardian of the oracle;
No man was better, none loved goodness more
Than he, no woman more devout than she.
And when Jove saw the world a waste of waters,
And of so many millions but one man,
And of so many millions but one woman
Alive, both innocent, both worshippers,

He bade the clouds disperse, the north wind drive
The storms away, and to the earth revealed
The heavens again and to the sky the earth.
Spent was the anger of the sea; the Lord
Who rules the main laid by his three-pronged spear
And calmed the waves and, calling from the deep
Triton, sea-hued, his shoulders barnacled
With sea-shells, bade him blow his echoing conch
To bid the rivers, waves and floods retire.
He raised his horn, his hollow spiralled whorl,
The horn that, sounded in mid ocean, fills
The shores of dawn and sunset round the world;
And when it touched the god's wet-bearded lips
And took his breath and sounded the retreat,
All the wide waters of the land and sea
Heard it, and all, hearing its voice, obeyed.
The sea has shores again, the rivers run
Brimming between their banks, the floods subside,
The hills emerge, the swelling contours rise;
As the floods lessen, larger grows the land,
And after many days the woods reveal
Their tree-tops bare and branches lined with mud.

   Earth was restored; but when Deucalion
Saw the deep silence of the desolate lands
And the wide empty wastes, in tears he said:
'Pyrrha, my dearest cousin, dearest wife,
Sole woman left alive, whom ties of blood
And family, then marriage, joined to me,
And now our perils join, in all the lands
The sun beholds from dawn to eve we two
Remain, their peoples—the sea has claimed the rest.
Yet even now our lives are scarce assured,
And still the clouds strike terror in my heart.
Suppose, poor soul, the Fates had rescued you
Alone, what would you feel, how could you face
Your fear without me? Who would staunch your grief?
Be sure that, if the sea had held you too,
I'd follow you; the sea would hold me too.
O for my father's magic* to restore
Mankind again and in the moulded clay

Breathe life and so repopulate the world!
Now on us two the human race depends—
So Heaven wills—us, patterns of mankind.'
They wept together; then resolved to pray
To Powers above and heavenly guidance seek
In oracles; and quickly, hand in hand,
Went to Cephisus' stream, whose current ran
Not limpid yet but in his wonted course,
And there, in ritual due with holy water
Sprinkling their heads and clothes, they turned their steps
Towards the holy shrine (a pale scum fouled
Its roofs; the altars stood without a flame).
They reached the temple steps and then, prostrate,
With timid lips both kissed the cold wet stone
And said: 'If righteous prayers may move and soften
The Powers divine, may turn their wrath away,
Tell, holy Themis, by what art our race,
Now lost, may be restored: in thy great mercy
Hear and grant succour to a world submerged.'
The goddess, pitying, gave her answer: 'Leave
My temple, veil your heads, loosen your robes,
And cast behind you your great mother's bones.'
Long did they wait bewildered, until Pyrrha,
Breaking the silence first, refused assent
And asked in trembling tones the goddess' pardon,
Not daring to offend her mother's ghost
By violence to her bones. In vain they sought
The hidden meaning, searching to and fro
The baffling words' blind coverts. Then at last
Prometheus' son calmed Epimetheus'* daughter
With words of cheer: 'Either my reasoning
Misleads me or in truth (since oracles
Are holy and will never counsel crime)
The earth is our great mother and the stones
Within earth's body surely are the bones
The oracle intends. These we must throw
Over our shoulders as Themis directs.'
So he interpreted, and Pyrrha's heart
Was warmed, but still hope wavered, such distrust
Oppressed them both; and yet what harm to try?

brother of Prometheus [handwritten marginal note]

They leave the temple, veil their heads, ungird
Their robes and, as the oracle commanded,
Behind them, past their footprints, throw the stones.
Those stones (who would believe did ancient lore
Not testify the truth?) gave up their hardness;
Their rigidness grew slowly soft and, softened,
Assumed a shape, and as they grew and felt
A gentler nature's touch, a semblance seemed
To appear, still indistinct, of human form,
Like the first rough-hewn marble of a statue,
Scarce modelled, or old uncouth images.
The earthy part, damp with some trace of moisture,
Was turned to flesh; what was inflexible
And solid changed to bone; what in the stones
Had been the veins retained the name of veins.
In a brief while, by Heaven's mysterious power,
The stones the man had thrown were formed as men,
Those from the woman's hand reshaped as women.
Hence we are hard, we children of the earth,
And in our lives of toil we prove our birth.

    All other forms of life the earth brought forth,
In diverse species, of her own accord,*
When the sun's radiance warmed the pristine moisture
And slime and oozy marshlands swelled with heat,
And in that pregnant soil the seeds of things,
Nourished as in a mother's womb, gained life
And grew and gradually assumed a shape.
So when the seven-mouthed Nile has left at last
The sodden acres and withdrawn its flow
Back to its ancient bed, and the fresh mud
Is warmed by the bright sunshine, farmers find,
Turning the clods, so many forms of life,
Some just begun, still in the stage of birth,
Others unfinished, short of proper parts,
And often, in one creature, part alive,
Part still raw soil. Because when heat and moisture
Blend in due balance, they conceive; these two,
These, are the origin of everything.
Though fire and water fight, humidity
And warmth create all things; that harmony,

So inharmonious, suits the springs of life.
Thus when the earth, deep-coated with the slime
Of the late deluge, glowed again beneath
The warm caresses of the shining sun,
She brought forth countless species, some restored
In ancient forms, some fashioned weird and new.
    Indeed the earth, against her will, produced
A serpent never known before, the huge
Python, a terror to men's new-made tribes,
So far it sprawled across the mountainside.
The Archer god, whose shafts till then were used
Only against wild goats and fleeing deer,
Destroyed the monster with a thousand arrows,
His quiver almost emptied, and the wounds,
Black wounds, poured forth their poison. Then to ensure
The centuries should have no power to dull
The lustre of that deed, Apollo founded
The sacred games,* the crowded contests, known
As Pythian from that serpent overthrown.
Here all whose hand or foot or wheel had won,
Received the honour of a wreath of oak.
Laurels were still unknown; Apollo then
The greenery of any tree would wear
For garlanding his long and lovely hair.

APOLLO AND DAPHNE

Daphne, Peneus' child, was the first love*
Of great Apollo, a love not lit by chance
Unwitting, but by Cupid's spiteful wrath.
The god of Delos,* proud in victory,
Saw Cupid draw his bow's taut arc, and said:
'Mischievous boy, what are a brave man's arms
To you? That gear becomes my shoulders best.
My aim is sure; I wound my enemies,
I wound wild beasts; my countless arrows slew
But now the bloated Python, whose vast coils
Across so many acres spread their blight.
You and your loves! You have your torch to light them!
Let that content you; never claim my fame!'

And Venus' son replied: 'Your bow, Apollo,
May vanquish all, but mine shall vanquish you.
As every creature yields to power divine,
So likewise shall your glory yield to mine.'
Then winging through the air his eager way
He stood upon Parnassus' shady peak,
And from his quiver's laden armoury
He drew two arrows of opposing power,
One shaft that rouses love and one that routs* it.
The first gleams bright with piercing point of gold;
The other, dull and blunt, is tipped with lead.
This one he lodged in Daphne's heart; the first
He shot to pierce Apollo to the marrow.
At once he loves; she flies the name of love,
Delighting in the forest's secret depths
And trophies of the chase, a nymph to vie
With heaven's virgin huntress, fair Diana;
A careless ribbon held her straying hair.

Many would woo her; she, rejecting all,
Manless, aloof, ranged through the untrodden woods
Nor cared what love, what marriage rites might mean.
Often her father said, 'My dearest daughter,
It is my due to have a son-in-law.'
Often her father said, 'It is my due,
Child of my heart, to be given grandchildren.'
She hated like a crime the bond of wedlock,
And, bashful blushes tingeing her fair cheeks,
With coaxing arms embraced him and replied:
'My dear, dear father grant I may enjoy
Virginity for ever; this Diana
Was granted by her father.' He, indeed,
Yielded, but Daphne—why, her loveliness
Thwarts her desire, her grace denies her prayer.

Apollo saw her, loved her, wanted her—
Her for his bride, and, wanting, hoped—deceived
By his own oracles; and, as the stubble
Flames in the harvest fields or as a hedge
Catches alight when some late wayfarer
Chances his torch too close or, in the dawn,
Discards its smouldering embers, so love's fire

Consumed the god, his whole heart was aflame,
And high the hopes that stoked his fruitless passion.
He sees the loose disorder of her hair
And thinks what if it were neat and elegant!
He sees her eyes shining like stars, her lips—
But looking's not enough!—her fingers, hands,
Her wrists, her half-bare arms—how exquisite!
And sure her hidden charms are best! But she
Flies swifter than the lightfoot wind nor stops
To hear him calling: 'Stay, sweet nymph! Oh, stay!
I am no foe to fear. Lambs flee from wolves
And hinds from lions, and the fluttering doves
From eagles; every creature flees its foes.
But love spurs my pursuit. Oh, you will fall
And briars graze your legs—for shame!—and I,
Alas, the cause of your distress! The ground
You race across is rough. You run too fast!
Check your swift flight, and I'll not chase so fast.
Yet ask who loves you. No rough forester
Am I, no unkempt shepherd guarding here
His flocks and herds. You do not know—you fly,
You madcap girl, because you do not know.
I am the lord of Delphi; Tenedos
And Patara and Claros are my realms.
I am the son of Jupiter. By me
Things future, past and present are revealed;
I shape the harmony of song and strings.
Sure are my arrows, but one surer still
Has struck me to the heart, my carefree heart.
The art of medicine I gave the world
And all men call me "healer"; I possess
The power of every herb. Alas! that love
No herb can cure, that skills which help afford
To all mankind fail now to help their lord!'
    More he had tried to say, but she in fear
Fled on and left him and his words unfinished.
Enchanting still she looked—her slender limbs
Bare in the breeze, her fluttering dress blown back,
Her hair behind her streaming as she ran;
And flight enhanced her grace. But the young god,

Could bear no more to waste his blandishments,
And (love was driving him) pressed his pursuit.
And as a beagle sees across the stubble
A hare and runs to kill and she for life—
He almost has her; now, yes now, he's sure
She's his; his straining muzzle scrapes her heels;
And she half thinks she's caught and, as he bites,
Snatches away; his teeth touch—but she's gone.
So ran the god and girl, he sped by hope
And she by fear. But he, borne on the wings
Of love, ran faster, gave her no respite,
Hot on her flying heels and breathing close
Upon her shoulders and her tumbling hair.
Her strength was gone; the travail of her flight
Vanquished her, and her face was deathly pale.
And then she saw the river, swift Peneus,
And called; 'Help, father, help! If mystic power
Dwells in your waters, change me and destroy
My baleful beauty that has pleased too well.'
Scarce had she made her prayer when through her limbs
A dragging languor spread, her tender bosom
Was wrapped in thin smooth bark, her slender arms
Were changed to branches and her hair to leaves;
Her feet but now so swift were anchored fast
In numb stiff roots, her face and head became
The crown of a green tree; all that remained
Of Daphne was her shining loveliness.
    And still Apollo loved her; on the trunk
He placed his hand and felt beneath the bark
Her heart still beating, held in his embrace
Her branches, pressed his kisses on the wood;
Yet from his kisses still the wood recoiled.
'My bride', he said, 'since you can never be,
At least, sweet laurel, you shall be my tree.
My lyre, my locks, my quiver you shall wreathe;
You shall attend the conquering lords of Rome
When joy shouts triumph and the Capitol
Welcomes the long procession; you shall stand
Beside Augustus' gates, sure sentinel
On either side, guarding the oak* between.

My brow is ever young, my locks unshorn;
So keep your leaves' proud glory ever green.'
Thus spoke the god; the laurel in assent
Inclined her new-made branches and bent down,
Or seemed to bend, her head, her leafy crown.

IO

There is a vale in Thessaly, enclosed
With hanging forests, steep on every side;
Men name it Tempe. Here Peneus rolls
At towering Pindus' foot his foaming course,
And from his mighty fall the swirling clouds
Of mist drift down in rain upon the trees,
And far the waters' wearying roar resounds.
Here is the home, the mansion, the retreat
Of that majestic river; seated here
Within a rock-hewn cavern he dispensed
Justice to all his waters and their nymphs.
Hither assemble first the neighbouring streams,
Restless Enipeus, old Apidanus,
Spercheus poplar-fringed, gentle Amphrysus
And Aeas, doubtful whether to console
Daphne's fond parent or congratulate.
Soon other rivers come, whose courses flow
Where'er their currents drive and lead at last
Their wandering waters weary to the sea.
But one is absent, Inachus, withdrawn
Deep in his cave and weeping tears that swell
His current, as he mourns in bitter grief
Io, his daughter lost. He cannot tell
Whether she lives or dwells among the shades,
And finding her nowhere thinks she must be
Nowhere and fear feeds fear when knowledge fails.*

 Io returning from her father's stream
Had caught Jove's eye. 'You charming girl', he said,
'Well worthy of Jove's love, happy is he,
Whoe'er he be, that wins you for his bed.
Go to the deep wood's shade'—he pointed to
The shady wood—'the hour is hot; the sun

Shines in his zenith. If you fear alone
To risk the wild beasts' lairs, a god will guard you
And in the deepest forest keep you safe—
No common god! The sceptre of the sky
Is mine to hold in my almighty hand;
I wield at will the roaming thunderbolts—
No, do not run!' For now the girl had run;
Through Lerna's meadows and the forest lands
Of high Lyrceus she sped until the god
Drew down a veil of darkness to conceal
The world and stayed her flight and ravished her.

 Juno meanwhile observed the land of Argos
And wondered that the floating clouds had wrought
In the bright day the darkness of the night.
These were no river mists! No clouds like these
The humid earth exhaled! She looked around
To find her husband; well she knew his tricks,
So often had caught him in his escapades;
And searched the sky in vain. 'If I'm not wrong',
She thought, 'I'm being wronged'; and gliding down
From heaven's height she lighted on the earth
And bade the clouds disperse. Jove had fore-sensed
His spouse's visit and transformed poor Io
Into a sleek white heifer (lovely still
Although a cow). Juno, against her will,
Admired the creature and asked whose she was,
And whence she came and to what herd belonged,
Pretending not to know the truth. He lied—
'The earth had brought her forth'—so to deflect
Questions about her birth. Then Juno begged
The heifer as a gift. What should he do?
Too cruel to give his darling! Not to give—
Suspicious; shame persuades but love dissuades.
Love would have won; but then—if he refused
His wife (his sister too) so slight a gift,
A cow, it well might seem no cow at all!

 The goddess won her rival, but distrust
Lingered and still she feared her husband's tricks,
Till, for safe-keeping, she had given the cow
To Argus—Argus of the hundred eyes,

All watching and on duty round his head,
Save two which took in turn their sleep and rest.
Whichever way he stood he looked at Io,
Io before his eyes behind his back!
By day he let her graze, but when the sun
Sank down beneath the earth he stabled her
And tied—for shame!—a halter round her neck.
She browsed on leaves of trees and bitter weeds,
And for her bed, poor thing, lay on the ground,
Not always grassy, and drank the muddy streams;
And when, to plead with Argus, she would try
To stretch her arms, she had no arms to stretch.
Would she complain, a moo came from her throat,
A startling sound—her own voice frightened her.
She reached her father's river and the banks
Where often she had played and, in the water,
Mirrored she saw her muzzle and her horns,
And fled in terror from the self she saw.
The Naiads did not know—not even her father
Knew who she was, but she, disconsolate,
Followed her sisters, followed her father, let
Them stroke her, offered herself to be admired.
Old Inachus picked grass and held it out;
She licked her father's hand, cow-kissed his palms;
Her tears rolled down; if only words would come,
She'd speak her name, tell all, implore their aid.
For words her hoof traced letters* in the dust—
I, O—sad tidings of her body's change.
'Alas, alack!' her father cried, and clasped
The moaning heifer's horns and snow-white neck.
'Alas, alack!' he groaned: 'Are you the child
I sought through all the world? Oh, lighter grief
You were unfound than found. You give no answer;
Silent, but from your heart so deep a sigh!
A moo—all you can say—is your reply!
I, knowing naught, made ready for your marriage,
Hoped for a son-in-law and grandchildren.
But now the herd must find your husband, find
Your child. For me death cannot end my woes.
Sad bane to be a god! The gates of death

Are shut; my grief endures for evermore.'
As thus they grieved, Argus, star-eyed, drove off
Daughter from father, hurrying her away
To distant pastures. Then himself, afar,
High on a mountain top sat sentinel
To keep his scrutiny on every side.

But now heaven's master could no more endure
Io's distress, and summoned Mercury,
His son, whom the bright shining Pleiad bore,*
And charged him to accomplish Argus' death.
Promptly he fastened on his ankle-wings,
Grasped in his fist the wand that charms to sleep,
Put on his magic cap, and thus arrayed
Jove's son sprang from his father's citadel
Down to the earth. There he removed his cap,
Laid by his wings; only his wand he kept.
A herdsman now,* he drove a flock of goats
Through the green byways, gathered as he went,
And played his pipes of reed. The strange sweet skill
Charmed Juno's guardian. 'My friend', he called,
'Whoever you are, well might you sit with me
Here on this rock; nowhere is lusher grass
To feed your flock, and see how cool the shade
Extends congenial for a shepherd's seat.'

So Mercury joined him, and with many a tale
He stayed the passing hours and on his reeds
Played soft refrains to lull the watching eyes.
But Argus fought to keep at bay the charms
Of slumber and, though many of his eyes
Were closed in sleep, still many kept their guard.
He asked too by what means this new design
(For new it was), the pipe of reeds, was found.

Then Mercury told this story: 'Once there lived
On the cold mountainsides of Arcady
A Naiad, who among the forest sprites
Of lofty Nonacris was most renowned.
Syrinx the Naiads called her. Many a time
She foiled the chasing satyrs and those gods
Who haunt the shady copses and the coverts
Of the lush countryside. In her pursuits—

And in her chastity—Syrinx revered
Diana; girt like her she well might seem
(So easy to mistake) Diana's self,
Were not her bow of horn, Diana's gold.
Indeed she was mistaken. Pan returning
From Mount Lycaeus, crowned with his wreath of pine,
Saw Syrinx once and said—' but what he said
Remained to tell, and how* the scornful nymph
Fled through the wilderness and came at last
To Ladon's peaceful sandy stream, and there,
Her flight barred by the river, begged her sisters,
The water-nymphs, to change her; and, when Pan
Thought he had captured her, he held instead
Only the tall marsh reeds, and, while he sighed,
The soft wind stirring in the reeds sent forth
A thin and plaintive sound; and he, entranced
By this new music and its witching tones,
Cried 'You and I shall stay in unison!'
And waxed together reeds of different lengths
And made the pipes that keep his darling's name.
The tale remained untold; for Mercury saw
All Argus' eyelids closed and every eye
Vanquished in sleep. He stopped and with his wand,
His magic wand, soothed the tired resting eyes
And sealed their slumber; quick then with his sword
Struck off the nodding head and from the rock
Threw it all bloody, spattering the cliff with gore.
Argus lay dead; so many eyes, so bright
Quenched, and all hundred shrouded in one night.

Juno retrieved those eyes to set in place
Among the feathers of her bird* and filled
His tail with starry jewels. At once her wrath
Flared up and soon her anger was fulfilled.
Before her rival's eyes and in her mind
She set a frightful Fury* and deep down
Plunged blinding goads of fear; and Io fled
A cowering fugitive through all the world.
Her boundless travails found their end at last
Beside the Nile; there, falling on her knees,
Her head thrown back, she raised towards the stars

All she could raise, her face; her groans and tears,
Her wild grief-laden lowings seemed to send
A prayer to Jove to end her sufferings.
And Jove pleaded with Juno, throwing his arms
Around her neck, to end the punishment
At last. 'Lay fear aside; never again',
He swore, 'shall Io give you cause to grieve',
And charged the pools of Styx to attest his oath.

　　The goddess was appeased. Io regained
Her shape, became once more what once she was.
The hair falls from her hide, her horns are gone,
Her great wide eyes contract, her gaping mouth
Shrinks small again, her arms and hands return,
Her cloven hoofs resume their fivefold form;
The heifer vanished, save her fair white grace.
The nymph, content to use two legs again,
Now walked erect, yet still afraid to speak
Lest, cow-like, she might moo, and timorously
Essayed the syllables so long disused.

　　She is a goddess now, famous, divine,
And linen-robed adorers throng her shrine.
To her a son was born, young Epaphus,
Sprung, it was thought, at last from Jove's begetting,
And in each town he shared his mother's shrines.

PHAETHON

His peer in pride and years was Phaethon,
Child of the Sun, whose arrogance one day
And boasts of his high parentage were more
Than Epaphus could bear. 'You fool', he said,
'To credit all your mother says; that birth
You boast about is false.' Then Phaethon
Flushed (though shame checked his rage) and took those taunts
To Clymene, his mother. 'And to grieve
You more, dear mother, I so frank', he said,
'So fiery, stood there silent. I'm ashamed
That he could so insult me and that I
Could not repulse him. But, if I indeed
Am sprung from heavenly stock, give me sure proof

Of my high birth, confirm my claim to heaven.'
He threw his arms around his mother's neck,
And begged her by his own and Merops' life,
His sisters' hopes of marriage, to provide
Some token that that parentage was true.
And Clymene, moved whether by his words
Or anger at the insult to herself,
Held out her arms to heaven and faced the Sun
And cried, 'By this great glorious radiance,
This beaming blaze, that hears and sees us now,
I swear, dear child, that he, the Sun, on whom
You gaze, the Sun who governs all the globe,
He is your father. If I lie, let him
Deny his beams, let this light be the last
My eyes shall ever see! And you may find
Your father's home with no long toil. The place
From which he rises borders our own land.
Go, make the journey if your heart is set,
And put your question to the Sun himself.'
Then up flashed Phaethon at his mother's words;
Heaven filled his happy thoughts; and journeying
Through his own Ethiopians* and the lands
Of India beneath their burning skies,
He quickly reached his father's rising-place.

Clymene rose her arms to the sky and is telling the gods to prove he is the son of the Sun.

– if she lies then she will be punished with not being able to see.

BOOK II

PHAETHON (continued)

THE palace of the Sun rose high aloft
On soaring columns, bright with flashing gold
And flaming bronze; the pediments were clothed
With sheen of ivory; the double doors
Dazzled with silver—and the artistry
Was nobler still. For Vulcan had engraved
The world's great orb, the seas that ring the world,
The sky that hangs above; and in the waves
The sea-gods dwelt, Aegaeon,* his huge arms
Entwined around the backs of giant whales,
Ambiguous Proteus,* Triton* with his horn;
And Doris* and her daughters might be seen,
And some were swimming, some on fishes rode,
Or sat on rocks to dry their sea-green hair.
Nor were their looks the same, nor yet diverse,
But like as sisters should be. On the land
People and cities, woods and beasts were graven,
Rivers and nymphs and rural deities,
And, set above them, the bright signs of heaven,
In glory shining, six upon each door.*
　　Then Phaethon, climbing the steep ascent,
Entered his father's palace (fatherhood
Uncertain still) and made his way direct
Into the presence and there stood afar,
Unable to approach the dazzling light.
Enrobed in purple vestments Phoebus sat,
High on a throne of gleaming emeralds.
Attending him on either side stood Day
And Month and Year and Century, and Hours
Disposed at equal intervals between.
Young Spring was there, with coronet of flowers,
And naked Summer, garlanded with grain;
Autumn was there with trampled vintage stained,
And icy Winter,* rime upon his locks.
　　Enthroned amidst, the Sun who sees all things

Beheld the boy dismayed by sights so strange,
And said 'What purpose brings, faring so far,
My son, a son no father would deny,
To this high citadel?' The boy replied
'O thou, Creation's universal light,
Phoebus, my father, if to use that name
Thou givest me leave, and Clymene spoke truth
And hides no guilt, give proof that all may know
I am thy son indeed, and end for ever
The doubt that grieves me.' Then his father laid
Aside the dazzling beams that crowned his head
And bade him come and held him to his heart:
'Well you deserve to be my son', he said,
'Truly your mother named your lineage;
And to dispel all doubt, ask what you will
That I may satisfy your heart's desire;
And that dark marsh* by which the gods make oath,
Though to my eyes unknown,* shall seal my troth.'
He scarce had ended when the boy declared
His wish—his father's chariot for one day
With licence to control the soaring steeds.
      Grief and remorse flooded his father's soul,
And bitterly he shook his glorious head:
'Rash have your words proved mine! Would that I might
Retract my promise, Phaethon! This alone
I would indeed deny you. Yet at least
I may dissuade you. Dangerous is your choice;
You seek a privilege that ill befits
Your growing years and strength so boyish still.
Mortal your lot—not mortal your desire;
This, to which even the gods may not aspire,
In ignorance you claim. Though their own powers
May please the gods, not one can take his stand
Above my chariot's flaming axle-tree
Save I. Even he whose hand hurls thunderbolts,
Olympus' mighty lord, may never drive
My team—and who is mightier than Jove?
      Steep is the way at first, which my steeds scarce
Can climb in morning freshness; in mid sky
The altitude is greatest and the sight

Of land and sea below has often struck
In my own heart an agony of fear.
The final part drops sheer; then above all
Control must be assured, and even she
Whose waters lie below to welcome me,
Tethys, waits fearful lest I headlong fall.
Besides, in constant flux the sky streams by,*
Sweeping in dizzy whirl the stars on high.
I drive against this force, which overcomes
All things but me, and on opposing course
Against its rushing circuit make my way.
Suppose my chariot yours: what then? Could you
Confront the spinning poles and not be swept
Away by the swift axis of the world?
Perhaps you fancy cities of gods are there
And groves and temples rich with offerings.
No! Wild beasts lie in wait and shapes of fear!*
And though you keep your course and steer aright,
Yet you shall meet the Bull, must brave his horns,
And face the Archer and the ravening Lion,
The long curved circuit of the Scorpion's claws,
The Crab whose claws in counter-menace wave.
My horses too, when fire within their breasts
Rages, from mouth and nostrils breathing flames,
Are hard to hold; even I can scarce restrain
Their ardent hearts, their necks that fight the rein.
But, O my son, amend, while time remains,
Your choice, so may my gift not be your doom.
Sure proof you seek of fatherhood; indeed
My dread sure proof affords: a father's fear
Proves me your father. Look into my eyes!
Would you could look into my heart and see
And understand your father's agony!
See, last, how rich the world around you lies,
The bounty of the lands, the seas, the skies;
Choose what you will of these—it shall be yours.
But this alone, not this! Bane truly named
Not glory, Phaethon—bane this gift not boon!
Why fold me in your arms, fond foolish boy?
By Styx I swore and I shall not refuse,

Whate'er your choice: but oh! more wisely choose!'
   So the Sun warned; but Phaethon would not yield
And held his purpose, burning with desire
To drive the chariot. Then his father, slow
And pausing as he might, led out the boy
To that high chariot, Vulcan's masterwork.
Gold was the axle, gold the shaft, and gold
The rolling circles of the tyres; the spokes
In silver order stood, and on the harness
Patterns of gorgeous gems and chrysolites
Shone gleaming in the glory of the Sun.
And while the daring boy in wonder gazed,
Aurora, watchful in the reddening dawn,
Threw wide her crimson doors and rose-filled halls;
The stars took flight, in marshalled order set
By Lucifer* who left his station last.
Then, when the Sun perceived the morning star
Setting and saw the world in crimson sheen
And the last lingering crescent of the moon
Fade in the dawn, he bade the nimble Hours
Go yoke his steeds, and they, swift goddesses,
Fastened the jingling harness and the reins,
As from the lofty stalls the horses came,
Filled with ambrosial food and breathing flame.
Then on his son's young face the father smeared
A magic salve to shield him from the heat,
And set the flashing sunbeams* on his head,
And with a heavy heart and many a sigh,
That told of grief to come, addressed the boy:
   'If this advice at least you will obey,
Spare, child, the whip and rein them hard; they race
Unurged; the task's to hold them in their zeal.
Avoid the road direct through all five zones;
On a wide slanting curve the true course lies
Within the confines of three zones;* beware
Alike the southern pole and northern Bear.
Keep to this route; my wheeltracks* there show plain.
Press not too low nor strain your course too high;
Too high, you'll burn heaven's palaces; too low,
The earth; the safest course lies in between.

And neither rightwards towards the twisting Snake
Nor leftwards swerve to where the Altar* lies.
Hold in the midst! To fortune I resign
The rest to guide with wiser wit than yours.
    See, dewy night upon the Hesperian shore
Even while I speak has reached her goal. No more
May we delay; our duty calls; the day
Dawns bright, all shadows fled. Come take the reins!
Or take, if yet your stubborn heart will change,
My counsel, not my chariot, while you may,
While still on firm foundations here you stand
Before you mount between my chariot wheels,
So ignorant, so foolish!—and let me
Give the world light that you may safely see.'
    But Phaethon mounted, light and young and proud,
And took the reins with joy, and looking down,
Thanked his reluctant father for the gift.
    Meanwhile the four swift horses of the Sun,
Aethon, Eous, Pyrois and Phlegon,*
Kick at the gates, neighing and snorting fire,
And Tethys* then, her grandson's fate undreamt,
Draws back the bars and makes the horses free
Of all the boundless heavens. Forth they go,
Tearing away, and cleave with beating hooves
The clouds before them, and on wings outride
The winds that westwards from the morning blow.
But lightly weighs the yoke; the chariot moves
With ease unwonted, suspect buoyancy;
And like a ship at sea unballasted
That pitches in the waves for lack of weight,
The chariot, lacking now its usual load,
Bounced driverless, it seemed, in empty leaps.
The horses in alarm ran wild and left
The well-worn highway. Phaethon, dazed with fear,
Could neither use the reins nor find the road,
Nor were it found could make the team obey.
Then first the sunbeams warmed the freezing Bear,
Who sought vain refuge in forbidden seas;*
The Snake that numb and harmless hitherto
Lay next the icy pole, roused by the heat,

- Phaethon loses control of his horses on the chariot and Zeus strikes him down.

In newly kindled rage began to burn;
The Wagoner* too, it's said, fled in dismay,
Though slow and hampered by his lumbering wain.

    And when poor hapless Phaethon from the height
Of highest heaven looked down and saw below,
Far, far below the continents outspread,
His face grew pale, his knees in sudden fear
Shook, and his eyes were blind with light so bright.
Would he had never touched his father's steeds,
Nor learnt his birth, nor won his heart's desire!
Oh, to be known as Merops' son! Too late!
He's swept away as when a barque is driven
Before the northern gales and in despair
The master leaves the helm, resigns his charge
To heaven. What shall he do? The sky behind
Stretches away so far; yet more in front.
He measures each in turn; ahead he sees
The west that fate ordains he shall not reach,
Then looks back to the east. Dazed and in doubt
He cannot hold the reins or let them fall
Or even recall the horses' names. And then
He sees in panic strewn across the sky
Monstrous gigantic shapes of beasts of prey.
There is a place* in which the Scorpion's claws
Curve in a double arc, with tail and legs
On either side crossing two signs* of heaven;
Sweating black venom, there before his eyes,
Circling its tail to strike, the creature lies.
His senses reel; he drops the reins aghast.
And when the reins fall loose upon their backs,
The horses swerve away and, unrestrained,
Gallop through tracts of air unknown and race
Headlong, out of control, running amok
Amid the stars fixed in the vault of heaven,
Hurtling the chariot where no road had run.
And now they climb to highest heaven, now plunge
Sheer in breakneck descent down to the earth.
The moon in wonder sees her brother's team
Running below her own; the scalding clouds
Steam; the parched fields crack deep, all moisture **dried,**

And every summit flames; the calcined meads
Lie white; the leaf dies burning with the bough
And the dry corn its own destruction feeds.
These are but trifles. Mighty cities burn
With all their ramparts; realms and nations turn
To ashes; mountains with their forests blaze.
Athos* is burning, Oeta is on fire,
And Tmolus and proud Taurus and the crest
Of Ida, dry, whose springs were once so famed,
And virgin* Helicon and Haemus, still
Unknown, unhonoured.* Etna burns immense
In twofold conflagration; Eryx flames
And Othrys and Parnassus' double peaks;
Cynthus and Dindyma and Mycale
And Rhodope, losing at last her snows,
And Mimas and Cithaeron's holy hill.
Caucasus burns; the frosts of Scythia
Fail in her need; Pindus and Ossa blaze
And, lordlier than both, Olympus flames
And the airy Alps and cloud-capped Apennines.

 Then Phaethon saw the world on every side
Ablaze—heat more than he could bear. He breathed
Vapours that burned like furnace-blasts, and felt
The chariot glow white-hot beneath his feet.
Cinders and sparks past bearing shoot and swirl
And scorching smoke surrounds him; in the murk,
The midnight murk, he knows not where he is
Or goes; the horses whirl him where they will.

 The Aethiops then turned black, so men believe,
As heat summoned their blood too near the skin.
Then was Sahara's dusty desert formed,
All water scorched away. Then the sad nymphs
Bewailed their pools and springs; Boeotia mourned
Her Dirce lost, Argos Amymone,
Corinth Pirene; nor were rivers safe
Though fortune's favour made them broad and deep
And their banks far apart; in middle stream
From old Peneus rose the drifting steam,
From Erymanthus too and swift Ismenus,
And Mysian Caicus and the Don;

Maeander playing on his winding way;
Tawny Lycormas, Xanthus doomed to burn
At Troy a second time;* Melas of Thrace,
That sable stream; Eurotas, Sparta's pride.
Euphrates burned, river of Babylon,
Phasis, Danube and Ganges were on fire,
Orontes burned and racing Thermodon;
Alpheus boiled, fire scorched Spercheus' banks.
The gold that Tagus carries in his sands
Ran molten in the flames, and all the swans
That used to charm the Lydian banks with song
Huddled in mid Cayster sweltering.
The Nile in terror to the world's end fled
And hid his head, still hidden;* his seven mouths
Gaped dusty, seven vales without a stream.
The same disaster dried the Thracian rivers,
Hebrus and Strymon, dried the lordly flow
Of western waters, Rhone and Rhine and Po,
And Tiber, promised empire of the world.
Earth everywhere splits deep and light strikes down
Into the Underworld and fills with fear
Hell's monarch and his consort; the wide seas
Shrink and where ocean lay a wilderness
Of dry sand spreads; new peaks and ranges rise,
Long covered by the deep, and multiply
The scattered islands of the Cyclades.
The fishes dive; the dolphins dare not leap
Their curving course through the familiar air,
And lifeless seals float supine on the waves;
Even Nereus, fathoms down, in his dark caves,
With Doris and her daughters, felt the fire.
Thrice from the waters Neptune raised his arm
And frowning face; thrice fled the fiery air.

But Mother Earth, encompassed by the seas,
Between the ocean and her shrinking streams,
That cowered for refuge in her lightless womb,
Lifted her smothered head and raised her hand
To shield her tortured face; then with a quake,
A mighty tremor that convulsed the world,
Sinking in shallow subsidence below

Her wonted place, in solemn tones appealed:
'If this thy pleasure and my due, why now,
Greatest of gods, lie thy dread lightnings still?
If fire destroy me, let the fire be thine:
My doom were lighter dealt by thy design!
Scarce can my throat find voice to speak' (the smoke
And heat were choking her). 'See my singed hair!
Ash in my eyes, ash on my lips so deep!
Are these the fruits of my fertility?
Is this for duty done the due return?
That I endure the wounds of pick and plough,
Year-long unceasing pain, that I supply
Grass for the flocks and crops, sweet sustenance,
For humankind and incense for you gods?
But, grant my doom deserved, what have the seas
Deserved and what thy brother?* Why shrinks the main,
His charge, and from the sky so far recoils?
And if no grace can save thy brother now,
Nor me, pity thine own fair sky! Look round!
See, each pole smokes; if there the fire should gain,
Your royal roofs will fall. Even Atlas fails,
His shoulders scarce sustain the flaming sky.*
If land and sea, if heaven's high palaces
Perish, prime chaos will us all confound!
Save from the flames whatever's still alive,
And prove you mean Creation to survive!'
    Then Earth could speak no more, no more endure
The fiery heat and vapour, and sank back
To her deep caverns next the Underworld.
But the Almighty Father, calling the gods
And him who gave the chariot to attest
Creation doomed were now his aid not given,
Mounted the highest citadel of heaven,
Whence he was wont to veil the lands with clouds*
And roll his thunders and his lightnings hurl.
But then no clouds had he the lands to veil,
Nor rain to send from heaven to soothe their pain.
He thundered; and poising high his bolt to blast,
Struck Phaethon from the chariot and from life,
And fire extinguished fire and flame quenched flame.

Zeus struck him down.

[handwritten margin note top: Phaethon's death ↓]

The horses in wild panic leapt apart,
Burst from the traces and flung off the yoke.
There lie the reins, the sundered axle there,
Here the spokes dangle from a shattered wheel,
And far and wide the signs of wreckage fly.
    And Phaethon, flames ravaging his auburn hair,
Falls headlong down, a streaming trail of light,
As sometimes through the cloudless vault of night
A star, though never falling, seems to fall.
Eridanus receives him, far from home,
In his wide waters half a world away,
And bathes his burning face. The Hesperian nymphs
Bury his smouldering body in a tomb
And on a stone engrave this epitaph:
'Here Phaethon lies, his father's charioteer;
Great was his fall, yet did he greatly dare.'
    His father, sick with grief, had hidden his face,
Shrouded in misery, and, if the tale
Is true, one day went by without the Sun.
The flaming fires gave light—some gain at least
In that disaster. Clymene, distraught
With sorrow, said whatever could be said
In woes so terrible and beat her breast,
And roamed the world to find his lifeless limbs
And then his bones, and found his bones at last
Buried beside a foreign river-bank.
And, prostrate there, she drenched in tears his name
Carved in the marble and hugged it to her breast.
His sisters too, the Sun's three daughters, wept
Sad tears, their futile tribute to the dead,
And long lay prostrate on their brother's tomb,
Bruising their breasts and calling day and night
Phaethon who never more would hear their moans.
Four times the waxing crescent of the moon
Had filled her orb, and, in their wonted way
(Wailing was now their wont) they made lament,
When Phaethusa, eldest of the three,
Meaning to kneel upon the ground, complained
Her feet were rigid. When Lampetie,
Her lovely sister, tried to come to her,

She found herself held fast by sudden roots;
The third, reaching to tear her hair, instead
Plucked leaves. One, in dismay, felt wood encase
Her shins and one her arms become long boughs.
And while they stood bewildered, bark embraced
Their loins and covered, inch by inch, their waists,
Breasts, shoulders, hands, till only lips were left,
Calling their mother. She, what can she do
But dart distractedly now here, now there,
And kiss them while she may. It's not enough.
She tries to tear the bark away and breaks
The tender boughs, but from them bloody drops
Ooze like a dripping wound. 'Stop, mother, stop!'
Each injured girl protests; 'I beg you, stop;
The tree you tear is me. And now, farewell!'
The bark lapped her last words. So their tears still
Flow on, and oozing from the new-made boughs,
Drip and are hardened in the sun to form
Amber and then the clear stream catches them
And carries them for Roman brides to wear.
    Cycnus,* the son of Sthenelus, was there
And saw this miracle. Now he was kin
To Phaethon through his mother, and in spirit
Closer than kin.* He left the realm he ruled,
Liguria's peoples and their mighty towns,
And filled Eridanus' green riverside
And poplar-rows, to which those sisters three
Were added, with his moans of misery.
His voice grew thin, white feathers hid his hair,
His neck stretched long, his fingers, turning red,
Were fastened by a web, wings draped his sides,
His mouth became a blunt unpointed beak.
He was a strange new bird, a swan, that fears
To trust the sky or Jove, remembering
The unfairness of that fiery bolt he hurled.
He haunts broad lakes and ponds, and, hating fire,
Finds in fire's opposite his fluid home.
    The Sun meanwhile, dishevelled, his bright sheen
Subdued as in the gloom of an eclipse,
Loathing himself, loathing the light, the day,

Gives way to grief, and, grief rising to rage,
Denies his duty to the world. 'Enough',
He cries, 'Since time began my lot has brought
No rest, no respite. I resent this toil,
Unending toil, unhonoured drudgery.
Let someone else take out my chariot
That bears my sunbeams, or, if no one will,
And all the gods confess they can't, let Jove
Drive it, and, as he wrestles with the reins,
There'll be a while at least when he won't wield
His bolt to rob a father of his son;
And, when he's tried the fiery-footed team
And learnt their strength, he'll know no one should die
For failing to control them expertly.'
Then all the deities surround the Sun
And beg him and beseech him not to shroud
The world in darkness. Jove, indeed, defends
His fiery bolt and adds his royal threats.
So the Sun took in hand his maddened team,
Still terrified, and whipped them savagely,
Whipped them and cursed them for their guilt that they
Destroyed his son, their master, that dire day.

CALLISTO

The Almighty Father made the anxious round
Of heaven's vast bastions to ensure that none,
Enfeebled by the fire's assault, should fall;
And seeing all were sound, their strength intact,
Surveyed the earth and the affairs of men.
His own Arcadia* was his weightiest care;
Her springs and rivers, fearing still to flow,
He primed anew, gave verdure to the fields,
Leaves to the trees and bade the ravaged woods
Grow green again. And as he came and went,
Busy, there caught his eye a country nymph
Of Nonacris* and love flared in his heart.
She was no girl to spin soft skeins of wool
Or vary her hair-style; a buckle held
Her dress, a plain white band her straggling hair.

She carried a light spear—sometimes a bow—
Diana's warrior; none so high as she
In Dian's favour on the mountain slopes
Of Maenalus; but favourites soon fall.
　　One afternoon, the sun still riding high,
She found a glade deep in the virgin woods
And there unstrung her bow, took off her quiver,
And lay down on the grass, the coloured case
A pillow for her head. Jove saw her there,
Weary and unprotected and alone.
'This prank', he thought, 'my wife will never learn,
Or should she, all her scolding's worth the prize.'
　　Taking at once Diana's form, her face
And dress, 'My dear', he said, 'best of my troop,
Which mountain coverts have you drawn?' The girl
Rose from the greensward; 'Hail, my queen', said she,
'Greater than Jove I say though Jove should hear.'
Jove heard and smiled, happy that she preferred
Him to himself, and kissed her on the lips—
No modest, maiden's kisses—checked her tale,
Seized her and by his outrage stood betrayed.
She fought, it's true, as hard as girls can fight;
(Would that Juno had watched, her wrath were less)
She fought, but how could any girl succeed,
How master Jove? Victorious, he retired
To heaven above; she loathed the forest glade,
The woods that knew, and, as she turned to go,
Nearly forgot her quiver and her bow.
　　And now Dictynna* across high Maenalus
Progressing with her troop, proud of her kills,
Observed the girl and called her. At the call
She shrank at first lest it were Jove again,
But then she saw the nymphs came with their queen,
And feared no trap and joined their company.
How hard it is for a face to hide its guilt!
She scarce could raise her eyes, nor as before
Stayed by her goddess' side and led the train.
Silent, her awkward blushes told her shame.
Diana, but for her own chaste innocence,
Might well have learnt by countless little signs

The guilty truth; no doubt the nymphs knew well.
    Nine times the crescent moon had filled her orb,
When Dian, wearied by her brother's beams
And by the chase, reached a cool shady grove,
Through which there flowed a babbling rivulet,
Whose gliding current shaped its shelving sands.
Charmed by the place, the goddess dipped her feet
Into the stream; and that was charming too.
'No spy is near', she said, 'here let us strip
And bathe.' The poor girl blushed; they all undressed;
One lingered waiting. As she hesitates,
They strip her body—and her secret—bare.
Aghast, she spread her hands to hide her shape.
'Begone!' Diana cried, 'you shall not stain
My stream!' and bade her quit her company.
    Juno, the Thunderer's consort, knew the truth
Long since, and had deferred until due time
Her dire revenge, and now the time was due.
Her rival bore a boy (*that* galled her most),
Arcas; on him the goddess turned her eyes,
Her anger. 'Strumpet, so it came to this,
That you gave birth, and published by that birth
My injury and proved my Jove's disgrace.
Now you shall pay! That loveliness, your joy,
The grace that won my lord, I shall destroy!'
She seized her by the hair and flung her flat
Upon the ground. The girl held out her arms
For mercy. Over those arms spread grisly fur,
Her nails lengthened to claws, her hands curved down
To serve as feet, the lips that Jove so praised
Were hideous jaws, and, lest her prayers prevail,
Her power of speech was quenched; a fearful growl,
Angry and menacing, came from her throat.
She was a bear, but kept her woman's heart;
Moan after moan proclaimed her misery.
She raised her hands (her paws!) towards the stars
And blamed, though wordless, Jove's ingratitude.
How often in the lonely woods she feared
To lay her head, and wandered to and fro
Before her home, through her familiar fields!

How often, when the baying hounds gave chase,
She fled across the scarps—the huntress fleeing
In panic from the horror of the hunt!
And many a time, forgetting what she was,
Hid from the creatures of the wild; a bear,
She shuddered to see bears on the high hills,
Feared wolves although her father* was a wolf.

   The years rolled on; Arcas was now sixteen,
His mother lost, her fate, her name unknown.
One day, out hunting in the forest glades
Of Erymanthus, as he placed his nets,
He chanced to meet her; seeing him she stopped
Stock still, seeming to recognize his face.
He shrank away; those eyes, unmoving, fixed
For ever on his own, froze the boy's heart
With nameless fear, and as she moved towards him
He aimed his javelin to strike her dead.
The Almighty stayed his hand and swept away
Both son and mother—with the threatened crime—
Whirled in a wind together through the void,
And set them in the sky as neighbouring stars.*

   Juno, in fury when that concubine
Shone midst the stars, descended to the sea,
To Tethys* and old Ocean, whom the gods
Greatly revere, and to their questioning
Replied: 'You ask why I, the queen of heaven,
Come hither from the mansions of the sky?
I am dethroned; another reigns; my words
Are false unless, when night darkens the world,
You see, new-honoured in heaven to injure me,
Twin constellations at the utmost pole,
Where earth in last and shortest circle turns.
Who now would hesitate to insult Juno?
Who fear to offend me, me whose punishment
Proves but preferment? Such is my success!
So vast my influence! She whom I forbade
To be a woman, made a goddess! Thus
The guilty pay! So great my sovereignty!
Let him unbeast the beast, her shape restore,
As Io's was, his other paramour!

Why not, deposing Juno, set instead
Lycaon's wanton daughter in my bed?
But you who reared me, if your hearts are touched
By my disgrace, debar from your green deeps
That sevenfold star* that at the price of shame
Was set in heaven, nor let that prostitute
Your waters' pure integrity pollute.'
The sea-gods gave assent, and Saturn's child
Departed heavenwards through the cloudless air
With her light chariot and her peacock team,
Her peacocks, painted bright with Argus' eyes,
Slain lately at the time* that garrulous bird,
The raven, which had formerly been white,
Was changed and suddenly made black as night.

THE RAVEN AND THE CROW

The raven once had been a silvery bird,
With snow-white wings, pure as the spotless doves,
His whiteness rivalling the wakeful geese
Whose voice would one day save the Capitol,*
And rivalling the swans that love the streams.
His ruin was his tongue; his chattering tongue
Turned that white colour to its opposite.
    In all the land of Thessaly no girl
Was lovelier than Coronis of Larissa.
She certainly was Phoebus' favourite,
So long as she was chaste—or not found out.
But Phoebus' bird* had found her faithlessness
And hastened to his master to reveal
The guilt she hid, ruthless to tell his tale.
To learn the latest news a garrulous crow
Flapped quickly after him, and when it heard
His journey's aim, 'To no good end', it said,
'You make your way. Heed my prophetic tongue!
See what I was, what I am now, and ask
Did I deserve it. Frank good faith you'll find
Was my undoing. Once upon a time
A baby, Erichthonius, was born
Without a mother.* Pallas hid the child

Safe in a box of wickerwork and gave
The box to Cecrops' three unmarried daughters,
With strict instructions not to pry inside.
I hid among the delicate foliage
Of a large leafy elm and watched to see
What they would do. Two, Pandrosos and Herse,
Impeccably observed their trust; but one,
Aglauros,* called them cowards and untied
The fastenings, and there inside they saw
The baby, and beside him stretched a snake.*
I told the goddess. All the thanks I got
Was to be banished from Minerva's sight,
Reduced to rank below the bird of night!
My punishment might well warn birds to watch
Their tongues and take no risks. No doubt you think
I pestered her, and not that *she* chose me:
Ask Pallas then herself! Of course she's angry,
But not too angry to admit the truth.

    My father was the famous king of Phocis,
Coroneus, as the world knows well enough,
And I was a princess, and I was wooed
(You must not laugh) by many a wealthy man.
My beauty doomed me. One day on the shore,
Pacing across the sand with long slow strides,
As I still do, the Sea-god saw me there,
And fell in love with me; and when his pleas
And winning words proved but a waste of time,
He tried to force me. In my flight I left
The hard firm beach and soon, in the soft sand,
Was quite worn out—in vain! I cried for help
To gods and men. No human heard my voice;
A virgin's anguish moved the Virgin's heart*
And Pallas brought her aid. I raised my arms
To heaven; along my arms a sable down
Of feathers spread. I strove to throw my cloak
Back from my shoulders: that was feathers too,
Deep-rooted in my skin. I tried to beat
My hands on my bare breast and had no hands
Nor bare breast any more. And then I ran,
And found the sand no longer clogged my feet;

I skimmed the surface; in a trice I soared
High up into the air; and I was given
To Pallas, her companion without stain.
But what good was it, if Nyctimene,
She who was made a bird for her foul sin,*
Supplants me in my place of privilege?
Or have you never heard the tale, renowned
All over Lesbos, how Nyctimene
Outraged her father's bed? Bird she may be,
But shuns the daylight and the watching eye,
Guilt-cursed, her shame shut in the dark unseen,
An utter outcast from the sky's bright sheen.'

    'Confound your croaks of doom!' the raven cried,
'I scorn false prophets!' and he held his course
And told his master Phoebus how he found
Coronis in the arms of some bright lad.
At that black charge her lover's bay-wreath slipped;
Composure, plectrum, colour, all were lost.
Swept in a storm of rage, he seized his bow,
By habit, strung the string, and shot a shaft
Unerring, inescapable, to pierce
Her breast whereon so often his own had lain.
She screamed and, as the arrow came away,
Her fair white skin was drenched in crimson blood.
'It could have been', she moaned, 'that I had borne
Your child before you punished me; but now
We two shall die together', and her life
Ebbed with her blood; she breathed her latest breath
And through her body stole the chill of death.

    Too late, alas, too late the lover rues
His cruel punishment, and hates himself
For lending ear and flaring up so fast.
He hates the bird who blithely forced on him
The knowledge of that guilt, that fount of grief.
He hates his bow, his arrows, hates his hand
So rash, so hasty, hugs her huddled there,
And tries if some late salve may vanquish fate,
And practises his healing art in vain.
And when he finds all fails, and sees the pyre
Stands ready and her body soon to burn

In the last funeral flames, then (since the gods
May never wet their cheeks with tears*) he groans
Deep from the very bottom of his heart,
As a cow groans* who sees, before her eyes,
Upon the forehead of her suckling calf
With echoing crash the high-held hammer fall.
He poured—unthanked—sweet perfumes on her breast,
Gave her a loving last embrace, and mourned
With all due obsequies her death undue.
But that his seed should perish in that fire
Phoebus could not endure, and snatched his son*
Out of his mother's womb, out of the flames,
And carried him to two-formed Chiron's cave.*
As for the raven, whose report was right
And hopes ran high, he turned him black as night,
Banned from the breed of birds whose colour's white.

OCYRHOE

The centaur was delighted with that child
Of heavenly stock, his honourable charge.
One day his daughter came, her auburn hair
Falling upon her shoulders, whom the nymph
Chariclo once had borne upon the bank
Beside a flowing river, and had named
Ocyrhoe.* The girl was not content
To know her father's art: she prophesied
The Fates' dark secrets. In the mystic mood
Of prophecy, when hidden in her heart
The heavenly fervour glowed, she fixed her eyes
Upon the child. 'Grow strong, dear boy,' she said
'Healer of all the world. Often to you
Men shall owe health and life, and yours shall be
The right to win again departed souls,
And, though you dare this once in heaven's despite,
Jove's bolt will thwart that gift a second time.
You, now divine, shall be a lifeless corpse,
And from a corpse become divine again,
And twice you shall renew your destiny.*
You too, dear father, you, immortal now

And destined by your birthright to live on
Through all eternity, will long to die
When you are tortured by the serpent's blood,*
That agonizing poison in your wounds;
And, saved from immortality, the gods
Shall put you in death's power, and the three
Goddesses* shall unloose your threads of fate.'
More prophecies remained, but then she sighed,
Sighed deeply, and as tears rolled down her cheeks
She cried, 'The Fates forestall me! I'm forbidden
To tell you more. My power of speech is stopped.
My arts—oh! never worth so much!—have brought
Heaven's wrath upon me. Would I'd never known
The future! Surely now my human shape
Is stolen away; the food I like is grass;
I feel the urge to frisk in open fields.
I'm changing to a mare—a family shape—
But why the whole of me? When plainly half
My father's human?' As she spoke, her last
Protests were almost meaningless, her words
Were all confused, sounds that seemed neither words
Nor whinnies, more like mimicking a mare.
Soon she was whinnying clearly, and her arms
Walked on the grass, and then her fingers joined,
And their five nails were bound in a light hoof
Of undivided horn; her mouth and neck
Increased in size; her trailing dress became
A tail; the hair that wandered on her neck
Fell as a mane down on the right-hand side;
And so her voice and shape alike were new,
And that weird change gave her a new name* too.

MERCURY AND BATTUS

Chiron, the centaur half-divine, invoked,
Weeping, the lord of Delphi, but in vain.
Apollo had no power to countermand
Great Jove's decrees and, had he had the power,
He was not there. No, he was dallying
In Elis and Messene's meadowlands.

That was the time when he wore shepherd's garb,
His left hand held a sturdy woodland staff,
His right a pipe of seven graded reeds;
And, while love* filled his thoughts and his pipe played
Soft soothing tunes, the flock he failed to watch
Wandered away, it's said, to Pylos' fields.
Mercury saw them there and drove them off
In his sly way and hid them in the woods.
No one had seen the theft save one old man,
A character of that green countryside,
Battus,* so named by all the neighbourhood.
In those lush glades and pastures he had charge
Of Neleus' mares, blood mares of a rich master.
Suspicious, Mercury drew the man aside
And coaxed him: 'My good friend, whoever you are,
If anyone enquires about this herd,
Say you've not seen them; and to thank you for
That service, take a cow for your reward.'
He gave the cow. The old man, taking it,
Replied, 'Proceed! You're safe; that stone will tell
Sooner than I', and pointed to a stone.
Then Mercury pretended to make off,
But soon returned with different voice and build,
And said, 'Good fellow, help me; if you've seen
Some cattle hereabouts, speak up, they're stolen;
And you shall have a cow and bull, a pair.'
The fee was doubled! So the old man said,
'There on yon hill they'll be'—and there they were.
Mercury laughed; 'You rogue, so you betray
Me to myself, me to myself, I say!'
And changed that treacherous heart into a stone,
A stone called tell-tale* still for all to see,
Marking, though guiltless, that old infamy.
   Then Mercury rose soaring on his wings,
And in his flight looked down upon the land
That Pallas loves and the Munychian fields
And the Lyceum's* cultivated groves.

THE ENVY OF AGLAUROS

It chanced that day was Pallas' festival
And virgins carried, in the accustomed way,
In baskets, flower-crowned, upon their heads
The sacred vessels to her hilltop shrine.
As they returned the winged god saw them there
And turned aside and circled overhead,
Like a swift kite* that sees a sacrifice
And, while the priests press round the victim, waits
Circling afraid, yet dares not go too far,
And hovers round his hope on hungry wings;
So Mercury above the citadel
Of ancient Athens wheeled his sweeping course
In circle after circle through the air.
   Even as the morning star more brilliant shines
Than all the stars, or as the golden moon
Outshines the morning star, so Herse walked
Among her comrades, lovelier than them all,
The fairest jewel of the festival.
Jove's son, breath-taken by her loveliness,
Was kindled as he hovered, like a lead
Slung from a Spanish sling, that as it flies
Glows with its speed and finds below the clouds
Heat not its own.* Swerving, he left the sky
And flew to earth, and there took no disguise—
Such trust in his good looks! Yet though his trust
Was sound, he spared no pains; he smoothed his hair,
Arranged his robe to hang aright, to show
The whole long golden hem, saw that his wand,
The wand he wields to bring and banish sleep,
Shone with a polish, and his ankle-wings
Were lustrous and his sandals brushed and clean.
   The house possessed in a secluded wing
Three chambers, richly inlaid with ivory
And tortoiseshell. The right was the abode
Of Pandrosos, Aglauros on the left
And Herse in between. Aglauros first
Marked Mercury's approach and boldly asked
The god his name and business. To her question

Pleione's grandson* answered: 'I am he
Who bears his father's mandates through the sky.
My father's Jove himself. I'll not invent
A reason. Only, if you'll be so good,
Stand by your sister and consent to be
Aunt to my child. For Herse's sake I'm here;
Favour a lover's hope!' She looked at him
With those hard eyes that spied not long ago
Fair-haired Minerva's mystery, and asked
A golden fortune for her services,
And pending payment forced him from the house.

    The warrior goddess* turned her angry eyes
Upon the girl and heaved a sigh so deep
That breast and aegis* shuddered. She recalled
It was Aglauros whose profaning hand
Laid bare that secret when the oath she swore
Was broken and she saw the infant boy,
Great Vulcan's child, the babe no mother bore;
And now she would find favour with the god
And with her sister too, and grow so rich
With all that gold her greed had planned to gain.
Straightway she sought the filthy slimy shack
Where Envy* dwelt deep in a dreary dale,
A gruesome sunless hovel, filled with frost,
Heart-numbing frost, its stagnant air unstirred
By any breeze, for ever lacking warmth
Of cheerful fire, for ever wrapped in gloom.
Reaching the place the virgin queen of war
Paused by the threshold, since she might not pass*
Beneath that roof, and struck upon the door
With her spear's point. The door flew wide and there
She saw foul Envy eating viper's flesh,
Fit food for spite, and turned her eyes away.
Slowly the creature rose, leaving the snakes
Half-eaten, and approached with dragging steps,
And when she saw the goddess' face so fair
And gleaming mail, she scowled and groaned in grief.

    Her cheeks are sallow, her whole body shrunk,
Her eyes askew and squinting; black decay
Befouls her teeth, her bosom's green with bile,

And venom coats her tongue. She never smiles
Save when she relishes the sight of woe;
Sleep never soothes her, night by night awake
With worry, as she sees against her will
Successes won and sickens at the sight.
She wounds, is wounded, she herself her own
Torture. Minerva, filled with loathing, forced
A few curt words: 'Inject your pestilence
In one of Cecrops' daughters; that I need;
Aglauros is the one.' That said, she soared,
Launched from her downthrust spear,* and sped to heaven.

    With sidelong glance the creature saw her fly
And muttered briefly, grieving to foresee
Minerva's triumph; then she took her staff,
Entwined with thorns, and, wrapped in a black cloud,
Went forth and in her progress trampled down
The flowery meads, withered the grass, and slashed
The tree-tops, and with filthy breath defiled
Peoples and towns and homes, until at last,
Brilliant and blessed with arts and wealth and peace,
Athens in happy festival appears—
And tears she sheds to see no cause for tears.

    Into the room of Cecrops' child she went
And did as she was bid. On the girl's breast
She laid her withering hand and filled her heart
With thorny briars and breathed a baleful blight
Deep down into her bones and spread a stream
Of poison, black as pitch, inside her lungs.
And lest the choice of woe should stray too wide,
She set before her eyes her sister's face,
Her fortune-favoured marriage and the god
So glorious; and painted everything
Larger than life. Such thoughts were agony:
Aglauros pined in private grief, distraught
All night, all day, in utter misery,
Wasting away in slow decline, like ice
Marred by a fitful sun. The happiness
Of lucky Herse smouldered in her heart
Like green thorns on a fire that never flame
Nor give good heat but wanly burn away.

Often she'd rather die than see such sights;
Often she meant, as if some crime, to tell
The tale to her strict father. In the end
She sat herself outside her sister's door
To bar the god's access. With honeyed words
He pressed his prayers and pleas. 'Enough', said she,
'I'll never move till you are forced away!'
'A bargain!' cried the god and with his wand,
His magic wand, opened the door. But she
Found, as she tried to rise, a numbing weight
Stiffened her muscles; as she strained to stand
Upright, her knees were stuck; an icy chill
Seeped through her limbs, the blood paled in her veins.
And as an evil growth beyond all cure
Creeps far and wide and wounds what once was well,
So by degrees the winter of dark death
Entered her heart and choked her breath and stopped
The lanes of life. She did not try to speak,
Nor, had she tried, was way still left for words.
Her throat, mouth, lips were hardened into stone;
And there, a lifeless statue she remained,
Nor was it white, but with her dark thoughts stained.
  Such was the punishment that Mercury dealt
Aglauros for her wicked words and will.
Then, leaving Athens, Pallas' fabled land,
He made his way to heaven on beating wings.

JUPITER AND EUROPA

Jove called his son aside and, keeping dark
His secret passion, 'Mercury', he said,
'Trusty executant of my commands,
Make haste, glide swiftly on your usual course
Down to the land that sees your mother's star
High in the southern sky, named by its people
The land of Sidon; in the distance there,
Grazing the mountain pastures, you will find
The royal herd; drive them to the sea-shore.'
And presently (as Jove had bidden) the herd,
Driven from the hillside, headed for the shore,

Where with her girls of Tyre for company
The great king's daughter often used to play.
   Ah, majesty and love go ill together,
Nor long share one abode! Relinquishing
Sceptre and throne, heaven's father, God of gods,
Who wields the three-forked lightning, at whose nod
The world is shaken, now transforms himself
Into a bull and, lowing, joins the herd,
Ambling—so handsome—through the tender grass.
His hide was white, white as untrodden snow
Before the south wind brings the melting rain.
The muscles of his neck swelled proud; below
The dewlap hung; his horns, though small, you'd swear
A master hand had made, so jewel-like
Their pure and pearly sheen; upon his brow
No threat, no menace in his eye; his mien
Peaceful. Europa marvelled at his beauty
And friendliness that threatened naught of harm.
Yet, gentle as he seemed, she feared at first
To touch him, but anon came up to him
And offered flowers to his soft white lips.
   Glad was the lover's heart and, till the joy
Hoped for should come, he kissed her hand, and then—
Hardly, oh, hardly, could postpone the rest!
And now he frolicked, prancing on the greensward;
Then on the yellow sand laid his white flank;
And gradually she lost her fear, and he
Offered his breast for her virgin caresses,
His horns for her to wind with chains of flowers,
Until the princess dared to mount his back,
Her pet bull's back, unwitting whom she rode.
Then—slowly, slowly down the broad dry beach—
First in the shallow waves the great god set
His spurious hooves, then sauntered further out
Till in the open sea he bore his prize.
Fear filled her heart, as, gazing back, she saw
The fast receding sands. Her right hand grasped
A horn, the other leant upon his back;
Her fluttering tunic floated in the breeze.*

BOOK III

NOW, safe in Crete, Jove shed the bull's disguise
And stood revealed before Europa's eyes.
Meanwhile her father, baffled, bade his son
Cadmus, set out to find the stolen girl
And threatened exile should he fail—in one
Same act such warmth of love, such wickedness!

CADMUS

He roamed the whole wide world, for who could trace
Jove's secret tricks? Shunning his father's wrath
And fatherland, an exiled fugitive,
He knelt before Apollo's oracle
And asked what country he should make his home.
'A cow will meet you in a lonely land',
The god replied, 'A cow that never wore
A yoke nor toiled to haul a curving plough.
With her to guide you make your way, and where
She rests upon the grass, there you must found
Your city's battlements, and name the place
Boeotia.'* Cadmus left the holy cave
And saw, almost at once, as he went down,*
A heifer ambling loose that bore no sign
Of service on her neck. He followed her
With slow and wary steps and silently
Worshipped Apollo, guardian and guide.
Now past Cephisus' shallows and the meads
Of Panope they wandered on, and there
The heifer stopped and raised towards the sky
Her graceful high-horned head and filled the air
With lowings; then, her big eyes looking back
Upon her followers, she bent her knees
And settled on her side on the soft grass.
Cadmus gave thanks and kissed the foreign soil,
Hailing the unknown hills and countryside.
Then meaning to make sacrifice to Jove,
He sent his henchmen forth to find a spring
Of living water for the ritual.

There stood an ancient forest undefiled
By axe or saw, and in its heart a cave
Close-veiled in boughs and creepers, with its rocks
Joined in a shallow arch, and gushing out
A wealth of water. Hidden in the cave
There dwelt a snake, a snake of Mars. Its crest
Shone gleaming gold; its eyes flashed fire; its whole
Body was big with venom, and between
Its triple rows of teeth its three-forked tongue
Flickered. The Tyrians* reached the forest glade
On their ill-fated quest and dipped their pails
Into the water. At the sound the snake
Thrust from the cave its long dark head and hissed—
A frightful hiss! Their blood ran cold. The pails
Fell from their hands and, horror-struck, they quaked
In shock and terror. Coil by scaly coil
The serpent wound its way, and, rearing up,
Curved in a giant arching bow, erect
For more than half its length, high in the air.
It glared down on the whole wide wood, as huge,
If all its size were seen, as in the sky
The Snake* that separates the two bright Bears.
Then in a trice it seized them, some in flight,
Some set to fight, some fixed too fast in fear
For either. Every man of them it slew,
With fang that struck or coil that crushed or breath
That dealt a putrid blast of poisoned death.

 The noonday sun had drawn the shadows small,
And Cadmus, wondering at his men's delay,
Followed their tracks, his mail a lion's skin,
His arms a javelin and lance that gleamed
Iron-tipped, his heart worth more than any arms.
He reached the glade and saw his murdered men,
And high in triumph that enormous foe,
Its blood-red tongue licking their sorry wounds.
'My faithful fallen friends!' he cried, 'Your deaths
I'll now avenge or share!' and lifting high
A rock above his head with all his might
He hurled the mighty missile, such a blow
As shatters towers and soaring battlements.

The snake, its scales like armour shielding it,
Stood fast unscathed; its hard black carapace
Bounced the blow back; but that hard armour failed
To foil the javelin that pierced its spine
Deep in the midmost coil, with the full length
Of iron buried in the serpent's side.
In agony it twisted back its head
To see the wound, and bit the deep-sunk shaft,
And straining it from side to side at last
Wrenched it away—but still the iron stuck fast.
   Now to its natural rage new source of rage
Was added. In its throat the arteries
Swelled huge; its poison fangs were flecked with foam;
Its scales scraped rasping on the rocks; its breath
Like the black blast that stinks from holes of Hell,
Befouled the fetid air. And now it coils
In giant spirals, now it towers up
Tall as a tree, now like a stream in spate
After a storm it rushes surging on,
And breasts aside the woods that bar its way.
Cadmus steps back; his lion's spoil withstands
The onslaught; his long lance's point,
Thrust forward, keeps the darting fangs at bay.
The snake is frenzied; on the unyielding iron
It wastes its wounds and bites the metal point.
Then from its venom-laden lips an ooze
Of blood began and spattered the green grass.
The wound was slight, for, shrinking from the thrust,
It turned its injured neck away and kept
The blow from piercing deep and striking home.
Cadmus pressed on and drove the firm-lodged lance
Deep in the creature's gullet, till an oak
Blocked its retreat and snake and oak were nailed
Together. Burdened by the serpent's weight
The tree bent curving down; its strong trunk groaned
Beneath the lashings of that writhing tail.
   Then as the victor contemplates his foe,
His vanquished foe so vast, a sudden voice
Is heard, its source not readily discerned,
But heard for very sure: 'Why, Cadmus, why

Stare at the snake you've slain? You too shall be
A snake and stared at.' For an age he stood
Rigid, frozen in fear, his hair on end,
His colour and his courage drained away.
But look, a guardian goddess! Gliding down
Out of the sky Pallas appears and bids
Him plough the soil and plant the serpent's teeth,*
From which a future people should arise.
Cadmus obeys, and with his plough's deep share
Opens wide furrows, then across the soil
Scatters the teeth, the seed of humankind.
The tilth (beyond belief!) began to stir:
First from the furrows points of spears were seen,
Next helmets, bright with nodding painted plumes,
Then shoulders, chests and weapon-laden arms
Arose, a growing crop of men in mail.
So, when the curtain at a theatre*
Is raised, figures rise up, their faces first,
Then gradually the rest, until at last,
Drawn slowly, smoothly up, they stand revealed
Complete, their feet placed on the fringe below.
    In fear of these new foemen Cadmus sprang
To arms. 'Lay down your arms!' a warrior cried,
One of the earth-born regiment, 'Take no part
In civil strife.' So saying, with his sword
He felled a soil-sprung brother by his side,
Then fell himself, struck by a far-flung lance.
He too who dealt him death was dead as soon,
And of that new-given lifebreath breathed his last.
In the same mould of madness all that host,
That sudden brotherhood, in battle joined,
With wound for wound fell dead. That prime of youth,
Whose lot was life so short, lay writhing on
Their mother's bloodstained bosom— all save five,*
Five who survived. Among them was Echion,*
Who at Minerva's bidding dropped his arms
And joined his brothers in a pact of peace.
These were his comrades when the Prince of Tyre,
Obedient to the oracle's command,
Founded his city in that foreign land.

DIANA AND ACTAEON

Now Thebes stood strong; now Cadmus might have seemed
Blessed in his exile. He had won for bride
The child of Mars and Venus.* Add besides
From such a glorious wife a dynasty,
So many sons and daughters, grandsons too,
Dear links of love, by now indeed young men.
But yet in truth one ever must await
A man's last day, nor count him fortunate
Before he dies* and the last rites are paid.
In his prosperity a grandson first
Was source of Cadmus' sorrow, whose young brow
Sprouted outlandish antlers and the hounds,
His hounds, were sated with their master's blood.
Though, if you ponder wisely, you will find
The fault was fortune's and no guilt that day,   → what Ovid is
For what guilt can it be to lose one's way?*   asking.
    Upon a mountainside, whose woodland coverts   – apply to
Were stained with many a kill of varied game,   Oedipus.
The shining noon had narrowed all the shade
And midway at his zenith stood the sun.
Then young Actaeon was content; he called
His comrades as they roamed the lonely woods:
'Come, friends, our nets are wet, our javelins
Drip with our quarries' blood; today has brought
Success enough; tomorrow, when the dawn
On saffron wheels leads on another day,
We'll start our work again; now the sun shines
Half-way upon his journey and his rays
Crack the parched countryside. Take up your nets;
Here let us end the work in hand.' The men
Obeyed his words and rested from their toil.
    There was a valley clothed in hanging woods
Of pine and cypress, named Gargaphie,
Sacred to chaste Diana, huntress queen.
Deep in its farthest combe, framed by the woods,
A cave lay hid, not fashioned by man's art,
But nature's talent copied artistry,
For in the living limestone she had carved

A natural arch; and there a limpid spring
Flowed lightly babbling into a wide pool,
Its waters girdled with a grassy sward.
Here, tired after the hunt, the goddess loved
Her nymphs to bathe her with the water's balm.
    Reaching the cave, she gave her spear and quiver
And bow unstrung to an attendant nymph;
Others received her robes over their arms;
Two loosed her sandals; more expert than these
Crocale tied the hair loose on her shoulders
Into a knot, her own hair falling free.
Then Nephele and Hyale and Rhanis
And Phiale and Psecas brought the water
In brimming jars and poured it over her.

queen of the fairies in a Midsummer Night's Dream.

And while Titania* bathed there in the pool,
Her loved familiar pool, it chanced Actaeon,
The day's hunt finished, idly wandering
Through unknown clearings of the forest, found
The sacred grove—so the Fates guided him—
And came upon the cool damp cave. At once,
Seeing a man, all naked as they were,
The nymphs, beating their breasts, filled the whole grove
With sudden screams and clustered round Diana
To clothe her body with their own. But she
Stood taller, a head taller than them all;
And as the clouds are coloured when the sun
Glows late and low or like the crimson dawn,
So deeply blushed Diana, caught unclothed.
Her troop pressed close about her, but she turned
Aside and looking backwards (would she had
Her arrows ready!) all she had, the water,
She seized and flung it in the young man's face,
And as the avenging downpour drenched his hair
She added words that warned of doom: 'Now tell
You saw me here naked without my clothes,
If you can tell at all!' With that one threat

Diana turned him into a deer.

Antlers she raised upon his dripping head,
Lengthened his neck, pointed his ears, transformed
His hands to hooves, arms to long legs, and draped
His body with a dappled hide; and last

Set terror in his heart. Actaeon fled,
Royal Actaeon, and marvelled in his flight
At his new leaping speed, but, when he saw
His head and antlers mirrored in a stream,
He tried to say 'Alas!'—but no words came;
He groaned—that was his voice; the tears rolled down
On cheeks not his—all changed except his mind.
What should he do? Go home, back to the palace,
Or stay in hiding in the forest? Shame
Forbade the first decision, fear the other.

he knows all of the dogs now. -notices them.

While thus he stood in doubt his hounds had seen him.
Blackfoot and Tracker first gave tongue, wise Tracker,
A Cretan hound, Blackfoot of Spartan breed;
Swift as the wind the rest came rushing on:
Glance, Glutton, Ranger (all from Arcady),
Fierce Rover, sturdy Stalker, moody Storm,
Flight unsurpassed for speed, Hunter for scent,
Bold Woodman lately wounded by a boar,
Dingle a slender bitch sired by a wolf,
Snatch with two pups, gaunt Catch from Sicyon,
And Shepherd, once a guardian of her flock;
Spot, Gnasher, Tigress, Courser, Lightfoot, Strong,
Dark-coated Sooty, Blanche with snowy hair,
Wolf and her nimble brother Cyprian,
Huge stalwart Spartan, Tempest never tired;
Clinch, his dark forehead crowned with a white star,
Blackie; rough-coated Shag; a couple of hounds
Born of a Cretan sire and Spartan dam,
Fury and Whitetooth; Barker, noisy bitch;
And many more too long to tell. The pack,
Hot in pursuit, sped on over fells and crags,
By walls of rock, on daunting trails or none.
He fled where often he'd followed in pursuit,
Fled his own folk, for shame! He longed to shout
'I am Actaeon, look, I am your master!'
Words failed his will; their baying filled the sky.
Blackhair bit first, a wound deep in his haunch;
Next Killer; Climber fastened on his shoulder.
These started late but cut across the hills
And gained a lead. They held their master down

he is still Actaeon, he sees himself in another body and his dogs point of view.

- his dogs took him down.

[handwritten left margin: no one heard him, his friends all cheered the dogs on. - looking for Acteon.]

Till the whole pack, united, sank their teeth
Into his flesh. He gave a wailing scream,
Not human, yet a sound no stag could voice,
And filled with anguished cries the mountainside
He knew so well; then, suppliant on his knees,
Turned his head silently from side to side,
Like arms that turned and pleaded. But his friends
With their glad usual shouts cheered on the pack,
Not knowing what they did, and looked around
To find Actaeon; each louder than the rest
Calling Actaeon, as though he were not there;
And blamed his absence and his sloth that missed
The excitement of the kill. Hearing his name,
He turned his head. Would that he were indeed
Absent! But he was there. Would that he watched,
Not felt, the hounds' (his hounds') fierce savagery!
Now they are all around him, tearing deep
Their master's flesh, the stag that is no stag;
And not until so many countless wounds
Had drained away his lifeblood, was the wrath,
It's said, of chaste Diana satisfied.

[handwritten left margin: this is an incomplete metamorphoses, he is still Acteon]

   As the tale spread views varied; some believed
Diana's violence unjust; some praised it,
As proper to her chaste virginity.
Both sides found reason for their point of view.

SEMELE AND THE BIRTH OF BACCHUS

Jove's wife alone said not a word of blame
Or praise; simply her heart rejoiced in that
Disaster fallen on Agenor's house.
Her hatred of that Tyrian concubine*
She turned against her kin. Yes, now a new
Offence followed the last, the grievous news
That Semele was pregnant by great Jove.
Harsh words rose to her lips, 'But what have words
Ever achieved?' she said. 'That girl herself
Must now be dealt with. Her, if I'm well named
Almighty Juno, if I'm fit to wield
My jewelled sceptre, if I'm queen of heaven,

Jove's wife and sister—sister certainly—
Her I'll destroy. Yet secret stolen love
May well be all she wants. My marriage bonds
Suffer brief harm. No! she's conceived—that crowns it!
Her bulging womb carries her glaring guilt.
She means to be a mother by great Jove—
Luck hardly ever mine! Such confidence
In her good looks! I'll see it lets her down.
I'm never Saturn's child if she's not swallowed
In Styx's waves, sunk by her Jove himself!'
       Then rising from her throne she wrapped herself
In a bright golden cloud and visited
The home of Semele, and kept the cloud
Till she'd disguised herself as an old woman,
With white hair on her forehead, wrinkled skin,
Bowed back and shaky steps, and speaking too
Like an old woman. She was Beroe,
The Epidaurian nurse of Semele.
They talked of many things and then the name
Of Jove came up. 'I pray it may be Jove',
She sighed, 'All these things frighten me. So often
Men, claiming to be gods, have gained the beds
Of simple girls. But even to be Jove
Is not enough; he ought to prove his love,
If he is Jove. In all the power and glory
That's his when heavenly Juno welcomes him,
Beg him to don his godhead and take you
In the same power and glory in his arms.'
       So Juno moulded Cadmus' daughter's mind.
The girl, unwitting, asked of Jove a boon
Unnamed. 'Choose what you will', the god replied,
'There's nothing I'll refuse; and should you doubt,
The Power of rushing Styx shall be my witness,
The deity whom all gods hold in awe.'
She, too successful, happy in her ruin,
Doomed by her lover's generosity,
Answered 'Give me yourself in the same grace
As when your Juno holds you to her breast
In love's embrace.' He would have locked her lips;
Too late: her words had hastened on their way.

He groaned: her wish could never be unwished,
His oath never unsworn. In bitterest grief
He soared ascending to the ethereal sky,
And by his nod called up the trailing clouds
And massed a storm, with lightnings in the squalls,
And thunder and the bolts that never miss.
Even so he tried, as far as he had power,
To curb his might, and would not wield the fire
With which he'd felled the hundred-handed giant.
That was too fierce. There is another bolt,
A lighter one, in which the Cyclops forged
A flame less savage and a lesser wrath,
Called by the gods his second armament.*
With this in hand he went to Semele
In Cadmus' palace. Then her mortal frame
Could not endure the tumult of the heavens;
That gift of love consumed her. From her womb
Her baby, still not fully formed, was snatched,
And sewn (could one believe the tale) inside
His father's thigh, and so completed there
His mother's time. Ino, his mother's sister,
In secret from the cradle nursed the child
And brought him up, and then the nymphs of Nysa
Were given his charge and kept him hidden away*
Within their caves, and nourished him on milk.

TIRESIAS

While down on earth as destiny ordained
These things took place, and Bacchus, babe twice born,
Was cradled safe and sound, it chanced that Jove,
Well warmed with nectar, laid his weighty cares
Aside and, Juno too in idle mood,
The pair were gaily joking, and Jove said
'You women get more pleasure out of love
Than we men do, I'm sure.' She disagreed.
So they resolved to get the views of wise
Tiresias. He knew both sides of love.
For once in a green copse when two huge snakes
Were mating, he attacked them with his stick,

And was transformed (a miracle!) from man
To woman; and spent seven autumns so;
Till in the eighth he saw the snakes once more
And said 'If striking you has magic power
To change the striker to the other sex,
I'll strike you now again.' He struck the snakes
And so regained the shape he had at birth.
Asked then to give his judgement on the joke,
He found for Jove; and Juno (so it's said)
Took umbrage beyond reason, out of all
Proportion, and condemned her judge to live
In the black night of blindness evermore.
But the Almighty Father (since no god
Has right to undo what any god has done)
For his lost sight gave him the gift to see
What things should come, the power of prophecy,
An honour to relieve that penalty.

✳NARCISSUS AND ECHO

So blind Tiresias gave to all who came
Faultless and sure reply and far and wide
Through all Boeotia's cities spread his fame.
To test his truth and trust the first who tried
Was wave-blue water-nymph Liriope,
Whom once Cephisus in his sinuous flow
Embracing held and ravished. In due time
The lovely sprite bore a fine infant boy,
From birth adorable, and named her son
Narcissus; and of him she asked the seer,
Would he long years and ripe old age enjoy,
Who answered 'If he shall himself not know'.
For long his words seemed vain;* what they concealed
The lad's strange death and stranger love revealed.
　　Narcissus now had reached his sixteenth year
And seemed both man and boy; and many a youth
And many a girl desired him, but hard pride
Ruled in that delicate frame, and never a youth
And never a girl could touch his haughty heart.
Once as he drove to nets the frightened deer

A strange-voiced nymph observed him, who must speak
If any other speak and cannot speak
Unless another speak, resounding Echo.
Echo was still a body, not a voice,
But talkative as now, and with the same
Power of speaking, only to repeat,
As best she could, the last of many words.
Juno had made her so; for many a time,
When the great goddess might have caught the nymphs
Lying with Jove upon the mountainside,
Echo discreetly kept her talking till
The nymphs had fled away; and when at last
The goddess saw the truth, 'Your tongue', she said,
'With which you tricked me, now its power shall lose,
Your voice avail but for the briefest use.'
The event confirmed the threat: when speaking ends,
All she can do is double each last word,
And echo back again the voice she's heard.
   Now when she saw Narcissus wandering
In the green byways, Echo's heart was fired;
And stealthily she followed, and the more
She followed him, the nearer flamed her love,
As when a torch is lit and from the tip
The leaping sulphur grasps the offered flame.
She longed to come to him with winning words,
To urge soft pleas, but nature now opposed;
She might not speak the first but—what she might—
Waited for words her voice could say again.
   It chanced Narcissus, searching for his friends,
Called 'Anyone here?' and Echo answered 'Here!'
Amazed he looked all round and, raising his voice,
Called 'Come this way!' and Echo called 'This way!'
He looked behind and, no one coming, shouted
'Why run away?' and heard his words again.
He stopped and, cheated by the answering voice,
Called 'Join me here!'* and she, never more glad
To give her answer, answered 'Join me here!'
And graced her words and ran out from the wood
To throw her longing arms around his neck.
He bolted, shouting 'Keep your arms from me!

Be off! I'll die before I yield to you.'
And all she answered was 'I yield to you'.
Shamed and rejected in the woods she hides
And has her dwelling in the lonely caves;
Yet still her love endures and grows on grief,
And weeping vigils waste her frame away;
Her body shrivels, all its moisture dries;
Only her voice and bones are left; at last
Only her voice, her bones are turned to stone.
So in the woods she hides and hills around,
For all to hear, alive, but just a sound.*

    Thus had Narcissus mocked her; others too,
Hill-nymphs and water-nymphs and many a man
He mocked; till one scorned youth, with raised hands, prayed,
'So may *he* love—and never win his love!'
And Nemesis approved the righteous prayer.

    There was a pool,* limpid and silvery,
Whither no shepherd came nor any herd,
Nor mountain goat; and never bird nor beast
Nor falling branch disturbed its shining peace;
Grass grew around it, by the water fed,
And trees to shield it from the warming sun.
Here—for the chase and heat had wearied him—
The boy lay down, charmed by the quiet pool,
And, while he slaked his thirst, another thirst
Grew; as he drank he saw before his eyes
A form, a face, and loved with leaping heart
A hope unreal and thought the shape was real.
Spellbound he saw himself, and motionless
Lay like a marble statue staring down.
He gazes at his eyes, twin constellation,
His hair worthy of Bacchus or Apollo,
His face so fine, his ivory neck, his cheeks
Smooth, and the snowy pallor and the blush;
All he admires that all admire in him,
Himself he longs for, longs unwittingly,
Praising is praised, desiring is desired,
And love he kindles while with love he burns.
How often in vain he kissed the cheating pool
And in the water sank his arms to clasp

The neck he saw, but could not clasp himself!
Not knowing what he sees, he adores the sight;
That false face fools and fuels his delight.
You simple boy, why strive in vain to catch
A fleeting image? What you see is nowhere;
And what you love—but turn away—you lose!
You see a phantom of a mirrored shape;
Nothing itself; with you it came and stays;
With you it too will go, if you can go!
   No thought of food or rest draws him away;
Stretched on the grassy shade he gazes down
On the false phantom, staring endlessly,
His eyes his own undoing. Raising himself
He holds his arms towards the encircling trees
And cries 'You woods, was ever love more cruel!
You know! For you are lovers' secret haunts.
Can you in your long living centuries
Recall a lad who pined so piteously?
My joy! I see it; but the joy I see
I cannot find' (so fondly love is foiled!)
'And—to my greater grief—between us lies
No mighty sea, no long and dusty road,
Nor mountain range nor bolted barbican.
A little water sunders us. He longs
For my embrace. Why, every time I reach
My lips towards the gleaming pool, he strains
His upturned face to mine. I surely could
Touch him, so slight the thing that thwarts our love.
Come forth, whoever you are! Why, peerless boy,
Elude me? Where retreat beyond my reach?
My looks, my age—indeed it cannot be
That you should shun—the nymphs have loved me too!
Some hope, some nameless hope, your friendly face
Pledges; and when I stretch my arms to you
You stretch your arms to me, and when I smile
You smile, and when I weep, I've often seen
Your tears, and to my nod your nod replies,
And your sweet lips appear to move in speech,
Though to my ears your answer cannot reach.
Oh, I am he! Oh, now I know for sure

The image is my own; it's for myself
I burn with love; I fan the flames I feel.
What now? Woo or be wooed? Why woo at all?
My love's myself—my riches beggar me.
Would I might leave my body! I could wish
(Strange lover's wish!) my love were not so near!
Now sorrow saps my strength; of my life's span
Not long is left; I die before my prime.
Nor is death sad for death will end my sorrow;
Would he I love might live a long tomorrow!
But now we two—one soul—one death will die.'*
    Distraught he turned towards the face again;
His tears rippled the pool, and darkly then
The troubled water veiled the fading form,
And, as it vanished, 'Stay', he shouted, 'stay!
Oh, cruelty to leave your lover so!
Let me but gaze on what I may not touch
And feed the aching fever in my heart.'
Then in his grief he tore his robe and beat
His pale cold fists upon his naked breast,
And on his breast a blushing redness spread
Like apples, white in part and partly red,
Or summer grapes whose varying skins assume
Upon the ripening vine a blushing bloom.
And this he saw reflected in the pool,
Now still again, and could endure no more.
But as wax melts before a gentle fire,
Or morning frosts beneath the rising sun,
So, by love wasted, slowly he dissolves
By hidden fire consumed. No colour now,
Blending the white with red, nor strength remains
Nor will, nor aught that lately seemed so fair,
Nor longer lasts the body Echo loved.
But she, though angry still and unforgetting,
Grieved for the hapless boy, and when he moaned
'Alas', with answering sob she moaned 'alas',
And when he beat his hands upon his breast,
She gave again the same sad sounds of woe.
His latest words, gazing and gazing still,
He sighed 'alas! the boy I loved in vain!'

And these the place repeats, and then 'farewell',
And Echo said 'farewell'. On the green grass
He drooped his weary head, and those bright eyes
That loved their master's beauty closed in death.
Then still, received into the Underworld,
He gazed upon himself in Styx's pool.
His Naiad sisters wailed and sheared their locks
In mourning for their brother; the Dryads too
Wailed and sad Echo wailed in answering woe.
And then the brandished torches, bier and pyre
Were ready—but no body anywhere;
And in its stead they found a flower—behold,
White petals clustered round a cup of gold!

✻PENTHEUS AND BACCHUS

News of this story brought the prophet fame,
Well-merited, in all the towns of Greece.
His name was great. Even so, one man alone,
Echion's son Pentheus, who scorned the gods,
Spurned him and mocked the old man's prophecies,
Taunting him with his blindness and the doom
Of his lost sight. Then, shaking his white head,
'How lucky you would be', the prophet warned,
'If you too lost this light, and never saw
The rites of Bacchus. For the day shall dawn,
Not distant I foresee, when here shall come
A new god, Liber,* son of Semele.
Unless you honour him with holy shrines,
You shall be torn to pieces; far and wide
You shall be strewn, and with your blood defile
The forests and your mother and her sisters.
So it shall come to pass. You will refuse
The god his honour due and mourn that I
In this my darkness saw too certainly.'
Even as he spoke, Pentheus thrust him away.
His words proved true; his forecast was fulfilled.

   Bacchus is there. The revellers' wild shrieks
Ring through the fields. The crowds come rushing out;
Men, women, nobles, commons, old and young

Stream to the unknown rites. 'What lunacy
Has stolen your wits away, you race of Mars,
You children of the serpent?' Pentheus cried.
'Can clashing bronze, can pipes of curving horn,
Can conjuror's magic have such power that men
Who, undismayed, have faced the swords of war,
The trumpet and the ranks of naked steel,
Quail before women's wailing, frenzy fired
By wine, a bestial rabble, futile drums?
You elders, you who sailed the distant seas
And founded here a second Tyre, made here
Your home in exile—shame on you, if you
Surrender them without a fight! You too,
Young men of sharper years, nearer my own,
Graced by your martial arms, not Bacchic wands,*
With helmets on your heads, not loops of leaves!
Recall your lineage, brace your courage with
The spirit of that snake who killed, alone,
So many. For his pool and spring he died.
You, for your honour, you must fight and win!
He did brave men to death. Now you must rout
Weaklings* and save your country's name! If fate
Refuses Thebes long life, I'd wish her walls
Might fall to brave men and their batteries,
And fire and sword resound. Our misery
Would have no guilt; our lot we'd need to mourn,
Not hide; our tears would never bring us shame.
But now an unarmed boy will capture Thebes,
And in his service not the arts of war,
Weapons and cavalry, but tender garlands,
Myrrh-scented tresses and embroidered robes
Of gold and purple. Only stand aside,
And here and now I'll force him to confess
His father's name is false, his rites a lie.
Why, if Acrisius* was man enough
To spurn his sham divinity and shut
The gates of Argos in his face, shall Pentheus
And all Thebes shudder at this newcomer?
Quick, now' (he bade his servants), 'bring him here,
Their ringleader, in chains, and waste no time.'

His grandfather and Athamas and all
His courtiers upbraided him and tried
Their best to stop him, but in vain. Their words
Of warning whetted him and his wild rage,
Stung by restraint, increased; endeavours to
Control him made things worse. So I have seen
A stream, where nothing blocks its course, run down
Smoothly with no great noise, but where it's checked
By trees or boulders in its way it foams
And boils and flows the fiercer for the block.

    Look now, the men come back spattered with blood,
And when he asks where Bacchus is, they say
Bacchus they did not see, 'But this man here,
His comrade and his acolyte, we seized';
And hand over a Maeonian, his arms bound
Behind his back, a follower of the god.
Pentheus, with terrible anger in his eyes,
Glared at the man and hardly could delay
His punishment. 'Before you die', he cried,
'And, dying, give a lesson to the rest,
Tell me your name,* your family, your country,
And why you practise this new cult of yours.'
He answered undismayed, 'My name's Acoetes,*
Maeonia's my country and my parents
Were humble folk. My father left me no
Acres for sturdy steers to turn and till,
No woolly sheep, no flocks, no herds at all.
He was poor too. He used to lure and catch
Fish with his lines and hooks, and with his rod
Drew them, leaping, to land: that skill of his
Was all his fortune. When he passed it on,
"You are my heir, successor to my craft",
He said; "receive my wealth and my estate."
And when he died he left me nothing but
The waters; that is all that I can call
My heritage. Soon after, to escape
Being stuck for ever on the self-same rocks,
I learnt as well the art of helmsmanship.*
My eyes studied the stars, the rainy Goat,
Taygete, the Hyads and the Bear;

Harbours and havens too and the winds' homes.
One day, making for Delos, I put in
To Chios; we rowed shrewdly to the shore;
A light leap, and I stood on the wet sand.
We spent the night there; in the first red glow
Of dawn I rose and sent my men for water,
Along a track that led them to a spring.
I, myself, climbed a knoll and gazed around
To judge the promise of the wind, then called
My shipmates, and so back to board the ship.
Opheltes, in the lead, crying "Here we are!"
Brought to the beach a prize (or so he thought),
Discovered in this lonely spot, a boy,
As pretty as a girl. He seemed to reel,
Half-dazed with wine and sleep, and almost failed
To follow along. I gazed at his attire,
His face, his bearing; everything I saw
Seemed more than mortal. I felt sure of it,
And said to my shipmates "What deity
Is in that frame, I'm doubtful, but for sure
Some deity is there. Whoever you are,
Be gracious, bless our labours, and forgive
These fellows!" "Spare your prayers for us",
Said Dictys (no man nimbler to swarm up
Right to the highest yard and slide back down
The stays) and Libys backed him, and Melanthus,
Our fair-haired prow-man, and Alcimedon,
Epopeus too, who called the rowers' time,
To pull or pause, and kept their spirits up,
And all the others to a man: so blind
Is greed for booty. "No!" I cried, "That freight
Is holy! Never shall I let my ship
Commit such sacrilege! I'm master here!"
I stood to block the gangway. Lycabas,
Of all the crew the boldest, was incensed.
(He had been banished from a Tuscan town,
Exiled for a foul murder.) As I stood,
He seized me by the throat and would have thrown
Me overboard, had I not, half-concussed,
Clung to a rescuing rope. That godless group

Applauded him and cheered him. Then at last
Bacchus (for it was he), aroused, no doubt,
From slumber by the shouting, and his wits
Regathered from the wine, cried "What's this noise?
What are you doing? How did I come here?
Where do you mean to take me?" "Have no fear",
Said Proreus; "Name the port you wish to reach;
You shall be landed at the place you choose."
"Naxos", said Bacchus, "set your course to Naxos.
That is my home,* that land will welcome you."
Then by the sea and every god they swore,
Those swindling rogues, it should be so, and bade
Me get the painted vessel under sail.
Naxos lay on the right, and for the right
I set my canvas. "Fool, what are you doing?"
Opheltes said; "What lunacy is this?
Steer to the left!" and every man of them
Supported him. They made their meaning clear
By nods and winks and some by whispers. I
Was staggered. "Someone else shall take the helm",
I said—I'd not let my skill serve their crime!
All the crew cursed me. "So you think our whole
Safety", Aethalion cried, "depends on you!"
He strode and took my duty at the helm,
And, turning course from Naxos, steered away.

   Then the god, making sport of them, as if
He'd only just perceived their treachery,
Gazed from the curving poop across the sea
And seemed in tears and said "That's not the shore
You promised me! That's not the shore I want!
What glory can you gain, if you strong men
Cheat a small boy, so many against one?"
I had been long in tears. The godless gang
Laughed at my tears, and rowed on hastily.
Now, by that god himself (for there's no god
Closer* than he) I swear I tell what's true,
As true as past belief: the ship stood still
Upon the sea as fixed as in dry dock.
The crew, bewildered, rowed with dogged strokes
And spread the sails, twin means to make her move.

But ivy creeping, winding, clinging, bound
The oars and decked the sails in heavy clusters.
Bacchus himself, grape-bunches garlanding
His brow, brandished a spear that vine-leaves twined,
And at his feet fierce spotted panthers lay,
Tigers and lynxes too, in phantom forms.
The men leapt overboard, all driven mad
Or panic-stricken. Medon's body first
Began to blacken and his spine was arched
Into a curve. "What magic shape is this?"
Cried Lycabas, but, even as he spoke,
His mouth widened, his nose curved out, his skin
Turned hard and scaly. Libys, trying to pull
The thwarting oars, saw his hands suddenly
Shrink—hands no longer—fins they might be called.
Another, when he meant to clasp his arms
Around a hawser, had no arms and jumped
Limbless and bending backwards into the waves.
His tail forked to a sickle-shape and curved
Like a half moon. All round the ship* they leapt
In showers of splashing spray. Time after time
They surfaced and fell back into the sea,
Playing like dancers, frolicking about
In fun, wide nostrils taking in the sea
To blow it out again. Of the whole twenty
(That was the crew she carried) I alone
Remained. As I stood trembling, cold with fear,
Almost out of my wits, the god spoke words
Of comfort: "Cast your fear aside. Sail on
To Naxos." Landing there, I joined his cult
And now am Bacchus' faithful follower.'

   'We've listened to this rigmarole', said Pentheus,
'To give our anger time to lose its force.
Away with him, you slaves! Rush him away!
Rack him with fiendish tortures till he dies
And send him down to the black night of Styx.'
So there and then Acoetes was hauled off
And locked in a strong cell; but while the fire,
The steel, the instruments of cruel death,
Were being prepared, all of their own accord

The doors flew open, all of their own accord
The chains fell, freed by no one, from his arms.
      Pentheus stood firm. This time he sent no scout,
But sallied forth himself to where Cithaeron,
The mountain chosen for the mysteries,
Resounded with the Bacchants' shouts and songs.
Like a high-mettled charger whinnying
When brazen-throated trumpets sound for war,
And fired with lust for battle, so the noise
Of long-drawn howls that echoed through the air
Excited Pentheus, and his anger flared.
      In the encircling forest, half-way up,
There lies a level clearing, bare of trees,
Open and in full view from every side.
Here, as his impious gaze was fixed upon
The mysteries, the first to see him, first
To rush in frenzy, first to hurl her staff,
Her Bacchic staff, and wound her Pentheus was
His mother. 'Here!' she called her sisters, 'Here!
That giant boar that prowls about our fields,
I'm going to kill that boar!' The whole mad throng
Rush at him, all united, and pursue
Their frightened quarry, frightened now for sure,
Now using less fierce language, blaming now
Himself, admitting now that he's done wrong.
Wounded, he cries, 'Help, Aunt Autonoe!
Mercy! Actaeon's ghost* should move your mercy!'
Actaeon's name's unknown. She tore away*
His outstretched hand, and Ino seized and wrenched
The other off. With no hands left to stretch
Out to his mother, 'Look, mother!' he cried,
And showed the severed stumps. And at the sight*
Agave howled and tossed her head and hair,
Her streaming hair, and tore his head right off,
And, as her bloody fingers clutched it, cried
'Hurrah for victory! The triumph's mine!'
As swiftly as the winds of autumn strip
From some tall tree its lightly-hanging leaves
That frosts have fingered, so those wicked hands
Tore Pentheus limb from limb. That lesson learnt*

By his example, the Theban women throng
The novel rites, honouring the god divine,
And offering incense in his holy shrine.

BOOK IV

THE DAUGHTERS OF MINYAS

NOT so in the judgement of Alcithoe,
Minyas' child: to her the god's wild rites
Were inadmissible. She still denied,
Rash girl, that Bacchus was the son of Jove,
And had her sisters too as allies in
That blasphemy. The priest had now ordained
A feast day: servant girls must be excused
From work, and with their mistresses must swathe
Their breasts in skins, let down their braided hair,
Garland their heads, and carry in their hands
The leafy staves; and fierce, he prophesied,
Would be his wrath if Bacchus were defied.
The women, old and young alike, obeyed.
Weaving, work-boxes and unfinished work
They put away, and, burning incense, called
On Bacchus by his many noble names:*
Lyaeus, Bromius; child of flaming fire;
Alone twice mothered and alone twice born;
Great lord and planter of the genial grape;
Nyseus too, and Lenaeus and Thyoneus,
Whose locks are never shorn; Nyctilius,
Iacchus, Euhan, father Eleleus;
And all the countless titles* that are yours,
Liber, throughout the lands of Greece. For you*
Have youth unfading; you're a boy for ever;
You shine the fairest in the firmament.
When you lay by your horns, your countenance
Is like a lovely girl's.* You hold in thrall
The Orient, even those remotest lands
Where Ganges waters dusky India.
You, most worshipful, sent to their doom
Lycurgus* with his two-edged battleaxe,
And Pentheus, both blasphemers; you consigned
The Tuscan sailors to the sea: you drive
Your pair of lynxes with bright coloured reins.

Bacchants and Satyrs are your followers,
And that old drunkard* whose stout staff supports
His tottering steps, who sits so insecure
Upon his sagging ass. Wherever your
Course leads you, young men's shouts and women's cries
Echo afar with noise of tambourines
And clashing bronze and long-bored pipes of box.
  'Come in thy mercy, come in gentleness!'
The Theban women cry and celebrate
The rites commanded. Only Minyas' daughters
Remain indoors and mar the festival
By their untimely spinning,* as they draw
The strands of wool and thumb the twisting threads,
Or ply their loom and keep the work-girls busy.
Then one, as her deft fingers drew the thread,
Suggested, 'While the others have ceased work
And throng those spurious rites, let us as well,
Busy for Pallas now, a better goddess,
Lighten our useful toil with talk, and tell
Some tale in turn to while the tedious hours
Away and give delight to idle ears.'
Her sisters both agreed and bade her start.
She pondered which to choose of many tales
(She knew so many), doubting should she tell
Of Dercetis of Babylon, whose shape
The Palestinians believe was changed—
Scales lapped her limbs and in a mere she moved;
Or of her daughter* who grew wings and spent
Her final years upon a tall white tower;
Or how a Naiad, using magic charms
And herbs too powerful, transformed young men
To silent fish, until she met that fate
Herself; or of the tree whose fruit, once white,
The touch of blood now dyes a dusky red.
This last she liked the best, because the tale
Was far from widely known,* and, as she span
Her wool, this is the story she began.

PYRAMUS AND THISBE

'Now Pyramus and Thisbe, he of all
The fine young men the handsomest, and she
The fairest girl of all the fabled East,
Lived next door to each other in that city*
Whose high brick walls Semiramis once built.
As neighbours, step by step acquaintance grew;
Love ripened; wedding torches would have flamed
But for their fathers' ban: yet never ban
Could quench the mutual flame that fired them both.
They spoke by signs; they had no go-between;
Their fire the more concealed, the fiercer raged.
Between the houses was a common wall,
Flawed with a narrow chink long years ago,
When it was built. This chink, so long unnoticed—
But what does love not see?—those lovers found
And made of it their voices' passageway,
And safely flowed the whispered words of love;
And often, when on her side Thisbe stood
And Pyramus on his, eager to catch
Each other's breath, they said "O jealous wall,
Why thwart fond hearts? Why grudge to let us meet,
Or open, at least, to give our kisses room?
Yet we are grateful, for we owe to you
A pathway for sweet words of lovers true."
So, on their separate sides, they talked in vain
Till nightfall, then "goodbye", and on the wall
Each printed kisses that could never meet.
The rising dawn had dimmed the lamps of night,
And the sun's beams had dried the frosty grass;
Back to their place they came; then whispering low
Their sorry troubles, they resolve, that night
When all is still, to elude their guardians,
Steal out of doors and, once outside, to leave
The city too, and lest they miss the way
In the open fields, to meet at Ninus' tomb*
And hide beneath a tree. A tree was there
Laden with snow-white fruit, a mulberry;
And close beside the tree a fresh cool spring.

They liked the plan. The sun—how slow he seemed!—
Plunged in the waves and from the waves rose night.
   It was dark, and deftly Thisbe turned the lock
And reached the street unseen and, closely veiled,
Came to the tomb and sat beneath the tree.
Love made her bold. But lo! a lioness,
Her jaws all bloody from a recent kill,
Came to the spring nearby to slake her thirst.
In the bright moonlight Thisbe watched her come
And fled in terror to a shadowy cave,
And running dropped her shawl. The savage beast
Drank deep and quenched her thirst, then, turning back
Into the woods, chanced on the delicate wrap
(But not the girl!) and with her bloody jaws
Tore it. Arriving later, Pyramus
Saw the beast's footprints plain in the deep dust,
And staggered and turned pale; then found the shawl
All bloody on the ground, and cried "One night
Two lovers shall destroy; she should have lived
A long and happy life; the guilt is mine.
Your death I caused, who bade you, piteous girl,
Alone, at night, go to this place of fear,
And came not first myself. My body rend,
My guilty flesh devour with your fierce fangs,
Ye lions whose lairs are here beneath this crag!
Yet but to wish for death's a cowardly thing."
He seized the shawl and bore it to the tree,
The shady trysting tree, and poured his tears
And kisses on the soft familiar silk,
And cried "Drink now a draught of my blood too!"
Then drew his sword and plunged it in his side
And quick from the warm wound withdrew the blade.
And as he lay outstretched his blood leaped high,
As when a pipe* bursts where the lead is flawed
And water through the narrow hissing hole
Shoots forth long leaping jets that cut the air.
The berries of the tree, spattered with blood,
Assumed a sable hue; the blood-soaked roots
Tinged with a purple dye the hanging fruits.
   But see! still fearful, Thisbe now returns

Lest Pyramus should miss her; eyes and heart
Search for her lover, and she longs to tell
The perils she has passed. She knows the place
And the tree's shape, but yet the berries' hue
Makes her uncertain—can this be the tree?
And while she doubts, she sees a twitching limb
Striking the bloody ground, and starts away
Paler than boxwood, shivering as the sea
Shivers beneath a little sliding breeze.
And then, at last, she sees it is her lover,
And screams, beating her breast, tearing her hair,
And takes him in her arms and bathes the wound
With gushing tears that mingle with his blood,
And prints her kisses on his death-cold lips,
Crying "My Pyramus, oh, what mischance
Has reft you from me? Answer, Pyramus!
Your dearest Thisbe calls you; lift your head!"
At Thisbe's name he raised his dying eyes
And looked at her, and closed his eyes again.

  Then, when she recognized the shawl, and saw
The ivory scabbard empty, "Hapless boy",
She said, "Your hand, your heart destroyed you; mine,
My hand, my heart are brave for this deed too.
Love will give strength to strike. To death I'll follow!
And men shall say of me, poor wretched Thisbe,
I was the cause and comrade of your fate,
And you whom death alone from me could sever,
Death now shall have no power to part us ever.
And yet, dear sorrowing parents, mine and his,
Grant us, we both implore, this last request,
That we whom love and life's last hour have joined
Be not denied to share the selfsame tomb.
And you, strange tree, whose boughs one body shade
And soon shall shade another, keep for aye
The marks of death, your fruit funereal,
Most fit for grief, the pledge of our twin blood."

  She fixed the sword's sharp point below her breast,
Then fell upon the blade still warm with blood.
The parents and the gods received her prayer:
The mulberry retains its purple hue;

One urn the ashes holds of lovers true.'
　　The tale had ended; a brief interval
Had followed; then, her sisters falling silent,
This time Leuconoe began her tale.

THE SUN IN LOVE

'Even the Sun, whose star-born radiance
Governs the world, became the thrall of love.
How the Sun fell in love, shall be my tale.
The Sun is thought to have been the first to see
Venus' adultery with Mars: the Sun
Is first to see all things. Shocked at the sight
He told the goddess' husband, Juno's son,
How he was cuckolded and where. Then Vulcan's heart
Fell, and from his deft blacksmith's hands fell too
The work he held. At once he forged a net,
A mesh of thinnest links of bronze, too fine
For eye to see, a triumph not surpassed
By finest threads of silk or by the web
The spider hangs below the rafters' beam.
He fashioned it to respond to the least touch
Or slightest movement; then with subtle skill
Arranged it round the bed. So when his wife
Lay down together with her paramour,
Her husband's mesh, so cleverly contrived,
Secured them both ensnared as they embraced.
Straightway Vulcan flung wide the ivory doors
And ushered in the gods. The two lay there,
Snarled in their shame. The gods were not displeased;
One of them prayed for shame like that. They laughed
And laughed; the joyful episode was long
The choicest tale to go the rounds of heaven.*
　　Venus did not forget. Him who revealed
And brought to ruin the love she hoped to hide
She punished with a love as ruinous.
What then availed Hyperion's proud son
His beauty's brilliance and his flashing beams?
Why, he, whose fires set all the world aglow,
Glowed with new fire, and he who should observe

All things gazed only on Leucothoe,
And fastened on one girl those eyes he owes
To all creation. In the eastern sky
Sometimes he rose too soon; sometimes too late
He sank beneath the waves, and, lingering
To look at her, prolonged a winter's day.
At times he failed; the fever in his heart
Infected his bright beams, and in the dark
Men groped in fear. Nor was his pallor's cause
The moon's round orb nearing the earth to mar
His light: that pale complexion came from love.

    She was his one delight. Not Clymene,
Nor Rhodos* now had power to hold his heart,
Nor Circe's lovely mother,* nor the girl,
Sad Clytie, who languished for his love,
Though scorned, and at that moment nursed her wound.
All were forgotten for Leucothoe.

    She was the child of fair Eurynome,
The fairest lady of the perfumed lands;*
And as the child grew up her loveliness
Surpassed her mother's as her mother's once
Surpassed all others. Orchamus, her father,
Was seventh in descent from ancient Belus,*
And ruled the country of the Achaemenids.*

    Beneath the far Hesperian sky extend
The pastures of the horses of the Sun.
For grass they graze ambrosia, to rebuild
Their strength, tired by the duties of the day,
Fresh for the morrow's toil. While his team there
Cropped heavenly pasturage and night took turn,
The Sun gained entrance to his loved one's chamber,
Taking the features of Eurynome,
Her mother. In the lamplight there she sat
Beside her wheel, spinning a slender thread,
And round the princess her twelve waiting-maids.
Then, as a mother kisses her dear child,
He kissed Leucothoe and said, "You maids,
Withdraw; I have a secret; please respect
A mother's right to speak in privacy."
They did his bidding. When the room was left

Without a witness, "I am he", he said,
"Who measures the long year, who sees all things,
By whom the whole earth sees all things, the eye
Of all the world. In truth you please me well."
Fear gripped her heart. Distaff and spindle fell
Unheeded from her hands. Her very fear
Enhanced her grace. The Sun, waiting no more,
Resumed his own true shape, his wonted splendour.
The girl, astounded by the sudden sight,
Yet vanquished by the glory of the god,
With no complaint accepted his assault.

   Then Clytie was jealous, for she loved
The Sun beyond all measure. Spurred with anger
Against that paramour, she published wide
The tale of shame and, as it spread, made sure
Her father knew. Brutal and merciless,
Despite her prayers, although she stretched her hands
Towards the Sun and cried "He ravished me
Against my will", her father buried her*
Deep in the earth and on her heaped a mound
Of heavy sand. Hyperion's proud son
Dispersed it with his beams and made a way
For her to raise her smothered head; but she,
Crushed by the weight of earth, had now no strength
To lift it and lay there a lifeless corpse.
Nothing since Phaethon's fiery death had grieved
So sore the master of the swift-winged steeds.
He tried if by the power of his beams
Warm life might be recalled to those cold limbs;
But destiny denied* the great attempt.
Then on her body and her burial-place
With long laments he sprinkled fragrant nectar,
And sighing said "Yet you shall touch the sky!"*
At once her body, anointed by the drops
Of heavenly nectar, melted and the earth
Was moistened with its fragrance. Then there rose
Slowly, its roots deep in the soil, its shoots
Piercing the mound, a shrub of frankincense.

   But Clytie, although her love might well
Excuse her grief and grief her tale-bearing,

The Lord of Light no longer visited;
His dalliance was done. She pined and languished,
As love and longing stole her wits away.
Shunning the nymphs, beneath the open sky,
On the bare ground bareheaded day and night,
She sat dishevelled, and for nine long days,
With never taste of food or drink, she fed
Her hunger on her tears and on the dew.
There on the ground she stayed; she only gazed
Upon her god's bright face as he rode by,
And turned her head to watch him cross the sky.
Her limbs, they say, stuck fast there in the soil;
A greenish pallor spread, as part of her
Changed to a bloodless plant, another part
Was ruby red, and where her face had been
A flower like a violet was seen.
Though rooted fast, towards the sun she turns;*
Her shape is changed, but still her passion burns.'

    That was the end; the miracle had held
Them fascinated; one denies such things
Could happen; others say true gods can do
All things—but Bacchus is not one of them.*
When they were quiet, Alcithoe was called.
Running her shuttle through the upright* warp,
'I'll not relate',* she said, 'the well-known love
Of Daphnis,* Ida's shepherd, whom a nymph
In anger at her rival turned to stone:
Such pain sears lovers' hearts! Nor will I speak
Of nature's laws relaxed and Sithon's* sex
Ambiguous, now a woman, now a man.
The tale of Celmis* too, hard granite now
But once the truest friend of infant Jove;
And the Curetes, sprung from a sharp shower;*
And Crocus with his Smilax* turned one day
To tiny flowers—these stories I'll pass by,
And hold you with a charming novelty.

SALMACIS AND HERMAPHRODITUS

Hear how the magic pool of Salmacis
Found its ill fame, and why its strengthless waters
Soften and enervate the limbs they touch.
All know its famous power but few the cause.
    To Hermes, runs the tale, and Aphrodite
A boy was born whom in Mount Ida's* caves
The Naiads nurtured; in his face he showed
Father and mother and took his name from both.
When thrice five years had passed, the youth forsook
Ida, his fostering home, his mountain haunts,
Eager to roam strange lands afar, to see
Strange rivers, hardships softened by delight.
The towns of Lycia he reached at last
And Caria's marching provinces; and there
He saw a pool, a limpid shining pool,
Clear to its very bottom; no marsh reed,
No barren sedge grew there, no spiky rush;
The water crystal clear, its margin ringed
With living turf and verdure always green.
A nymph dwelt there, not one to bend the bow
Or join the hunt or run to win the race;
She was the only water-sprite unknown
To swift Diana. Many a time her sisters
Chid her: "Come, Salmacis, get out your spear
Or painted quiver; vary your hours of ease
With hardships of the chase." Yet never spear
She took nor painted quiver, nor would vary
Her hours of ease with hardships of the chase;
But in her pool would bathe her lovely limbs,
And with a comb of boxwood dress her hair,
And, gazing long, take counsel of the waters
What style were best. Now on the soft green grass
Or on soft leaves in gauzy dress she lay;
Now gathered flowers—and, gathering, chanced to see
The boy and seeing, saw her heart's desire.
Yet though her heart would haste she paused awhile
Till, dress inspected, all in order placed,
Charm in her eyes set shining, she deserved

To look so lovely, then began to speak:
  "Fair boy* you seem—how worthily you seem!—
A god, and, if a god, Cupid himself,
Or if a mortal, happy pair are they
Who gave you birth; blest is your brother, blest
Indeed your sister, if you have one, and the nurse
Who suckled you, but far, oh far, more blest
She, your betrothed, found worthy of your love!
If there *is* one, let stolen joy be mine;
If none, let me be her, make me your bride!"
  This said, she held her peace. A rosy blush
Dyed the boy's cheeks; he knew not what love was;
But blushes well became him; like the bloom
Of rosy apples hanging in the sun,
Or painted ivory, or when the moon
Glows red beneath her pallor and the gongs
Resound in vain to rescue her eclipse.*
Then the nymph pleaded, begged, besought at least
A sister's kiss, and made to throw her arms
Around his ivory neck. "Enough!" he cried
"Have done! or I shall quit this place—and you."
Fear struck her heart; "I yield the place", she said,
"Stranger, to you" and turned away as if
To leave him, then, with many a backward glance,
She vanished in the leafy undergrowth
And crouched in hiding there. The boy, alone
(He thought) on the empty sward and unobserved,
Strolled to and fro and in the rippling water
Dipped first his toes, then ankle deep, and soon,
Charmed by the soothing coolness of the pool,
Stripped his light garments from his slender limbs.
  Then Salmacis gazed spellbound, and desire
Flamed for his naked beauty and her eyes
Blazed bright as when the sun's unclouded orb
Shines dazzling in a mirror. She scarce could bear
To wait, hardly postpone her joy, she longed
To embrace him, scarce contained her frenzied heart.
He clapped his hollow palms against his sides
And dived into the pool and, as he swam
Arm over arm, gleamed in the limpid water

Like, in a guarding dome of crystal glass,
White lilies or a figure of ivory.
"I've won, he's mine!" she cried, and flung aside
Her clothes and plunged far out into the pool
And grappled him and, as he struggled, forced
Her kisses, willy-nilly fondled him,
Caressed him; now on one side, now the other
Clung to him as he fought to escape her hold;
And so at last entwined him, like a snake
Seized by the king of birds and borne aloft,
Which, as it hangs, coils round his head and claws
And with its tail entwines his spreading wings;
Or ivy wrapping round tall forest trees;
Or, in the sea, a squid whose whipping arms
Seize and from every side surround their prey.
The youth fought back, denied the nymph her joy;
She strained the more; her clinging body seemed
Fixed fast to his. "Fool, fight me as you will",
She cried, "You'll not escape! Ye Gods ordain
No day shall ever dawn to part us twain!"
    Her prayer found gods to hear;* both bodies merged
In one, both blended in one form and face.
As when a gardener sets a graft and sees
Growth seal the join and both mature together,
Thus, when in fast embrace their limbs were knit,
They two were two no more, nor man, nor woman—
One body then that neither seemed and both.
So when he saw the waters of the pool,
Where he had dived a man, had rendered him
Half woman and his limbs now weak and soft,
Raising his hands, Hermaphroditus cried,
His voice unmanned, "Dear father and dear mother,
Both of whose names I bear, grant me, your child,
That whoso in these waters bathes a man
Emerge half woman, weakened instantly."
Both parents heard; both, moved to gratify
Their bi-sexed son, his purpose to ensure,
Drugged the bright water with that power impure.'

THE DAUGHTERS OF MINYAS TRANSFORMED

The tale was done but still the girls worked on,
Scorning the god, dishonouring his feast,
When suddenly the crash of unseen drums
Clamoured, and fifes and jingling brass
Resounded, and the air was sweet with scents
Of myrrh and saffron, and—beyond belief!—
The weaving all turned green, the hanging cloth
Grew leaves of ivy, part became a vine,
What had been threads formed tendrils, from the warp
Broad leaves unfurled, bunches of grapes were seen,
Matching the purple with their coloured sheen.
    And now the day was spent, the hour stole on
When one would doubt if it were light or dark,
Some lingering light at night's vague borderlands.
Suddenly the whole house began to shake,
The lamps flared up, and all the rooms were bright
With flashing crimson fires, and phantom forms
Of savage beasts of prey howled all around.
Among the smoke-filled rooms, one here, one there,
The sisters cowered in hiding to escape
The flames and glare, and, as they sought the dark,
A skinny membrane spread down their dwarfed limbs,
And wrapped thin wings about their tiny arms,
And in what fashion they had lost their shape
The dark hid from them. Not with feathered plumes
They ride the air, but keep themselves aloft
On parchment wings; and when they try to speak
They send a tiny sound that suits their size,
And pour their plaints in thin high squeaking cries.
Houses they haunt, not woods; they loathe the light;
From dusk they take their name,* and flit by night.

ATHAMAS AND INO

So then Bacchus' divinity was hymned
Throughout all Thebes, and Ino everywhere
Told of the god's (her nephew's) mighty power.
Of all the sisters* she alone was spared

Sorrow except her sorrow for their sake.
Her pride was high, pride in her children, pride
In Athamas, her husband and the god,
Her foster-child;* and this in Juno's sight
Was more than she could bear. 'That strumpet's child',
She mused, 'had power to change those mariners
And sink them in the sea; to make a mother
Murder the son she bore; to wrap those three
Daughters of Minyas in fantastic wings.
Can Juno then do nothing but lament
Wrongs unavenged? Is that enough for me?
Is that my only power? But he himself
Teaches me what to do (one may be taught
Even by one's enemy). The power of madness
Is demonstrated more than well enough
By Pentheus' murder. Why should Ino not
Be stung to madness too, and take the road
Of frenzy where her kin have shown the way?'

    There is a dropping path in twilight gloom
Of deadly yews; it leads through silent slopes
Down to the Underworld, where sluggish Styx
Exhales his misty vapours. By that path
New ghosts, the duly buried dead, descend.
There in a wan and wintry wilderness
The new wraiths grope to find the way that leads
To Hades' city and the cruel court
Of swarthy Dis. Countless broad entrances
That city* has and portals everywhere
Open, and, as the sea from every land
Receives the rivers, so that place receives
The spirits, every one; no multitude
Finds it too small; it never knows a crowd.
There the shades wander without flesh or blood
Or bones; some gather in the central square;
Some throng the courts of Hell's infernal king;
Some busy with their skills that mimic life,
And some enduring their due punishment.*

    Hither Queen Juno forced herself to go*
(So huge her hate and anger) from her home
In heaven. She entered and the threshold groaned*

Under her holy tread. Immediately
Cerberus sprang at her with his three heads
And gave three barks together. Juno called
The Sisters* born of Night, divinities
Implacable, doom-laden. There they sat,
Guarding the dungeon's adamantine doors,
And combed the black snakes hanging in their hair;
And when they recognized her through the gloom,
The Sisters rose. 'The Dungeon of the Damned'*
That place is called. There giant Tityus*
Lies stretched across nine acres and provides
His vitals for the vultures; Tantalus
Can never catch the water, never grasp
The overhanging branches; Sisyphus
Chases and heaves the boulder doomed to roll
For ever back; Ixion's wheel revolves,
Always behind himself, always ahead.
The Danaids who dared to do to death
Their cousin-husbands carry endlessly
The water that their sieves can never hold.
    At all of them, but chiefly at Ixion,
The child of Saturn glared, then turned her gaze
To Sisyphus and 'Why should he', she said,
'Of all the brothers* suffer punishment
For ever, while proud Athamas resides
In a rich palace, he who with his wife
Has always held me in contempt?' She explained
Her hatred's cause, and why she came, and what
She wanted. What she wanted was the fall
Of Cadmus' house and Athamas dragged down
To crime and horror by those Sisters three.
Prayers, promises and orders, all in one,
She poured and begged their aid. When she had done,
Tisiphone,* dishevelled as she was,
Shook her white hair and tossed aside the snakes
That masked her face. 'There is no need', she said,
'Of rigmaroles. Count your commands as done.
Leave this unlovely realm and make your way
Back home to the more wholesome airs of heaven.'
Juno went blithely back and Thaumas' child,*

The Rainbow, as she entered heaven again,
Purged her with sprinkled drops of cleansing rain.
    Losing no time, malign Tisiphone
Seized a torch steeped in blood, put on a robe
All red with dripping gore and wound a snake
About her waist, and started from her home;
And with her as she went were Grief and Dread,
Terror, and Madness too with frantic face.
She stood upon the threshold of the palace;
The door-posts shook, it's said; the maple doors
Turned pale, the sunlight fled. The monstrous sight
Terrified Ino, terrified Athamas.
They made to leave the palace; in the entrance
The baleful Fury stood and barred their way,
Stretching her arms entwined with tangled snakes,
And shaking out her hair. The snakes, dislodged,
Gave hissing sounds; some crawled upon her shoulders;
Some, gliding round her bosom, vomited
A slime of venom, flickering their tongues
And hissing horribly. Then from her hair
She tore out two and with a doom-charged aim
Darted them. Down the breasts of Athamas
And Ino, winding, twisting, they exhaled
Their noisome breath; yet never any wound
To see, the fateful fangs affect their minds.
Tisiphone brought with her poisons too
Of magic power: lip-froth of Cerberus,
The Hydra's* venom, wild deliriums,
Blindnesses of the brain, and crime and tears,
And maddened lust for murder; all ground up,
Mixed with fresh blood, boiled in a pan of bronze,
And stirred with a green hemlock stick. And while
They shuddered there, she poured the poisoned brew,
That broth of madness, over both their breasts
Right down into their hearts. Then round and round
She waved her torch, fire following brandished fire.
And so, her task accomplished, victory won,
Back to great Pluto's realm of wraiths she went,
And loosed the snake she'd fastened round her waist.
    Then raving through the palace Athamas

Shouted 'Here in this copse, friends, spread the nets!
I've seen a lioness with her two cubs!'
And, in his madness hunting her, tracked down
His wife and snatched Learchus from her arms,
His little laughing son with hands outstretched,
And like a slinger whirled him round and round
And wildly smashed the baby's head against
A granite block; and then his mother, crazed
By grief or by the sprinkled poison's power,
Screamed madly and with streaming hair rushed out
With tiny Melicerta in her arms,
And shouted 'Bacchus! Bacchus!'; at the name
Of Bacchus Juno smiled, 'Well done, the brat
You fostered, to bestow a boon like that!'

   A cliff hung by the shore; the bottom part
Was hollowed by the waves and formed a roof
To shield the waters from the storms; the top
Stood hard and high and faced the open sea.
Here Ino climbed (her madness gave her strength)
And with her burden launched herself, unchecked
By any thought of fear, out and away,
And where she fell the waves were white with spray.

   But Venus, pitying her grandchild's* woes,
So undeserved, addressed with winning words
Her uncle: 'Lord of waters, whose power yields
To heaven alone, great Neptune, what I ask
Is much indeed, but pity those I love,
Now tossing in the vast Ionian sea,
And make them gods to join your company.
I too should find some favour with the sea,
For in its holy depths in days gone by
From sea-foam I was formed, and still from foam
I take my name* in Greece.' Her prayer was granted.
Neptune removed their mortal essences,
Clothed them in majesty and awe, and changed
Features and names alike, the boy to be
Palaemon, and his mother Leucothoe.

   Ino's attendants, following her tracks
At their best speed, saw her last footprints there
At the cliff's edge. Not doubting of her death,

They mourned the house of Cadmus, beat their breasts
And tore their hair and garments. They reviled
Juno for her injustice and her rage
Too cruel to her rival. Such abuse
The goddess would not stand. 'You'll be', said she,
'The best memorials of my cruelty!'
Deeds followed words. The most devoted girl
Cried 'I shall join my queen amid the waves',
And tried to leap but could not move at all,
And stood fixed fast upon the cliff. Another,
Trying to beat her bosom as before,
Found her arms locked and stiff; one who had stretched
Her hands towards the waves, now, turned to stone,
Still stretches out her hands towards the waves;
One, as she reached to tear her hair, you'd see
Suddenly the fingers in her hair set hard.
Each in whatever gesture she was caught,
So she was fixed. And some were changed to birds;
And so the Theban women still today
Skim on their wings the waters of the bay.

THE TRANSFORMATION OF CADMUS

Now Cadmus never knew that his dear child
And grandson had become sea-deities;
But overcome by sorrow and his train
Of troubles and so many warning signs,
He left the city, Thebes, that he had founded,
As if that city's fortune, not his own,
Were crushing him, and with his pilgrim wife,
After long wanderings reached Illyria.
And now, worn by their woes and weight of years,
The two were talking of their early times,
The fortune of their house and their sad toils,
And Cadmus said 'Was that a sacred snake
My spear transfixed when I had made my way
From Sidon's walls and scattered on the soil
The serpent's teeth, those seeds of magic power?
If it is he the jealous gods avenge
With wrath so surely aimed, I pray that I

May be a snake* and stretch along the ground.'
Even as he spoke he was a snake that stretched
Along the ground. Over his coarsened skin
He felt scales form and bluish markings spot
His blackened body. Prone upon his breast
He fell; his legs were joined, and gradually
They tapered to a long smooth pointed tail.
He still had arms; the arms he had he stretched,
And, as his tears poured down still human cheeks,
'Come, darling wife!' he cried, 'my poor, poor wife!
Touch me, while something still is left of me,
And take my hand while there's a hand to take,
Before the whole of me becomes a snake.'
    More he had meant to say, but suddenly
His tongue was split in two; words failed his will;
And every time he struggled to protest,
He hissed; that was the voice that nature left.
Beating her naked breast, his wife cried out
'Stay, Cadmus, stay! Throw off that monstrous shape!
Cadmus, what now? Your feet, your shoulders, hands
Where are they? And your colour and your shape,
And, while I'm speaking, everything? Ye Gods,
Why don't you turn me too into a snake?'
He licked his poor wife's cheeks, and glided down
To her dear breasts, as if familiar there,
And coiled, embracing, round the neck he knew.
All who were there—and courtiers were there—
Were terrified; but she caressed and stroked
Her crested dragon's long sleek neck, and then
Suddenly there were two, their coils entwined.
They crawled for cover to a copse nearby;
And still, what they once were, they keep in mind,
Quiet snakes, that neither shun nor harm mankind.
    But ample solace for their altered shape
They both found in their grandson, conqueror
Of India, worshipped in the new-built shrines
Of Greece. Only Acrisius,* Abas' son,
Of the same lineage, barred him from his city,
Argos, by force of arms, and still denied
Jove was his father, just as he denied

Perseus could be Jove's son, whom Danae
Conceived in that gold shower.* Yet ere long
(So sure the power of truth) Acrisius
Repented of his violence to the god
And his rejection of his grandson's claim.
Bacchus was placed among the gods of heaven.

PERSEUS AND ANDROMEDA

But Perseus, with the snake-haired monster's* head,
That famous spoil, in triumph made his way
On rustling pinions* through the balmy air
And, as he hovered over Libya's sands,
The blood-drops from the Gorgon's head dripped down.
The spattered desert gave them life as snakes,
Smooth snakes of many kinds, and so that land
Still swarms with deadly serpents to this day.
    Thence through the firmament the warring winds
Propelled him like a rain-cloud back and forth.
From heaven's height he gazed down on the lands
Far, far below and flew the whole world over.
Three times he saw the icy Bears, three times
The Crab's* long claws, and often to the east
And often to the west was whirled away.
And now at dusk, fearing to trust the night,
He landed on the far Hesperian shore,
The realm of Atlas, seeking rest awhile
Until the Morning Star should wake the Dawn,
And Dawn call forth the chariot of day.
    Atlas surpassed all men in giant size.
He ruled the world's last lands and that far sea
That greets the panting horses of the sun
And welcomes their tired wheels. A thousand herds
Roamed on his pastures and a thousand flocks,
Unchecked, untroubled by a neighbour's bounds;
And there were trees whose glittering leaves of gold
Clothed golden apples under golden boughs.
'Good friend', Perseus addressed him, 'if renown
Of lineage may count, I take my line
From Jove, my father; or if deeds can win

Your admiration, mine you will admire.
I ask for rest and lodging.' But the giant
Recalled the oracle* which on Parnassus
Themis had given: 'Atlas, a time shall come
When from your tree the gold shall be despoiled,
And of that spoil a son of Jove shall boast.'
In fear he had walled his orchards all around
With massive ramparts and for guardian
Set an enormous dragon; and drove off
All strangers from the borders of his realm.
To Perseus too 'Away! Begone!' he cried,
'Or you shall find no joy in that renown
Your lies invent, no joy in Jupiter',
And added force to threats, as Perseus tried
Fair words at first, then bravely grappled him.
But when he found his strength surpassed (for who
Could match the strength of Atlas?) 'Very well!'
He taunted, 'If you rate my thanks so low,
Accept a gift!' and turned his face away
And on his left held out the loathsome head,
Medusa's head. Atlas, so huge, became
A mountain; beard and hair were changed to forests,
Shoulders were cliffs, hands ridges; where his head
Had lately been, the soaring summit rose;
His bones were turned to stone. Then each part grew
Beyond all measure (so the gods ordained)
And on his shoulders rested the whole vault
Of heaven with all the innumerable stars.

   Now in their age-old prison Aeolus
Had locked the winds, and brilliant in the dawn
The Morning Star had mounted high, the star
That wakes the world to work. Then Perseus laced
His feet again with plumes on either side,
And girded on his curving sword* and clove
With beating ankle-wings the flowing air.
Below on either hand he left behind
Unnumbered nations till he saw the land
Where Cepheus ruled the Ethiopians.
There, innocent, by Jove's unjust decree
Condemned to suffer for her mother's tongue,*

Andromeda was pinioned to a rock.
When Perseus saw her, had a wafting breeze
Not stirred her hair, her eyes not overflowed
With trembling tears, he had imagined her
A marble statue. Love, before he knew,
Kindled; he gazed entranced; and overcome
By loveliness so exquisite, so rare,
Almost forgot to hover in the air.

He glided down. 'Shame on those chains!' he cried;
'The chains that you deserve link lovers' hearts.
Reveal, I beg, your name and this land's name
And why you wear these shackles.' She at first
Was silent, too abashed to face a man,
So shy she would have held her hands to hide
Her blushing cheeks had not her hands been chained;
But weep she might and filled her eyes with tears.
Then, as he urged again, lest it should seem
Her own offence she dreaded to confess,
She told her name, her country and the tale
Of her proud mother's beauty—boast and bane.
Ere all was told a noise came from the sea,
And from the ocean's depths a monstrous beast
Loomed up, its breast spread wide across the waves.
She screamed. Her wretched father stood close by,
Her mother with him, both in dire distress,
Though she with juster cause. They brought no aid,
But wailed and wrung their hands, as well they might,
And clasped the shackled girl; and, as they clung,
The stranger spoke: 'Long time is left for tears,
But short the hour for succour. I, Perseus,
The son of Jove and her whom, in her prison,
Jove's golden shower made fertile; I, Perseus,
The snake-haired Gorgon's victor; I, who dared
On soaring wings to ride the winds of heaven—
If I should woo this damsel, none for sure
Could be my rival as your son-in-law.
To dower so glorious I aim to add,
With heaven's help, my service; and I strike
A bargain—if my valour's bold design
Avail to rescue her, she shall be mine.'

They take his terms—for who would hesitate?—
Beseech his aid and add as dower their realm.
   Look! As a galley with its pointed prow
Furrows the sea when rowers sweat and strain,
The beast breasts on and rolls the waves aside.
And now it was no further from the cliff
Than Spanish slings can hurl the flying lead
Across the sky, when Perseus suddenly
Sprang from the ground and soared into the clouds.
The monster saw his shadow on the sea
And savaged what it saw. And as Jove's bird* *eagle*
Spies in some empty field a dusky snake
Sunning itself and strikes it from behind,
And, lest it turn its deadly fangs, secures
With eager claws its writhing scaly neck,
So Perseus, swooping headlong through the void,
Attacked the monster's back and, as it roared,
Deep in its shoulder sank his crescent blade.
Wounded so sore, the beast now reared upright,
High in the air, now dived below the waves,
Now turned like a fierce boar in frenzy when
The pack bays all around. On his swift wings
Perseus eludes the snapping fangs and strikes
The parts exposed and plunges his curved sword
Between its ribs and in its back, all rough
With barnacles, and where its tapering tail
Ends in a fish. The beast belched purple blood,
Sea spume and blood together. Perseus' plumes
Were soaked with spray, so heavy he could trust
His ankle-wings no longer; then he saw
A rock, bare in still water but awash
In rising seas. On this he braced himself,
His left hand on a ridge, and with his sword
Stabbed time and time again the monster's groin.
Cheers filled the shore and echoed round the halls
Of heaven. Cepheus and Cassiope
With rapturous hearts saluted their new son,
The stay and saviour of their house. The girl,
Released, stepped forth unfettered from her chains,
The cause, the recompense of all his pains.

Water was brought and Perseus washed his hands,
Triumphant hands, and, lest the snake-girt head
Be bruised on the hard shingle, made a bed
Of leaves and spread the soft weed of the sea
Above, and on it placed Medusa's head.
The fresh seaweed, with living spongy cells,
Absorbed the Gorgon's power and at its touch
Hardened, its fronds and branches stiff and strange.
The sea-nymphs tried the magic on more weed
And found to their delight it worked the same,
And sowed the changeling seeds back on the waves.
Coral still keeps that nature; in the air
It hardens; what beneath the sea has grown
A swaying plant, above it, turns to stone.
    Then he built three turf altars to three gods,
The left to Mercury, the middle Jove's,
The right the warrior queen's, and sacrificed
A cow to Pallas,* to the wing-foot god
A calf and to the king of heaven a bull.
Then to his heart he took Andromeda,
Undowered, she herself his valour's prize.
With waving torches Love and Hymen lead
The wedding, full and fat the perfumed fires
Of incense burn and garlands deck the beams.
Lyre, flute and song resound on every side,
Glad proof of happiness. The noble doors
Flung wide reveal the whole great golden hall,
And there, a gorgeous banquet spread, the chiefs
Of Cepheus' realm attend his royal feast.
    The banquet at an end and hearts aglow
With Bacchus' noble gift, Perseus enquired
About the country and its character,
The manners and the spirit of its men,
And Cepheus answered him, and asked in turn:
'My gallant Perseus, tell me by what craft,
What courage, you secured the snake-tressed head.'
And Perseus told him of the place that lies,
A stronghold safe below the mountain mass
Of icy Atlas;* how at its approach
Twin sisters, Phorcys' daughters,* lived who shared

A single eye, and how that eye by stealth
And cunning, as it passed from twin to twin,
His sly hand caught, and then through solitudes,
Remote and trackless, over rough hillsides
Of ruined woods he reached the Gorgons'* land,
And everywhere in fields and by the road
He saw the shapes of men and beasts, all changed
To stone by glancing at Medusa's face.
But he, he said, looked at her ghastly head
Reflected in the bright bronze of the shield
In his left hand, and while deep sleep held fast
Medusa and her snakes, he severed it
Clean from her neck; and from their mother's blood
Swift-flying Pegasus and his brother* sprang.

He told them too of many a peril passed,
Perils in truth, on his long journeyings,
What lands and seas he saw from his great height,
What stars on soaring pinions he had touched;
But all too soon was silent. Then a chief,
One of their number, asked why* she alone
Among her sisters wore that snake-twined hair,
And Perseus answered: 'What you ask is worth
The telling; listen and I'll tell the tale.
Her beauty was far-famed, the jealous hope
Of many a suitor, and of all her charms
Her hair was loveliest; so I was told
By one who claimed to have seen her. She, it's said,
Was violated in Minerva's shrine
By Ocean's lord.* Jove's daughter turned away
And covered with her shield her virgin's eyes,
And then for fitting punishment transformed
The Gorgon's lovely hair to loathsome snakes.
Minerva still, to strike her foes with dread,
Upon her breastplate* wears the snakes she made.'

BOOK V

PERSEUS' FIGHT IN THE PALACE OF CEPHEUS

WHILE Danae's heroic son enthralled
The chiefs of Cepheus' court, a noisy mob
Crowded into the palace—not the sound
Of happy wedding songs, but heralding
Battle and blood; the banquet suddenly
Transformed to tumult, like a quiet sea
That winds in fury rouse to raging waves.
Phineus was first, rash ringleader of war,
And, brandishing his bronze-tipped ashen spear,
'I'm here! I'm here!' he cried; 'I've come to avenge
My stolen bride!* Your wings won't save you now,
Nor Jove's gold counterfeit',* and as he aimed,
'What are you doing?' Cepheus cried; 'Is this
Your thanks for such great service? This the dower
You pay for her life saved? It was not Perseus
Who took her from you, if you want the truth;
It was the Nereids and Neptune's wrath,
It was horned Ammon, it was that sea-monster
Who came to feast upon my flesh and blood.
You lost her *then*, then when her death was sure,
Unless her death indeed is what you want
And mean my grief to ease your cruel heart.
Maybe it's not enough, then, that you watched
While she was chained and brought no aid at all,
You, her betrothed, her uncle? Must you grieve,
Besides, that someone saved her? Must you steal
The prize he won? If that now seems so fine,
You should have tried to gain it from the cliff
Where it was shackled. Now permit the man
Who gained it, who has saved my life's last years
From childlessness, to keep what both my word
And his deserts confirm; and be assured
It's not to you that he has been preferred;
No—Perseus was preferred to certain death.'
　　From Phineus not a word. He gazed in turn

At Cepheus and at Perseus, wondering
At which of them to aim. A moment's pause;
And then with all the force that fury gave
He hurled his spear at Perseus—but in vain;
It stuck fast in the couch; and then at last
Perseus flashed up and hurled the weapon back,
And would have pierced his enemy to the heart,
Had Phineus not dodged back behind the altar*—
Shelter (for shame!) to shield the criminal.
Even so the weapon found a mark and struck
Rhoetus full on the forehead. Down he fell
And, as the iron was dragged out of his skull,
His heels drummed on the ground and his red blood
Spattered the banquet-board. And then for sure
The rabble blazed with wrath unquenchable.
Spears flew. Some called for Cepheus' death beside
His son-in-law, but he by now had left
The hall, calling Faith, Justice and the Gods
Of Hospitality to bear him witness*
That what was done defied his word and will.
Minerva, warrior goddess, then appeared
To guard her brother Perseus with her shield
And give him heart.

              There was an Indian lad,
Athis, whom Ganges' nymph, Limnaee, bore
Beneath her crystal waters. His fine looks
Were striking and enhanced by rich attire.
He was sixteen, full-grown, and wore a cloak
Of Tyrian purple with a golden fringe;
A chain of gold adorned his neck, a fine
Circlet his lovely sleek myrrh-scented hair.
Expert he was to hurl the javelin,
However far the mark, more expert still
To draw the bow; and, this time, as he bent
The springing crescent, Perseus seized a brand
That smoked upon the altar there, and struck
The lad and smashed his face to shattered bones.
   Assyrian Lycabas, his closest friend,
His comrade and his lover* long confessed,
Saw those praised features writhing there in blood

And Athis gasping out his life beneath
That bitter wound, and wept hot tears, and seized
The bow *he*'d drawn and cried, 'I'll fight you now!
The fight's with me! You shan't find joy for long
In that lad's death that brings you more disgrace
Than honour!' While he spoke, the piercing shaft
Flashed from the string, but missed the mark and hung
From Perseus' billowing tunic. Perseus turned
On him the blade Medusa's death had proved
And plunged it in his breast; then, as he died,
His eyes that swam in death's dark night looked round
For Athis, and he lay down by his side,
Solaced among the shades to share his death.

　Next Phorbas of Syene, Metion's son,
And Libyan Amphimedon, intent
To join the fray, fell slipping in the blood
That wet and warmed the whole huge floor; the sword
Cut short their rising, one pierced through the ribs,
The other through the throat. But Eurytus,
Whose weapon was a two-edged battleaxe,
Perseus did not attack with his curved sword,
But lifting high in his two hands a huge
Bowl of enormous massive weight, embossed
In bold relief, he crashed it on the man.
Spewing up scarlet blood and dying on
His back, he beat his head upon the ground.

　Then Polydaemon, scion of the line
Of Queen Semiramis, and Abaris
Of Caucasus and long-haired Helices,
Lycetus too whose lands Spercheus laved,
And Phlegyas and Clytus—all of them
Perseus laid low and trod the piles of dead.
And Phineus dared not fight him hand to hand,
But flung his javelin, which missed and struck
Idas, who all in vain had held aloof
And followed neither side. He glared at Phineus;
'Since I am forced to join the fight', he cried,
'Know I'm your foe and pay with wound for wound!'
He pulled the shaft out of his side to hurl
It back, but crumpled faint from loss of blood.

And then Hodites, next to the king in rank,
Fell by the sword of Clymenus; Hypseus
Struck Prothoenor, Lyncides Hypseus.
Emathion was there, a grand old man,
Who honoured justice and revered the gods.
He, since his years forbade the battle, fought
With voice and tongue, and striding forwards, cursed
Their wicked fighting. As his shaking hands
Embraced the altar,* Chromis drew his sword
And struck his head off. On the altar down
It dropped and there the still half-conscious tongue
Maintained its maledictions as it breathed
Its last life-breath amidst the altar fires.*
   Next two twin brothers fell by Phineus' hand,
Ammon and Broteas, invincible
Boxers, could but the gloves subdue the sword,
And Ceres' priest, Ampycus, with the white
Bands round his brow; Lampetides as well
Not meant for business such as this, but for
Pursuits of peace with viol, lute and song.
His duty was to entertain the feast
And sing the festal songs and, as he stood
Apart, his peaceful viol in his hand,
Pettalus mocked him; 'Sing the rest', he cried,
'To Styx's shades!' and stabbed him in the head.
He fell and still his dying fingers swept
The strings and sorrow sounded in his fall.
But not to let his death go unavenged,
Lycormas snatched in fury from the door
The right crossbar and crashed it down upon
Pettalus' neck, and he dropped like an ox
Slaughtered in sacrifice. Pelates tried to wrench
The left crossbar away, and, as he tried,
Corythus speared his hand and pinned it to
The post, and Abas* thrust him through the side;
Nor did he fall, but died there as he hung,
His hand nailed to the wood. Then Melaneus
Of Perseus' camp was slain, and Dorylas,
The richest lord of Nasamonia,
Lord of rich acres; none possessed such wide

Domains or harvested so many heaps
Of incense. In his groin, a fatal spot,
A spear lodged sideways. He who gave the wound,
Halcyoneus of Bactria, saw him roll
His eyes and gasp his life away, and cried
'Of all your acres keep the ground you grasp!'
And left the lifeless corpse. But Perseus, swift
For vengeance, seized the spear from the warm wound
And hurled it back; it pierced his nose and neck
And stuck out back and front. And then he slew,
While fortune favoured, Clytius and Clanis,
Born of one mother, dead of different wounds.
The ash-spear brandished by his mighty arm
Pinned Clytius' two thighs, and Clanis' teeth
Clenched on a javelin. And Celadon
Of Mendes died, and Astreus died, whose mother
Was Syrian and his father never known;
Aethion died, once wise in things to come
But then misled by lying auguries;
And with them Cepheus' page, Thoactes, died;
Agyrtes too, the scandalous parricide.

Worn as he was, yet more remained. They all
Were bent on his one murder; on all sides
The united ranks assailed him, in a cause
Opposed to just deserts and plighted word.
On his side, in support, were King Cepheus,
Loyal in vain, and his new bride and her
Mother, who filled the hall with their shrill screams.
But high above them rose the din of arms
And groans of them that fell; and all the while
Bellona fouled the gods of hearth and home
With flooding gore and stirred fresh scenes of strife.

Alone! And Phineus and his thousand men
All round him! Thick and fast as winter hail
The spears are flying, past his eyes and ears,
To right and left. Against a huge stone column
He set his back and, sheltered from behind,
Faced the attack and held the fierce assault.
The left assault Chaonian Molpus led,
Ethemon of Arabia the right;

And as a tigress, spurred by hunger, hears
Two herds of cattle lowing* in a dale,
Two separate herds, and doubts which one to attack
And burns to attack them both, so Perseus weighed
The right, the left, in doubt; and then dismissed
Molpeus with a deep leg-wound and was glad
To let him go, because, no respite given,
Ethemon charged in frenzy, aiming high
To wound him in the neck, but, striking wild,
Shattered his sword against the column's edge.
The leaping blade lodged in its owner's throat,
Yet not a blow of power enough to cause
His death. But as he trembled, stretching out
His empty hands for mercy, Perseus struck
And thrust him through with Mercury's curved blade.

　　Yet Perseus saw* that valour could not vie
With weight of numbers. 'You, yourselves', he cried,
'Compel me! I'll seek succour from my foe!
If any friend is present, turn away
Your face!' And he held up the Gorgon's head.
'Find someone else to fear your miracles!'
Said Thescelus, aiming his lance of doom,
And in that pose he stayed, a marble statue.
Next Ampyx lunged his sword at Perseus' heart,
That great and valiant heart, and as he lunged
His hand, rigid, moved neither back nor forth.
But Nileus, he who falsely claimed descent
From sevenfold Nile and bore a shield embossed
In gold and silver with those seven streams,
Cried 'See the source of my proud lineage!
You'll get great solace in the silent shades
To know you fell by my proud hand.' His voice
Was cut off in mid speech, his parted lips
Seemed to frame words, but never a word could pass.
Then Eryx cursed them: 'It's your cowardice
That holds you frozen, not the Gorgon's power.
Charge him with me, charge him, and bring him down,
Him and his magic weapon!' As he charged,
The floor fastened his feet, and there he stayed
Stock still, a man in armour turned to stone.

These paid the proper price, but there was one,
A warrior on Perseus' side, Aconteus,
Who, fighting for his lord, looked at the head,
Medusa's head, and hardened into stone.
Astyages, who thought him still alive,
Hit him with his long sword, and loud and shrill
The long sword rang. And he, gazing aghast,
Took the same stoniness, caught there and fixed
With blank amazement in his marble face.
To name the rank and file who fought and died
Would take too long; two hundred still survived,
Two hundred saw that head and turned to stone.
    Now Phineus rues his battle so unjust—
At last. But what is he to do? He sees
Statues in many poses, knows they are
His men, calls each by name and begs his aid.
In disbelief he touched those nearest him:
Marble they were! He turned away, his hands
Held abject in defeat, his arms outstretched
Sideways* for mercy. 'You have won', he said,
'Put down your monstrous magic! Put it down,
Your Gorgon's head whoever she may be,
That makes men marble! Put it down, I beg!
I fought you not because I hated you,
Or wanted royal power. For my betrothed
I battled. Time gave me the better claim,
Your merits you. Would I had given way!
You, bravest of the brave, grant me but this,
My life! The rest—let everything be yours.'
He dared not look at Perseus as he spoke;
And Perseus answered 'Cowardest of cowards!
What I have power to grant, I grant; and great
The guerdon to your craven soul. Fear not!
No steel shall work you woe. Oh, no! My gift
Shall be an everlasting monument.
In Cepheus' palace men shall gaze at you
For ever, and my wife take comfort from
The sight of her betrothed.' And as he speaks,
He thrusts the Gorgon's head in Phineus' face,
His wincing face. Even then he tries to turn

His eyes away, but now his neck is stiff,
His moist eyes fixed and hard and stony. There
With frightened pleading face and abject hands,
In cringing pose the marble statue stands.
    Perseus returned in triumph with his wife
To Argos, his ancestral city. There
To champion and avenge his grandfather,
Acrisius, despite his ill-deserts,
He challenged Proetus. (Proetus had usurped*
Argos' high stronghold and expelled his brother
By force of arms.) But neither force of arms
Nor stronghold, basely seized, availed against
The ghastly snake-haired Gorgon's glaring eyes.
Yet Polydectes,* lord of small Seriphos,
Remained unsoftened by the sufferings
Of Perseus and the prowess that his feats,
So many feats, proclaimed. His hate was hard
And unrelenting and his baseless rage
Unending. He belittled Perseus' praise
And even claimed Medusa's death a lie.
'I'll give you proof conclusive', Perseus cried,
'Friends, shield your eyes!' and with Medusa's face
He changed the king's face to a bloodless stone.

MINERVA MEETS THE MUSES ON HELICON

Minerva thus far had accompanied
Her gold-born brother. Now she left Seriphos,
Wrapped all about in cloud, and on the right
Passed Gyaros and Cythnos,* setting course,
Her shortest course, across the sea to Thebes
And Helicon, the Muses' mountain home.
Alighting there she stopped and thus addressed
The learned sisters: 'There has reached my ears
A tale of a new fountain that burst forth
Beneath the hooves of flying Pegasus.
That is my journey's purpose, my desire
To see the miracle. I saw that horse
Brought into being from his mother's blood.'*
Urania replied: 'Whatever cause

May bring you to our home, you find our hearts
Most welcoming. The tale indeed is true;
The author of the spring is Pegasus.'
She led Minerva to the sacred spring.
The waters issuing from his hoof's hard stroke*
Long held her wondering eyes; then she gazed round
At the green bowers of the ancient woods,
The caves and grottoes and the spangled lawns
With all their countless flowers. Blest, she said,
The Muses were alike in their pursuits
And in their home. And one of them replied:
'Had not thy valour, Pallas, led thee on
To greater tasks, thou wouldst be numbered with
Our company. Thy words are true; our arts,
Our happy home deserve thy praises; blest
Indeed our fortune here, were we but safe.
But crime is so unchecked that everything
Frightens our virgin hearts. Brutal Pyreneus*
Haunts me; in truth I've not recovered yet.
He brought his savage Thracian soldiery
And captured Daulis and the countryside
Of Phocis and retained his ill-gained realm.
One morning we were travelling towards
The temple on Parnassus;* on the road
He saw us and, pretending reverence
For our divinity, "Wait here a while",
He said, "blest Muses" (knowing who we were)
"Beneath my roof and shelter from the rain"
(For rain was falling) "and the angry sky.
You must not scruple: often gods of heaven
Have entered humbler homes."* Swayed by his words
And by the weather we agreed and went
Inside the entrance hall. The rain now ceased,
The south wind yielding to the northern breeze;
The dark clouds fled, the sky was clean and clear;
We meant to go. Pyreneus locked the door
To do us violence, which we escaped
By taking wing.* As if he meant to follow
He climbed a battlement. "Whichever way
You take", he said, "I'll take the same" and leapt,

The madman, from the highest pinnacle,
And pitched head foremost, shattering his skull
Upon the ground, red with his wicked blood.'
    The Muse was speaking still when in the air
A whirr of wings was heard, and from high boughs
There came a greeting voice.* Jove's child looked up
To see whence came the tongue that spoke so clear,
Thinking it was a man. It was a bird:
Nine of them there had perched upon the boughs,
Lamenting their misfortune, master-mimics,
Nine magpies.* As Minerva gazed in wonder,
The Muse began (one goddess to another)
To tell this tale. 'Not long ago these, too,
Worsted in contest, swelled the tribe of birds.
Their father was rich Pierus, a squire
Of Pella, and Paeonian* Euippe
Their mother. To her aid nine times she called
Lucina and nine times she bore a child.
This pack of stupid sisters, puffed with pride
In being nine, had travelled through the towns,
So many towns, of Thessaly and Achaea
And reached us here at last and challenged us:
"Cease cheating with that spurious charm of yours
The untutored rabble. If you trust your powers,
Contend with us, you Thespian goddesses.*
In voice and skill we shall not yield to you;
In number we are equal. If you lose,
You leave Medusa's spring and Aganippe,*
Or we the plains of Macedonia
Up to Paeonia's snowy mountainsides;
And let the judgement of the nymphs decide."
    Of course it was a shame to strive with them
But greater shame to yield. The choice of nymphs
Was made; they took the oath by their own streams,
And sat on benches shaped from living stone.
Then, without drawing lots, the one who claimed
To challenge sang of the great war in heaven,*
Ascribing spurious prowess to the giants,
Belittling all the exploits of the gods:
How Typhon,* issuing from earth's lowest depths,

Struck terror in those heavenly hearts, and they
All turned their backs and fled, until they found
Refuge in Egypt and the seven-mouthed Nile.
She told how earth-born Typhon even there
Pursued them and the gods concealed themselves
In spurious shapes;* "And Jove became a ram",
She said, "lord of the herd, and so today
Great Lybian Ammon's shown with curling horns.*
Phoebus hid as a raven,* Bacchus a goat,*
Phoebe a cat, Juno a snow-white cow,
Venus a fish* and Mercury an ibis."*
   So to her lyre she sang and made an end.
Then we were called. But maybe you've no time
Or leisure now to listen to our song?'
'No, to be sure', said Pallas; 'sing your song,
Sing it right through', and took her seat beneath
The trees' light shade. The Muse resumed her tale.
'We appointed one of us our champion,
Calliope.* She rose, her flowing hair
Bound in an ivy wreath, and with her thumb
Tuning the plaintive chords, began this song,
Accompanying her voice with sweeping strings.

THE RAPE OF PROSERPINE

"Ceres first turned the earth with the curved plough;
She first gave corn and crops to bless the land;
She first gave laws;* all things are Ceres' gift.
Of Ceres I must sing. Oh that my song
May hymn the goddess' praise as she deserves,
A goddess who deserves high hymns of praise.
   The huge three-angled isle of Sicily
Lies piled upon the body of the giant,
Typhon, whose hopes had dared heaven's palaces,
And holds him fast beneath its mighty mass.
Often he strives and strains to rise again
But on his right hand long Pelorus stands,
And on his left Pachynus; Lilybaeum*
Crushes his legs, Etna weighs down his head,
Where, face upturned, his fierce throat vomits forth

Cinders and flames. Often he strains his strength
To heave earth's weight aside, to roll away
The mountain ranges and the teeming towns.
Then the land quakes and even the king who rules
The land of silence shudders lest the ground
In gaping seams should open and the day
Stream down and terrify the trembling shades.*

    In dread of such disaster Hades' king
Had left his dark domains and to and fro,
Drawn in his chariot and sable steeds,
Inspected the foundations of the isle.
His survey done, and no point found to fail,
He put his fears aside; when, as he roamed,
Venus of Eryx, from her mountain throne,
Saw him and clasped her swift-winged son, and said:
'Cupid, my child, my warrior, my power,
Take those sure shafts with which you conquer all,
And shoot your speedy arrows* to the heart
Of the great god to whom the last lot* fell
When the three realms were drawn. Your mastery
Subdues the gods of heaven and even Jove,
Subdues the ocean's deities and him,
Even him, who rules the ocean's deities.
Why should Hell lag behind? Why not there too
Extend your mother's empire and your own?
The third part of the world's at stake, while we
In heaven (so long-suffering!) are despised—
My power grows less, and less the power of Love.
Do you not see how Pallas and Diana,
Queen of the chase, have both deserted me?
And Ceres' daughter, if we suffer it,
Will stay a virgin too—her hope's the same.
So for the sake of our joint sovereignty,
If that can touch your pride, unite in love
That goddess with her uncle.'* So she spoke.
Then Cupid, guided by his mother, opened
His quiver and of all his thousand arrows
Selected one, the sharpest and the surest,
The arrow most obedient to the bow,
And bent the pliant horn* against his knee

And shot the barbed shaft deep in Pluto's heart.
    Not far from Henna's* walls there is a lake,
Pergus by name, its waters deep and still;
It hears the music of the choiring swans
As sweet as on Cayster's gliding stream.
Woods crown the waters, ringing every side,
Their leaves like awnings* barring the sun's beams.
The boughs give cooling shade, the watered grass
Is gay with spangled flowers of every hue,
And always it is spring. Here Proserpine
Was playing in a glade and picking flowers,
Pansies and lilies, with a child's delight,
Filling her basket and her lap to gather
More than the other girls, when, in a trice,
Dis saw her, loved her, carried her away—
Love leapt in such a hurry! Terrified,
In tears, the goddess called her mother, called
Her comrades too, but oftenest her mother;
And, as she'd torn the shoulder of her dress,
The folds slipped down and out the flowers fell,
And she, in innocent simplicity,
Grieved in her girlish heart for their loss too.
Away the chariot sped; her captor urged
Each horse by name and shook the dark-dyed reins
On mane and neck. On through deep lakes he drove,
On through Palica's* sulphurous pools that boil
In reeking chasms, on past Syracuse,
Where settlers once from Corinth's isthmus built
Between two harbours their great battlements.
    A bay confined by narrow points of land
Lies between Arethusa and Cyane.*
And there lived Cyane, the most renowned
Of all the nymphs of Sicily, who gave
Her pool its name. Out of her waters' midst
She rose waist-high and recognized the goddess.
'Stop, Pluto, stop!' she cried, 'You cannot take
This girl to wife against Queen Ceres' will!
She ought to have been wooed, not whirled away.
I too, if humble things may be compared
With great, was loved; Anapus* married me;

But I was wooed and won, not, like this girl,
Frightened and forced.' She held her arms outstretched
To bar his way. But Saturn's son restrained
His wrath no longer. Urging on his steeds,
His terrible steeds, and brandishing aloft
His royal sceptre in his strong right arm,
He hurled it to the bottom of the pool.
The smitten earth opened a way to Hell
And down the deep abyss the chariot plunged.
    But Cyane, heartbroken at the rape
Of Proserpine and at her pool's outrage,
In silence carried in her heart a wound
Beyond consoling, and in endless tears
She wasted all away. Into the pool—
Her pool and she but now its deity—
She spread dissolved. You might have seen her limbs
Soften, her bones begin to bend, her nails
Losing their hardness. All the slenderest parts,
Her wave-blue hair, her fingers, legs and feet
Were liquid first; the change is slight and short
From delicate limbs to chilly water. Next
Her shoulders, back and sides and breast dissolved
In slender rivulets and disappeared,
And last, in place of warm and living blood,
Water flows in along her wasted veins
And nothing now that you could grasp remains.
    Ceres meanwhile in terror sought her child
Vainly in every land, o'er every sea.
Never the Dawn rising with dewy hair,
Nor ever the Evening Star saw her at rest.
She lit pine-torches, one in either hand,
At Etna's fires, and through the frosty dark
Bore them unsleeping. When the friendly day
Had dimmed the stars, she sought her daughter still
From sunrise until sunset hour by hour.
Weary she was and thirsty, for no spring
Had wet her lips, until she chanced to see
A little cottage thatched with straw, and knocked
On its low door; then an old crone came out
And looked at her, and when she asked for water

Brought a sweet barley-flavoured drink, and, while
She drank, a saucy bold-faced boy stood by
And laughed and called her greedy. She in anger
Threw the unfinished drink with all the grains
Of barley in his face. His cheeks came out
In spots, and where his arms had been legs grew;
A tail was added to his altered limbs
And then, to keep his power of mischief small,
He shrank till he was tinier than a lizard.
The crone, amazed, in tears, bent down to touch
The changeling creature, but it fled to find
A hiding-hole. It has a name to suit
Its coloured skin—a starry-spotted newt.*
      Through what far lands and seas the goddess roved
Were long to tell; the whole world failed her search.
She turned again to Sicily and there,
In wanderings that led her everywhere,
She too reached Cyane; who would have told
All, had she not been changed. She longed to tell
But had no mouth, no tongue, nor any means
Of speaking. Even so she gave a clue,
Clear beyond doubt, and floating on her pool
She showed the well-known sash which Proserpine
Had chanced to drop there in the sacred spring.
How well the goddess knew it! Then at last
She seemed to understand her child was stolen,
And tore her ruffled hair and beat her breast.
Where the girl was she knew not, but reproached
The whole wide world—ungrateful, not deserving
Her gift of grain—and Sicily in chief
Where she had found the traces of her loss.
So there with angry hands she broke the ploughs
That turned the soil and sent to death alike
The farmer and his labouring ox, and bade
The fields betray their trust, and spoilt the seeds.
False lay the island's famed fertility,
Famous through all the world. The young crops died
In the first blade, destroyed now by the rain
Too violent, now by the sun too strong.
The stars and winds assailed them; hungry birds

Gobbled the scattered seeds; thistles and twitch,
Unconquerable twitch, wore down the wheat.
      Then that fair nymph* whom once Alpheus loved
Rose from her pool and brushed back from her brow
Her dripping hair, and said: 'O thou, divine
Mother, who through the world hast sought thy child,
Mother of crops and harvest, cease at last
Thy boundless toil and end thy savage rage
Against the land that has kept faith with thee.
The land is innocent; against its will
It opened for that rape. Nor is it mine,
This land I plead for—I, a stranger here.
My land is Pisa and I trace my stock
From Elis. Here in Sicily I dwell
An alien, but no land in all the world
Is dearer now to me. I, Arethusa,
Have here my home, my heart. This land, I pray,
Goddess most gentle, cherish and preserve.
Why I forsook my home and fared so far
O'er the vast ocean to Ortygia,*
A fitting time will come to tell, when cares
Are lightened and thine eyes are bright. The earth
Opened a way for me and I was borne
Below its deepest caverns, until here
I raised my head and saw the stars again.
And so it was that, while beneath the earth
I glided in my Stygian stream, I saw,
Myself with my own eyes, your Proserpine.
Her looks were sad, and fear still in her eyes;
And yet a queen, and yet of that dark land
Empress, and yet with power and majesty
The consort of the sovereign lord of Hell.'*
      The mother heard in horror, thunderstruck
It seemed and turned to stone. Then as her shock
So great gave way to grief as great, she soared,
Borne in her chariot, to the sky's bright realms
And stood, with clouded face and hair let loose,*
Indignant before Jove and said: 'I come
To plead for my own flesh and blood, yours too;
And if the mother finds no favour, let

At least the daughter move her father's heart;
Love her not less because I gave her birth.
Behold, the daughter I have sought so long
Is found, if "found" is surer loss, or if
But to know where she is is finding her.
Her theft I'll bear if he'll but bring her back;
A thief, a kidnapper's no proper husband
For child of yours, even if she's mine no more.'
And Jove replied: 'The child is yours and mine,
Our common care and love. If we allow
Things proper names, here is no harm, no crime,
But love and passion. Such a son-in-law,
If you, Ma'am, but consent, will not disgrace us.
To be Jove's brother, what a splendid thing!—
If that were all! What then, when that's not all,
When he yields place to me only because
The lots so fell? But if your heart's so set
To part them, Proserpine shall reach the sky
Again on one condition, that in Hell
Her lips have touched no food; such is the rule
Forestablished by the three fate-goddesses.'

    So Jove replied; but Ceres was resolved
To win her daughter back. Not so the Fates
Permitted, for the girl had broken her fast
And wandering, childlike, through the orchard trees
From a low branch had picked a pomegranate
And peeled the yellow rind and found the seeds
And nibbled seven.* The only one who saw
Was Orphne's* son, Ascalaphus, whom she,
Not the least famous of Avernus' nymphs,
Bore once to Acheron in her dusky bower.
He saw and told, in spite, and by his tale
Stole her return away. The queen of Hell
Groaned in distress and changed the tale-bearer
Into a bird. She threw into his face
Water from Phlegethon,* and lo! a beak
And feathers and enormous eyes! Reshaped,
He wears great tawny wings, his head swells huge,
Long claws curve down, he stretches clumsily
The plumes new-sprouted on his lazy arms—

A loathsome bird, ill omen for mankind,
A skulking screech-owl, sorrow's harbinger.
   That tell-tale tongue of his no doubt deserved
The punishment. But Achelous' daughters,
Why should it be that they have feathers now
And feet of birds, though still a girl's fair face,
The sweet-voiced Sirens?* Was it not because,
When Proserpine was picking those spring flowers,
They were her comrades there, and, when in vain
They'd sought for her through all the lands, they prayed
For wings to carry them across the waves,
So that the seas should know their search, and found
The gods were gracious, and then suddenly
Saw golden plumage clothing all their limbs?
Yet to preserve that dower of glorious song,
Their melodies' enchantment, they retained
Their fair girls' features and their human voice.
   Then Jove, to hold the balance fair between
His brother and his sister in her grief,
Portioned the rolling year in equal parts.
Now Proserpine, of two empires alike
Great deity, spends with her mother half
The year's twelve months and with her husband half.
Straightway her heart and features are transformed;
That face which even Pluto must have found
Unhappy beams with joy, as when the sun,
Long lost and hidden in the clouds and rain,
Rides forth in triumph from the clouds again.

ARETHUSA

Now Ceres had regained her Proserpine
And, light at heart, enquired of Arethusa
The reason of her flight and why she was
A sacred spring. The waters of her pool
Fell silent; from the depths their goddess raised
Her head and, combing her green tresses dry,
Told the old story of Alpheus' love.
   'One of the nymphs whose home is in Achaea*
I used to be, and none more keen than I

To roam the glades, more keen to place the nets.
Though I was strong and brave and never sought
Beauty's renown, yet I was known for beauty,
Nor did its praise—too praised—once profit me.
That dower of beauty, other girls' delight,
Brought but a bumpkin's blushes to my cheeks
And in my thoughts it seemed a crime to please.

    I was returning tired, I well remember,
From hunting in the woods; the heat was great
And doubled by my toil. I found a stream*
That glided with no eddy, with no sound,
Clear to the bottom, each pebble in its depths
Easy to count; it hardly seemed to move.
Poplars fed by the stream and silvery willows
Gave to the shelving banks a natural shade.
I reached the water's edge and dipped my feet;
Then to my knees, and not content with that
Took off my light soft clothes and laid them by
On a curved willow branch and, naked, dropped
Into the water, plunging to and fro
In countless twists and turns; and as I flung
My arms and gaily gambolled there, I heard,
Deep in the stream, a strange rough rumbling sound,
And leapt in terror on the nearer bank.
"Whither so fast?" It was Alpheus' voice,
Calling me from his waters. "Whither so fast,
Fair Arethusa?" his harsh voice called again.
I fled, just as I was, unclothed—my clothes
There on the other bank. He chased the hotter;
I seemed the readier in my nakedness.
As doves on fluttering wings flee from a hawk,
And as a hawk pursues a fluttering dove,
So did I run, so fiercely he gave chase.
On past Orchomenus,* past Elis' towers
And Psophis and Cyllene and the combes
Of Maenalus and icy Erymanthus*
I held my flight, nor did he gain on me;
Until, my strength outmatched, the pace was more
Than I could long endure, and he still fresh.
Yet on through moors and tree-clad mountainsides,

Over crags and cliffs and trackless wastes I ran.
The sun was at our backs: I saw in front—
Or it was fear that saw—a giant shadow.
For sure I heard his frightful footfalls, felt
His panting breath upon my braided hair.
Exhausted, "Save me! Save thy hunting-nymph,
Diana",* I cried, "to whom so oft thou gavest
Thy bow to bear, thy arrows and thy quiver!"
The goddess heard and, choosing a thick cloud,
Draped it about me; and the river, baulked,
Circled me wrapped in darkness, quested round
The hollow cloud, stood twice, at fault, beside
My hiding-place and twice called "Arethusa!
Hey, Arethusa!" Oh! poor wretched me!
What heart had I! Was I not like a lamb
That hears the wolves howling around the fold,
Or like a hare that, hiding in the brake,
Sees the hounds' deadly jaws and dares not stir?
Alpheus waited; at that place he saw
My footprints stopped; he watched the cloud, the place.
Trapped and besieged! A cold and drenching sweat
Broke out and rivulets of silvery drops
Poured from my body; where I moved my foot,
A trickle spread; a stream fell from my hair;
And sooner than I now can tell the tale
I turned to water. But the river knew
That water, knew his love, and changed again,
His human form discarding, and resumed
His watery self to join his stream with me.*
Diana cleft the earth. I, sinking down,
Borne through blind caverns reached Ortygia,
That bears my goddess' name, the isle I love,
That first restored me to the air above.'

TRIPTOLEMUS

Her tale was done. Then bounteous Ceres yoked
Her pair of dragons to her chariot,
And fixed the curbing bits and made her way
Between the earth and sky to Pallas' city,

And brought the chariot to Triptolemus,*
And gave him seed and bade him scatter it
Partly in virgin land and part in fields
Long fallow. Soaring high the young prince rode
Through Europe and the realms of Asia till
He came to Scythia, where Lyncus* ruled,
And entered the king's palace. Lyncus asked
How he had come, his journey's cause, his name
And country. 'Famous Athens* is my country',
He answered, 'and my name Triptolemus.
No sail brought me by sea, nor foot by land,
The sky lay wide to give me way. I bring
The gifts of Ceres. If you sow them wide
Over your ploughland, they will give you back
Bountiful harvests, gentle nourishment.'*
That barbarous king was jealous, and to gain
Himself the credit for that gift so great
Lavished his hospitality, and when
His guest was sunk in sleep, attacked him with
A dagger. As he tried to stab his heart,
Ceres transformed the king into a lynx;
Then bade the prince of Athens drive her pair
Of sacred dragons homeward through the air."

Such was the song our leading sister sang;
She finished and the nymphs with one accord
Declared the goddesses of Helicon
The winners. As the losers hurled abuse,
"So then it's not enough", I said, "that your
Challenge has earned you chastisement; you add
Insult to injury. Our patience has
Its limits; we'll proceed to punishment.
Where anger calls, we'll follow." Those nine girls*
Laughed and despised my threats and, as they tried
To speak and shout and scream and shake their fists,
Before their eyes their fingers sprouted feathers,
Plumage concealed their arms, and each of them
Saw in the face of each a hard beak form,
All weird new birds to live among the woods;
And as they beat their breasts their flapping arms
Raised them to ride the air—and there they were,

Magpies, the copses' saucy scolds. Now still
As birds they keep their former eloquence,
Their endless raucous chattering, as each
Indulges in her passionate love of speech.'

BOOK VI

ARACHNE

PALLAS had listened to the tale she told
With warm approval of the Muses' song
And of their righteous rage. Then to herself—
'To praise is not enough; I should have praise
Myself, not suffer my divinity
To be despised unscathed.' She had in mind
Arachne's* doom, the girl of Lydia,
Who in the arts of wool-craft claimed renown
(So she had heard) to rival hers. The girl
Had no distinction in her place of birth
Or pedigree, only that special skill.
Her father was Idmon* of Colophon,
Whose trade it was to dye the thirsty wool
With purple of Phocaea. She had lost
Her mother, but she too had been low-born
And matched her husband. Yet in all the towns
Of Lydia Arachne's work had won
A memorable name, although her home
Was humble and Hypaepae where she lived
Was humble too. To watch her wondrous work
The nymphs would often leave their vine-clad slopes
Of Tmolus, often leave Pactolus' stream,
Delighted both to see the cloth she wove
And watch her working too; such grace she had.
Forming the raw wool first into a ball,
Or fingering the flock and drawing out
Again and yet again the fleecy cloud
In long soft threads, or twirling with her thumb,
Her dainty thumb, the slender spindle, or
Embroidering the pattern—you would know
Pallas had trained her. Yet the girl denied it*
(A teacher so distinguished hurt her pride)
And said, 'Let her contend with me. Should I
Lose, there's no forfeit that I would not pay.'

Pallas disguised herself as an old woman,

A fringe of false grey hair around her brow,
Her tottering steps supported by a stick,
And speaking to the girl, 'Not everything
That old age brings', she said, 'we'd wish to avoid.
With riper years we gain experience.
Heed my advice. Among the world of men
Seek for your wool-craft all the fame you will,
But yield the goddess place, and humbly ask
Pardon for those rash words of yours; she'll give
You pardon if you ask.' With blazing eyes
Arachne stared at her and left her work.
She almost struck her; anger strong and clear
Glowed as she gave the goddess (in disguise)
Her answer: 'You're too old, your brain has gone.
You've lived too long, your years have done for you.
Talk to your daughters, talk to your sons' wives!
My own advice is all I need. Don't think
Your words have any weight. My mind's unchanged.
Why doesn't Pallas come herself? Why should
She hesitate to match herself with me?'
Then Pallas said, 'She's come!' and threw aside
The old crone's guise and stood revealed. The nymphs
And Lydian women knelt in reverence.
Only Arachne had no fear. Yet she
Blushed all the same; a sudden colour tinged
Her cheeks against her will, then disappeared;
So when Aurora rises in the dawn,
The eastern sky is red and, as the sun
Climbs, in a little while is pale again.
　　She stood by her resolve, setting her heart,
Her stupid heart, on victory, and rushed
To meet her fate. Nor did the child of Jove
Refuse or warn her further or postpone
The contest. Then, with no delay, they both,
Standing apart, set up their separate looms
And stretched the slender warp. The warp is tied
To the wide cross-beam; a cane divides the threads;
The pointed shuttles carry the woof through,
Sped by their fingers. When it's through the warp,
The comb's teeth, tapping, press it into place.

Both work in haste, their dresses girdled tight
Below their breasts; the movements of their arms
Are skilled and sure; their zeal beguiles their toil.
Here purple threads that Tyrian vats have dyed
Are woven in, and subtle delicate tints
That change insensibly from shade to shade.
So when the sunshine strikes a shower of rain,
The bow's huge arc will paint the whole wide sky,
And countless different colours shine, yet each
Gradation dupes the gaze, the tints that touch
So similar, the extremes so far distinct.
Threads too of golden wire were woven in,
And on the loom an ancient tale was traced.

   The rock of Mars in Cecrops' citadel*
Is Pallas' picture and that old dispute*
About the name of Athens. Twelve great gods,
Jove in their midst, sit there on lofty thrones,
Grave and august, each pictured with his own
Familiar features: Jove in regal grace,
The Sea-god standing, striking the rough rock
With his tall trident, and the wounded rock
Gushing sea-brine, his proof to clinch his claim.
Herself she gives a shield, she gives a spear
Sharp-tipped, she gives a helmet for her head;
The aegis guards her breast, and from the earth,
Struck by her spear, she shows an olive tree,
Springing pale-green with berries on the boughs;
The gods admire; and Victory ends the work.
Yet to provide examples to instruct
Her rival what reward she should expect
For her insensate daring, she designed
In each of the four corners four small scenes
Of contest, brightly coloured miniatures.
There in one corner Thracian Rhodope
And Haemon,* icy mountains now, but once
Mortals, who claimed the names of gods most high.
Another showed the Pygmy matron's* doom,
Her pitiable doom, when Juno won
The contest and transformed her to a crane
And made her fight her folk, her kith and kin.

Antigone* she pictured too, who once
Challenged the royal consort of great Jove.
And Juno changed her to a bird, and Troy
Availed her nothing nor Laomedon,
Her father—no! with snowy feathers clothed,
In self-applause she claps her stork's loud bill.
In the last corner Cinyras,* bereaved,
Embraced the temple steps, his daughters' limbs,
And lying on the marble seemed to weep.
All round the border ran an olive-branch,
The branch of peace.* That was the end, and she
Finished her picture with her own fair tree.
   Arachne shows* Europa cheated by
The bull's disguise, a real bull you'd think,*
And real sea. The girl was gazing at
The shore she'd left and calling to her friends,
Seeming to dread the leaping billows' touch,
Shrinking and drawing up her feet in fear.
Asterie* in the struggling eagle's clutch
She wove, and pictured Leda as she lay
Under the white swan's wings, and added too
How Jove once in a satyr's guise had got
Antiope with twins, and, as Amphitryon,
Bedded Alcmena; in a golden shower
Fooled Danae, Aegina in a flame,*
And as a shepherd snared Mnemosyne,*
And as a spotted serpent Proserpine.*
Neptune she drew, changed to a savage bull
For love of Canace; and Neptune too
Sired, as Enipeus, the Aloidae;*
Bisaltes' child* he cheated as a ram;
The corn's most gracious mother,* golden-haired,
Suffered him as a horse, and, as a bird,
The snake-tressed mother* of the flying steed;
And poor Melantho knew him as a dolphin.
To all of them Arachne gave their own
Features and proper features of the scene.
She wove too Phoebus in a herdsman's guise,*
And how he sometimes wore a lion's skin,
Sometimes hawk's plumage;* how he fooled Isse,

Macareus' daughter, as a shepherd; how
Bacchus with bunches of false grapes deceived
Erigone,* and Saturn, as a horse,
Begot* the centaur Chiron. Round the edge
A narrow band of flowers she designed,
Flowers and clinging ivy intertwined.
　　In all that work of hers Pallas could find,
Envy could find, no fault. Incensed at such
Success the warrior goddess, golden-haired,
Tore up the tapestry, those crimes of heaven,
And with the boxwood shuttle in her hand
(Box of Cytorus) three times, four times, struck
Arachne on her forehead. The poor wretch,
Unable to endure it, bravely placed
A noose around her neck; but, as she hung,
Pallas in pity raised her. 'Live!' she said,
'Yes, live but hang, you wicked girl, and know
You'll rue the future too: that penalty
Your kin shall pay to all posterity!'
And as she turned to go, she sprinkled her
With drugs of Hecate,* and in a trice,
Touched by the bitter lotion, all her hair
Falls off and with it go her nose and ears.
Her head shrinks tiny; her whole body's small;
Instead of legs slim fingers line her sides.
The rest is belly; yet from that she sends
A fine-spun thread and, as a spider, still
Weaving her web, pursues her former skill.

NIOBE

All Lydia rang; the story raced abroad
Through Phrygia's towns and filled the world with talk.
Before her marriage Niobe had known
Arachne, when she lived in Lydia,
Near Sipylus, while still a girl. Even so
She took no warning from the punishment
Of her compatriot to give the gods
Their proper place and moderate her tongue.
Much made her haughty. Yet her husband's skill,*

The high birth of them both, their kingdom's power,
Though all indeed gave pleasure, none could give
Such pleasure as her children. Niobe
Must have been thought the happiest of mothers,
Had she not thought so too. The prophetess,
Manto,* Tiresias' daughter, had been spurred
By heavenly promptings. Through the city's streets
She cried her holy call: 'Women of Thebes,
Come in your throngs, with bay wreaths round your hair,
And give Latona and her children twain
Incense and reverent worship. Through my lips
Latona calls!' And, in obedience, all
The Theban women wreathe their brows and bring
Their prayers and incense to the holy shrine.

But here, escorted by a multitude
Of courtiers, comes Niobe, superb
In a shining Phrygian gown of woven gold.
Lovely she was, as far as rage allowed,
Tossing her graceful head and glorious hair
That fell upon her shoulders either side.
She stopped, and in her full height cast her gaze,
Her haughty gaze, around. 'What lunacy
Makes you prefer a fabled god', she said,
'To gods you see? Latona, why should her
Shrine be revered, when my divinity
Lacks incense still? My father's Tantalus,*
The only mortal gods in heaven allowed
To share their banquet-board. My mother* ranks
As sister of the Pleiads. That great giant,
Atlas,* whose shoulders bear the circling sky,
Is one grandfather; Jupiter the other,*
My husband's father too I'm proud to say.
The Phrygian nation fears me. I am mistress
Of Cadmus' royal house; our city's walls,
Built by my husband's music, and our people
Are ruled by him and me.* Enormous wealth
I see throughout my home wherever I turn
My gaze; and godlike beauty too is mine.
Then add my seven sons and seven daughters
And soon my sons' wives and my sons-in-law.

Now ask yourselves the reason for my pride,
And dare prefer me to that Titan's child,
Whom Coeus sired, whoever he may be,
Latona whom the great globe once refused
The smallest spot to give her children birth.*
Not earth, nor sky, nor water would accept
Your goddess, outcast from the world, until
Delos took pity on her wanderings
And said, "You roam the land and I the sea,*
Homeless", and gave her drifting refuge there.
She bore two children;* so her womb was worth
A seventh part of mine. O happy me!
(Who would deny it?) and happy I'll remain
(Who could doubt *that*?). My riches make me safe.
Yes, I'm too great to suffer Fortune's blows;
Much she may take, yet more than much she'll leave.
My blessings banish fear. Suppose some part
Of this my clan of children could be lost,
And I bereft, I'll never be reduced
To two, Latona's litter—near enough
Childless! Away with you! Enough of this!
Remove those laurels from your hair!' With wreaths
Removed, they left the ritual unfinished.
They worshipped, as they might, in silent words.
    The goddess was outraged; upon the peak
Of Cynthus* she addressed her pair of twins:
'I, here, your mother, proud to have borne you both,
I, who will give no goddess precedence
Save Juno, find that my divinity
Is doubted and unless you children help
I'm barred from shrines and altars evermore.
Nor is this all that hurts. To injury
Tantalus' child adds insults. Yes, she dares
Set her own children above you, and calls
Me childless—may that fall on her own head!
Her wicked tongue shows her paternity!'*
To this sad tale Latona had in mind
To add too her entreaties, when 'Enough!'
Said Phoebus, 'Long complaints do but delay
The punishment', and Phoebe said the same.

Then clothéd in cloud they glided swiftly down
And reached the citadel of Cadmus' town.
   Beside the walls there spread a practice-ground,
A broad flat level, trampled endlessly
By horses, all the surface sandy-soft
Beneath the hard hooves and the thronging wheels.
Some of Amphion's seven sons had there
Mounted their mettled chargers, reining them
With bright gold-studded bridles, and astride
Caparisons of purple pageantry.
The first-born son, Ismenus, with tight rein
And foaming bit, was circling round the ring,
When suddenly he cried in pain—an arrow
Had pierced him to the heart. His dying hands
Let the reins fall and slowly he sank down,
Collapsing sideways from his mount's right flank.
Next Sipylus who heard in the empty air
A quiver's rattling sound, shook out his reins,
As when a master of a ship has seen
Storm-clouds and runs for safety, crowding on
All canvas to catch every breath of wind.
He shook the reins, but inescapable
The arrow followed him and in his nape
Stuck quivering, and from his throat in front
The bare steel thrust. Hunched forward as he was,
Over the flying mane and racing legs
He pitched and fouled the ground with his hot blood.
Then ill-starred Phaedimus, and Tantalus
Endowed with his grandfather's name, had made
An end to their habitual exercise
And turned to wrestling, shining sport of youth,
And now were locked and struggling breast to breast,
When, sped from the taut string, an arrow pierced
The pair of them, close clinching as they were.
Both gave a groan, both writhed in pain and fell;
Both, as they lay there, rolled their dying eyes,
And both together breathed their lives away.
Alphenor saw them, beat and bruised his breast,
And flew to lift their cold limbs in his arms,
And in that loyal service fell. Apollo

Severed his vitals with a shaft of doom,
And, as it was withdrawn, part of his lung
Was dragged out on the barbs and life and blood
Streamed forth into the air. But Damasichthon,
A long-haired lad, was wounded more than once,
Struck first just where the lower leg begins,
That soft and sinewy spot behind the knee,
And while he struggled to extract the shaft,
The fatal shaft, a second arrow struck
And drove right to the feathers through his throat:
The blood expelled the arrow,* spurting high
In a long leaping jet that bored the air.
Ilioneus, last, held out his arms in prayer,
Prayer profitless, crying 'All ye Gods in heaven',
Not knowing that he need not ask them all,
'Have mercy!' and the Archer-god was moved—
Too late: the shaft was now beyond recall.
Yet was the wound that laid Ilioneus low
The least; the arrow barely pierced his heart.

　　Rumours of havoc, sorrow in the streets,
Her household's tears brought Niobe the news,
News of her sudden ruin. She was shocked
That it could happen, angry that the gods
Had dared so far, that they possessed such power.
(The father, Amphion,* had already plunged
A dagger in his heart and by his death
Ended both life and grief.) Ah, Niobe!
Alas! how unlike now that Niobe
Who drove the Thebans from Latona's shrine,
Who walked her city's streets with head so high,
The envy of her friends—whom now her foes,
Even her foes, must pity! On the cold
Corpses she threw herself and gave her last
Kisses convulsively to all her sons.
Then raising her bruised arms to heaven, she cried
'Feast, cruel Latona, feast upon my grief!
Yes, glut your savage heart! On seven biers
I'm borne. Exult! Triumph in victory!
Even so, why victory? My wretchedness
Still gives me more than you your happiness:

After so many deaths I triumph still!'
    Hard on her words a bowstring twanged, and all
Were terrified, save only Niobe.
Disaster made her bold. In robes of black,
With hair unbound, beside their brothers' biers
The sisters stood. One of them, as she wrenched
An arrow from her vitals, swooned away,
Her cheek upon her brother. One, who tried
To comfort her poor mother, suddenly
Was silent, doubled by an unseen wound.
One, in vain flight, collapsed; another died
Upon her sister. One concealed herself,
One trembled there for all to see. So six
With one wound or another met their deaths.
The last was left. Her mother shielded her
With her whole body, her whole dress, and cried,
'Leave me my one, my littlest! Of them all
I crave this one, my littlest!' As she begged,
The one she begged for fell. She sat bereft
Amid her sons, her daughters and her husband,
All lifeless corpses, rigid in her ruin.
Her hair no breeze can stir; her cheeks are drained
And bloodless; in her doleful face her eyes
Stare fixed and hard—a likeness without life.
So too inside; that tongue of hers congeals;
Her palate's hard; no pulse beats in her veins;
No way for neck to bend nor arms to wave
Nor feet to walk; and all within is stone.
Yet still she weeps, and in a whirling wind
Is swept back to her homeland. Fastened there
Upon a mountain peak* she pines away,
And tears drip from that marble to this day.
    Then every man and woman, all of them,
Dreaded the goddess' wrath made manifest,
And worshipped more devoutly the divine
Power of the mother of the heavenly pair.
And, as will happen, new tales bring back old,
And one of them this story then retold.

THE LYCIAN PEASANTS

'In Lycia's fertile fields once, long ago,
The peasants scorned Latona—not unscathed.
It's not a thing well known—the men of course
Being low-born louts*—but marvellous all the same.
I saw with my own eyes the lake and place
Famed for the miracle. For my old father,
Too old by then, too worn to take the road,
Had charged me to retrieve some special steers
And given me a Lycian for guide.
With him I traversed those far pasture-lands,
When, standing in the middle of a mere,
And black with ash of sacrifice, behold
An ancient altar, ringed with waving reeds.
My guide stood still and muttered anxiously
"Be gracious to me!" and I muttered too
"Be gracious!"; then I asked him if the altar
Was built to Faunus or the Naiads or
Some local god, and he gave this reply.
"Not so, my lad, no mountain deity
Enjoys this altar; it is claimed by her
Whom once the queen of heaven barred from the world,
Whom drifting Delos scarcely dared consent
To harbour, when that island swam the sea.
There, leaning on a palm and Pallas' tree,*
Latona in spite of Juno bore her twins;
From there again she fled the wife of Jove,
Hugging her new-born infants, both divine.
And now in Lycia, the Chimaera's* land,
The flaming sun beat down upon the fields;
The goddess, tired by her long toil, was parched
With thirst, so hot heaven's torrid star; the babes
Had drained their mother's milk and cried for more.
She chanced to see, down in the dale below,
A mere of no great size. Some farmfolk there
Were gathering reeds and leafy osiers
And sedge that marshes love. Reaching the edge,
Latona knelt upon the ground to drink
The cooling water, knelt to drink her fill.

The group of yokels stopped her. 'Why?' said she,
'Why keep me from the water? Everyone
Has right to water.* Nature never made
The sunshine private nor the air we breathe,
Nor limpid water. No! A common right
I've reached. Even so I ask, I humbly ask,
Please give it me. I do not mean to wash,
Or bathe my weary limbs, only to quench
My thirst. My mouth is dry, as I am speaking,
My throat is parched, words hardly find a way.
A drink of water—nectar it will be,
And life, believe me, too; life you will give
With water. And these babies here, who stretch
Their little arms, must touch your hearts.' It chanced*
The twins stretched out their arms. Whom could those words,
Those gentle words the goddess spoke, not touch?
Despite her pleas they stopped her, adding threats
Unless she went away, and insults too.
And, not content with that, they even stirred
The pond with hands and feet, and on the bottom
Kicked the soft mud about* in spiteful leaps.
    Her thirst gave way to anger. Of such boors
She'd ask no favour now, nor speak again
In tones beneath a goddess. Raising her hands
To heaven, 'Live in that pool of yours', she cried,
'For evermore!' And what she wished came true.
They love to live in water; sometimes all
Their bodies plunge within the pool's embrace;
Sometimes their heads pop up; often they swim
Upon the surface, often squat and rest
Upon the swampy bank and then jump back
To the cool pond; but even now they flex
Their squalid tongues in squabbling,* and beneath
The water try to croak a watery curse.
Their voice is harsh, their throats are puffed and swollen;
Their endless insults stretch their big mouths wide;
Their loathsome heads protrude, their necks seem lost;
Their backs are green; their bodies' biggest part,
Their bellies, white; and in the muddy pond
They leap and splash about—new-fangled frogs." '

MARSYAS

Then, when whoever it was had told the doom
Those Lycian peasants met, someone recalled
The satyr who had lost to Leto's son
The contest when he played Minerva's pipe,
And paid the penalty. 'No! no!' he screamed,
'Why tear me from myself? Oh, I repent!
A pipe's not worth the price!' and as he screamed
Apollo stripped his skin; the whole of him
Was one huge wound, blood streaming everywhere,
Sinews laid bare, veins naked, quivering
And pulsing. You could count his twitching guts,
And the tissues as the light shone through his ribs.
The countryfolk, the sylvan deities,
The fauns and brother satyrs and the nymphs,
All were in tears,* Olympus* too, still loved,
And every swain who fed his fleecy flocks
And long-horned cattle on those mountainsides.
The fertile earth grew moist and, moistened, held
Their falling tears and drank them deep into
Her veins and, changing them to water there,
Issued them forth into the open air;
And thence a river hurries to the sea
Through falling banks, the river Marsyas,
The freshest, clearest stream of Phrygia.

PELOPS

From tales like these the townsfolk quickly turned
To present things and mourned Amphion dead,
Perished with all his line. The blame was laid
Upon the mother. Even then one man,
Pelops, they say, shed tears for her, and when
He tore his robe apart revealed his left
Shoulder of ivory. This at his birth
Was flesh and matched the colour of his right,
And later, when his father* carved him up,
The gods rejoined the parts and all were found

Save one between the neck and upper arm.
An ivory block was inset to replace
The missing piece, and that made Pelops whole.

TEREUS, PROCNE, AND PHILOMELA

Leaders from neighbouring lands assembled there
And cities near at hand besought their kings
To visit Thebes with words of sympathy—
Mycenae, Pelops' pride, Argos and Sparta;
Messene fierce in battle; Calydon,
Not yet* the victim of Diana's hate;
Fertile Orchomenus, and Corinth famed
For bronzes*; Patrae, humble Cleonae,
And Pylos, Neleus' town, and Troezen too,
Where Pittheus later reigned;* and all the towns
The twin-sea'd Isthmus locks, and all the towns
Outside at which the twin-sea'd Isthmus looks.
Athens alone (who could believe it?) lagged.
War thwarted such a service. Sea-borne bands
Of wild barbarians held her walls in fear.
Tereus of Thrace with his relieving force
Had routed them and won a victor's fame;
And, seeing he was strong in wealth and men
And, as it happened, traced his lineage
From Mars* himself, Pandion gave his child,
Procne, in marriage, thus to link their lines.
When they were married, Juno was not there*
To bless the rite, nor Hymen nor the Graces.
The Furies held the torches, torches seized
From mourners' hands; the Furies made their bed.
An unclean screech-owl like a nightmare sat
Above their chamber on the palace roof.
That bird* haunted the couple's union,
That bird haunted their parenthood. Of course
Tereus' and Procne's marriage gave delight
To Thrace, and they too gave the gods their thanks;
And those glad days when that illustrious prince
Married Pandion's child, and when their son,
Itys, was born were named as holidays:

So deep men's true advantage lies concealed.
    Now season followed season, as the sun
Led on the years; five autumns glided by,
And Procne coaxed her husband, 'If my love
Finds any favour, give me leave to visit
My sister, or invite my sister here,
Giving my father your sure word that she
Will soon return. To see her once again
Will be a gift most precious.' So her husband
Had his ship launched, and gained by sail and oar
Athens' great port and reached Piraeus' shore.
    There King Pandion gave him audience,
And hand clasped hand, their meeting seemed set fair.
He had begun to speak of Procne's plan,
The reason of his visit, and to pledge
Her sister's swift return, when suddenly
In entered Philomela, richly robed
In gorgeous finery, and richer still
Her beauty; such the beauty of the nymphs,
Naiads and Dryads, as we used to hear,
Walking the woodland ways, could one but give
The nymphs such finery, such elegance.
The sight of her set Tereus' heart ablaze
As stubble leaps to flame when set on fire,
Or fodder blazes, stored above the byre.
Her looks deserved his love; but inborn lust
Goaded him too, for men of that rough race
Are warm for wenching:* Thracian villainy
Joined flaring with his own. An impulse came
To bribe her retinue, suborn her nurse,
Even assail the girl herself with gifts,
Huge gifts, and pay his kingdom for the price—
Or ravish her and then defend the rape
In bloody war. Nothing he would not do,
Nothing not dare, as passion drove unreined,
A furnace barely in his heart contained.
    Now he'll not linger and turns eagerly
To Procne's plan again, and under hers
Forwards his own. Love made him eloquent;
And, if at times he pressed his pleas too far,

Why, Procne wished it so; he even wept,
As if she'd ordered tears. Ye Gods above,
How black the night that blinds our human hearts!
The pains he took for sin appeared to prove
His loyalty; his villainy won praise.
Why, Philomela had the same desire,
And threw her arms around her father's neck,
And begged him, as he wished her happiness,
(Alas for happiness!) to let her go.
As Tereus watched, already in his thoughts
He fondled her, and when he saw her kisses
And how she hugged Pandion, everything
Thrust like a goad, his passion's food and fire.
As she embraced her father, would he were
Himself her father! Nor would his sin be less!

　　Pandion yields, since both his daughters plead,
And, filled with joy, she thanks him. Hapless girl,
She thinks they both have won a victory,
Though what both won will end in tragedy.

　　Now the Sun's team, the day's toil nearly done,
Were pounding down the slope that led them home.
A royal banquet was arrayed, with wine
In golden goblets, and anon they lay
Relaxed in slumber. But the Thracian king,
Though he too had retired, was simmering
With thoughts of her, as he recalled her face,
Her hands and gestures, and his mind's eye shaped,
To suit his fancy, charms he'd not yet seen.
He fuelled his own fire, and, as he lay,
The turmoil in his heart drove sleep away.

　　Daylight had come, and now, as Tereus left,
Pandion wrung him by the hand and gave
His daughter to his trust with many a tear:
'My son, since links of love leave me no choice,
And both have set their hearts (and your heart too,
My son, is set), I give her to your keeping;
And I beseech you by your honour, by the ties
Of family and by the gods above,
To guard her with a father's love and send
Back soon (each waiting day will be so long)

The darling solace of my sombre age.
And you too, Philomela, if you love
Your father, come back soon—it is enough
That your dear sister is so far from home.'
So he adjured them, weeping tenderly,
And kissed his child goodbye, and took their hands
And joined them, his and hers, to seal their pledge
And charged them to remember his fond love
To Procne and his grandson far away.
He scarce could say farewell for sobs and tears,
Such dire forebodings filled his soul with fears.

Once Philomel was on the painted ship
And the oars struck and thrust the land away,
'I've won!' he cried, 'I've won! My dearest wish
Is mine on board with me!' His heart leapt high;
The brute could hardly wait to seize his joys,
And never turned his eyes away from her.
So, when Jove's bird of prey* has caught a hare
And in his talons carries it aloft
To his high nest, the captive has no chance
Of flight, the captor gloats over his prize.

The voyage now is done, and now they leave
The weary ship and land on their own shore;
And then the king drags off Pandion's daughter
Up to a cabin in the woods, remote
And hidden away among dark ancient trees,
And there pale, trembling, fearing everything,
Weeping and asking where her sister was,
He locked her, and revealed his own black heart
And ravished her, a virgin, all alone,
Calling and calling to her father, calling to
Her sister, calling, even more, to heaven above.
She shivered like a little frightened lamb,
Mauled by a grizzled wolf and cast aside,
And still unable to believe it's safe;
Or as a dove, with feathers dripping blood,
Still shudders in its fear, still dreads the claws,
The eager claws that clutched it. In a while,
When sense returned, she tore her tumbled hair,
And like a mourner bruised her arms, and cried

With outstretched hands, 'You brute! You cruel brute!
Do you care nothing for the charge, the tears
Of my dear father, for my sister's love,
For my virginity, your marriage vows?
All is confused! I'm made a concubine,
My sister's rival; you're a husband twice,
And Procne ought to be my enemy!
You traitor, why not take, to crown your crimes,
My life as well? Would God you'd taken it
Before you wreaked your wickedness: my ghost
Had then been free from guilt. Yet, if the gods
Are watching, if heaven's power means anything,
Unless my ruin's shared by all the world,
You'll pay my score one day. I'll shed my shame
And shout what you have done. If I've the chance,
I'll walk among the crowds: or, if I'm held
Locked in the woods, my voice shall fill the woods
And move the rocks to pity. This bright sky
Shall hear, and any god that dwells on high!'

    In anger at her words and fear no less,
Goaded by both, that brutal despot drew
His dangling sword and seized her by the hair,
And forced her arms behind her back and bound
Them fast; and Philomela, seeing the sword,
Offered her throat and hoped she would have died.
But as she fought, outraged, for words and called
Her father's name continually, he seized
Her tongue with tongs and, with his brutal sword,
Cut it away. The root jerked to and fro;
The tongue lay on the dark soil muttering
And wriggling, as the tail cut off a snake
Wriggles, and, as it died, it tried to reach
Its mistress' feet.* Even after that dire deed
Men say (could I believe it), lusting still,
Often on the poor maimed girl he worked his will.

    After this bestial business he returns,
Brazen, to Procne. When they meet, she asks
Her husband for her sister, and he groans
As if in grief and tells a lying tale
About her death, with tears to prove it true.

Then Procne snatches off her gleaming robe,
With its wide golden fringe, and clothes herself
In weeds of black and builds a cenotaph,
With offerings to the ghost that is no ghost,
And mourns her darling sister's tragedy,
And right she was to mourn—though differently.

   Through all the twelve bright signs of heaven the sun
Had journeyed and a whole long year had passed.
But what could Philomela do? A guard
Closed her escape, the cabin's walls were built
Of solid stone, her speechless lips could tell
No tale of what was done. But there's a fund
Of talent in distress, and misery
Learns cunning. On a clumsy native loom
She wove a clever fabric, working words
In red on a white ground to tell the tale
Of wickedness, and, when it was complete,
Entrusted it to a woman and by signs
Asked her to take it to the queen; and she
Took it, as asked, to Procne, unaware
What it contained. The savage monarch's wife
Unrolled the cloth and read the tragic tale*
Of her calamity—and said no word
(It seemed a miracle, but anguish locked
Her lips). Her tongue could find no speech to match
Her outraged anger; no room here for tears;
She stormed ahead, confusing right and wrong,
Her whole soul filled with visions of revenge.

   It was the time of Bacchus' festival,
Kept by the Thracian women each three years.
Night knows their sacraments; at night the peaks
Of Rhodope resound with ringing bronze;
At night the queen, arrayed to celebrate
The rites, went forth with frenzy's weaponry.
Vines wreathed her head, a light spear lay upon
Her shoulder and a deerskin draped her side.
Wild with her troop of women through the woods
She rushed, a sight of terror, frenzied by
The grief that maddened her, the image of
A real Bacchanal. At last she reached

The lonely hut and, screaming Bacchic cries,
Broke down the door, burst in and seized her sister,
Garbed her in Bacchic gear and hid her face,
Concealed in ivy leaves, and brought the girl
Back, in a daze, inside her palace wall.
    Then Philomela, when she realized
That she had reached that house of wickedness,
Shuddered in horror and turned deathly pale.
And Procne, in a private place, removed
The emblems of the revels and revealed
Her sister's face, a face of misery
And shame, and took her in her arms. But she,
Convinced that she had wronged her, could not bear
To meet her eyes and, gazing on the ground,
She made her hands speak for her voice, to swear
By all the gods in heaven that her disgrace
Was forced on her. Then Procne,* in a flame
Of anger uncontrolled, sweeping aside
Her sister's tears, 'This is no time for tears,
But for the sword', she cried, 'or what may be
Mightier than the sword. For any crime
I'm ready, Philomel! I'll set on fire
These royal roofs and bury in the blaze
That scheming fiend. I'll gouge his wicked eyes!
I'll pluck his tongue out, cut away those parts
That stole your honour, through a thousand wounds
I'll sluice his guilty soul! Some mighty deed
I'll dare, I'll do, though what that deed shall be,
Is still unsure.' As Procne spoke, her son,
Itys, approached—she knew what she could do!
Looking at him with ruthless eyes, she said
'You're like, so like your father!' and she planned
In silent rage a deed of tragedy.
Yet as the boy came close and greeted her
And hugged her, as she stooped, in his small arms,
And mingled kisses with sweet childish words
Of love, her mother's heart was touched, her rage
Stood checked and broken, and, despite herself
Her eyes were wet with tears that forced their way.
But then she felt her will was faltering—

She loved him well, too well—and turned again
To Philomel, and gazing at them both
In turn, 'Why, why', she cried, 'can one of them
Speak words of love and the other has no tongue
To speak at all? Why, when he calls me mother,
Does she not call me sister? See, just see,
Whom you have married, you, Pandion's daughter!
Will you betray your birth? For such a husband,
For Tereus, love and loyalty are crimes!'
Then—with no pause—she pounced on Itys, like
A tigress pouncing on a suckling fawn
In the dark jungle where the Ganges glides,
And dragged him to a distant lonely part
Of the great house. He saw his fate and cried
'Mother! Mother!' and tried to throw his arms
Around her neck. She struck him with a knife
Below his ribs, and never even looked
Away; one wound sufficed to seal his fate.
And Philomela slit his throat. Alive,
And breathing still, they carved and jointed him,
And cooked the parts; some bubbled in a pan,
Some hissed on spits; the closet swam with blood.

Then to the banquet Procne called her husband,
Unwitting, unsuspecting, and dismissed
The courtiers and servants: on this day,
So she pretended, at her father's court,
This holy day, the husband dines alone.
So, seated high on his ancestral throne,
King Tereus dines and, dining, swallows down
Flesh of his flesh, and calls, so dark the night
That blinds him, 'Bring young Itys here to me!'
Oh joy! She cannot hide her cruel joy,
And, bursting to announce her deed of doom,
'You have him here', she cries, 'inside!' and he
Looks round, asks where he is, and, as he asks
And calls again, in rushes Philomel,
Just as she is, that frantic butchery
Still spattered in her hair, and throws the head
Of Itys, bleeding, in his father's face.
She never wanted more her tongue to express

Her joy in words that matched her happiness!
    With a great shout the Thracian king thrust back
The table, calling from the chasms of Hell
The snake-haired Furies. Gladly, if he could,
He'd tear himself apart to vomit back
That frightful feast, that flesh of his own flesh.
He wept and wailed and called himself his son's
Disastrous tomb, then with his naked sword
Pursued Pandion's daughters. As they flee,
You'd think they float on wings. Yes, sure enough,
They float on wings! One daughter seeks the woods,
One rises to the roof;* and even now
The marks of murder show upon a breast
And feathers carry still the stamp of blood.
And he, grief-spurred, swift-swooping for revenge,
Is changed into a bird that bears a crest,
With, for a sword, a long fantastic bill—
A hoopoe, every inch a fighter still.

BOREAS AND ORITHYIA

His sorrow sent Pandion to the shades
Of Tartarus before his time, before
His long old age had reached its last full term.
Erechtheus held the sceptre and control,
A prince whose excellence might seem no less
In justice than in arms. Four sons he had,
Four daughters also, two of whom were matched
In beauty; Procris was the happy bride
Of Cephalus, but Boreas, whose love
Was Orithyia,* found the ill-repute
Of Tereus and his Thracians damaging,
And long he'd been without his heart's desire
While he preferred to woo with words not force.
But when fair speeches failed him, anger stormed,
The north wind's too familiar mood at home.
'Yes, I deserved it! Why, oh, why', he said,
'Did I give up my armoury, my wrath,
My blustering threats, my force, my savagery,
And take to grovelling and disgrace myself?

Force is what fits me, force! By force I drive
The weeping clouds, by force I whip the sea,
Send gnarled oaks crashing, pack the drifts of snow,
And hurl the hailstones down upon the lands.
I, when I meet my brothers in the sky,
The open sky, my combat field, I fight
And wrestle with such force that heaven's height
Resounds with our collisions and a blaze
Of fire struck from the hollow clouds leaps forth.
I, when I've pierced earth's vaulted passageways
And in her deepest caverns strain and heave
My angry shoulders, I put ghosts in fear,
And with those tremors terrify the world.*
Such means I should have used my wife to gain;
By force I should have won, not wooed in vain!'
With words like these or others no less high,
He waved his wings and, as they beat, the whole
World felt the blast and all the wide sea surged.
Trailing his dusty cloak across the peaks,
He swept the ground and, clothed in darkness, wrapped
Terrified Orithyia in his wings,
His loving tawny wings,* and as he flew
His fire was fanned and flared. The ravisher
Held on his airy course until he reached
The peopled cities of the Cicones.
There the princess of Attica became
Wife of the icy king and mother too,
Mother of twins, who had their father's wings,
Though all else from their mother. Yet the boys
Weren't born, it's said, with wings and, while their beards
Were still ungrown below their auburn locks,
Both Calais and Zeto were unwinged.
But later as their cheeks grew yellow down,
So, like a bird, wings lapped them on each side.
And thus it was that when their boyhood years
Gave place to manhood, with the Argonauts,
On that first ship* across the unknown sea
They sailed to seek the gleaming Golden Fleece.

BOOK VII

MEDEA AND JASON

AND now the Argonauts from Thessaly
Were cutting through the billows. They had seen
Old Phineus* dragging out his helpless age
In endless night and Boreas' two sons
Had driven the Harpies from his piteous lips.
At last illustrious Jason and his men
Reached after many travails the swift stream
Of muddy Phasis.* Going to the king,*
They claimed the famous Golden Fleece* and learnt
The fearful terms and monstrous toils imposed.
And then it was Medea, the king's daughter,
Conceived a mastering passion; long she fought
Her frenzy, but the voice of reason failed.
'Oh, vain!' she cried, 'Medea, is your struggle;
Some deity must thwart you. Strange if this—
Or something surely like—is not called love.
Else why do my father's orders seem too harsh?
Too harsh they are indeed! Why do I dread
His death whose face I first have seen today?
What cause, what reason for a fear so great?
Thrust down the flames that burn your virgin heart,
If you have strength!——Such strength would be my cure!
But against my will some force bewitches me;
One way desire, another reason calls;
The better course I see and do approve—
The worse I follow.*——Why long thus for him,
A princess for a stranger, why admit
Wild thoughts of wedlock with an alien world?
This land too offers what may win your love.
Whether he live or die, the gods decide.——
Yet may he live! That prayer, though I loved not,
Were surely licit. What has Jason done?
What heart would not be touched by Jason's youth,
His prowess, his proud birth? Who, if all else
He lacked, would not be moved by Jason's beauty?

My heart for sure is moved! Unless I help,
The bulls' hot breath will blast him; he will meet
Fierce foes of his own sowing, earth-created,
Or to the dragon be cast for prey and prize.
If I permit such things, I'll surely own
A tigress* was my dam and in my heart
I nurture iron and stone!*——Yet why not watch*
Him dying there, my gazing guilty eyes
Sharing the crime? Why not urge on the bulls,
The earth-born warriors and the unsleeping dragon?——
The gods forfend! Yet it's not what I pray
But what I do! Shall I betray* my father's throne,
And by my aid preserve some nameless stranger,
Who, saved by me, without me sails away
To win another wife across the sea
And I, Medea, am left to pay the price!
Could he do this, could he prefer another,
Then let him die!——But no—his countenance,
His manly grace, his soul's nobility
Tell me I need not fear his treachery,
Promise he'll not forget my due deserts.
And he shall pledge his troth; I'll make the gods
Witnesses of our pact. Why do you fear
What's safe and sure? Act now! Why hesitate?
Jason shall owe himself always to you,
And you shall be his bride; you shall be hymned
On every mother's tongue in every town
Of glorious Greece—Jason's deliverer!——
So shall I sail away and leave for ever
Sister and brother, father, gods and home?
In truth my father's cruel, my native land
Is barbarous, my brother still a child,
My sister shares my hopes. The mightiest god*
Is in my heart! Great things I shall not leave,
Great things I go to. Glory shall be mine—
To have saved the youth of Greece! And I shall know
A better land and cities whose fair fame
Lives even here, and arts and elegance
And him, my love, whom I would never leave
For all the wide world holds, beloved Jason;

He'll be my husband; men shall call me blest,
Fortune's darling: my head shall touch the stars!——
But what of those strange tales of cliffs that clash*
In the open sea, Charybdis' whirling waves
That suck and spew to sink the ships she hates,
And greedy Scylla,* girt with savage hounds
Baying beside the seas of Sicily?
Yes! In his arms and holding him I love
On the far seas I'll fare; in his embrace
If aught I fear, I'll only fear for him,
My husband.——No, Medea, not your husband!
With that fair name you cloak your infamy.*
Look long and see how great, how vile the crime
That lies ahead—and flee the guilt in time.'
And then before her eyes duty and honour
Stood clear and love, defeated, turned away.

   Now to the ancient shrine of Hecate,*
Deep in the forest in a shady grove,
She made her way. Now she was strong and brave,
Her vanquished passion cool, when she saw Jason,
And straight the smouldering flame was lit again.
Deeply she blushed, and fire suffused her face;
And as a little spark, that lies unseen
Beneath the ash, feeds on a fanning breeze
And grows and rises to its former strength,
So her faint love which now had seemed to fail
Leapt, as he stood before her, into flame.
By chance that day on Jason's features shone
Uncommon grace; her love could find excuse.
She gazed, her eyes fixed on his face as if
Not ever seen before; in her wild thoughts
His features seemed not mortal; motionless
She stood there; then, when he began to speak
And grasped her hand and in low tones besought
Her aid and promised marriage, her hot tears
Burst forth. 'I see', she cried, 'the thing I do;
It's love not ignorance leads me astray.
My help shall save you; only—saved—fulfil,
Fulfil your promise!' Then by the pure rites
Of Hecate and by whatever Power

Dwelt in that grove he swore, and by the Sun,
Her father's father* who sees all the world,
And by his triumphs and his perils passed.
Then she was sure; and straight the magic herbs
She gave into his hands and taught their use;
And blithely he returned to his abode.

Now dawn has put the twinkling stars to flight;
The people throng to the sacred field of Mars*
And fill the heights around; amid them sits
The king himself in purple splendour throned.
Look! There the bulls* with brazen hooves come forth,
Their adamantine nostrils snorting fire,
That scorches the green grass; and, as a furnace
Roars or as in a kiln the slaking lime
Hisses and burns beneath the watery spray,
So roared the imprisoned flames that rolled within
Their burning chests and throats. But Jason went
Forward to meet them. As he came they lowered
Their terrible muzzles and their iron-tipped horns;
Their cloven hooves stamped on the dusty ground
And smoky bellowings filled the waiting field.*
The Greeks were stiff with terror. On he went
And never felt the snorted flames, such power
The magic charms possessed; with daring hand*
He stroked their hanging dewlaps; on their necks
Fitted the yoke and forced the beasts to draw
The heavy plough and cut a furrow deep
Across the sacred ground never ploughed before.
The Colchians were amazed; the shouting Greeks
Cheered on their prince; then from the brazen helm
He took the serpent's teeth* and scattered them
Over the new-ploughed tilth; the waiting earth
Softened the seeds, in powerful venom steeped,
And the teeth formed new creatures in the soil;
And as a baby in his mother's womb
Takes human shape and, part by part within,
Is perfected and not until the hour
Is ripe issues into the common air,
So, when within the dark and pregnant earth
The forms of men were finished, up they rose

From the whole teeming field and each came forth
Clashing—most wonderful—the arms of war.
Then when the Greeks beheld the multitude
With sharp spears poised to hurl at Jason's head,
Their brave hearts failed; fear was on every face;
She too who had made him safe was filled with dread,
And when she saw him there alone, attacked
By foes so many, sudden terror drained
Her blood away, and cold and faint she sat;
And lest her herbs should fail she reinforced*
Them with her spells and summoned secret charms.
He hurled a heavy rock* amidst his foes
And thereby turned their onslaught from himself
On to each other; then by mutual wounds
In civil strife the earthborn brethren died.
The Greeks acclaimed the victor and embraced
Their glorious prince with eager arms; and she,
The foreign witch, longed to embrace him too,
But modesty—and her fair name—forbade.
With silent secret joy her heart was full
And gratitude to her triumphant spells
And to the gods who gave their magic power.
     The task remained to charm the dragon to sleep,
That ever-wakeful beast with threatening crest
And three-forked tongue and curving poison-fangs,
The ghastly guardian of the golden* tree.
Then with the opiate herb's Lethean juice
Jason sprinkled the creature and pronounced
Three times the words that bring deep peaceful sleep,
That stay the troubled seas, the swollen streams,
And on those sleepless eyes sleep fell at last.
And Jason won the famous Golden Fleece
And proudly with his prize, and with her too,
His second prize, who gave him mastery,
Sailed home victorious to his fatherland.

MEDEA AND AESON

In Thessaly, for their sons' safe return,
The mothers and the aged fathers brought
Gifts to the gods and burnt the high-heaped incense
And the vowed victim with his gilded horns
Was slain; but one was absent from the throng,
Aeson, now near to death, weary and worn
By weight of years. Then said his fond son, Jason:
'Dear wife, to whom I owe my own return,
You who have given me all, whose bounteous favours
Exceeded all my faith—yet, if this thing
Your spells can do—for what can they not do?—
Take from my youthful years some part and give
That part to my dear father', and his tears
Fell unrestrained. His love touched his wife's heart—
How different from his!—and she recalled
Her own deserted father far away.
But close she kept her troubled thoughts and answered:
'How vile a crime has fallen from your lips!
So I have power to transfer to another
A period of your life! This Hecate
Forbids; not right nor fair is your request.
But more than your request, a greater boon,
I'll aim to give; not with your years I'll dare
The attempt but by my arts, to win again
Your father's years long gone, if but her aid
The three-formed goddess gives and with her presence
Prospers the bold tremendous enterprise.'

   Three nights remained before the moon's bright horns
Would meet and form her orb; then when she shone
In fullest radiance and with form complete
Gazed down upon the sleeping lands below,
Medea, barefoot, her long robe unfastened,
Her hair upon her shoulders falling loose,
Went forth alone upon her roaming way,
In the deep stillness of the midnight hour.
Now men and birds and beasts in peace profound
Are lapped; no sound comes from the hedge; the leaves
Hang mute and still and all the dewy air

Is silent; nothing stirs; only the stars
Shimmer. Then to the stars she stretched her arms,
And thrice she turned about and thrice bedewed
Her locks with water, thrice a wailing cry
She gave, then kneeling on the stony ground,
'O night', she prayed, 'Mother of mysteries,
And all ye golden stars who with the moon
Succeed the fires of day, and thou, divine
Three-formèd Hecate, who knowest all
My enterprises and dost fortify
The arts of magic, and thou, kindly Earth,
Who dost for magic potent herbs provide;
Ye winds and airs, ye mountains, lakes and streams,
And all ye forest gods and gods of night,
Be with me now! By your enabling power,
At my behest, broad rivers to their source
Flow back, their banks aghast; my magic song
Rouses the quiet, calms the angry seas;
I bring the clouds and make the clouds withdraw,
I call the winds and quell them; by my art
I sunder serpents' throats; the living rocks
And mighty oaks from out their soil I tear;
I move the forests, bid the mountains quake,
The deep earth groan and ghosts rise from their tombs.
Thee too, bright Moon, I banish, though thy throes
The clanging bronze* assuage; under my spells
Even my grandsire's chariot grows pale
And the dawn pales before my poisons' power.
You at my prayer tempered the flaming breath
Of the dread bulls, you placed upon their necks,
Necks never yoked before, the curving plough;
You turned the warriors, serpent-born, to war
Against themselves; you lulled at last to sleep
The guardian that knew not sleep, and sent
Safe to the homes of Greece the golden prize.
Now I have need of essences whose power
Will make age new, bring back the bloom of youth,
The prime years win again. These you will give.
For not in vain the shimmering stars have shone,
Nor stands in vain, by wingèd dragons drawn,

My chariot here.' And there the chariot stood,*
Sent down from heaven her purpose to fulfil.
    She mounted, stroked the harnessed dragons' necks,
Shook the light reins and soared into the sky,
And gazing down beheld, far far below,
Thessalian Tempe; then the serpents' course
She set for regions that she knew of old.*
The herbs that Pelion and Ossa bore,
Othrys and Pindus and that loftiest peak,
Olympus, she surveyed, and those that pleased
Some by the roots she culled, some with the curve
Of her bronze blade she cut; many she chose
Beside Apidanus' green banks and many
Beside Amphrysus; nor was swift Enipeus
Exempt; Peneus too and the bright stream
Of broad Spercheus and the reedy shores
Of Boebe gave their share, and from Anthedon
She plucked the grass of life, not yet renowned
For that sea-change the Euboean merman* found.
    And now nine days had seen her and nine nights
Roaming the world, driving her dragon team.
Then she returned; the dragons, though untouched
Save by the wafting odour of those herbs,
Yet sloughed their aged skins of many years.
Before the doors she stopped nor crossed the threshold;
Only the heavens covered her; she shunned
Jason's embrace; then two turf altars built,
The right to Hecate, the left to Youth,
Wreathed with the forest's mystic foliage,
And dug two trenches in the ground beside
And then performed her rites. Plunging a knife
Into a black sheep's throat she drenched the wide
Ditches with blood; next from a chalice poured
A stream of wine and from a second chalice
Warm frothing milk and, chanting magic words,
Summoned the deities of earth and prayed
The sad shades' monarch and his stolen bride
That, of their mercy, from old Aeson's frame
They will not haste to steal the breath of life.
    And when in long low-murmured supplications

The deities were appeased, she bade bring out
The old exhausted king, and with a spell
Charmed him to deepest sleep and laid his body,
Lifeless it seemed, stretched on a bed of herbs.
Away! she ordered Jason and Away!
The ministrants, and warned that eyes profane
See not her secrets; then with streaming hair,
Ecstatic round the flaming altars moved,
And in the troughs of blood dipped cloven stakes
And lit them dripping at the flames, and thrice
With water, thrice with sulphur, thrice with fire
Purged the pale sleeping body of the king.

    Meanwhile within the deep bronze cauldron, white
With bubbling froth, the rich elixir boils.
Roots from the vales of Thessaly and seeds
And flowers she seethes therein and bitter juices,
With gem-stones from the farthest Orient
And sands that Ocean's ebbing waters wash,
And hoar-frost gathered when the moon shines full,
And wings and flesh of owls and the warm guts
Of wolves that change at will to human form.
To them she adds the slender scaly skins
Of Libyan water-snakes and then the livers
Of long-living gazelles and eggs and heads
Of ancient crows, nine generations old.
With these and a thousand other nameless things
Her more than mortal purpose she prepared.
Then with a seasoned stick of olive wood
She mixed the whole and stirred it. And behold!
The old dry stick that stirred the bubbling brew
Grew green and suddenly burst into leaf,
And all at once was laden with fat olives;
And where the froth flowed over from the pot
And the hot drops spattered the ground beneath,
Fair springtime bloomed again, and everywhere
Flowers of the meadow sprang and pasture sweet.
And seeing this Medea drew her blade
And slit the old king's throat and let the blood
Run out and filled his veins and arteries
With her elixir; and when Aeson drank,

Through wound and lips, at once his hair and beard,
White for long years, regained their raven hue;
His wizened pallor, vanquished, fled away
And firm new flesh his sunken wrinkles filled,
And all his limbs were sleek and proud and strong.
Then Aeson woke and marvelled as he saw
His prime restored of forty years before.
    Bacchus had seen from heaven this miracle,
So marvellous, and, learning that his own
Nurses* could have their youth restored, obtained
That boon and blessing from the Colchian.

MEDEA AND PELIAS: HER FLIGHT

Then, to continue with her witch's tricks,*
Medea, feigning enmity between
Herself and Jason, fled as suppliant
To Pelias, and there, since weight of years
Burdened the king, his daughters welcomed her.
In a brief while the crafty Colchian
Had won them with a false display of friendship.
She told, among her most deserving feats,
How she had banished Aeson's blighting years,
And, as she dwelt on that, led Pelias' daughters
To hope the like skill might rejuvenate
Their father too; and this they begged, and bade
Her name her price, a price unlimited.
She, for a time, was silent and appeared
To hesitate and kept them in suspense
By what seemed weighty thoughts, but in a while,
Giving her promise, 'To increase', she said,
'Your confidence, the leader of your flock,
Your oldest sheep, my drugs shall make a lamb.'
At once a shaggy ram was brought, a ram
Worn out by untold years, with curving horns
Upon his hollow temples. With her knife,
Her knife of Thessaly, Medea slit
His scrawny throat (his scanty blood just smeared
The blade), then in a vat of bronze the witch
Plunged the ram's carcass with her powerful drugs.

They shrank his body, burnt his horns away,
And with his horns his years. Then down inside
The vat was heard a small soft bleating sound;
And in a moment, while they marvelled at
The bleats, out jumped a lamb and skipped away,
Frisking to find a mother's milky teat.
The daughters were amazed: her promises
Had proved their truth. They urged her all the more.
    Three times had Phoebus now unyoked his team
When they had plunged in Ebro's* sunset stream.
It was the fourth night and the shining stars
Were shimmering as that false enchantress placed
A pot of water on a crackling fire,
Plain water then and herbs that had no power.
And now in sleep like death the old king lay
Relaxed and with their king the royal guard,
Sleep given by her magic chants and spells.
The daughters entered at Medea's bidding,
And stood around the bed. 'Why wait?' she said,
'Why stand there idle? Draw your swords and drain
His ancient blood, that I with young fresh blood
May fill his empty veins. His age, his life,
Is in your hands. If love and loyalty
Move you at all, unless hope springs in vain,
Do him this service. By those blades of yours
Expel old age; plunge in your steel, I say,
And let his sorry fluid flow away!'
    So urged, each in her loving loyalty
Vied in disloyalty, and each, in fear
Of guilt, was guilty. Yet not one of them
Could bear to see her blows. They looked away;
The wounds they gave, those savage wounds, were blind.
The old king, streaming blood, yet raised himself
Upon his elbow; butchered as he was,
He tried to rise from bed. Amid those swords,
So many swords, he stretched his pallid arms,
'Daughters, what are you doing? What has armed you',
He cried, 'to kill your father?' Their hearts failed;
Their hands fell. As he spoke again, the witch
Cut short the words and windpipe in his throat

And plunged him, butchered, in the boiling pot.
   Had she not soared away with her winged dragons,
She surely must have paid the price. Aloft,
Over the peak of shady Pelion,
Old Chiron's home, she fled,* and over Othrys
And those fair uplands that Cerambus'* fate
Made famous long ago. (By the nymphs' aid
Wings bore him through the air, and when the earth's
Great mass was whelmed beneath Deucalion's flood,
He escaped unflooded by the sweeping sea.)
She flew past Pitane of Aeolis,
Down on the left, where the long dragon* lay,
A shape of stone; past Ida's* grove where once
Bacchus had hidden, in a deer's disguise,
The steer his son had stolen; past the tomb
Of Paris buried in the shallow sand;
The meadowlands that Maera* terrified
With monstrous barks; Eurypylus' fair town
Where wives of Cos wore horns when Hercules*
Left with his troops; Rhodes, Phoebus' favourite;*
Ialysos where lived the vile Telchines*
Whose evil eyes had blighted everything,
Till Jove, in loathing, sank them all beneath
His brother's waves. And then she passed the walls
Of old Carthaea* where Alcidamas
Would marvel that a gentle dove was given
Birth from his daughter's body. Then she saw
Lake Hyrie and the idyllic vale renowned
When Cycnus* suddenly became a swan.
At that boy's bidding Phyllius had brought
Birds and a savage lion that he'd tamed;
Ordered to tame a bull, he tamed that too,
And, angry that his love was spurned so long,
Refused the boy the bull, that last best gift.
Pouting, he cried 'You'll wish you'd given it!'
And leapt from a high headland. Everyone
Thought he had fallen: he was made a swan
And floated in the air on snowy wings.
But Hyrie, his mother, unaware
That he was saved, in tears dissolved away

And made the lake that keeps her name today.
Nearby is Pleuron, where on fluttering wings
Combe,* the child of Ophius, escaped
Her son's assault. And next Medea saw
Calauria's fields, Latona's isle, that knew
Her king changed with his consort into birds.*
Then on her right Cyllene where Menephron
Like a wild beast would share his mother's bed;
And in the distance she looked back upon
Cephisus* weeping for his grandson made
A bloated seal, and on Eumelus'* home
Who mourned his son, a denizen of the air.

At last, borne on her dragons' wings, she reached
Corinth, Pirene's town, where ancient lore
Relates that mortals, when the world was young,
Emerged from mushrooms* rising after rain.
But when* her witch's poison had consumed
The new wife, and the sea on either side*
Had seen the royal palace all in flames,
Her wicked sword was drenched in her son's blood;
And, winning thus a mother's vile revenge,
She fled from Jason's sword. Her dragon team,
The Sun-god's dragons, carried her away
To Pallas' citadel, which once had seen
Phene, so righteous, and old Periphas
Winging together, and the granddaughter
Of Polypemon floating on new wings.*
There Aegeus welcomed her, in that one act
At fault: to be his guest was not enough;
He joined her in the bond of matrimony.

THESEUS

Theseus had come, whose prowess had brought peace
Throughout the twin-sea'd Isthmus, son whom yet
His father did not know. For that son's death
Medea mixed her poisoned aconite,
Brought with her long ago from Scythia's shores,
Said to be slobbered by the Hound of Hell.
There is a cavern yawning dark and deep,

And there a falling track where Hercules
Dragged struggling, blinking, screwing up his eyes
Against the sunlight and the blinding day,
The hell-hound Cerberus, fast on a chain
Of adamant. His three throats filled the air
With triple barking, barks of frenzied rage,
And spattered the green meadows with white spume.
This, so men think, congealed and, nourished by
The rich rank soil, gained poisonous properties.
And since they grow and thrive on hard bare rocks
The farmfolk call them 'flintworts'—aconites.*
This poison Aegeus, by Medea's guile,
Offered to Theseus as his enemy,
Father to son. As Theseus held the cup
In ignorance, his father recognized
The royal crest on his sword's ivory hilt
And from his lips dashed down that cup of guilt.

     Medea fled, swathed in a magic mist
Her spells had made. But Aegeus, happy in
His son's deliverance, yet horrified
By what small margin wickedness so great
Might have succeeded, fed the altar fires
And filled the shrines with gifts, as garlands wreathed
The bulls and axes struck their brawny necks.
No day, it's said, at Athens ever dawned
A happier festival; elders and common folk
Feasted and, wine inspiring eloquence,
Sang hymns of praise.* 'Great Theseus, mighty prince,
You Marathon admires, since you destroyed
The bull of Crete.* Your work, your gift it is
That safe from that fierce sow the farmers till
The fields of Cromyon.* Through you the land
Of Epidaurus saw the Club-Bearer*
Laid low; Cephisus' river banks
Saw cruel Procrustes* slain, and Ceres' town,
Eleusis, saw the death of Cercyon.*
Sinis, too, died who used his giant strength
For evil ends; he could bend trees and forced
Tall pines down to the ground to spring apart
And tear and strew his victims far and wide.

The road to Megara lies open now
And safe and free since Sciron's* put to rest;
That bandit's bones both land and sea alike
Refused, and long they tossed till time at last
Made them rock-hard, hard rocks that keep his name.
Your years, your glories, should we wish to count—
Your feats surpass your years. For you, our prince,
Our valiant prince, we bring a nation's prayers,
To you we drink, we drain our draughts of wine.'
With cheering crowds and cries of well-wishers
From end to end the royal halls resound;
No place of grief in all the city's found.

MINOS, AEACUS, THE PLAGUE AT AEGINA, THE MYRMIDONS

And yet, since no delight is unalloyed,
And troubles will intrude on happiness,
King Aegeus' pleasure in his son's return
Was not unworried. Minos* threatened war.
Strong as he was in men and strong in ships,*
Yet surest was his anger, to avenge
By righteous arms the murder of his son,*
Androgeos. But first by force he sought
Alliances and in his flying fleet,
His power's base, he roamed the Aegean sea.*
He gained Astypalaea and Anaphe,
The first by force, by promises the other;
He gained low Myconos, Cimolos' fields,
Those chalky fields, and Syros where the thyme
Flowers everywhere, Seriphos' level plain
And Paros' marble isle, that Arne* once
Betrayed. (She grasped the gold her greed had claimed
And changed into a bird, that still loves gold,
A jackdaw, black of foot and black of wing.)
But neither Oliaros nor Didymae,
Nor Gyaros nor Andros, no, nor Tenos,
Nor Peparethos lush with shining olives,
Would help the Cretan fleet. Then, steering west,

King Minos headed for Oenopia,
The kingdom of the house of Aeacus;
Oenopia the ancients called it till
Aeacus himself gave it his mother's name,
Aegina.*
                 Crowds poured out to get a glimpse
Of such a famous man; and greeting him
Were Telamon, Peleus his younger brother,
And Phocus youngest. Aeacus* himself
Came slowly forth in all his weight of years
And asked the purpose of his presence there.
The ruler of a hundred cities sighed,
Reminded of that grief of his, and answered,
'I beg your aid to join my arms and fight
For my son's sake, as love and duty lead.
Peace in the tomb I claim.' 'You ask in vain',
Said Aeacus, 'what my state cannot do.
No land is bound by closer ties than we
To Athens: ours are treaties of such force.'
And he in gloom, 'Your treaties' force will cost
You dear', and sailed away. He judged the threat
Of war more valuable than waging war
And wasting there his martial strength too soon.

   While from Aegina's walls they still could watch
The Cretan fleet, an Attic ship appeared
Under full sail and reached the friendly port
With Cephalus on board and greetings from
His countrymen. Though last seen long ago,
The princes recognized him, grasped his hand,
And led him to their father's court. All eyes
Were on him. Traces of his striking looks
He still retained, and held an olive branch,
His country's tree,* and, as he entered, brought
On either side two men of younger age,
Clytos and Butes, Pallas'* noble sons.

   Then, after gracious words of greeting given,
Cephalus expounded Athens' purposes,
Recalled their treaties and ancestral ties,
And asked their aid, adding that Minos aimed
At sovereignty throughout the lands of Greece.

His eloquence did service to his cause,
And Aeacus, his left hand leaning on
His sceptre's hilt, replied, 'Take, Athens, take
Our help, don't ask it! Never hesitate
To count as yours what might this island holds
And all that these affairs of mine afford.
Strength is not short; my troops suffice and more
For me and for my foes. Thanks to the gods,
The times are fair and find me no excuse.'
'So may it ever be!' said Cephalus,
'And may your city multiply! Just now,
On my way here, my heart rejoiced to see
Young men so handsome, so alike in age,
Coming to meet me. Even so I miss
Many I saw when you last welcomed me
Here in your city.' Aeacus gave a groan
And said in tones of grief, 'A tragedy
Befell us first but better fortune followed.
Would I could speak of that without the other!
I'll tell the tale in order with no long
Digressions to detain you. Bones and ashes
They lie, for whom your memory enquires,
And with them died so much of this my realm!
Upon my people fell a fearsome plague*
Through Juno's unfair rage, who hated us
Because our country took her rival's* name.
While the disease seemed part of nature's plan,
And the disaster's baleful cause lay hid,
We fought with physic's remedies. The ruin
Routed every resource: all faced defeat.
At first the sky weighed down upon the earth,
Black and unbroken, and the clouds shut in
Exhausting heat. Four times the crescent moon
Filled her round orb, four times from her full orb
She shrank and waned, and all that weary while
The hot south wind blew furnace blasts of death.
The vile infection spread, as all agree,
Through springs and pools, and in the untilled fields
Thousands of serpents swarmed and with their poison
Polluted rivers. The power of the disease,

So sudden, was first grasped in deaths of dogs
And birds, sheep, cattle and wild animals.
The ill-starred ploughman is aghast to see
His strong bulls stagger as they work and lie
There in mid-furrow. From the fleecy sheep,
Bleating so sickly, wool falls off unclipped
As bodies waste away. The racehorse, once
High mettled, famous on the dusty course,
Betrays his blood, forgets his victories,
Groans in his stall and waits a weary death.
The boar forgets to rage, the stag to trust
His speed, the bear to fall on battling herds.
Languor and lethargy! In woods, fields, roads
Foul corpses lie, their stench tainting the air,
And—what was wondrous—no grey wolves, no dogs,
No hungry birds would touch them; rotting there,
They decomposed and as they putrefied
Their effluence spread the infection far and wide.
    The doom weighed heavier as the plague attacked
The wretched farmfolk and gained mastery
Within the city's walls. The fever first
Inflamed the intestines: symptoms were short breath
And flushing skin. The tongue was furred and swollen;
The mouth gaped open, parched by the hot wind,
Straining to gulp the suffocating air.
Bedclothes and coverings of any kind
Were unendurable; upon the ground
They placed their bony bodies, but the earth
Gave no relief and gained their fevered heat.
Unchecked and uncontrolled! The savage plague
Broke out among the doctors; their own skill
Disqualified their owners. Why, the more
Closely and faithfully men served the sick,
The rapider their road to doom. As hope
Of safety fades and they foresee the end
Of the disease is death, they indulge their lusts,
Not caring what might help, since nothing helps.
By fountains, wells, brooks, rivers, everywhere
They huddle unashamed; their thirst is quenched
Only with life; so gross and bloated then

That many cannot rise and die right in
The water; others drink it all the same.
Finding their loathsome beds unbearable,
Poor wretches, they jump out or, if too weak
To stand, roll to the floor. Each flees from home,
For every home seems fatal: since the cause
Lies hid, the yards and garrets bear the guilt.
You could have seen them drifting half-alive
Along the streets, while they had strength to stand,
And others weeping, lying on the ground,
Their tired eyes turning in a last appeal,
Their arms stretched starwards to the hanging sky,
Here, there, each breathes his last where caught to die.
   What heart had I? Was it not natural
To loathe my life and long to join my own?
Wherever my gaze turned, the people lay
As rotten apples fall from swaying boughs
Or acorns under oaks that storms have tossed.
You see that temple, soaring high above
Its sweeping flight of steps: Jove's shrine it is.
Who did not offer on the altars there
Incense—in vain? How often while they prayed,
Husband for wife, father for son, they breathed
Their last in that inexorable shrine,
Hands holding still some incense unconsumed!
How often too inside the temple, while
The priest intoned and poured the holy wine
Between the horns, before the knife could strike
The bulls dropped dead. When I made sacrifice
To Jove for my own self, my fatherland
And my three sons, the victim raised its voice,
A voice of doom, and suddenly collapsed
With never a blow, and, when the blood was let,
Its feeble trickle barely stained the blade.
The entrails too, diseased, had lost the signs*
Of truth, the warnings of the gods: the plague
Had penetrated to the inmost parts.
Bodies I saw thrown by the temple doors;
Before the altars, even, to put the gods
To greater shame, some hanged themselves, and fled

By death the fear of death, and called their fate
That came uncalled. Corpses were never given
A proper funeral, too many biers
To jostle through the gates. Either they lay
Unburied or were heaped on high-raised pyres
Unhonoured. Now all reverence was lost;
They fought for pyres, used other people's flames.
No one was left to mourn. Unwept, unwailed,
Ghosts—old men, youths, brides, mothers—drifted round;*
And timber failed for fires, for graves the ground.
    Distraught by such a whirling storm of woes,
I cried "Great Jove, unless it's but a lie
That thou didst hold Aegina in thine arms,
And thou, Almighty Father, art ashamed
To be my parent, give my people back
To me, or send me to the grave myself!"
Thunder and lightning gave the god's assent.
"I accept the signs", I said, "and may they mark
Thy grace. I take the omen as thy pledge."
It chanced that close at hand there stood an oak,
Jove's sacred tree, a special spreading tree,
Sprung from Dodona's seed. Here, hard at work,
My eyes fell on an endless train of ants,
Huge loads in tiny mouths, all following
Their private path across the wrinkled bark.
In wonder at their numbers, "Grant", I said,
"Thou best of sires, so many citizens
To me and stock again my empty walls!"
The tall oak trembled; in the still calm air
The branches swayed and rustled.* Terror-struck
I shuddered, hair on end. And yet I kissed
The ground, the oak. I'd not admit my hopes,
Even so I hoped and wishes warmed my heart.
Night came. Our care-worn frames were lapped in sleep.
Before my eyes the same oak seemed to stand,
With boughs as many, on the boughs as many
Insects, and, trembling as before, it shook
The gleaning column to the field below.
And suddenly the creatures grew and grew,
Larger and larger; rising from the ground,

They stood erect; they shed their many legs,
Their leanness and their blackness and assumed
A human shape. Sleep left me. As I woke,
I scorned my dream and grumbled at the gods
Who gave no help. But from the palace came
A rumbling roar, men's voices, as I thought,
Long unfamiliar. I supposed this too
Was in my dream, when Telamon rushed in,
Threw the door wide, and "Father!" he burst out,
"A sight beyond our hopes, beyond belief!
Come out!" And out I went, and there I saw
And recognized the men, for all the world
Just as I'd dreamt: they greeted me as king.
I paid my vows to Jove, and to my new
Subjects shared out my city and the lands
Left vacant by their former husbandmen.
I call them Myrmidons,* a name to tell
In truth their origin. Their build you saw;
Their traits they keep, a thrifty toiling lot,
Grasping their gains and hoarding what they've got.
These, matched in mind and years, will follow you
To war when the east wind that brought you here
So happily' (that wind had brought them there)
'Changes and homeward from the south blows fair.'
    So with their talk and tales the livelong day
Was occupied; the light's last lingering hours
Were given to feasting and the night to sleep.
The golden sun had spread his shining beams
And still the east wind blew and checked their sails.

CEPHALUS AND PROCRIS

The sons of Pallas now joined Cephalus,
Their elder; with the two he waited on
The king, but sleep, deep sleep, still claimed the king.*
Under the portal Phocus welcomed them,
The youngest son, for Telamon and his brother
Were busy mustering their men for war.
Prince Phocus led them through the inner court
To the fine private rooms and all sat down.

He saw that Cephalus carried in his hand
A javelin of unknown wood with point
Of gold. They talked a while; then Phocus said:
'Hunting and forestry are in my blood,
But I've been wondering what kind of wood
That shaft you hold is made of. If of ash,
It would be brown, or if of cornel-wood,
It surely would be knotted. Whence it comes
I cannot tell, but never have my eyes
Beheld a javelin more beautiful.'
One of the brothers answered: 'Even more
You'll marvel at its flight; it cannot fail
To find its mark; chance never guides its course;
And red with blood it flies back unretrieved.'
So then young Phocus asked him everything,
Who gave so fine a gift and whence and why,
And Cephalus told him, but for shame withheld
The price he paid.* Silent and filled with grief
For his lost wife, he wept and said in tears:

   'This weapon, heaven-born prince (who could believe?)
Makes me shed tears and long will make me, if
Fate grants me long to live; this javelin
Destroyed my darling wife and me; this gift
I wish to heaven had never been bestowed!
   Procris, my wife, if Orithyia's name
May be the more familiar,* was the sister
Of ravished Orithyia, and if the two
Are judged in looks and nature, Procris was
The worthier prize. In marriage she and I
Were joined, and she and I were joined in love.
Men called me happy; happiness was mine.
The gods thought otherwise, or else perhaps
I should be happy still. Within two months
After our marriage, while I spread my nets
To catch the antlered deer, the saffron Dawn,*
Above Hymettus' ever-flowery peak,
Saw me at daybreak as the twilight fled,
And carried me away against my will.
And may the goddess pardon me, if I
Say what is true: her rosy cheeks are fair,

She rules the borderlands of dark and day,
She drinks the nectar's honeydew, but I
Loved Procris, Procris ever in my heart,
And Procris on my lips. I spoke of bonds
Of holy wedlock, of love's fresh delights,
My vows so new and my deserted bride,
Until in rage the goddess cried: "Enough
Of your complaining! Have your Procris! But,
If I can see the future, you will rue
The day you had her", and so sent me back.

    On my way home the goddess' prophecy
Rang in my mind and fear began to form,
Fear that my wife had failed her marriage vows.
Her youth and beauty bade my heart believe
Her guilt; her character forbade belief.
Still, I had been away; yes, I'd just left
A divine example of unfaithfulness,
And lovers' hearts imagine every fear.
Intent on heartbreak I resolved to test
Her loyalty with presents. And the Dawn
Favoured my fears and changed my form and face
(I felt the change) and so I entered Athens
Unrecognizable and made my way
Back home. At home nothing amiss; no trace
Of guilt; only distress for their lost lord.
By countless stratagems I gained at last
A meeting. When I saw my wife again,
My heart was overcome and my resolve
To test her love and honour almost failed;
I hardly stopped myself confessing all,
Stopped myself kissing her as she deserved.

    Her looks were sad in grief and longing for
Her husband snatched away, yet in her sadness
No girl could ever look more beautiful.
Imagine, Prince, how lovely was her grace,
When grief itself so graced her loveliness.
Why should I tell how often her loyalty
Rejected my attempts, how often she said,
"I keep myself for one alone; for him
Where'er he be, alone I keep my love."

Who in his senses would have failed to find
Such proof of loyalty enough? But I,
Unsatisfied, fought on—to wounds and woe.
I offered her a fortune, added more,
For a night's favours, till at last my wife
Wavered—I'd won, ill victory! I cried
"Shame on you! Your seducer is a sham!
I was your husband. My eyes' evidence
Convicts you, traitress, of your perfidy!"
She, not a word; silent and crushed with shame
She fled her wicked husband and that house
Of trickery and, hating for my hurt
The sight of men, among the mountains roved,
Devoted to the arts Diana loved.

Then I, deserted, felt the fire of love
Fiercer and deeper in my heart. I begged
My wife's forgiveness, owned that I had sinned,
That I too might have yielded to such gifts,
Had I been offered gifts so wonderful.
At this confession, when she had avenged
Her wounded honour, she came back to me
And we spent years in bliss and harmony.
She gave me too, as though herself were gift
Of small account, a hound her own Diana
Had given her, saying "He'll outrun them all".
The javelin too she gave me which you see.
You ask the story of the other gift?*
I'll tell a tale to take your breath away.

The riddle* that had baffled earlier brains
Was solved by Oedipus and headlong down
The Sphinx had fallen, her mysteries forgotten.
At once a second plague was launched on Thebes,
A savage beast* that killed and feasted on
The farmfolk and their flocks. We, the young squires,
Ringed the broad pastures with our hunting nets,
But with a bound the beast was over them,
Clearing the tops of our entanglements.
We slipped our dogs; the beast, as they gave chase,
Fled like a bird and mocked our hundred hounds.
With one accord my comrades called to me

For Whirlwind (my fine gift-hound), who for long
Had fought the leash that checked him. He was loosed
And straightway lost to sight; the hot dust held
His footprints; he had vanished; not so swift
A lance's flight or bullets from a sling
Or slender arrows from a Cretan bow.
Some rising ground commanded the wide fields;
I climbed the top and gained a grandstand view
Of that strange chase; one moment the beast's caught,
The next the death-wound's missed him—he's escaped.
His course was cunning, never straight for long;
He doubled back and circled to deceive
The chasing jaws, to foil his foe's assault.
The hound pressed close, clung step for step; it seemed
He'd got him, but he failed and snapped the air.
My javelin must help, I thought, and while
I weighed it in my hand and tried to fit
My fingers in the loop,* I glanced aside,
And when I looked again—amazing sight!—
There in the open plain below I saw
Two marble statues, one of them, you'd swear,
In flight, the other pouncing on its prey.
Some god,* if gods were watching, must have willed
That both should be unbeaten in that chase.'

 He stopped in silent thought. 'Your javelin,
Of what crime was that guilty?' Phocus asked;
And Cephalus told him of his weapon's crime.

 'My happiness, Prince Phocus, was the start
Of all my sorrows; I'll describe it first.
What pleasure to recall that blessed time,
Those early years, when, rightly, I had joy
In my dear wife and she had joy in me.
We shared the bonds of love and love's concern;
Not Jove's embraces would have pleased her more
Than mine, and me no other could have won,
Not Venus' self. The same love fired us both.
I would go hunting when the sun's first beams
Coloured the hilltops,* as a young man will,
Roving the woods alone; I never took
Servants or horses or keen-scented hounds

Or knotted nets to help me; I was safe
To have my javelin. And when my hand
Had had its fill of sport I used to seek
The coolness of the shade and of the breeze,
The zephyr* breathing from the chilly dales.
I sought the gentle zephyr in the heat,
I waited for the zephyr, for its balm,
My labour's rest. "Come, zephyr", I would call,
(How I remember!) "soothe me, welcome guest,
Come to my breast, relieve, as is your way,
The heat with which I burn." And I might add
(So the Fates led me on) more blandishments.
"You comfort and refresh me. For your sake
I love the lonely places and the woods;
Your breath I seek for ever on my lips."
Some fool who overheard my words mistook
The double sense and thought that zephyr called
So often was a nymph, and I in love.
    This hasty tell-tale hurried off to Procris
And told in whispers my supposed offence.
Love will believe too soon. In sudden grief
She swooned, they told me, then, restored at last,
Bemoaned her misery, her cruel fate,
Accused my honour and, imagining
A false offence, feared a mere nothing, feared
An insubstantial name, poor soul, and grieved
As over a true rival paramour.
Yet she had doubts and in her wretchedness
Hoped she was wrong, refusing to accept
The tale or, till her eyes had evidence,
Convict her husband of such villainy.
    Next day the gleam of dawn had banished night
And out into the woods I went and found
Good sport and, lying on the grass, I called
"Come, zephyr, come and soothe my weariness!"
And suddenly, as I spoke, I seemed to hear
A sound of moaning, but I called again
"Come, best and loveliest!" A falling leaf
Made a slight rustle and I thought it was
Some lurking beast and hurled my javelin.

It was my wife! Clutching her wounded breast,
"Ay me! Ay me!" she cried. I knew her voice,
My Procris' voice, and like a madman rushed
Headlong towards the sound. And there, half-dead,
Her clothes blood-spattered, plucking from the wound
The gift (heaven help me!) she had given me,
I found her. Cradled in my arms, I raised
Her body, dearer than my own to me, and tore
Her dress away and bound the cruel wound,
Trying to staunch the blood, and begged her not
To leave me, not condemn me by her death.
Exhausted then and dying, these few words
She forced herself to murmur: "By our vows
Of wedlock, by the gods of home and heaven,
By my deserts, if I have well deserved,
By my death's cause, my own still-living love,
I beg you, I implore you, not to take
Zephyr to be your wife in place of me."
And then at last I learnt of her mistake,
And told her all. But what did telling help?
She slipped away; what little strength was left
Ebbed with her failing blood; and while her eyes
Had power still to gaze, she gazed at me,
And on my lips her life's last breath was spent;
But she looked glad and seemed to die content.'
　　In tears the hero told his tragic tale,
In tears they heard. Then Aeacus arrived
With his two sons and new-raised soldiery,
Whom Cephalus welcomed with their valiant arms.

BOOK VIII

SCYLLA AND MINOS

THE morning star revealed the shining day,
Night fled, the east wind fell, the rain-clouds rose,
A steady south wind speeded the return
Of Cephalus with the Aeginetan force.
Their passage prospered and the fair breeze brought
Them sooner than their hopes to Athens' port.
Minos by now was laying waste the shores
Of Megara, testing his martial strength
Against the city of Alcathous,*
Where Nisus reigned, a venerable king
Upon whose head, crowning his locks of white,
There gleamed a purple tress, the talisman
And magic guarantee of his great realm.

   Six times the crescent of the rising moon
Had climbed the sky and still the fate of war
Hung in the balance, and on doubtful wings
Long hovered victory between each side.
There was a royal turret, built above
The singing walls where once Latona's son,
So the tale goes, laid down his golden lyre
And still its music lingers in the stones.*
Here Nisus' daughter often used to climb
And with a little pebble set the stones
A-singing; that was in the days of peace.
And when war came, she often used to watch
From there the stubborn strife and clash of arms;
And, as the war dragged on, she came to know
The captains' names, their blazons, arms and steeds,
And Cretan quivers. Best of all she knew—
Knew more than well enough—their general,
Europa's son, King Minos. When he wore
His fine plumed casque that hid his face, she thought
Him splendid helmeted; if he put on
His shield of shining bronze, the shining shield
Enhanced his beauty; when with arm drawn back

He hurled his long lithe spear, the girl admired
His strength and skill; and if he drew the string
And set an arrow to his long curved bow,
She swore Apollo, shafts in hand, stood so.
But when, unhelmed, he showed his face and rode
In royal purple on his milk-white steed,
With trappings gay, and reined the foaming bit,
Ah, then she gazed almost beside herself,
Almost out of her mind. Happy, she thought,
The javelin he touched, happy the reins
He gathered in his hands. An impulse came
To make her way, were that allowed, across
The hostile lines, a girl among the foe;
A wild impulse to leap down from the turret
Into the Cretan camp, or open wide
The bronze-barred gates, or any other thing
Minos might wish. And as she sat and watched
The white pavilions of the Island king,
'This tragic war', she thought, 'I cannot tell
Whether it brings my heart more grief or joy;
Grief that Minos, my love, should be my foe;
Yet, save the war, I had not seen his face.
Still, if he held me hostage, he could end
The fighting; I should be his comrade; I
The pledge of peace. If she* who gave you birth,
Most beautiful of kings, were like yourself,
Well she deserved to fire a god with love!
Thrice blest were I, if, winging through the air,
I stood within the camp of Knossos' king,
Confessed my love, and asked what he required
For dowry—so be it not my fatherland.
Perish my hope of marriage, if the price
Were treachery! Yet many in defeat
Find profit through a victor's clemency.
The war he wages for his murdered son
Is just; his cause is strong and strong the arms
That back his cause. Yes, our defeat is sure!
And if that doom awaits our city, why
Should his assault unlock those walls of mine
And not my love? Better that he should win

Now, with no slaughter, no delay, no cost
Of his own blood. Then, Minos, I'd not fear
Some blundering oaf might wound you! Oaf—for who
Could have the heart, well knowing what he did,
To aim his spear, his cruel spear, at you?
My start is sound: I stand on my resolve
To give myself and as my dowry give
My country too, and so will end the war.
But more than will is needed. Sentries guard
Every approach; the gates are locked; the keys
My father keeps. My father! Him alone,
Alas, I fear; alone he thwarts my hopes.
Would God I had no father! Everyone
Is his own god, for sure. Fortune rejects
A faint-heart's prayers. Fired with such love as mine
Another girl would blithely have destroyed,
Oh! long ago, whatever crossed her love.
Why should I be less brave? Through fire and sword
I'd dare to go. Yet here there is no need
Of fire or sword: I need my father's tress,
That purple tress, more precious now to me
Than gold; that tress will bring me blessedness,
Will give me power to win my heart's desire.'
    Then night, the surest nurse of troubled souls,
Advanced and with the dark her courage grew.
It was the quiet hour when slumber first
Enfolds men's hearts, tired by the long day's toil.
Into her father's chamber silently
The daughter crept and stole (oh, deed of doom!)
His life-tress and, her wicked booty won,
Crossed through the Cretan lines (so sure her trust
In her deserts) and reached the startled king,
And told her tale. 'Love led me to this deed.
I am King Nisus' daughter, Princess Scylla.
I offer you myself, my home, my country;
I ask for no reward except yourself.
Take for my love's sure proof this purple tress
And know I give you—not my father's tress—
I give his head!' And in her guilty hand
She offered him the tress. But Minos shrank

In horror from the gift, that monstrous gift,
And answered: 'You disgrace of our fair age!
May the gods purge you from their world! May land
And sea be barred to you! My land of Crete,
The isle that cradled Jove, I swear shall never
Feel the contagion of so foul a fiend!'
  Then Minos , justest of lawgivers, imposed
Terms on his captive enemies and bade
His fleet weigh anchor and the rowers man
The bronze-bound ships. And Scylla, when she saw
The vessels launched and knew the king refused
Her crime's reward, her prayers exhausted, turned
To storming fury and with streaming hair
And hands outstretched in passionate rage she cried:*
'Whither away so fast, leaving behind
Her who achieved so much, deserves so well,
You who were more to me than father, more
Than fatherland? Whither away, so cruel,
Whose triumph is my crime and my deserts?
The gift I gave, my love for you, my hopes
Built all on you alone, do they not move you?
Where can I turn abandoned? Turn again
Home to my fatherland? It lies in ruins.
Suppose it stands, its gates are closed to me
By my betrayal. Back to my father's arms?
He was my gift to you! My countrymen
Hate me and have good cause. The neighbouring cities
Fear my example. I from all the world
Am banished: Crete alone is open now.
If you forbid me Crete, ungrateful wretch,
And leave me here, you're not Europa's son.
Your mother was the Syrtes'* desolate sands,
A tigress of Armenia, or Charybdis,*
Lashed by the wild south wind. Jove's not your father,
Coaxing his darling in a bull's disguise.
That fable's false. It was a real bull
Begot you. Nisus, father, punish me!
Take your revenge! Ye towers and battlements
That I betrayed rejoice in my distress!
Yes, I have earned your joy! And I deserve

To die. But let my death come at the hand
Of one my wrong has injured. Why should you
Impeach my crime, who triumphed by my crime?
My sin against my father and my country
Take as my service done! Fit mate were you
Of that adulteress* who in a cow
Of wood beguiled a savage bull and bore
A monster in her womb! Do my words reach
Your ears or do the winds blow them to waste?
Those winds, ungrateful wretch, that fill your sails!
No wonder your Pasiphae preferred
Her bull to you: you were the fiercer beast.
Oh, my heart breaks! He bids them haste away;
Oars strike the sounding waves; the shore recedes
And I too on the shore. All to no end!
In vain have you forgotten my deserts;
Against your will I'll follow.* I shall clutch
Your curving poop and you shall carry me
Across the seas' long swell.' And, as she spoke,
She leapt into the waves (her passion gave
Her strength) and swam after the ship and clung—
Vile shipmate—to the Cretan galleon.
　　Her father saw her as he hovered near
(Changed to an osprey now with tawny wings)
And swooped to seize and tear her, as she clung,
With his hooked beak. She loosed her hold in terror,
And, as she fell, the light breeze seemed to bear
Her safe above the sea. It was her wings:
Changed to a feathered bird she rode the air—
A Shearer, named from that shorn* tress of hair.

THE MINOTAUR

Minos reached harbour in the isle of Crete
And, disembarking, paid his vows to Jove,
A hundred bulls, and hung the spoils of war
To adorn his palace walls. His dynasty's
Disgrace had grown; the monstrous hybrid beast
Declared the queen's obscene adultery.
To rid his precincts of this shame the king

Planned to confine him shut away within
Blind walls of intricate complexity.
The structure was designed by Daedalus,
That famous architect. Appearances
Were all confused; he led the eye astray
By a mazy multitude of winding ways,
Just as Maeander plays among the meads
Of Phrygia and in its puzzling flow
Glides back and forth and meets itself and sees
Its waters on their way and winds along,
Facing sometimes its source, sometimes the sea.
So Daedalus in countless corridors
Built bafflement, and hardly could himself
Make his way out, so puzzling was the maze.

    Within this labyrinth Minos shut fast
The beast, half bull, half man, and fed him twice
On Attic blood, lot-chosen each nine years,
Until the third choice mastered him.* The door,
So difficult, which none of those before
Could find again, by Ariadne's aid
Was found, the thread that traced the way rewound.
Then Theseus, seizing Minos' daughter, spread
His sails for Naxos, where, upon the shore,
That cruel prince abandoned her and she,
Abandoned, in her grief and anger found
Comfort in Bacchus' arms. He took her crown
And set it in the heavens to win her there
A star's eternal glory; and the crown
Flew through the soft light air and, as it flew,
Its gems were turned to gleaming fires, and still
Shaped as a crown their place in heaven they take
Between the Kneeler* and him who grasps the Snake.

DAEDALUS AND ICARUS

Hating the isle of Crete and the long years
Of exile,* Daedalus was pining for
His native land, but seas on every side
Imprisoned him. 'Though land and sea', he thought,
'The king may bar to me, at least the sky

Is open; through the sky I'll set my course.
Minos may own all else; he does not own
The air.' So then to unimagined arts
He set his mind and altered nature's laws.
    Row upon row of feathers he arranged,
The smallest first, then larger ones, to form
A growing graded shape, as rustic pipes
Rise in a gradual slope of lengthening reeds;
Then bound the middle and the base with wax
And flaxen threads, and bent them, so arranged,
Into a gentle curve to imitate
Wings of a real bird. His boy stood by,
Young Icarus, who, blithely unaware
He plays with his own peril, tries to catch
Feathers that float upon the wandering breeze,
Or softens with his thumb the yellow wax,
And by his laughing mischief interrupts
His father's wondrous work. Then, when the last
Sure touch was given, the craftsman poised himself
On his twin wings and hovered in the air.
    Next he prepared his son. 'Take care', he said,
'To fly a middle course, lest if you sink
Too low the waves may weight your feathers; if
Too high, the heat may burn them. Fly half-way
Between the two. And do not watch the stars,
The Great Bear or the Wagoner or Orion,
With his drawn sword, to steer by. Set your course
Where I shall lead.' He fixed the strange new wings
On his son's shoulders and instructed him
How he should fly; and, as he worked and warned,
The old man's cheeks were wet, the father's hands
Trembled. He kissed his son (the last kisses
He'd ever give) and rising on his wings
He flew ahead, anxious for his son's sake,
Just like a bird that from its lofty nest
Launches a tender fledgeling in the air.
Calling his son to follow, schooling him
In that fatal apprenticeship, he flapped
His wings and watched the boy flapping behind.
    An angler fishing with his quivering rod,

A lonely shepherd propped upon his crook,
A ploughman leaning on his plough, looked up
And gazed in awe, and thought they must be gods
That they could fly. Delos and Paros lay
Behind them now; Samos, great Juno's isle,
Was on the left, Lebinthos on the right
And honey-rich Calymne, when the boy
Began to enjoy his thrilling flight and left
His guide to roam the ranges of the heavens,
And soared too high. The scorching sun so close
Softened the fragrant wax that bound his wings;
The wax melted; his waving arms were bare;
Unfledged, they had no purchase on the air!
And calling to his father as he fell,
The boy was swallowed in the blue sea's swell,
The blue sea* that for ever bears his name.
His wretched father, now no father, cried
'Oh, Icarus, where are you? Icarus,
Where shall I look, where find you?' On the waves
He saw the feathers. Then he cursed his skill,
And buried his boy's body in a grave,
And still that island* keeps the name he gave.

PERDIX

Now while he laid his poor dear son to rest
A chattering partridge in a muddy ditch
Watched him and clapped its wings and crowed for joy—
A bird unique and never seen before,
A new creation and a long reproach
To Daedalus. His sister, never guessing
The fate in store, had given her boy to him
For training, twelve years old and quick to learn.
This lad observed the backbone of a fish
And copied it; he cut a row of teeth
In a slim blade of iron and a saw
Was his invention. He too was the first
To fasten with a joint two metal arms
So that, keeping a constant space apart,
While one stood still the other traced a circle.

In jealous rage his master hurled him down
Headlong from Pallas' sacred citadel,*
Feigning a fall; but Pallas, who sustains
Talent, upheld him, changed him to a bird
And clothed the lad with feathers as he fell.
Even so his talent's darting quickness passed
To wings and feet; he kept his former name.*
But this bird never lifts itself aloft,
Nor builds its nest on boughs or high tree-tops,
But flits along the ground and lays its eggs
In hedgerows, dreading heights for they recall
The memory of that old fearful fall.

MELEAGER AND THE CALYDONIAN BOAR

Now Etna's land gave weary Daedalus
Welcome, and Cocalus* who took up arms
On his behalf was kindly. Athens now
Had ceased—all praise to Theseus—to expend
Her tearful tribute. Shrines were garlanded,
And Pallas, Jove and all the gods were hymned
With offerings in their honour, victims' blood
And heaps of incense. Flying fame had spread
The name of Theseus through the towns of Greece,
And in their perils rich Achaea's realms
Implored his aid.* His aid even Calydon,
Who owned her Meleager, in distress
Begged and besought—the cause of her distress
A boar, Diana's boar, her instrument
Of enmity and vengeance. For the king,
Oeneus,* it's said, when plenty blessed the year,
To Ceres gave the first-fruits of the corn,
To Bacchus poured his wine, to golden-haired
Pallas her oil from her own holy tree.
The prized oblations, given first to gods
Of farm and field, reached all the gods of heaven.
Only Diana's altars* (so men say)
Were left uncensed, unserviced and ignored.
The gods feel anger too. 'This shall not pass
Unpunished. No!' she cried, 'I may be seen

Unhonoured, true, but never unavenged!'
The smarting goddess sent a giant boar,
Huge as the bulls that grassy Epirus breeds,
Dwarfing the bulls of fertile Sicily;
His eyes ablaze with fire and blood; his neck
Solid and steep; his bristles long and sharp,
Rigid as spearshafts; his broad sweeping flanks
Flecked, as he hissed and snorted, with hot foam.
His tusks were huge as Indian elephants';
His mouth flashed lightning and his burning breath
Seared the green leaves. Now the young growing corn
He trampled in the blade, and now cut short
The harvest in the ear, and laid to ruin
The farmers' ripened hopes. In vain the threshers,
In vain the barns await the promised crop.
Down fall the heavy grapes, the trailing vine,
Down fall the olive's berries, down the boughs.
Flocks too he savages, beyond the help
Of dogs or shepherds, nor can bulls, fierce bulls,
Defend their herds. The people fled; they felt
No safety save within a city's walls
Till Meleager and his heroes came,
A chosen band,* all fired by hopes of fame.
    There were the twins,* the sons of Tyndareus,
One famed for boxing, one for horsemanship;
Jason who fashioned the first ship; Theseus
Came with Pirithous, blest pair of friends,
And Thestius' two sons,* and swift Idas,
Idas with Lynceus, sons of Aphareus;
Caeneus, no woman then,* and fierce Leucippus;
Acastus famous for his javelin;
Hippothous and Dryas; Phoenix too,
Amyntor's son; Phyleus whom Elis sent,
And Actor's pair.* There too was Telamon
And great Achilles' father;* Pheres' son;*
Boeotian Iolaus, and Echion
That peerless sprinter, with Eurytion
Untiring; Panopeus, Lelex of Locri,
Fierce Hippasus and Hyleus; Nestor too,
Still in his prime;* and those Hippocoon

Had sent* from old Amyclae; and Ancaeus
From Arcady; and Laertes, and the son
Of Ampycus* so wise, and Amphiaraus
As yet unruined* by his wicked wife;
And with them from Arcadia's highland race
A Tegean girl,* the green glades' pride and grace.

    A plain brooch pinned the collar of her dress,
Her hair was simple, gathered in a knot;
From her left shoulder a quiver of ivory
Hung rattling* and her left hand held a bow.
So she was dressed; her features in a boy
You'd think a girl's and in a girl a boy's.
When Meleager saw her, in a flash
His heart leapt high (while Heaven opposed) and deep
He drank love's flame. Happy indeed, he thought,
The man whom *she* deems worthy of her hand!
But time and modesty allowed no more;
The high task pressed, the challenge of the boar.

    Dense woodland through long ages never felled
Rose from a valley with a wide prospect
Of sloping pasture. Reaching this wild wood
The heroes spread their nets, unleashed their hounds,
And followed the fresh footprints, each intent
To find his danger. There was a deep gully
When rain-fed freshets often used to fall,
Its swampy bottom full of supple willows,
Soft sedges, marshy flags and osiers,
With rushes rising high above small reeds.
Here they put up their quarry. Out he rushed
Straight at his enemies, like lightning struck
When clouds collide. His headlong charge broke down
The forest; sounds of crashing echoed through
The shattered wood. The huntsmen gave a shout,
Brave hands held spears thrust forward, their broad points
Glinting. On rushed the boar, scattering the hounds
That faced his fury, striking, as they bayed,
Swift slanting strokes and tossing them aside.

    The first spear thrown, hurled by Echion's hand,
Missed him and lightly grazed a maple trunk.
The next, aimed at his back by Jason, must

Have lodged there had his throw not been too strong.
It overshot. Then 'Phoebus!' Mopsus cried,
'If I have been and am thy worshipper,
Grant that my spear fail not to find its mark!'
His prayer, so far as Phoebus had the power,
Was granted. The spear struck—but made no wound.
There in mid flight Diana stole the steel,*
The wooden shaft arrived without its point.
Now the boar's anger flashed like lightning; flames
Blazed from his eyes; flames issued from his throat;
And as a ball flies from a catapult
Aiming at walls and towers packed with troops,
So, devastating, irresistible,
The beast charged those young men. Eupalamon
And Pelagon who guarded the right flank
He laid prostrate; and as they lay their friends
Dragged them away. But yet Enaesimus,
Son of Hippocoon, could not escape
The fatal blow; the sinews of his knees
Were severed and his leg-muscles collapsed.
And Nestor might perhaps have perished too
Before the time of Troy, had he not leapt,
Vaulting on his long spear, into a tree
That stood at hand, and there in safety gazed
Down on the enemy that he'd escaped.
Whetting his tusks on the oak's trunk, the brute
Raged high for havoc. Sure of his new-honed
Weapons, his curving snout ripped through the thigh
Of mighty Hippasus. But now the twins,
Not stars of heaven as yet,* came cantering up,
Both brothers striking, both on snow-white steeds;
And both poised quivering spears with flashing points;
They would have wounded him had not the boar,
The bristly brute, reached the dense woodland trees
Where neither spear nor horse could penetrate.
Telamon followed, careless, all too keen,
And tripping on a forest root, fell flat.
As Peleus picked him up, the Tegean girl
Set a swift arrow to her string and shot
From her bent bow. Just grazing the beast's back

The shaft lodged fast below his ear, and blood,
A bloody trickle, dyed his bristles red.
Yet she was not more glad of her success
Than Meleager. He, it's thought, was first
To see the blood and first to point it out
To his companions, shouting 'Bravely done!
All praise for manly prowess!' The men flushed;
All urged each other on, their courage raised
With shouts and cries, and hurled their spears unplanned,
A self-defeating stream that blocked its blows.
But look! the Arcadian with his double axe,
Raging for doom beyond his destiny,
Cried 'Learn how far the weapons of a man
Surpass a girl's and leave this task to me!
Even though Diana shields him from the blow,
Despite Diana, mine shall lay him low!'
Such was Ancaeus' braggart brazen boast,
And raising in both hands his double axe
He balanced on his feet and stood tiptoe.
Brave and bold! but the beast struck first and plunged
Both tusks high in his groin, the shortest road
To death, and down he fell and, disembowelled,
His guts gushed out and soaked the ground with gore.
Pirithous, Ixion's son, strode out
To meet the foe, but Theseus cried 'Hold back!
Twin soul of mine, life dearer than my own!
Brave men may keep their distance. His rash heart
Destroyed Ancaeus.' As he spoke, he hurled
His heavy cornel spear with point of bronze,
Well aimed and bound to reach its mark, had not
A leafy branch of chestnut blocked its flight.
And Jason threw his javelin, but luck
Waylaid it and it doomed an innocent hound,
Pierced through the flank and pinned fast to the ground.
    Now it was miss and hit for Meleager.
Two spears he sped; the first stood in the earth,
The second fair and square in the boar's back.
He roared, he raged, he twisted round and round,
Slavering blood afresh and hissing foam,
And in a trice the wielder of the wound

Was on his foe and, baiting him to fight,
Deep through his shoulder sank his shining blade.
All shout their joy with cheers of victory
And crowd to clasp the victor's hand and gaze
In awe and wonder at the monstrous brute
That lies there at such length, still half-afraid
To touch him, but each hero bloods his blade.
   Then Meleager, one foot placed upon
That head of doom and death, said 'Take the prize
That's mine to give, fair girl of Arcady,
And share the glory of the day with me!'
And there and then gave her the spoils, the skin
Barbed with stiff bristles and the head, that head
So striking with its two enormous tusks.
The gift delighted her, the giver too.
The rest were jealous and among them all
A murmur rose, and Thestius' two sons
Shouted with angry gestures, 'Put them down,
Woman, and don't usurp the right that's ours;
Don't be deluded by your lovely looks—
In case your doting donor lets you down!'
They took the gift from her, the right to give
From him. The son of Mars,* outraged beyond
Endurance, bursting in anger, shouted 'Learn,
You robbers of another's rights, how deeds
Differ from threats!' and, as Plexippus stood
Suspecting nothing, plunged his wicked sword
Deep in his heart; and Toxeus too, in doubt,
Eager for vengeance but afraid to share
His brother's fate, soon found his doubt dispelled,
As Meleager, while his blade was warm
With that first murder, made it warm once more
With double murder and a brother's gore.

ALTHAEA AND MELEAGER

Now in the shrine Althaea was offering
Thanksgiving for the victory of her son,
When she beheld her brothers brought in dead.

She beat her breast and filled the town with cries
Of grief and changed her golden gown for black.
But when she heard whose hand had dealt them death,
Away with tears, all sorrow fell away;
Her heart's desire was vengeance from that day.

   There was a log which, when Althaea lay
In childbirth with her son, the Sisters* three
Placed in her blazing hearth and as they spun,
With thumbs firm-pressed, the thread of fate, they said
'To you, babe newly born, and to this log
We give the same life-span.' This prophecy
Pronounced, the Sisters vanished, and at once
The mother snatched the burning brand away
And quenched the flame. The brand, for years concealed
In deepest secrecy, had been kept safe
And kept the lad's life safe. And now at last
She brought it out and called for kindling wood
And fired the kindling with a flame of hate.
Four times she steeled herself to throw the brand
Into the flames; four times she stayed her hand.
Mother and sister fought, two claims of kin
Dividing her one heart. Often her cheeks
Paled at the fearful prospect of her crime;
Often her eyes blazed as her anger flared.
At times her face cried out for cruelty;
At times a look of pity seemed to appear.
And when her heart's wild heat had dried her tears,
Yet tears were found again; and as a ship
That drives before the breeze against the tide
Will feel twin forces and obey them both,
So with both feelings, swaying back and forth,
In turn Althaea lulled and roused her wrath.

   She began a better sister than a mother,
Determined to appease with blood the shades
Whose blood was hers, for love's sake crushing love.
Yes, as the baleful fire gained strength, she cried
'Let that pyre burn flesh of my flesh' and stood
Before the funeral altar with the brand,
The fateful brand, held in her murderous hand,
And cried, poor ill-starred soul, 'Ye Furies three,

Ye goddesses of vengeance, see and mark
My rite of doom. My vengeance is my guilt:*
Death must be paid with death, crime piled on crime,
Bloodshed on bloodshed. Sorrow mountain-high
Must overwhelm this house of wickedness.
Is happy Oeneus to enjoy his son's
Triumph, while Thestius is twice bereft?
Better that both should mourn!* Only be sure,
Shades of my brothers, ghosts new-made, to mark
My service and accept my sacrifice
Made at such cost, my womb's most bitter birth.——
Ay me! Where am I swept so fast? Forgive,
Brothers, a mother's heart—my hands refuse!
Death, true, he well deserves, but I to be
His death's designer—that I cannot bear!——
So shall he go unscathed? And shall he live
In triumph, swollen with success, and rule
In royal Calydon, while you lie dead,
A little meagre ash, cold shivering ghosts?
I'll not endure it! No! that criminal
Shall perish and drag down his father's hopes,
His kingdom and his fatherland in ruins.——
Where is my mother's heart, the love, the claims
Of parenthood, the pangs that nine long months
I bore? Would God the flame had burnt you then,
When you were born, and I'd allowed it! My
Gift was your life—now you shall die by your
Desert. Receive your deed's reward. Give back
The life I gave you twice, first at your birth,
Next when I seized the brand; or count me too
A corpse beside my brothers' sepulchres.
I would, I want—and can't. What shall I do?
Before my eyes I see my brothers' wounds,
The picture of that slaughter—yet, again,
A mother's loyal love rends my resolve.
Oh my heart breaks! Your triumph is tragedy,
Yet take your triumph, brothers! Only let
Me follow you and him whom I give you,
Your solace and my own!' With trembling hand
And eyes averted, full into the flames

She threw the fatal brand. The log itself
Groaned, or it seemed to groan, as there it lay
Licked by the unwilling flames and burned away.
    Unknowing, absent, Meleager burned,
Burned with those flames and felt a hidden fire
Scorching his vitals and courageously
Suppressed his agony. Even so he grieved
To fall with no blood shed, no action fought,
And thought Ancaeus lucky with his wounds.
Groaning in pain, he called with his last breath
His wife, his brothers, his devoted sisters,
His aged father—perhaps his mother too.
The fire, the pains increase, then sink again;
Both die away together; gradually
In the light air his spirit slips away
As over the embers spreads a veil of grey.
    Low lies high Calydon. Young men and old,
Nobles and commons mourned and made lament;
Beside Euenus* mothers tore their hair
And beat their breasts. And Meleager's father,
On the ground prostrate, dirtied in the dust
His old white hair, his aged face, and cursed
His life too long. For haunted by her deed,
Her dreadful deed, his mother had atoned
By her own hand—a dagger in her heart.
    Not if a god* gave me a hundred mouths,
A hundred tongues, commanding genius
And all high Helicon, could I rehearse
His sorrowing sisters' threnodies of woe.
All decency forgotten, black and blue
They beat their breasts, and, while his corpse remained,
That corpse they fondled, fondled hour by hour;
They kissed their brother, kissed their brother's bier;
Then ashes—and his ashes in their urn
They held tight to their hearts, and threw themselves
Down on his tomb and clasped his name engraved;
And on that name poured forth their flooding tears.
At last Diana, sated with the ruin
Of Oeneus' house, raised up the sisters (all
Save Gorge and the wife of Hercules),*

Clothed them in plumage and along their arms
Spread wings and in their faces, once so fair,
Set beaks and launched them, changed, into the air.*

ACHELOUS AND THE NYMPHS

Theseus meanwhile, who had shared his comrades' toil,
Was on his way to Pallas' citadel,
Erechtheus' kingdom, but his road was cut
And progress halted by the swollen stream
Of Achelous. 'Enter my abode,
Illustrious prince of Athens', said the river;
'Risk not my ravening torrent. It transports
So often massive trees and sweeps away
Huge boulders headlong with a mighty roar.
Tall stables standing by the banks I've seen
Borne down, their cattle with them. In that flood
No strength could save the ox, no speed the horse.
And when the mountains free their snows, this spate
Drowns many a strong man in its swirling waves.
Rest will be safer, till the stream resumes
Its usual bounds, till its own bed contains
A slender flow.' And Aegeus' son agreed;
'Your counsel', he replied, 'and your kind home,
Both I'll accept', and he accepted both.
    Of porous pumice and rough tufa-rock
The residence* was built. The floor was damp
And soft with moss, the ceiling diapered
With shells of conch and murex laid in turn.
And now the sun had measured two long thirds
Of daylight. Theseus with his company
Reclined on couches, here Ixion's son,*
There Lelex, Troezen's hero, greying hair
Already on his temples; others too
Whom the Acarnanian* river-god had deemed
Deserving of like honour, overjoyed
Himself to entertain so great a guest.
Soon barefoot river-nymphs arranged the tables
And spread the banquet-board, and when the feast
Was cleared they set a jewelled bowl of wine.

Then glorious Theseus, gazing out to sea,
Pointed and asked 'What place is that? And tell me
What is that island's name, although it seems
Not one but more?' The river answered 'No,
What you observe is not one island. Five
Lie there, but distance blurs their difference.
What great Diana did when she was scorned,
Need not surprise you. These five islands once
Were nymphs. Ten bullocks they had sacrificed
And called the rustic gods to share the rite
With festal dance, but me they all forgot.
I swelled in anger, high as when my flood
Flows at its highest, merciless alike
In rage and waters. Fields I tore from fields,
Forests from forests, and the nymphs, at last
Mindful of me, with the ground beneath their feet
I rolled right out to sea. The ocean's surge
And mine broke up that spit of land to form
The five Echinades* whose number now
You mark amid the waves. But, as you see,
There lies one island in the distance, look,
There in the distance, one that's dear to me,
Named Perimele by the mariners.
She was my loved one and to me she lost
Her maidenhead. Hippodamas, her father,
In outrage hurled his daughter to her doom
From a high cliff. I caught her; as she swam
I held her up and prayed, "O thou whose lot
Won the world's second share, the wandering waves,
God of the Trident, thou to whom at last
All we pure holy rivers make our way,
Neptune, be present now and hear my prayer.
Her whom I hold, I wronged. Hippodamas,
If he were fair, if he were fatherlike,
If he were less unloving, less a brute,
He ought to pity her and pardon me.
Since from the land her father's savagery
Has sundered her, grant her to have a place,
Or be herself a place, that I'll embrace!"
The ruler of the ocean gave assent

And every wave was shaken by his nod.
The nymph was terrified, but still she swam,
And as she swam I touched her trembling breasts,
Quivering in fear and, as I fondled her,
Her body all grew hard beneath my hand
And she lay buried by the rising land.'
   The river finished and fell silent. All
Were moved and marvelled at the miracle.
Ixion's son, a daredevil who scorned
The gods,* laughed at their gullibility.
'Fables!' he said, 'You make the gods too great,
Good Achelous, if they chop and change
The shapes of things.'* All were aghast; such talk
They all condemned, Lelex especially,
Mature in years and mind, and he spoke up.

PHILEMON AND BAUCIS

'The power of heaven is great and has no bounds;
Whatever the gods determine is fulfilled.
I give you proof. Among the Phrygian hills
An oak tree and a lime grow side by side,
Girt by a little wall. I saw the place
With my own eyes when Pittheus ordered me
To Pelops' land where once his father reigned.*
Not far from these two trees there is a marsh,
Once habitable land, but water now,
The busy home of divers, duck and coot.
Here once came Jupiter, in mortal guise,*
And with his father herald Mercury,
His wings now laid aside. A thousand homes
They came to seeking rest; a thousand homes
Were barred against them; yet one welcomed them,
Tiny indeed, and thatched with reeds and straw;
But in that cottage Baucis, old and good,
And old Philemon (he as old as she)
Had joined their lives in youth, grown old together,
And eased their poverty by bearing it
Contentedly and thinking it no shame.
It was vain to seek master and servant there;

They two were all the household, to obey
And to command. So when the heavenly ones
Reached their small home and, stooping, entered in
At the low door, the old man placed a bench
And bade them sit and rest their weary limbs,
And Baucis spread on it a simple rug
In busy haste, and from the hearth removed
The ash still warm, and fanned yesterday's embers
And fed them leaves and bark, and coaxed a flame
With her old breath; then from the rafters took
Split billets and dry twigs and broke them small,
And on them placed a little copper pan;
Then trimmed a cabbage which her spouse had brought
In from the stream-fed garden. He reached down
With a forked stick from the black beam a chine
Of smoke-cured pork,* and from the long-kept meat
Cut a small piece and put it in to boil.
    Meanwhile their talk beguiles the passing hour
And time glides unperceived. A beechwood bowl
Hung by its curving handle from a peg;
They fill it with warm water and their guests
Bathe in the welcome balm their weary feet.
They place a mattress of soft river-sedge
Upon a couch (its frame and feet were willow)
And spread on it their drapes, only brought out
On holy days, yet old and cheap they were,
Fit for a willow couch. The Gods reclined.
Then the old woman, aproned, shakily,
Arranged the table, but one leg was short;
A crock adjusted it, and when the slope
Was levelled up she wiped it with green mint.
Then olives, black and green, she brings, the fruit
Of true Minerva, autumn cherry plums
Bottled in wine lees, endive, radishes,
And creamy cheese and eggs turned carefully
In the cooling ash; all served in earthenware.
Next a wine-bowl, from the same "silver" chased,
Is set and beechwood cups, coated inside
With yellow wax. No long delay; the hearth
Sends forth the steaming feast and wine again

Is brought of no great age, then moved aside,
Giving a space to bring the second course.
Here are their nuts and figs, here wrinkled dates,
And plums and fragrant apples in broad trugs,
And sweet grapes gathered from the purple vines,
And in the midst a fine pale honeycomb;
And—over all—a zeal, not poor nor slow,
And faces that with smiling goodness glow.
    Meanwhile they saw, when the wine-bowl was drained,
Each time it filled itself, and wine welled up
All of its own accord within the bowl.
In fear and wonder Baucis and Philemon,
With hands upturned, joined in a timid prayer
And pardon sought for the crude graceless meal.
There was one goose, the trusty guardian
Of their minute domain and they, the hosts,
Would sacrifice him for the Gods, their guests.
But he, swift-winged, wore out their slow old bones
And long escaped them, till at last he seemed
To flee for sanctuary to the Gods themselves.
The deities forbade. "We two are gods",
They said; "This wicked neighbourhood shall pay
Just punishment; but to you there shall be given
Exemption from this evil. Leave your home,
Accompany our steps and climb with us
The mountain slopes." The two old folk obey
And slowly struggle up the long ascent,
Propped on their sticks. A bowshot from the top
They turn their eyes and see the land below
All flooded marshes now except their house;
And while they wonder and in tears bewail
Their lost possessions, that old cottage home,
Small even for two owners, is transformed
Into a temple; columns stand beneath
The rafters, and the thatch, turned yellow, gleams
A roof of gold; and fine doors richly carved
They see, and the bare earth with marble paved.
    Then Saturn's son in gentle tones addressed them:
"Tell us, you good old man, and you, good dame,
His worthy consort, what you most desire."

Philemon briefly spoke with Baucis, then
Declared their joint decision to the Gods:
"We ask to be your priests and guard your shrine;
And, since in concord we have spent our years,
Grant that the selfsame hour may take us both,
That I my consort's tomb may never see
Nor may it fall to her to bury me."
Their prayer was granted. Guardians of the shrine
They were while life was left, until one day,
Undone by years and age, standing before
The sacred steps and talking of old times,
Philemon saw old Baucis sprouting leaves
And green with leaves she saw Philemon too,
And as the foliage o'er their faces formed
They said, while still they might, in mutual words
"Goodbye, dear love"* together, and together
The hiding bark covered their lips. Today
The peasants in those parts point out with pride
Two trees from one twin trunk grown side by side.

    This tale I heard from staid old men who had
No reason to deceive. I saw myself
Wreaths on the boughs and hung a fresh one there,
And said: "They now are gods, who served the Gods;
To them who worship gave is worship given." '*

    He said no more. The tale—the teller too—
Had moved them all, Theseus especially.*
More marvels of the gods he wished to hear,
And thereupon the Calydonian river,
Propped on his elbow, turned to him and said:

ERYSICHTHON AND HIS DAUGHTER

'Some, my brave Theseus, have been changed the once
And keep their changeling shape; some have the gift
To change and change again in many forms,
Like Proteus,* creature of the encircling seas,
Who sometimes seemed a lad, sometimes a lion,
Sometimes a snake men feared to touch, sometimes
A charging boar, or else a sharp-horned bull;
Often he was a stone, often a tree,

Or feigning flowing water seemed a river
Or water's opposite a flame of fire.
   That gift of changing Erysichthon's daughter*
Also possessed. Her father was a man
Who spurned the gods and never censed their shrines.
His axe once violated Ceres' grove,
His blade profaned her ancient holy trees.
Among them stood a giant oak, matured
In centuries of growing strength, itself
A grove; around it wreaths and garlands hung
And votive tablets, proofs of prayers fulfilled.
Often beneath its shade the Dryads danced
In festival and often hand in hand
Their line circled its trunk, full fifty feet
Of giant girth; it towered as high above
The woodland trees as they above the grass.
Yet even so that wicked man refused
To spare his blade, and bade his woodmen fell
That sacred oak, and when he saw them slow
To obey he seized the axe himself, and cried
"Be this the tree the goddess loves, be this
The goddess' very self, its leafy crown
Shall touch the ground today", and poised his axe
To strike a slanting cut. The holy tree
Shuddered and groaned, and every leaf and acorn
Grew pale and pallor spread on each long branch.
And when his impious stroke wounded the trunk,
Blood issued, flowing from the severed bark,
As when a mighty bull is sacrificed
Before the altar and from his riven neck
The lifeblood pours. All stood aghast, but one
Was bold to thwart the crime, to stay the steel.
Then Erysichthon glared at him: "Take this
For pious thoughts" he cried and turned the axe
Against the man and struck the man's head off,
And, blow on blow, attacked the oak again.
Then deep from the tree's heart there came a voice:
"I, Ceres' nymph, Ceres' most favourite nymph,
Dwell in this oak, and, dying, prophesy
That punishment is nigh for what you do,

To comfort me in death." But he pursued
His crime, till weakened by so many blows,
Hauled down by ropes, at last the giant oak
Crashed and its weight laid low the trees around.
    Heartbroken by their loss—the grove's loss too—
Her sister Dryads, clad in mourning black,
Going to Ceres, prayed for punishment
On Erysichthon. That most lovely goddess
Assented and the teeming countryside,
Laden with harvest, trembled at her nod.
A punishment she planned most piteous,
Were pity not made forfeit by his deed—
Hunger to rack and rend him; and because
Ceres and Hunger—so the Fates decree—
May never meet,* she charged a mountain sprite,
A rustic oread, to take her message.
"There is a place", she said, " a freezing place,
At Scythia's farthest bounds, a land of gloom,
Sad barren soil with never crop nor tree;
This is the numb wan home of Cold and Ague
And starving Hunger; go, bid Hunger sink
Deep in the belly of that impious wretch,
And let no plenty ever vanquish her,
Nor strength of mine prevail against her dearth,
And lest the distance daunt you, take my chariot
And dragons here to drive across the sky."
She gave the chariot; riding through the air
The oread reached Scythia; on a peak
Of granite men call Caucasus she unyoked
The dragons and set out in search of Hunger,*
And found her in a stubborn stony field,
Grubbing with nails and teeth the scanty weeds.
Her hair was coarse, her face sallow, her eyes
Sunken; her lips crusted and white; her throat
Scaly with scurf. Her parchment skin revealed
The bowels within; beneath her hollow loins
Jutted her withered hips; her sagging breasts
Seemed hardly fastened to her ribs; her stomach
Only a void; her joints wasted and huge,
Her knees like balls, her ankles grossly swollen.

Eyeing her from a distance, fearing to go
Closer, the nymph gave her the goddess' orders
And hardly waiting, though some way away,
Though just arrived, she felt, or seemed to feel,
Hunger and seized the reins and soaring high
She drove the dragons back to Thessaly.

Hunger did Ceres' bidding, though their aims
Are ever opposite, and, wafted down
The wind, reached the king's palace and at once
Entered the scoundrel's room and, as he slept
(The hour was midnight), wrapped him in her arms
And breathed upon him, filling with herself
His mouth and throat and lungs, and channelled through
His hollow veins her craving emptiness;
Then, duty done, quitting the fertile earth
Returned to her bleak home, her caves of dearth.

Still gentle sleep on wings of quietness
Soothed Erysichthon. In his sleep he dreamed
Of food and feasting, chewed and champed on nothing,
Wore tooth on tooth, stuffed down his cheated gullet
Imaginary food, and course on course
Devoured the empty air. But when he woke,
And peace had fled, a furious appetite
Reigned in his ravenous throat and burning belly.
At once whatever sea or land or air
Can furnish he demands, and when the board
Groans he complains he's starving; while he feasts
Calls for more courses; what could satisfy
Cities or realms is not enough for one;
The more he crams his guts, the more he craves.
And as from every land the rivers flow
To fill the insatiate sea, which never fills
For all those far-flung streams; or as a fire
Never refuses fuel and, ravening, burns
Logs beyond counting, and the more it gets
The more it wants and, glutted, grows on greed;
So wicked Erysichthon's appetite
With all those countless feasts is stoked—and starves;
Food compels food; eating makes emptiness.

Now hunger and his belly's deep abyss

Exhausted his ancestral wealth, but still
Hunger was unexhausted and the flame
Of greed blazed unappeased, until at last,
His fortune sunk and swallowed, there remained
His daughter, undeserving such a father.
Her too he sold; but she, a highborn girl,
Would be no master's slave and, stretching her hands
Towards the sea near by, "Save me", she cried,
"From slavery, thou who didst steal the prize
Of my virginity!" The thief was Neptune,
Who did not spurn her prayer and, though her master
A moment past had seen her, changed her shape—
She was a man, clothed like a fisherman.
    Her master looked at her and said "Good sir,*
You expert of the rod and line, who bait
The dangling hook, tell me—and may the sea
Be smooth for you, the fish bite well, the bait
Hook every bite—where is that ragged girl
With tousled hair, who stood here on the beach
A moment past? I saw her on the beach
Standing just here, and here her footprints stop."
So Neptune's charm was working! Jubilant
To find herself being asked about herself,
She answered "Pardon me, whoever you are,
I've never turned my eyes from this lagoon
And all my mind was on my task. I swear,
So may the Sea-god aid my skill* today,
No man, or woman either, this long time
Has stood here on the beach except myself."
Her master took her at her word and turned,
Baffled, across the sand; the girl regained
Her former shape. But when her father saw
His daughter had this changeability,*
He often sold her and away she went
A mare, a cow, a bird, a deer, and brought
Her glutton father food, unfairly gained.
Yet when his wicked frenzy had consumed
All sustenance and for the dire disease
Provision failed, the ill-starred wretch began
To gnaw himself, and dwindled bite by bite

As his own flesh supplied his appetite.
    But why spend time on tales of others? I
Myself, young friends, also possess the power
Of changing, though my choice is limited.
At times you see me as I am; at times
I twist into a snake; at times a bull
That leads the herd, my strength set in my horns.*
Horns!—while I could!—but now one side, you see,
Has lost its weapon.' And he gave a groan.

BOOK IX

WHY the god groaned and how his brow was maimed
Theseus enquired, and Calydon's great river,
His tangled tresses bound with reeds, began:
'Sad is the task you set. For who would wish
To chronicle the battles that he lost?
Yet the whole tale* I'll tell. It was less shame
To lose than glory to have fought the fight:
Much comfort comes from such a conqueror.
You may perhaps have heard* of Deianira,
Once a most lovely girl, the envied hope
Of many a suitor. I was one of them
And entered the king's palace hopefully
And "Sire", I said, "I crave your daughter's hand."
So, too, said Hercules. The others all
Gave way to us, us two. He told his tale,
How Jove would be her father-in-law,* the fame
Of his great labours, the accomplishment
Of Juno's orders. I, opposing, said,
"Disgrace it is if gods give way to men."
(He was not yet a god.) "In me you see
The master of the waters that descend
In winding courses through your royal realm;
No stranger son-in-law from foreign shores,
But one of your own folk, your own affairs.
Let it not damage me that royal Juno
Does not detest me, that no toils imposed
Have ever punished me! You, Hercules,
Alcmena's son, who claim your father's Jove—
That tale's untrue, or true to your disgrace:
A father through your mother's sin. So choose
Which you prefer, either that fatherhood
Is false or you were born in infamy."
While I was speaking, all the time, he scowled,
And, failing to control his flaring rage,
Gave me his curt reply: "This hand of mine

Is better than my tongue. Win, if you may,
With words, provided I prevail in deeds!''
And on he rushed in fury. My fine words
Made me ashamed to flinch. I threw aside
My green cloak, raised my arms and poised my hands
Half-curled before my chest and stood to fight.
He scooped up dust and threw it over me,*
And he was yellowed too with my gold sand.
Now at my neck, now at my twinkling legs
He lunged (or feinted), pressing his attack
At every point. My weight protected me;
I stood unscathed, like a huge rock that waves
Beat with a roaring crash, and there it stands
Fast in the safety of its mighty mass.
We drew apart a little, then again
Joined battle, standing rooted, both resolved
Never to yield an inch. Foot locked with foot,
Fingers with fingers, brow to brow, I pressed
Him down half-prone; as I've seen battling bulls
Collide in contest for the sleekest cow
Of all the countryside; the herd looks on
In fear and awe not knowing which of them
The victory and the sovereignty await.
Three times with no success did Hercules
Struggle and strain to break my lock; the fourth
Shook off my hold and loosed my clinching arms,
And, striking with his fist (I mean to tell
The truth) he whirled me round and clung with all
His weight upon my back. If you'd believe
(I seek no fame from fiction), crushing me
I seemed to have a mountain. Even so
I managed to insert my sweating arms,
I managed to dislodge his iron grip.
He charged as I stood breathless, gave me no
Chance to recover, and got me round my neck.
At last, forced to my knees, I bit the sand.
    Outmatched, out'man'ned, I used that art of mine:
Changed to a long smooth snake I slid from him.*
In circling sinuous coils I wound myself
And flickering my forked tongue hissed horribly.

He laughed and mocked my magic. "Mastering snakes
Is child's play,* Achelous! Yes, if you
Were champion serpent, how could you compare
With Lerna's Hydra, you a single snake?
It throve on wounds: of all its hundred heads
I cut off none but from its neck two more
Sprang to succeed it, stronger than before!
Yes, though it branched with serpents sprung from death,
And multiplied on doom, I mastered it,
And, mastered, I dispatched it. What's in store
For you, d'you think, no proper snake at all,
No weapons of your own, just skulking in
A shape you've begged and borrowed?" As he spoke,
He locked his fingers round my neck; I felt
My windpipe in a vice; in agony
I fought to free my gullet from his thumbs.
Vanquished again, my third shape still remained,
A savage bull.* A bull! And I fought back!
On my left side he threw his arms around
My bulging neck and, as I raced along,
Kept pace and dragged me down and forced my horns
Right into the hard ground and laid me low
In the deep sand. Even that was not enough:
He grasped my strong stiff horn in his fierce hand,
Broke it, and wrenched it off—my brow was maimed!
My Naiads filled it full of fragrant flowers
And fruits, and hallowed it. From my horn now
Good Plenty* finds her wealth and riches flow.'

　　His tale was done. One of the serving nymphs,
Dressed in Diana's simple style, her hair
Flowing on either side, came bearing in
The horn with all its wealth, all autumn there,
Fruits in perfection for our second course.
Dawn came, and, when the sun's first rising beams
Struck on the peaks, the young men went their way,
Not waiting till the river had regained
Its peace and placid flow and all the flood
Had fallen. Achelous hid his face,
His rustic face, and head with missing horn
Beneath his waters. Humbled though he was

To lose that elegance, all else was sound,
And he concealed his loss with willow leaves
Or reeds and rushes worn upon his head.

HERCULES, NESSUS, AND DEIANIRA

But savage Nessus lost his life for love
Of that same lady, when an arrow flew
To pierce his side. When Jove's son, Hercules,
Was making for his native city's* walls
With his new bride, he reached the rushing waters
Of broad Euenus, high beyond its wont.
The river, swollen by the winter's rains
And full of whirlpools, poured impassable.
And as he stood there, fearless for himself
But anxious for his wife, Nessus approached,
Mighty in muscle and knowing the fords well.
'With my help she'll stand safe on the far side',
He volunteered: 'You, use your strength and swim!'
To Nessus then the Theban hero gave
His bride of Calydon, pale and afraid,
Dreading the river, dreading the centaur too.
And then, just as he was, with all the weight
Of lion-skin and quiver (club and bow
He'd thrown across), 'Since I've begun', he cried,
'I'll beat one river more!' and never paused
To take his time or pick the kindest water,
And scorned to use the current's services.
And now on the far bank and stooping for
The bow he'd thrown, he heard a voice, his wife's,
Calling and sure that Nessus had in mind
A breach of trust, 'You raping ravisher!'
He cried, 'Where are you going? So confident
In your four feet! Nessus, you centaur, listen!
Hold off from me and mine. Maybe you feel
No dread of me—at least your father's* wheel
Should hold you back from lust and lechery.
Trust horse-strength if you will, you'll not escape.
With wounds not feet I'll follow!' His last words
Were proved at once: an arrow flew and pierced

The fleeing centaur's back: out from his breast
The barbed point stuck. He wrenched the shaft away,
And blood from both wounds spurted, blood that bore
The Hydra's poison.* Nessus caught it up.
'I'll not die unavenged', he thought and gave
His shirt soaked in warm gore to Deianira,
A talisman, he said, to kindle love.

   Long years had passed, and Hercules' great deeds
Had filled the world and sated Juno's hate.
Fresh from his triumph in Oechalia
He had made plans to pay his vows to Jove
At Cenaeum, when rumour* rode ahead—
Rumour who talks and loves to tangle true
With false, and from near nothing flourishes
On her own lies—and swiftly reached the ears
Of Deianira, rumour that her lord
Was held in thrall by love of Iole.*
Her doting heart believed. This latest love
Filled her with fear. First she gave way to weeping,
Flooding her pain away, poor soul, in tears.
Then soon 'Why do I weep?' she said, 'Those tears
Will gladden that girl's heart. Since she must come,
I must make haste, devise some stratagem
While time allows, before that paramour
Is settled in my bed. Shall I protest?
Shall I be dumb? Go back to Calydon?
Or wait here? Leave the house? Or stand at bay,
If nothing better? Why, remembering
I'm Meleager's sister, why not plan
Some deed of doom, and strangle her and prove
The power of pain, the power of slighted love?'
Swaying from plan to plan, at last she chose
To send the shirt imbued with Nessus' blood
To fortify her husband's failing love.
Not knowing what she gave, she entrusted her
Sorrow to Lichas (ignorant no less)
And charged him with soft words (poor piteous soul!)
To take it to her lord. And Hercules
Received the gift and on his shoulders wore,
In ignorance, the Hydra-poisoned gore.

THE DEATH AND APOTHEOSIS OF HERCULES

The flame was lit; he offered words of prayer
And incense, pouring on the marble altar
Wine from the bowl. That deadly force grew warm.
Freed by the flame, it seeped and stole along,
Spreading through all the limbs of Hercules.
While he still could, that hero's heart of his
Stifled his groans, but when the agony
Triumphed beyond endurance, he threw down
The altar, and his cries of anguish filled
The glades of Oeta.* Desperately he tried
To tear the fatal shirt away; each tear
Tore his skin too, and, loathsome to relate,
Either it stuck, defeating his attempts
To free it from his flesh, or else laid bare
His lacerated muscles and huge bones.
Why, as the poison burned, his very blood
Bubbled and hissed as when a white-hot blade
Is quenched in icy water. Never an end!
The flames licked inwards, greedy for his guts;
Dark perspiration streamed from every pore;
His scorching sinews crackled; the blind rot
Melted his marrow. Hands raised to the stars,
'Feast', he cried, 'Juno! Feast upon my doom!
Gaze down from heaven in your cruelty
Upon my torment. Glut your savage heart!
If even from my foes, if even from you,
Some pity I deserve, take, take away
My hateful life, tortured so terribly,
Life born to labour. Death a boon will be,
A boon a stepmother gives fittingly!

Was it for this,* that I subdued Busiris,*
Whose temples he defiled with strangers' blood?
That I uprooted fierce Antaeus* from
His mother's nourishment? Faced unafraid
Cerberus' triple heads, the triple heads
Of Geryon?* That you, my hands, forced down
The great bull's* horns, you gave deliverance
To Elis,* to Parthenius'* high glades,

To Stymphalus'* broad waters, and your valour
Secured the gold-chased belt of Thermodon*
And the apples* guarded by the unsleeping snake?
The centaurs* quailed before me, and the boar*
That wasted Arcady; the Hydra's gain
From loss, with doubled strength, was all in vain.
Yes, when I saw the Thracian's horses* fat
On human blood and mangers full of flesh,
Torn flesh, did I not smash them down and slay
Master and steeds together? By these arms
Nemea's giant lion lay destroyed;
This neck sustained the sky.* Jove's savage wife
Is tired of setting tasks: I'm still untired.
But now this latest torture! That no courage,
No weapons can withstand! Deep in my lungs
Roams the devouring fire, through all my frame
It feeds. Yet King Eurystheus flourishes
Alive and well! And men can still believe
In gods!'* In wounded agony he roamed
The heights of Oeta, like a bull that bears
Deep in its side a hunting-spear, when he
Who dealt the wound has fled. Time after time
You could have seen him trying to tear away
The fatal shirt, roaring great cries of pain,
Cursing the mountain, crashing down the pines,
Or raising hands to heaven, his father's home.
    Then Lichas* caught his eye, look, cowering
In panic in a cave. 'Lichas!' he cried,
Pain mounting up to madness, 'It was you
Gave me this gift of doom! Yes, you'll be my
Murderer!' Lichas paled and shuddering
In terror tried to stammer his excuse,
And made to clasp his master's knees. But he
Snatched him away and whirled him round and round,
And flung him like a sling-shot out to sea,
The Euboean sea. Along that airy path
He hardened, as in icy winds,* it's said,
Raindrops congeal and turn to snow, and snow,
Soft swirling flakes of snow, combine to form
Round stones of hail; so Lichas, hurled away

By those gigantic shoulders through the void,
Blood-drained by fear, all living moisture lost,
The old tale tells, was turned to flinty rock.
Now from Euboea's waves a short rock-shelf
Projects with traces still of human shape,
'Lichas'* to mariners who, in belief
It feels them, fear to tread upon that reef.

   Then Jove's illustrious son cut down the trees
That clothed steep Oeta's side and built a pyre,
And ordered Poeas' son,* whose service set
The flame beneath, to take his mighty bow,
His quiver and his arrows that should see
Troy's realm a second time.* And, as the flames
Licked the great timber pile, he spread the skin
Of the Nemean lion high on top,
And, pillowed on his club, lay there at ease,
As at a feast* with friends he might recline,
Flower-garlanded amid the flowing wine.

   Now strong and spreading on all sides the flames
Were crackling, licking at those carefree limbs,
That heart that scorned them. Gods in heaven feared
For earth's defender. Conscious of their thoughts,
Jove, well content, addressed them:* 'These your fears
Are my delight. Gladly do I rejoice
With my whole heart that you, my grateful people,
Call me your lord and father, that my issue
Finds the protection of your favour too.
For though you pay this tribute to his own
Achievements, I myself am in your debt.
Indeed let not your faithful hearts be filled
With needless terror. Spurn those flames on Oeta!
He who has conquered all will conquer too
The fires you see. He'll not feel Vulcan's power
Save in his mother's part. What he derived
From me is everlasting, stands beyond
The sting of death, unscathed by any flame.
That part, now done with earth, I shall receive
On heaven's shores, and I am confident
My action will give joy to every god.
If anyone, however—anyone—

Is going to be distressed that Hercules
Is made a god and grudges that award,
The gift was well deserved and that he'll know,
And, though it hurts, consent to have it so.'
    The gods agreed. His royal consort too
Seemed not to mind his words, until the last,
Aimed at herself, received an angry frown.
Meanwhile whatever parts the flames could ravage
Mulciber had removed; of Hercules
No shape remained that might be recognized,
Nothing his mother gave him, traces now
Only of Jove. And as a snake will slough
Age with its skin and revel in fresh life,
Shining resplendent in its sleek new scales,
So Hercules, his mortal frame removed,
Through all his finer parts* gained force and vigour,
In stature magnified, transformed into
A presence clothed in majesty and awe.*
The Almighty Father carried him away,
Swept in his four-horsed chariot through the clouds,
And stationed him among the shining stars.
Atlas could feel his weight.
                                    But even now
Eurystheus' rage did not relax. His hate,
From father turned to children, cruel hate,
Was still at work. Anxiety had long
Distressed Alcmena, but in Iole
She found a confidante whom she could trust
With an old lady's troubles, and relate
Her son's world-famous labours and her own
Story. Obeying Hercules' commands,
Hyllus had welcomed Iole in love
And wedlock; in her swelling womb she bore
His noble child. Alcmena spoke to her:

THE BIRTH OF HERCULES

'May the gods favour *you* when your time comes,
With no long painful waiting when you call
On Ilithyia,* who attends the pangs

And fears of labour. To myself she was
By Juno's influence most difficult.
For when the natal day of Hercules,
My greatly-toiling son, drew close and now
The sun had reached the tenth of heaven's signs,
My burden strained my womb, and what I bore
Was huge: you could be sure that hidden weight
Was Jove's begetting. Then my pains grew worse,
More than I could endure. Why, even now
I feel cold shudders as I speak, and pain
Recalled is pain renewed. For seven nights,
For seven days in torture, overwhelmed
In agony, I stretched my arms to heaven
And called Lucina and the Gods of Birth.
I called and called. She came, indeed, but bribed
Beforehand, ready to donate my life
To spiteful Juno. On that altar there,
Before the door, she sat and heard my groans.
Legs crossed, right over left, and fingers locked,
She barred the birth,* and chanted silent spells,
Spells that held back the birth as it began.
I strained and struggled; mad with pain I screamed
Abuse in vain at Jove's ingratitude.
I longed to die; my protests would have moved
A block of granite. Theban matrons came
To add their prayers and comfort my distress.
One of my maids was there, a low-born girl,
My golden-haired Galanthis, always active
To do my bidding and a favourite
For her good services. She realized
That spiteful Juno had some plot in hand,
And on her frequent errands in and out
She saw the goddess sitting by the altar,
Arms round her knees and fingers linked, and said
"Whoever you may be, congratulate
Our mistress; Lady Alcmena is delivered,
Her prayers are answered and her babe is born."
Up sprang the great Birth-goddess in dismay,
And loosed her linking hands, and as the bonds
Were loosed I was delivered of my child.

Galanthis laughed at the goddess she'd deceived
(So is the story told) and, as she laughed,
The cruel goddess seized her by the hair
And dragged her to the ground and when she tried
To rise prevented her and changed her arms
To forelegs. Though her shape is different,
She's active now as ever, and her back
Still keeps her golden colour, and because
Out of her mouth came lies that aided birth,
Out of her mouth* her young are born. My door
She's in and out* of as she was before.'

DRYOPE

She sighed, remembering her former maid,
And as she sorrowed Iole began:
'Yet, mother, she whose ravished shape you mourn
Was not of *our* blood. What if I should tell you
My sister's fate, so strange; though tears and pain
Impede my tongue and check my tale. My sister!
The loveliest girl of all Oechalia,
Dear Dryope, her mother's only child
(Mine was a different mother). He who rules
Delphi and Delos* had assaulted her;
Andraemon welcomed her, a maid no more,
And he was counted lucky in his wife.
There is a lake* whose shelving sides had shaped
A sloping shore, and myrtles crowned the ridge.
There Dryope had come, not dreaming of
The Fates' design, and, what must make you more
Indignant, bringing garlands for the nymphs.
She carried at her breast her little boy,
A darling burden not a twelvemonth old,
And fed him with her milk. Near the lakeside
A water-lotus flowered, its crimson blooms
Like Tyrian dye, fair hope of fruit to come.
Dear Dryope had picked a posy of
These flowers to please her boy. I meant to do
The same (for I was there), when I saw drops
Of blood drip from the blossoms and the boughs

Shiver in horror. For this shrub, you see
(Too late the peasants told us), was the nymph
Lotis* who fled Priapus' lechery
And found changed features there but kept her name.
    Nothing of this my sister knew. She'd said
Prayers to the nymphs and now in terror tried
To turn away and leave, but found her feet
Rooted. She fought to free herself, but failed
To move below her bosom. Gradually
Up from the soil right round her legs and loins
Bark climbed and clung; and, seeing it, she tried
To tear her hair, but found leaves filled her hand,
Leaves covered her whole head. Her little boy,
Amphissos (Eurytus, his grandfather,
Had named him so) could feel his mother's breasts
Grow hard; the milky flow failed as he sucked.
And I stood there, a helpless onlooker,
Watching her cruel fate. As best I could,
I clasped my sister in my arms and stayed
The growing trunk and boughs, and longed to see—
Yes, longed—the selfsame bark envelop me.
    And then in sore distress her husband came,
Andraemon, and her father too to look
For Dryope; for Dryope I showed
The lotus* there. Upon the still-warm wood
They printed kisses; prostrate on the ground,
They hugged their dear tree's roots, that darling tree.
Of my sweet sister naught that was not tree
Remained except her face. Her tears, poor soul,
Bedewed the leaves she'd grown; and, while she might,
While lips would let words pass, her protests poured:
"If misery can win belief, I swear
By heaven I've not deserved this wickedness.
Guiltless I'm punished; all my life has been
Innocent. If I lie, let all my leaves
Be parched and lost, let axes cut me down,
Let me be burnt. But take this baby from
His mother's boughs and give him to a nurse.
And see that often underneath my tree
He takes his milk and underneath my tree

He often plays, and, when he's learnt to talk,
See that he greets his mother, knows to say
Sadly 'My mother's hidden in this trunk.'
Let him beware of pools and never pick
Blossoms from trees, but fancy every bush
A goddess in disguise. And now farewell
Dear husband, farewell sister, farewell father.
Yet, if you love me, keep my foliage
Secure from wounding blades and browsing flocks.
And, since I'm not allowed to bend to you,
Reach up to me and let me kiss you still
While you can touch my lips, and lift my son,
My little son, to me. And now no more!
Over my snow-white throat the smooth rind creeps;
Up to the crown I'm swathed. Let no hands touch
My lids: without your service let the bark
Envelop in its shroud my dying eyes!"
Her words, her life, together ceased to flow;
Her changeling boughs long held her body's glow.'

IOLAUS AND THE SONS OF CALLIRHOE

When Iole had told her wondrous tale,
Alcmena dried her tears (in tears herself),
Then all their sorrows were arrested by
A strange surprise. In the high doorway stood
A youth, almost a boy, his cheeks it seemed
Still downy, Iolaus,* now restored
In form and features to his early prime.
This guerdon was the gift of Juno's daughter,
Hebe, to gratify her husband's* wish.
She meant to swear not to bestow such gifts
On any man thereafter, but was stopped
By Themis.* 'Civil war', she said, 'embroils
Thebes now and save by Jove's might Capaneus*
Shall not be conquered: brothers* shall be paired
In wounds; the prophet* yet alive shall see
His ghost as earth gapes open; and his son*
Parent on parent shall avenge, a deed
Of loving duty and a deed of crime.

Distraught with troubles, driven from his mind
And home, the Furies and his mother's ghost
Shall hound him till his consort shall demand
The fatal golden necklace, and the sword
Of Phegeus* drain the blood of kith and kin.
And then at last Callirhoe, the child
Of Achelous, for her infant sons
Shall beg those years* from Jove on bended knee,
To speed their vengeance for the victor's death.
And, at her suit, Jove shall foreclaim that gift
Of his stepdaughter,* and her sons shall be
Transformed to manhood from their infancy.'

   As Themis, who foreknew the future, spoke
These prophecies, a rumbling argument
Arose in heaven, the gods all grumbling why
Others should not be allowed to grant such gifts.
Aurora grumbled at her husband's age,
And gentle Ceres that Iasion
Was going grey; and Mulciber required
New life for Erichthonius.* Venus too,
Worried about the future,* staked a claim
To have Anchises' years made young again.
Each of them had some favourite. A storm
Of rivalry and discord swelled, till Jove
Unlocked his lips. 'If you at all', he said,
'Hold me in honour, what possesses you?
Does anyone suppose he has the power
To conquer fate?* It was the will of fate
That Iolaus gained his years again;
To fate the children of Callirhoe
Will owe their manhood, not to canvassing
Or conflict. You yourselves, yes, me myself
(If that may give you comfort) fate controls.
If I could alter it, my Aeacus
Would not be stooping in his last late years,
And Rhadamanthus would enjoy the flower
Of youth for ever and my Minos too,
Whom now the bitter burden of old age
Has brought to scorn, who'll never know again
The majesty in which he once held reign.'

Jove's words were moving. No god could complain
When he saw Aeacus and Rhadamanthus
And Minos worn with years. Why, in his prime
The very name of Minos had struck fear
In mighty nations, but by then his strength
Was failing and he feared Apollo's son,
Miletus, proud in all the power of youth
And parentage, and thought he planned to rise
Against his throne, yet feared to force him from
His fatherland. But of his own accord
Miletus fled and in his speeding ship
Crossed the Aegean Sea and on the shores
Of Asia built the battlements that keep
Their founder's name; where, as she strolled beside
Maeander's winding banks, her father's stream,
That turns so often back upon its course,
He joined in love a nymph of beauty rare,
Cyanee, who one day bore him there
Byblis and Caunus, twins, a tragic pair.

BYBLIS

The tale of Byblis shows* that girls should love
As law allows, Byblis who lost her heart
To great Apollo's grandson, her twin brother.
Hers was no sister's love; her love was wrong.
At first she failed to understand at all
What her heart felt and never thought it sin
To kiss him often or to throw her arms
Around her brother's neck, and long mistook
The lying semblance of a sister's love.
Then gradually her passion warped. She dressed
With care to meet her brother, keen, too keen,
To look her loveliest, and envious
If ever some girl there was lovelier.
She still had no clear picture of herself,
Her heart still formed no prayer, though inwardly
Passion burned high. She addressed him as 'My lord'*
And, hating words of kinship, wanted him
Always to call her Byblis, never sister.

Even so she dared not let her waking thoughts
Admit her wanton hopes. But when she sank
Relaxed in quiet rest, she often saw
The object of her love, and fancied too
She lay with him and blushed even in her sleep.
She woke and long lay still, as she recalled
The vision of her slumber. Troubled thoughts
Perplexed her. 'Wretched me! What can it mean
This dream the still night sends? It must not be!
Why do I have such dreams? True, his good looks
Even jealous eyes admit; I like him well,
And I could love him were he not my brother;
He's worth my love—but kinship ruins me.
So long as I, awake, try no such thing,
May sleep return with many such a dream!
Sleep has no spy, imagined joy no sin.
O Venus, O winged God of Love, what joy,
What bliss was mine! How real my ecstasy!
Oh, how I lay dissolved in my delight!
What rapture to remember! Though the thrill
Of pleasure was so fleeting and the night
Sped rushing on and grudged what we began.
Oh, could I change my name and join my heart
With yours, how good a daughter I could be,
Dear Caunus, to your father, you, how good
A son to mine! We would share everything,
If heaven allowed, except our ancestry—
I'd want you to be better born than me!
Some other girl, my fairest love, will be—
I know not who—the mother of your sons,
But I, whose ill luck made your parents mine,
In you have but a brother. That alone
Is ours to share, that thing that severs us.
    What do my dreams portend? What weight have dreams?
Do dreams have weight at all? The gods forbid!
Yet gods have loved their sisters; yes, indeed!
Why, Saturn married Ops, his kin by blood,
And Ocean Tethys, and Olympus' lord,
Jove, married Juno. But the gods above
Are laws unto themselves. Why try to fit

The different rules of heaven to modes of men?
This flame I'll force, forbidden, from my breast,
Or, if I fail, oh, let me perish first,
And as I'm laid dead on my bier, then let
My brother kiss me. Yet for what I want
Two minds must meet: suppose it brings delight
To me, it must be sinful in his sight.
But then no scruples held the fabled sons
Of Aeolus* from their six sisters' beds!
How do I know these stories? Why so pat
These precedents?* What will become of me?
Away, perverted passion! Let me love
My brother with a proper sister's love!
Yet if *his* love had first been fired by me,
Maybe his madness would have found me willing.
Well then, if I were willing had he wooed,
I'll woo myself. Can I speak out? Can I
Confess? Love will compel me! Yes, I can.
Or if shame locks my lips, then I'll reveal
By private letter love my lips conceal.'
     The plan seemed sound and won her wavering mind.
Raising herself, she leant on her left arm.
Let him be judge, she thought; now I'll confess
My love so mad. Ay me! How I do fall!
What fire my heart has caught! With trembling hand
She starts the sentences her thoughts have framed.
Her right hand holds the pen, her left the wax.
She starts, she pauses, writes and thinks it wrong,
Restarts, erases, alters, likes, dislikes,
Puts down the tablet, picks it up again,
Not knowing what she wants, and finding fault
With everything as soon as settled. Shame
Mingles with resolution in her face.
'Your sister' she had written, but decided
'Sister' were best erased, and on the wax,
Its surface smoothed, incised these sentences:
     'Good health to you from one who'll have no health,
Unless you grant it, one who loves you well!
Shame, shame withholds her name, and should you ask
What I so long for, nameless I would wish

To plead my cause and not be recognized
As Byblis till my hope was safe and sure.
Proof of my wounded soul you must have seen:
My face so pale and haggard, my sad eyes
So full of tears, my senseless-seeming sighs,
My fond caresses and—had you but felt—
My kisses that no sister's lips should press.
Yet, though my wound was grievous, though the flame
Of passion flared within me, everything
I tried (the gods bear witness) to regain
My sanity at last, and struggled long
To foil Cupid's assault. Alas! I've borne
More than you'd think a girl could bear. Defeat
I'm forced to own, your aid with trembling prayers
I'm forced to supplicate. A loving heart
Now you alone can save, alone destroy.
Choose which you will. Your suppliant's no foe,
No foe, but one who, though she's nearest you,
Longs to be nearer, to be bound to you
By closer bonds. Let old men know the law,*
Examine what's allowed, what's right and wrong,
Study the statutes. Love that heeds no rules
Suits our young years. As yet we have not learnt
What is allowed, think everything's allowed,
And follow the examples of the gods.
No father's rules, no fears for our fair name,
No qualms shall thwart us. Were there cause for qualms,
Brother and sister, sweet companionship,
The world will note, veiling our secret joy.
I am at liberty to speak with you
In private; we embrace, kiss openly;
The rest—how much is that? Pity a girl
Who speaks her love, and would not, did its fire,
Its sovereign fire, not force her. On my tomb,
Oh, do not earn the title that to you,
When men shall carve the cause, my death was due!'
     The words she traced—and traced in vain—had filled
The tablets and the final sentence clung
Close to the margin. With her signet-gem
Straightway she sealed the tale of guilt—her tears

Had served to moisten it; her tongue was dry—
Then, shamefaced, called a slave and nervously,
With honeyed words, 'Take these, good faithful friend',
She said, 'and give them to'—a long and anxious pause—
'My brother.' As she handed them, they slipped
And fell. The omen troubled her, but still
She sent them all the same. The serving-man
Delivered, when he found a fitting time,
The message that confessed her love. Aghast,
In sudden rushing rage, young Caunus threw
The tablets down, half read, and hardly kept
His fingers from the trembling servant's throat.
'Be off, you rogue! Off, while you may!' he cried,
'You pimp of lawless lust! But that your fate
Involved my shame, your death had paid for this!'
The servant fled in fear and told his mistress
Her brother's fierce reply. When Byblis heard
Her love repulsed, she shivered and turned pale,
Seized by an icy chill. But when anon
Her faculties came back, back came as well
Her wild desire. In whispers hardly heard
She breathed, 'Yes! I deserved it! Why, oh why
Did I reveal my wound so rashly? Why
So quickly put in writing—in such haste—
What should have been concealed? I should have first
Tested his feelings, using words that might
Mean nothing. To make sure the wind blew fair,
I should have set small sail and kept good watch,
And so fared safely on the sea, but now
I've spread full sail to winds untried, unknown.
So on the rocks I'm cast and overturned;
Shipwrecked and sunk beneath the boundless main,
My sails will never bring me home again.
   Why! By the clearest omens I was warned
Not to indulge my love, when, as I bade
The man deliver them, the tablets fell
And so made sure that all my hopes should fall.
Indeed that day—or else my whole intent—
But better, yes! that day—should have been changed.
The god himself was warning me with signs,

Had I not lost my senses, crystal clear.
Of course I should have spoken, not have risked
Myself in writing,* should in person have
Revealed my passion. Then he would have seen
The tears I shed, have seen my looks of love;
Words could have told him more than wax could hold.
Against his will I could have thrown my arms
Around his neck and, were I thrust away,
I could have seemed near death and clasped his feet,
And on my bended knees begged for my life.
I could have done so many many things,
Which one by one might fail, but all together
Could not have failed to turn his stubborn heart.

    Perhaps the man I sent made some mistake,
Approached him clumsily, chose, I dare say,
An awkward moment, did not wait until
The hour was free, his thoughts unoccupied.
These things have harmed me. He's no tigress' son,*
No heart of flint or iron or adamant
Beats in his breast, no lioness's milk
Has given him suck. He *shall* be overcome.
He must be wooed again. I shall not shrink
From what I've started, while my breath remains.
Best were—could I undo what I have done—
Not to have started; now my second best
Is to fight on and what I've started win.
For he, though I give up my hopes, can never
Fail to remember what my hopes have dared,
And I shall seem, because I give them up,
Fickle and frivolous, even to have tried
To tempt and trap him, or for sure he'll think
Lust overcame me, not the God of Love,
Whose sovereign fiery flame my passion drove.
In short I've sinned and can't unsin my sin;
I wrote, I wooed, I wanted wickedness.
Though no more's done, I'll not seem innocent.
What lies ahead may little add of sin,
But much, oh much, of happiness to win.'

    Her thoughts were so uncertain, so confused,
That what she wished she'd never tried, she meant

To try again. Poor girl, she passed all bounds,
Kept offering herself to his rebuffs,
And soon, no end in sight, her brother fled,
Fled from his country and the scene of shame
To found a city* in a foreign land.
    Then Byblis was beside herself with grief.
She beat herself in frenzy and tore down
The tunic from her breast. Now openly
She raved with no attempt to hide her hope
Of lawless love, and in despair forsook
The home she hated and her fatherland
To trace her brother, find that fugitive.
Like Thracian women maddened each three years
By Bacchus' wand in holy ecstasy,
Byblis ran howling through the countryside,
Watched by the wives of Bubasis,* then on
Through Caria and Lycia she roamed,
Among the warrior Leleges, and now
Cragus* was far behind her and the streams
Of Limyre* and Xanthos* and the scarp
Where the Chimaera prowled with lungs of fire
And lion's breast and head and dragon's tail.
The forest failed; on the hard ground she fell,
Exhausted by her quest, and lay face down,
With tumbled hair, among the fallen leaves.
Often the wood-nymphs tried to cradle her
In their soft arms and often sought to salve
The fever of her love, and comforted
With soothing words her heart that heard no more.
She lay in silence, clutching the small sedge,
And watering the greensward with her tears.
And these, men say, the Naiads made a rill,
For ever flowing—what could they give more?
At once, as resin drips from damaged bark,
Or asphalt oozes from the earth's dark womb,
Or, when the west wind breathes its balm, the sun
Unlocks the water that the frost has bound,
So, wasting by her weeping all away,
Byblis became a spring.* Still in that dale
It keeps its mistress' name, still mournfully

Trickles below the tall dark ilex tree.
    The tale of this strange miracle might well
Have been the talk* of all the hundred towns
Of Crete, had not that island lately known
In Iphis' change a marvel nearer home.

IPHIS AND IANTHE

Now once upon a time in Phaestos town,
Not far from royal Knossos, lived a man,
Ligdus by name, of humble family,
Freeborn but hardly known, nor did his purse
Surpass his pedigree, though none could blame
His life or probity. His wife was soon
To bear a child and when her time was near
He spoke a word of warning: 'In my prayers
I ask two things, that your delivery
Be swift and easy and the child you bear
May be a boy. Girls are more burdensome,
And fate denies our means. If—heaven forbid!—
The babe should chance to be a girl, she must—
It breaks my heart to say it—Oh, may love
Of kith and kin forgive me!—she must die!'*
Their cheeks were wet with streaming tears, both his
Who gave the dire decree and hers who heard.
Yet Telethusa begged him, begged again
And prayed her husband not to halve her hopes—
In vain; Ligdus' resolve was steadfast. Now
The time was ripe, the weight within her womb
She scarce could carry, when, as midnight came,
She saw before her bed, or seemed to see
As in a dream, great Isis with her train*
Of holy deities. Upon her brow
There stood the crescent moon-horns, garlanded
With glittering heads of golden grain, and grace
Of royal dignity; and at her side
The baying dog Anubis,* dappled Apis,*
Sacred Bubastis* and the god who holds
His finger to his lips for silence' sake;
Osiris* too for whom the endless search

Is never satisfied, and holy timbrels
And foreign snakes whose venom soothes to sleep.
Now she seemed wide awake and what she saw
As clear as day, and then the goddess spoke:
'My Telethusa, whom I count among
My faithful, lay your carking cares aside;
Play false your husband's order; when the toils
Of birth are done, be sure you rear the babe,
Whatever it shall be. I answer prayers;
I am the goddess of good hope; I help
In time of need; you never shall complain
You worshipped an ungrateful deity.'
Her guidance given, she vanished from the room.
With happy heart the Cretan girl rose up
And held her hands towards the stars and prayed
The promise of her vision might prove true.
Her pains increased; her burden forced itself
To birth; a girl was born (unknown to Ligdus),
And Telethusa bade them tend the boy.
Trust hid the truth, and no one knew the trick
Except the nurse. The father paid his vows
And named the child after its grandfather,*
Iphis, a name that gave its mother joy:
It meant no fraud—it could be a girl or boy.
　　So the long lie that love began lay hid.
She dressed her as a boy, and, whether judged
As boy or girl, the child was beautiful.
Time rolled apace and thirteen years passed by,
And then her father found Iphis a bride,
Telestes' charming daughter, golden-haired
Ianthe, highest praised of all the girls
Of Phaestos for her dower of loveliness.
Equal in age they were, equal in looks,
And both from the same masters had received
The first instruction of their early years;
And so it was that both their simple hearts
Love visited alike and both alike
Were smitten—but their hopes how different!
Ianthe longed to fix the wedding day,
To be a wife and take to be her man

Her Iphis, whom she took to be a man.
Poor Iphis loved a girl, girl loving girl,
And knew her love was doomed and loved the more.
Almost in tears, 'What will become of me?'
She said, 'possessed by love unheard of, love
So monstrous, so unique? If the gods mean
To spare me, they should spare me. If they mean
To ruin me, at least they should have sent
Some natural ill, some normal malady.
Cows never yearn for cows, nor mares for mares;
The ewe follows the ram, the hind her hart;
So the birds mate, so every animal;
A female never fires a female's love.
Would I were not a girl!* That Crete should lack
No monstrous birth, the daughter* of the Sun
Once loved a bull—a female with a male.
The madness of my love, if truth be told,
Is more than hers. At least her love had hope;
At least her bull, tricked by that bogus cow,
Served her—she had a male to lead astray.
Though all the skill and wisdom of the world
Were gathered here, though Daedalus himself
Flew back on wax-bound wings, what could he do?
Could all the arts he learnt change me from girl
To boy? Ianthe, could he alter you?
    Steady your heart, Iphis, compose your thoughts,
Smother, you must, that foolish futile flame.
See what you were from birth, unless you dupe
Even yourself; seek what the law allows
And love as every woman ought to love.
It's hope that fires and hope that fosters love,
But hope the facts refuse. No watch and ward,
No husband's cautious care, no father's force
Keeps you from her dear arms, nor she herself
Refuses you; but yours she cannot be.
Nor, though all things befall, though gods and men
Toil for your sake, can you gain happiness.
Even now none of my prayers is vain; the gods
Have gladly given what was theirs to give,
And what I wish is her wish and the wish

Of both our fathers. Only nature stands
Unwilling, nature mightier than them all—
To work my woe. See now the longed-for time
Is come, the day to link our love dawns bright;
Ianthe shall be mine. . . . It cannot be!
No, in the midst of water I shall thirst.
Ay me! why should the Wedding-god preside
Without a groom, with both of us a bride!'
She said no more. The other girl, in love
As eager, prayed the Wedding-god to haste.

　　What she so longed for, Telethusa feared.
First she postponed the date, then gained delay
Pleading some malady, and often made
A dream or omen her excuse. At last,
All stratagems exhausted, hard at hand
The ceremony stood, so long deferred.
One day was left. Then, letting down her hair,
And taking from her head (her daughter's too)
The bands of braid and clinging to the altar,
'O Isis,* gracious lady of the lands
Of Mareotis and the isle of Pharos
And Paraetonium and the seven streams
Of holy Nile', she prayed, 'bring me thy help,
And heal, oh heal, my fear. Thee, thee I saw
And these thy symbols once, so long ago,
And recognized them all, thy holy train,
The timbrels' sound, the torches; and my heart
Retained thine orders. That my daughter sees
The light of day, that I am not chastised,
Is thine, thy gift and guidance. Show us both
Thy pity! Save us with thy power!' The tears
Streamed as she prayed. The goddess seemed to move
Her altar; yes, it moved! The temple doors
Trembled, the sound of timbrels filled the shrine,
The moon-shaped horns shone bright. Then, anxious still,
But heartened by the omens' signs of hope,
The mother left the temple. At her side
Walked Iphis, as she went, with longer strides
Than usual, her cheeks of darker hue,
Her features firmer, limbs more powerful,

Her hanging tresses shorter and her strength*
Greater than woman's wont. She who had been
A girl a moment past was now a boy.
Rejoice, rejoice, with fearless faith! Go, bring
Your offerings to the holy shrine! They brought
Their offerings and beside them placed a plaque,
And on the plaque a couplet was inscribed:
   'These offerings, vowed by Iphis as a maid,
   By Iphis, now a man, are gladly paid.'
   The morning's radiance revealed the world;
Venus, Juno and Hymen joined to bless
The wedding rite; their love was sanctified,
And Iphis gained Ianthe, groom and bride.

marriage of poetic forms

very heroic

BOOK X

ORPHEUS AND EURYDICE

THENCE Hymen came, in saffron mantle clad,
At Orpheus' summons through the boundless sky
To Thessaly, but vain the summons proved.
True he was present, but no hallowed words   *a lot of foreshad-*
He brought nor happy smiles nor lucky sign;   *owing*
Even the torch he held sputtered throughout
With smarting smoke, and caught no living flame
For all his brandishing. The ill-starred rite
Led to a grimmer end. The new-wed bride,   *she ate 6*
Roaming with her gay Naiads through the grass, *pomogranite seeds*
Fell dying when a serpent struck her heel.   *6 in Hades*
And when at last the bard of Rhodope   → *poet*   *(winter)*
Had mourned his fill in the wide world above,   *Green world*
He dared descend through Taenarus'* dark gate
To Hades to make trial* of the shades;
And through the thronging wraiths and grave-spent ghosts
He came to pale Persephone and him,   → *goddess of*
Pluto ← Lord of the shades,* who rules the unlovely realm, *agriculture,*
And as he struck his lyre's sad chords he said: *daughter of*
'Ye deities who rule the world below,   *Ceres*
Whither we mortal creatures all return,   *6 mons in Hades.*
If simple truth, direct and genuine,
May by your leave be told, I have come down
Not with intent to see the glooms of Hell,   *Apollo - god of*
Nor to enchain the triple snake-haired necks   *music, poetry*
stepped on ⌐ Of Cerberus, but for my dear wife's sake,   *and medicine.*
a snake ⌐ In whom a trodden viper poured his venom   *ideal nature,*
And stole her budding years. My heart has sought   *perfection.*
Strength to endure; the attempt I'll not deny;
But love has won, a god whose fame is fair   *- poetic form*
In the world above; but here I doubt, though here
Too, I surmise; and if that ancient tale
Of ravishment is true,* you too were joined
In love. Now by these regions filled with fear,
By this huge chaos, these vast silent realms,

calliope- she is mother of
heroic poetry
- most important

Reweave, I implore, the fate unwound too fast ⎤
Of my Eurydice. To you are owed   ⎦ *
Ourselves and all creation; a brief while
We linger; then we hasten, late or soon,
To one abode; here one road leads us all;
Here in the end is home; over humankind
Your kingdom keeps the longest sovereignty.
She too, when ripening years reach their due term,
Shall own your rule. The favour that I ask
Is but to enjoy her love; and, if the Fates
Will not reprieve her, my resolve is clear
Not to return: may two deaths give you cheer.'
    So to the music of his strings he sang,
And all the bloodless spirits wept to hear;
And Tantalus* forgot the fleeing water,
Ixion's wheel was tranced; the Danaids
Laid down their urns; the vultures left their feast,
And Sisyphus sat rapt upon his stone.
Then first by that sad singing overwhelmed,
The Furies' cheeks, it's said, were wet with tears;
And Hades' queen and he whose sceptre rules
The Underworld could not deny the prayer,
And called Eurydice. She was among
The recent ghosts and, limping from her wound,
Came slowly forth; and Orpheus took his bride
And with her this compact that, till he reach
The world above and leave Avernus' vale,
He look not back or else the gift would fail.
    The track climbed upwards, steep and indistinct,
Through the hushed silence and the murky gloom;
And now they neared the edge of the bright world,
And, fearing lest she faint, longing to look,
He turned his eyes—and straight she slipped away.
He stretched his arms to hold her—to be held—
And clasped, poor soul, naught but the yielding air.
And she, dying again, made no complaint
(For what complaint had she save she was loved?)
And breathed a faint farewell, and turned again
Back to the land of spirits whence she came.
    The double death of his Eurydice

[handwritten annotations:]

-he just recited a poem.

he wants to make sure she is there.

to see if she is alright, Orpheus cares for her and she slips away

Ovid   Orpheus and ↑

love makes Orpheus a poet. Love and lack, he can't grasp her. Love and lack makes poetry to reach the ultimate desire.

Stole Orpheus' wits away; (like him* who saw
In dread the three-necked hound of Hell with chains
Fast round his middle neck, and never lost
His terror till he lost his nature too
And turned to stone; or Olenos, who took
Upon himself the charge and claimed the guilt
When his ill-starred Lethaea trusted to
Her beauty, hearts once linked so close, and now
Two rocks on runnelled Ida's mountainside).
He longed, he begged, in vain to be allowed
To cross the stream of Styx a second time.
The ferryman repulsed him. Even so
For seven days he sat upon the bank,
Unkempt and fasting, anguish, grief and tears
His nourishment, and cursed Hell's cruelty.
Then he withdrew to soaring Rhodope
And Haemus* battered by the northern gales.

Three times the sun had reached the watery Fish
That close the year,* while Orpheus held himself
Aloof from love of women, hurt perhaps
By ill-success or bound by plighted troth.
Yet many a woman burned with passion for
The bard, and many grieved at their repulse.
It was his lead that taught the folk of Thrace
The love for tender boys,* to pluck the buds,
The brief springtime, with manhood still to come.

There was a hill, and on the hill a wide
Level of open ground, all green with grass.
The place lacked any shade. But when the bard,
The heaven-born bard, sat there and touched his strings,
Shade came in plenty. Every tree was there:*
Dodona's holy durmast,* poplars once
The Sun's sad daughters,* oaks with lofty leaves,
Soft limes, the virgin laurel* and the beech;
The ash, choice wood for spearshafts, brittle hazels,
The knotless fir, the ilex curving down
With weight of acorns, many-coloured maples,
The social* plane, the river-loving willow,
The water-lotus, box for ever green,
Thin tamarisks and myrtles double-hued,

all the trees
are meta-
mor phosed
into humans
in poetry.

nature → human by POETRY

Viburnums bearing berries of rich blue.
Twist-footed ivy came and tendrilled vines,
And vine-clad elms, pitch-pines and mountain-ash,
Arbutus laden with its blushing fruit,
Lithe lofty palms, the prize of victory,
And pines, high-girdled, in a leafy crest,
The favourite of Cybele, the gods'
Great mother, since in this tree Attis doffed
His human shape* and stiffened in its trunk.

CYPARISSUS

Amid the throng the cone-shaped cypress stood,
A tree now, but in days gone by a boy,
Loved by that god who strings both lyre and bow.
Once, sacred to the nymphs who dwell among
Carthaea's* fields, there was a giant stag,
Whose spreading antlers shed a screen of shade
Upon his head. Those antlers gleamed with gold
And from his silky neck a collar hung
Over his shoulders, set with precious stones.
Upon his brow, secured by slender strings,
A silver medal swayed, given at his birth,
And round his hollow temples, gleaming bright,
From either ear a pearly pendant hung.
Quite fearless, all his natural shyness lost,
He often visited the homes of men,
And he'd let even strangers stroke his neck.
But of them all he was the favourite
Of Cyparissus, Cea's fairest lad.
And he it was who used to lead the stag
To pasture and the waters of the spring.
Flowers of many colours he would weave
Around his horns or, mounted on his back,
A happy cavalier, ride up and down,
Guiding his tender mouth with crimson reins.
    It was high noon upon a summer's day;
The sun's bright beams were burning as the Crab,
That loves the shore-line, spread his curving claws.
The stag lay down upon the grass to rest

And breathed the coolness of the spinney's shade.
There, unaware, with his sharp javelin
Young Cyparissus pierced him to the heart.
And as he saw him dying of the wound,
So cruel, he resolved to die himself.
What words of comfort did not Phoebus give!
What warnings not to yield to grief so sore,
So ill-proportioned!* Still he groaned and begged
A last boon from the gods, that he might mourn
For evermore. And now, with endless sobs,
With lifeblood drained away, his limbs began
To take a greenish hue; his hair that curled
Down from his snowy brow rose in a crest,
A crest of bristles, and as stiffness spread
A graceful spire gazed at the starry sky.
Apollo groaned and said in sorrow 'I
Shall mourn for you, for others you shall mourn;
You shall attend when men with grief are torn.'

GANYMEDE

Such was the grove the bard assembled. There
He sat amid a company of beasts,
A flock of birds, and when he'd tried his strings
And, as he tuned, was satisfied the notes,
Though different, agreed in harmony,
He sang this song: 'From Jove,* great Mother Muse,
Inspire my song: to Jove all creatures bow;
Jove's might I've often hymned in days gone by.
I sang the giants* in a graver theme
And bolts victorious in Phlegra's plains.
But now I need a lighter strain, to sing
Of boys beloved of gods and girls bewitched
By lawless fires who paid the price of lust.
    The King of Heaven once was fired with love
Of Ganymede,* and something was devised
That Jove would rather be than what he was.
Yet no bird would he deign to be but one
That had the power to bear his thunderbolts.
At once his spurious pinions beat the breeze

And off he swept the Trojan lad; who now,
Mixing the nectar, waits in heaven above
(Though Juno frowns) and hands the cup to Jove.
    Hyacinth,* too, Apollo would have placed
In heaven had the drear Fates given time
To place him there. Yet in the form vouchsafed
He is immortal. Year by year, when spring
Drives winter flying and the Ram succeeds
The watery Fish,* he rises from the earth
And in the greensward brings his bloom to birth.

HYACINTH

Hyacinth was my father's* favourite,
And Delphi, chosen centre of the world,
Lost its presiding god, who passed his days
Beside Eurotas in the martial land
Of unwalled* Sparta, and no more esteemed
Zither or bow. Forgetting his true self,
He was content to bear the nets, to hold
The hounds in leash and join the daylong chase
Through the rough mountain ridges, nourishing
His heart's desire with long companionship.
    One day, near noon, when the high sun midway
Between the night past and the night to come
At equal distance stood from dawn and dusk,
They both stripped off their clothes and oiled their limbs,
So sleek and splendid, and began the game,
Throwing the discus; and Apollo first
Poised, swung and hurled it skywards through the air,
Up, soaring up, to cleave the waiting clouds.
The heavy disk at longest last fell back
To the familiar earth, a proof of skill,
And strength with skill. Then straightway Hyacinth,
Unthinking,* in the excitement of the sport,
Ran out to seize it, but it bounded back
From the hard surface full into his face.
The god turned pale, pale as the boy himself,
And catching up the huddled body, tried
To revive him, tried to staunch the tragic wound

And stay the fading soul with healing herbs.
His skill was vain; the wound was past all cure.
And as, when in a garden violets
Or lilies tawny-tongued or poppies proud
Are bruised and bent, at once they hang their heads
And, drooping, cannot stand erect and bow
Their gaze upon the ground; so dying lies
That face so fair and, all strength ebbed away,
His head, too heavy, on his shoulder sinks.

   "My Hyacinth", Apollo cried, "laid low
And cheated of youth's prime! I see your wound,
My condemnation, you my grief and guilt!
I, I have caused your death; on my own hand,
My own, your doom is written. Yet what wrong
Is mine unless to join the game with you
Were wrong or I were wrong to love you well?
Oh, would for you—or with you—I might give
My life! But since the laws of fate forbid,
You shall be with me always; you shall stay
For ever in remembrance on my lips,
And you my lyre and you my song shall hymn.
A new flower you shall be with letters marked
To imitate my sobs, and time shall come
When to that flower the bravest hero born*
Shall add his name on the same petals writ."

   So with prophetic words Apollo spoke,
And lo! the flowing blood that stained the grass
Was blood no longer; and a flower* rose
Gorgeous as Tyrian dye, in form a lily,
Save that a lily wears a silver hue,
This richest purple. And, not yet content,
Apollo (who had wrought the work of grace)
Inscribed upon the flower his lament,
AI AI, AI AI, and still the petals show
The letters written there in words of woe.
And Sparta's pride in Hyacinth, her son,
Endures undimmed; with pomp and proud display
Each year his feast* returns in the ancient way.

   But should you ask ore-laden Amathus*
If her Propoetides have brought her pride,

She would reject alike both them and those
Whose brows twin horns made hideous, whence their name,
Cerastae. Once an altar stood before
Their doors to Jove, the God of Hospitality.
A newcomer who did not know their guilt,
Seeing that altar stained with blood, would think
That suckling calves or lambs of Amathus
Were offered there. It was the blood of guests!
Kind Venus, outraged by these wicked rites,
Prepared to leave her cities and the land
Of Cyprus. "Yet", she said, "these towns of mine,
These charming places, what have they done wrong?
Rather this impious race shall pay the price
By death or exile or some means half-way
Between the two, and that, what can it be*
Except to change their shape to something new?"
What change to choose, she wondered; then, her eyes
Lighting upon their horns, she realized
Those could be left to them, and she transformed
Their bulky bodies into savage bulls.
    Even so the obscene Propoetides had dared
Deny Venus' divinity. For that
The goddess' rage, it's said, made them the first*
Strumpets to prostitute their bodies' charms.
As shame retreated and their cheeks grew hard,
They turned with little change to stones of flint.

PYGMALION transformation of material.

Pygmalion had seen these women spend
Their days in wickedness, and horrified
At all the countless vices nature gives
To womankind lived celibate and long
Lacked the companionship of married love.
Meanwhile he carved his snow-white ivory
With marvellous triumphant artistry
And gave it perfect shape, more beautiful   *he carved a woman*
Than ever woman born. His masterwork   *and fell in love*
Fired him with love. It seemed to be alive,   *with her.*
Its face to be a real girl's, a girl

Who wished to move—but modesty forbade.
Such art his art concealed.* In admiration
His heart desired the body he had formed.
With many a touch he tries it—is it flesh
Or ivory? Not ivory still, he's sure!
Kisses he gives and thinks they are returned;
He speaks to it, caresses it, believes
The firm new flesh beneath his fingers yields,
And fears the limbs may darken with a bruise.
And now fond words he whispers, now brings gifts
That girls delight in—shells and polished stones,
And little birds and flowers of every hue,
Lilies and coloured balls and beads of amber,
The tear-drops of the daughters of the Sun.*
He decks her limbs with robes and on her fingers
Sets splendid rings, a necklace round her neck,
Pearls in her ears, a pendant on her breast;
Lovely she looked, yet unadorned she seemed
In nakedness no whit less beautiful.
He laid her on a couch of purple silk,
Called her his darling, cushioning her head,
As if she relished it, on softest down.

　　Venus' day came, the holiest festival
All Cyprus celebrates; incense rose high
And heifers, with their wide horns gilded, fell
Beneath the blade that struck their snowy necks.
Pygmalion, his offering given, prayed
Before the altar, half afraid, "Vouchsafe,
O Gods, if all things you can grant, my bride
Shall be"—he dared not say my ivory girl—
"The living likeness of my ivory girl."
And golden Venus (for her presence graced
Her feast) knew well the purpose of his prayer;
And, as an omen of her favouring power,
Thrice did the flame burn bright and leap up high.
And he went home, home to his heart's delight,
And kissed her as she lay, and she seemed warm;
Again he kissed her and with marvelling touch
Caressed her breast; beneath his touch the flesh
Grew soft, its ivory hardness vanishing,

And yielded to his hands, as in the sun
Wax of Hymettus softens and is shaped
By practised fingers into many forms,
And usefulness acquires by being used.
His heart was torn with wonder and misgiving,
Delight and terror that it was not true!
Again and yet again he tried his hopes—
She was alive! The pulse beat in her veins!
And then indeed in words that overflowed
He poured his thanks to Venus, and at last
His lips pressed real lips, and she, his girl,
Felt every kiss, and blushed, and shyly raised
Her eyes to his and saw the world and him.
The goddess graced the union she had made,
And when nine times the crescent moon had filled
Her silver orb, an infant girl was born,
Paphos, from whom the island takes its name.

MYRRHA

Her son was Cinyras, who might have been
Numbered among the fortunate, had he
Been childless. Terrible my tale will be!
Away, daughters!* Away, parents! Away!
Or, if my singing charms you, hold *this* tale
In disbelief; suppose the deed not done;
Or, with belief, believe the punishment.
If nature does allow such crimes at least
How happy are our countrymen, this land
Of Thrace,* this world of ours, to be so far
From realms that rear such sin. Panchaia* may
Enjoy her wealth of mace and cinnamon,
Her oozing incense and her balsam's balm,
And all her spicy blooms, so long as she
Grows myrrh as well! That new tree cost too much!
Cupid himself denies his arrows hurt
Myrrha and clears his torch of that offence.
One of the three dread Sisters* blasted her
With viper's venom and firebrands of Hell.
To hate one's father is a crime; this love

A greater crime than hate.
                                    From everywhere
The eager suitors came; the golden youth
Of all the Orient vied to win her hand.
Choose, Myrrha, one among that company
So long as *one* among them shall not be!
In truth she fought the love she felt was foul.
"What are these thoughts?" she asked herself; "My aim,
What is it? May the gods, may duty's bond,
The sacred rights of parents, stop this crime,
If it is crime. Yet surely duty's bond
They say does not condemn such love as this.
Why, other creatures couple as they choose
Regardless. If a heifer's mounted by
Her father, that's no shame; a horse becomes
His daughter's husband; goats will mate with kids
They've sired themselves; why, even birds conceive
From seed that fathered them. How blest are they
That have such licence! Human nicety
Makes spiteful laws. What nature will allow,
Their jealous code forbids. Yet there exist*
Peoples, it's said, where sons will marry mothers
And daughters fathers, and their doubled love
Increases duty's bond. But I, poor me,
Was not so lucky—I was not born there.
The chance of birthplace injures me.——Oh, why
Hark back to things like that? Away, away,
Forbidden hopes! He's worthy of my love,
Yes, but as father.——Well then, were I not
Great Cinyras's daughter, I could lie
With Cinyras. But now because he's mine,
He isn't mine! Propinquity itself
Does damage; I'd do better not so near.
I'd wish to go away and leave afar
My native borders, could I flee from crime.
But evil fires hold my heart here, to keep
Beloved Cinyras before my eyes,
To touch him, speak with him, and kiss him too,
If nothing more's allowed. What more? Can you
Set more before your eyes, you wicked girl?

Think of the tangled knot of ties and names!
Will you become your father's concubine,
Your mother's rival? Shall men label you
Your brother's mother, sister of your son?
Surely the snake-haired Sisters frighten you,
Whom guilty souls see aiming at their eyes
Their fiendish flaming torches. Come, while yet
No sin's committed, banish thoughts of sin,
Nor ever foul great nature's covenant
By that forbidden act! Wish as you may,
The facts forbid. He's righteous! Yes, he'll not
Forget the claim of duty. Oh, to see
In him the same mad fire that flames in me!"
   Now Cinyras, confronted with a crowd
Of worthy suitors, doubting what to do,
Asked Myrrha herself, enquiring name by name
Whom she would have for husband. She at first
Was silent, gazing in her father's face, her thoughts
In turmoil, hot tears welling in her eyes.
And Cinyras, who thought her tears were but
A girl's misgiving, told her not to cry,
And dried her cheeks and kissed her on the lips.
His kisses! Joy too thrilling! Then he asked
What kind of husband she would like, and she
Said "One like you". He did not understand
And praised her: "May you never lose your love
So dutiful!" At "dutiful" the girl
Lowered her eyes, too conscious of her guilt.
   Midnight had come and sleep relaxed the limbs
And cares of men, but Myrrha lay awake,
A prey to ungoverned passion, and resumed
Her frenzied longings, sometimes in despair,
Sometimes resolved to try, at once ashamed
And yearning, vainly groping for some plan.
And as a huge tree, wounded by an axe,
Only the last stroke left, will wait in doubt
Which way to fall and every side's in fear,
So Myrrha's mind, weakened by wound on wound,
Wavered uncertainly this way and that,
Nodding on either side and found no end,

No respite for her love except in death.
Death it shall be! She rises up resolved
To hang herself. Tying her girdle to
A beam, "Goodbye, dear Cinyras!" she moans,
"Goodbye, and understand why I must die",
And fits the noose around her death-pale neck.

They say some sound, some whisper of her words
Came to her nurse's ears, her faithful nurse,*
Guarding her Myrrha's room. The old nurse rose,
Opened the door and saw the means of death.
She shrieked and beat her breast and tore her robe,
And in the same short moment, seizing the noose,
Snatched it from Myrrha's neck. Then she had time
At last for tears, and took her in her arms
And asked the reason for the rope. The girl
Was silent, dumb, her gaze fixed on the ground,
Distraught that her attempt had been found out
And death too late. The old nurse pressed her hard,
Baring her white locks and her empty breasts,
And begged her by her cradle, by the feeds
Of her first days, to trust her with the cause
Of her distress. She groaned and turned away.
Resolved to find the truth, the old nurse pledged
Not only secrecy. "Tell me", she said,
"And let me help you. My old age is not
Inactive. If your mind's unhinged, my herbs
And spells can cure it; if you've been bewitched,
You shall be purified with magic rites;
If it's gods' anger, angry gods may be
Appeased by sacrifice. What else, I wonder?
Your fortunes and your home are safe, I'm sure,
And all goes as it should. Your mother's well,
Your father too." At "father" Myrrha sighed,
Sighed from the bottom of her heart. But still
The nurse imagined nothing villainous,
But sensed some love affair, and persevered
And begged the girl, whatever it might be,
To tell it her; and raised her as she wept
To her old bosom and, enfolding her
Thus in her feeble arms, "I know", she said,

"You are in love. Don't be afraid! In this
My diligence may serve you very well.
Your father shall know nothing." With a bound
Myrrha, beside herself, sprang up and sank
Face-down among the pillows. "Go away!"
She pleaded, "Spare my misery and shame!"
And, as the nurse pressed, "Go!" she screamed, "or stop
Asking what tortures me. It is a crime
You work so hard to know." Shocked and aghast,
The good old woman stretched her trembling hands,
Shaking with age and dread, and falling on
Her knees before her darling's feet she tried
Now winning words, now fear to make her share
Her secret, threatening to report the noose
And death-attempt, and promising her best
Service if she'll confide her love to her.
Then Myrrha raised her head; her gushing tears
Rained down her nurse's bosom. Many a time
She attempted to confess and many a time
Bit her words back, and held her dress to hide
Her face of shame. Then "Mother", came the words,
"How happy in your husband!" Nothing more
Except a groan. An icy shudder ran
Through the old woman's frame (she understood)
And every hair upon her snowy head
Stood stiff on end; and many many words
She poured to expel that passion if she could,
So terrible. The girl well knew the truth
Of what she warned; but still her purpose held
To die unless she had her heart's desire.
"'Live then", the nurse replied, "and have your—"* not
Daring to utter "father", she stopped short
In silence, then she called the gods of heaven
To ratify the promise she had given.
    The time of Ceres' festival had come,
In duty kept by mothers every year,
When, robed in white, they bring their firstfruit gifts
Of wheat in garlands, and for nine nights count
Love and the touch of men forbidden things.
The king's wife Cenchreis was there among

The worshippers and joined the sacred rites.
So while the king's bed lacked a lawful wife,
The old bad-busy nurse found Cinyras
Well-wined and gave him tidings of a girl
Who loved him truly (naming a false name),
And when he asked her age, "The same", she said,
"As Myrrha's". So he bade her bring the girl,
And she, returning home, "My darling child,
Rejoice!" she said, "we've won." The ill-starred girl
Felt no whole-hearted joy. Forebodings filled
Her soul with sadness; even so joy too
Was there—her warring thoughts were so confused.
    It was the hour when all the world is silent,
And high between the Bears the Wagoner*
With slanting shaft had turned his starry Wain.
Now to her deed she went. The golden moon
Fled from the sky;* the stars lay hid behind
A canopy of cloud; night's fires were lost.
(The first to hide his face was Icarus,
And with him dutiful Erigone,
Who loved her father and was raised to heaven.)
Three times a boding stumble warned her back,
Three times a screech-owl, bird of doom, declared
The omen with its deadly threnody.
Yet on she went, the darkness of the night
Dwindling her shame. Her left hand held her nurse,
Her right groped the blind passage. Now she's reached
The room, now found the door and opened it,
And now she's led inside. Her shaking knees
Give way, blood fails her cheeks, and as she goes
Her senses reel. The nearer to her crime,
The more her horror. Would she'd never dared!
Would she could steal away unrecognized!
As she hung back, the old nurse took her hand
And led her to the high-raised couch and said
"She's yours,* your Majesty. Take her"; and joined
The pair in doom. In that incestuous bed
The father took his flesh and blood, and calmed
Her girlish fears and cheered her bashfulness.
Maybe, to suit her age, he called her "daughter"

And she him "father"—names to seal the crime.
     Filled with her father Myrrha left the room,
His wicked seed within her tragic womb,
The crime conceived. The next night saw the deed
Doubled, and that was not the end. At last,
After so many times, eager to know
Who was the girl who loved him, Cinyras
Brought in a lamp* and saw his crime and her,
His daughter. Dumb in agony, he drew
His flashing sword that hung there. Myrrha fled.
The darkness and the night's blind benison
Saved her from death. Across the countryside
She wandered till she left the palm-fringed lands
Of Araby and rich Panchaia's fields.
Nine times the crescent of the moon returned
And still she roamed, and then she found at last
Rest for her weariness on Saba's* soil;
She scarce could bear the burden of her womb.
And then, not knowing what to wish, afraid
Of death and tired of life, she framed these words
Of prayer: "If Powers of heaven are open to
The cries of penitents, I've well deserved—
I'll not refuse—the pain of punishment,
But lest I outrage, if I'm left alive,
The living, or, if I shall die, the dead,
Expel me from both realms; some nature give
That's different; let me neither die nor live!"*
Some Power is open to a penitent;
For sure her final prayer found gods to hear.*
For, as she spoke, around her legs the earth
Crept up; roots thrusting from her toes
Spread sideways, firm foundations of a trunk;
Her bones gained strength; though marrow still remained,
Blood became sap, her fingers twigs, her arms
Branches, her skin was hardened into bark.
And now the growing tree had tightly swathed
Her swelling womb, had overlapped her breast,
Ready to wrap her neck. She would not wait,
But sinking down to meet the climbing wood,
Buried her face and forehead in the bark.

Though with her body she had forfeited
Her former feelings, still she weeps and down
The tree the warm drops ooze. Those tears in truth
Have honour; from the trunk the weeping myrrh
Keeps on men's lips for aye the name of her.
　　The child conceived in sin had grown inside
The wood and now was searching for some way
To leave its mother and thrust forth. The trunk
Swelled in the middle with its burdened womb.
The load was straining, but the pains of birth
Could find no words, nor voice in travail call
Lucina. Yet the tree, in labour, stooped
With groan on groan and wet with falling tears.
Then, pitying, Lucina stood beside
The branches in their pain and laid her hands
Upon them and pronounced the words of birth.
The tree split open and the sundered bark
Yielded its living load; a baby boy
Squalled, and the Naiads laid him on soft grass
And bathed him in his mother's flowing tears.
Envy herself would praise his looks; for like
The little naked Loves that pictures show
He lay there, give or take the slender bow.

VENUS AND ADONIS

Time glides in secret and his wings deceive;
Nothing is swifter than the years. That son,
Child of his sister and his grandfather,
So lately bark-enswathed, so lately born,
Then a most lovely infant, then a youth,
And now a man more lovely than the boy,
Was Venus' darling (Venus'!) and avenged
His mother's passion. Once, when Venus' son
Was kissing her, his quiver dangling down,
A jutting arrow, unbeknown, had grazed
Her breast. She pushed the boy away.
In fact the wound was deeper than it seemed,
Though unperceived at first. Enraptured by
The beauty of a man, she cared no more

For her Cythera's shores nor sought again
Her sea-girt Paphos nor her Cnidos, famed
For fish, nor her ore-laden Amathus.
She shunned heaven too: to heaven she preferred
Adonis. Him she clung to, he was her
Constant companion. She who always used
To idle in the shade and take such pains
To enhance her beauty, roamed across the hills,
Through woods and brambly boulders, with her dress
Knee-high like Dian's, urging on the hounds,
Chasing the quarry when the quarry's safe—
Does and low-leaping hares and antlered deer—
But keeping well away from brigand wolves
And battling boars and bears well-armed with claws
And lions soaked in slaughter of the herds.
She warned Adonis too, if warnings could
Have been of any use, to fear those beasts.
"Be brave when backs are turned, but when they're bold,
Boldness is dangerous. Never be rash,
My darling, to my risk; never provoke
Quarry that nature's armed, lest your renown
Should cost me dear. Not youth, not beauty, nor
Charms that move Venus' heart can ever move
Lions or bristly boars or eyes or minds
Of savage beasts. In his curved tusks a boar
Wields lightning; tawny lions launch their charge
In giant anger. Creatures of that kind
I hate." And when Adonis asked her why,
'I'll tell", she said, "a tale to astonish you
Of ancient guilt and magic long ago.
But my unwonted toil has made me tired
And, look, a poplar, happily at hand,
Drops shade for our delight, and greensward gives
A couch. Here I would wish to rest with you"
(She rested) "on the ground", and on the grass
And him she lay, her head upon his breast,
And mingling kisses with her words began.

ATALANTA

"You may perchance have heard how in the races
A girl outran the men who ran to win.
That was no idle tale; she always won.
Nor could one say her gift of glorious speed
Was more surpassing than her loveliness.
An oracle that once she had consulted*
About a husband had declared 'No husband,
Fair Atalanta, is for you; refuse
A husband's kisses; yet you'll not refuse,
And you, while still you live, yourself shall lose.'
The fate foretold appalled her, and she lived
Alone, unwedded in the shady woods,
And angrily repulsed the pressing throng
Of suitors with a challenge: 'No man's wife
Am I', she said, 'unless he wins the race.
Contend with me in speed. For speed the prize
Is wife and wedlock; for the slow the price
Is death: upon that rule the race is run.'
Her heart was pitiless, yet, such the power
Of beauty, on that rule rash lovers thronged.

    To watch the unequal race Hippomenes
Sat in his seat and scoffed 'Would any man
At such dire peril wish to win a wife?'
And blamed the young men for their love's excess.
But when he saw her face and, now unrobed,*
Her body's beauty, beauty such as mine,
Adonis, or as yours were you a girl,
He marvelled and, with hands upraised, exclaimed
'Forgive my censuring words; I had not known
The peerless prize you seek.' And with his praise
Love burgeoned and he prayed that none would run
Faster than she, and fear and envy filled
His heart. 'But why', he thought, 'do I not try
Myself my fortune in this rivalry?
The gods help those who dare.' And, while he mused,
On wingèd feet the glorious girl flew by.
And though her speed seemed like an arrow's flight,
Yet more he marvelled at her glowing grace—

And running gave her grace; the breeze blew back
The ribbons* from her ankles and her knees
In fluttering colours; down her ivory back
Her long hair streamed behind; a rosy flush
Painted the girlish pallor of her limbs,
As when a scarlet awning in the sun
Is drawn above a marble vestibule*
And dyes, or seems to dye, the coloured shade.
These things the newcomer Hippomenes
Marked well; and then the final lap was run
And Atalanta with the festal wreath
Of victory was crowned; the losers groaned
And duly paid the appointed penalty.
    But young Hippomenes was undismayed
By the others' fate and in the midst stood forth
And fixed his eyes upon the girl, and said
'Why seek an easy fame defeating sluggards?
Contend with me. If fortune favours me,
There'll be no shame to yield the victory.
My father's Megareus of Onchestus;*
His grandfather was Neptune; great-grandson
Of Ocean's king am I, nor does my birth
Exceed my prowess—or, if I should fail,
The victor of Hippomenes shall win
A memorable name, a great renown.'
And as he spoke King Schoeneus' daughter gazed
With tender eyes and doubted in her heart
Whether this time she wished to win or lose.
'What god', she thought, 'who envies beauty's charms,
Desires his death and bids him seek a bride
At hazard of his own dear life? So much
Is more than I am worth. It's not his beauty
That touches me (though that could touch me too);
But he is still a boy; it's not himself
That moves me but his tender years, his youth.
Think of his courage, unafraid of death,
His lineage, fourth from Ocean's mighty lord,
His love that counts our wedlock worth so much
That he would die, if fate denied my love.
Go, stranger, while you may! Blood stains my bed;*

Oh cruel bane were I your bride! But you
None will refuse; some wiser girl than I
One happy day will wish to be your bride.——
But why do I care for you, when other men
Have died before, so many, for my sake?
So fend then for yourself! Yes, let him die
Since by so many deaths he is not warned
And wearies of his life!——Then shall he perish
Because he longed to live with me, and pay
The price of love in death so undeserved?
My victory will bring more bitterness
Than I can bear! And yet the fault's not mine!
Would that your heart might change, or, since your heart
Is crazed, you might outrun me in the race!
Oh, how his boy's fair face is like a girl's!
Oh, poor Hippomenes, that you should ever
Have looked on me! How you deserved to live!
Were I not so ill-starred, would fate but yield
And not deny me marriage, you alone
I'd choose to be companion of my bed.'
Artless she was, and when at last love came,
She burned, but never thought it was love's flame.

     And now her father and the townspeople
Called for the usual race, and Neptune's prince,
Hippomenes, with anxious voice, invoked
My help and prayed: 'Come, lovely Cytherea,
Prosper the deed I dare and with thy grace
Nourish the flame of love that thou hast lit.'
A kindly breeze wafted his charming prayer;
It moved me, I admit, and little time
Was left to succour him. There is a field
The people call the close of Tamasus,
The richest part of all the isle of Cyprus,
Which long ago was hallowed in my name
And added as endowment to my shrine.
A tree stands in the close with leaves of gold
And golden branches* rustling in the breeze.
On my way thence it chanced that in my hand
I held three golden apples I had picked
And I stood by Hippomenes, unseen

Except by him, and taught* the apples' use.

The trumpets sound the start; both crouching low
Flash from their marks and skim the sandy course
With flying feet; it seemed that they could race
Dry-shod across the surface of the sea*
And over the standing heads of harvest corn.
The shouting crowd cheered on the newcomer:
'Run, run, Hippomenes! Now is your chance!
Now! Faster! Faster! Run with all your speed!
You're going to win!' And hard it was to know
Who liked their words the more, Hippomenes
Or Atalanta. Many a time she slowed
When she might pass and gazed into his eyes,
And with a heavy heart left him behind.
And now he flagged, his breath came fast and dry
And there was far to go; so then he threw
One of the three gold apples from the tree.
She was amazed and, eager to secure
The gleaming fruit, swerved sideways from the track
And seized the golden apple as it rolled.
He passed her and the benches roared applause.
She with a burst of speed repaired her waste
Of time and soon again left him behind.
He threw the second apple and again
She stopped, and followed, and again ran past.
And so the last lap came. 'Be with me now,
Goddess', he prayed, 'who gavest me the gift.'
And then with all the strength of youth he threw
The shining gold far out across the field,
The longer to delay the girl; and she
Seemed undecided, but I made her chase
The rolling apple and increased its weight,
And by its weight alike and loss of speed
I hindered her. And, not to make my tale
More lengthy than the race, she lost the day
And he, victorious, led his prize away.

And I, Adonis, did I not deserve
Especial thanks and incense in my honour?
But he forgot; he gave no thanks and burnt
No incense; then to sudden wrath I turned.

Stung by his scorn and lest I be despised
In days to come, I set my heart against
Them both, to warn the world by their example.
A temple stands hidden in shady woods,
Which once Echion* to fulfil a vow
Had raised to the great Mother of the Gods.
There they had journeyed and were glad to rest;
And there ill-timed importunate desire,
Roused by my power, possessed Hippomenes.
Beside the temple was a dim-lit grotto,
A gloomy cavern, roofed with natural rock,
An ancient holy shrine, filled by the priest
With wooden statues* of the gods of old.
He entered here and with forbidden sin
Defiled the sanctuary. The holy statues
Turned their shocked eyes away and Cybele,
The tower-crowned Mother, pondered should she plunge
The guilty pair beneath the waves of Styx.
Such punishment seemed light.* Therefore their necks,
So smooth before, she clothed with tawny manes,
Their fingers curved to claws; their arms were changed
To legs; their chests swelled with new weight; with tails
They swept the sandy ground; and in their eyes
Cruel anger blazed and growls they gave for speech.
Their marriage-bed is now a woodland lair,
And feared by men, but by the goddess tamed,
They champ—two lions—the bits of Cybele.
And you, my darling, for my sake beware
Of lions and of every savage beast
That shows not heels but teeth; avoid them all
Lest by your daring ruin on us fall."
　　Her warning given, Venus made her way,
Drawn by her silver swans across the sky;
But his bold heart rebuffed her warning words.
It chanced his hounds, hot on a well-marked scent,
Put up a boar, lying hidden in the woods,
And as it broke away Adonis speared it—
A slanting hit—and quick with its curved snout
The savage beast dislodged the bloody point,
And charged Adonis as he ran in fear

For safety, and sank its tusks deep in his groin
And stretched him dying on the yellow sand.
Venus was riding in her dainty chariot,
Winged by her swans, across the middle air
Making for Cyprus, when she heard afar
Adonis' dying groans, and thither turned
Her snowy birds and, when from heaven on high
She saw him lifeless, writhing in his blood,
She rent her garments, tore her lovely hair,
And bitterly beat her breast, and springing down
Reproached the Fates: "Even so, not everything
Shall own your sway. Memorials of my sorrow,*
Adonis, shall endure; each passing year
Your death repeated in the hearts of men
Shall re-enact my grief and my lament.
But now your blood shall change into a flower:
Persephone of old was given grace
To change a woman's form to fragrant mint;*
And shall I then be grudged the right to change
My prince?" And with these words she sprinkled nectar,
Sweet-scented, on his blood, which at the touch
Swelled up, as on a pond* when showers fall
Clear bubbles form; and ere an hour had passed
A blood-red flower arose, like the rich bloom
Of pomegranates* which in a stubborn rind
Conceal their seeds; yet is its beauty brief,
So lightly cling its petals, fall so soon,
When the winds blow that give the flower its name.'*

Orpheus is denying himself of love.

BOOK XI

THE DEATH OF ORPHEUS

WHILE Orpheus sang his minstrel's songs* and charmed *resumes the story.*
The rocks and woods and creatures of the wild
To follow, suddenly, as he swept his strings
In concord with his song, a frenzied band
Of Thracian women, wearing skins of beasts, *Thracis a country northeast of Macedonia*
From some high ridge of ground caught sight of him.
'Look!' shouted one of them, tossing her hair
That floated in the breeze, 'Look, there he is,
The man who scorns us!'* and she threw her lance *Virgil 'no love, no thought, no marriage moved his mind.'*
Full in Apollo's minstrel's face, but, tipped
With leaves,* it left a bruise but drew no blood.
Another hurled a stone; that, in mid air, *entheus waves an olive-branch*
Was vanquished by the strains of voice and lyre
And grovelled at his feet, as if to ask
Pardon for frenzy's daring. Even so
The reckless onslaught swelled; their fury knew
No bounds; stark madness reigned. And still his singing
Would have charmed every weapon, but the huge *country in Asia Minor*
Clamour, the drums, the curving Phrygian fifes,
Hand-clapping, Bacchic screaming drowned the lyre.
And then at last, his song unheard, his blood
Reddened the stones. The Maenads first pounced on
The countless birds still spellbound by his song,
The snakes, the host of creatures of the wild,
His glory and his triumph. Next they turned
Their bloody hands on Orpheus, flocking like *epic simile*
Birds that have seen a midnight owl abroad
By day, or in the amphitheatre* *these wild beast hunts began the program. draws attention to NATURE.*
Upon the morning sand a pack of hounds
Round a doomed stag. They rushed upon the bard,
Hurling their leaf-dressed lances, never meant
For work like that; and some slung clods, some flints,
Some branches torn from trees. And, lest they lack
Good weapons for their fury, as it chanced,
Oxen were toiling there to plough the land

And brawny farmhands digging their hard fields
Not far away, and sweating for their crop.
Seeing the horde of women, they fled and left
Their labour's armoury, and all across
The empty acres lay their heavy rakes,
Hoes and long-handled mattocks. Seizing these,
Those frantic women tore apart the oxen*
That threatened with their horns, and streamed to slay
The bard. He pleaded then with hands outstretched
And in that hour for the first time his words
Were useless and his voice of no avail.
In sacrilege they slew him. Through those lips
(Great Lord of Heaven!) that held the rocks entranced,
That wild beasts understood, he breathed his last,
And forth into the winds his spirit passed.

    The sorrowing birds, the creatures of the wild,
The woods that often followed as he sang,
The flinty rocks and stones, all wept and mourned
For Orpheus;* forest trees cast down their leaves,
Tonsured in grief, and rivers too, men say,
Were swollen with their tears,* and Naiads wore,
And Dryads too, their mourning robes of black
And hair dishevelled. All around his limbs
Lay scattered. Hebrus'* stream received his head
And lyre, and floating by (so wonderful!)
His lyre sent sounds of sorrow and his tongue,
Lifeless, still murmured sorrow, and the banks
Gave sorrowing reply. And then they left
Their native river, carried out to sea,
And gained Methymna's shore on Lesbos' isle.
There, as his head lay on that foreign sand,
Its tumbled tresses dripping, a fierce snake*
Threatened, until at last Apollo came
To thwart it as it struck and froze to stone
That serpent's open mouth and petrified,
Just as they were, its jaws that gaped so wide.
    The ghost of Orpheus passed to the Underworld,
And all the places that he'd seen before
He recognized again and, searching through
The Elysian fields, he found Eurydice*

And took her in his arms with leaping heart.
There hand in hand they stroll, the two together;
Sometimes he follows as she walks in front,
Sometimes he goes ahead and gazes back—
No danger now—at his Eurydice.
　　Bacchus did not permit this crime to pass
Unpunished, unavenged.* Distressed to lose
The minstrel of his mysteries, at once
He fastened in the woods by twisting roots
All the women who had seen that wickedness,
Each at the place of her pursuit, their toes
Drawn down to points forced deep in the firm soil.
And as a bird, its foot held in a snare
Hidden by a clever fowler, feels it's caught
And flaps its wings and by its flutterings
Tightens the trap, so each of them was stuck
Fast in the soil and struggled, terrified,
In vain, to escape and as she jerked away,
The lithe root held her shackled. When she asked
Where were her toes, her nails, her feet, she saw
The bark creep up her shapely calves. She tried,
Distraught, to beat her thighs and what she struck
Was oak, her breast was oak, her shoulders oak;
Her arms likewise you'd think were changed to long
Branches and, thinking so, you'd not be wrong.
　　For Bacchus this was not enough. He left
Those Thracian fields and with a worthier train
Made for the slopes and vineyards of his own
Beloved Tmolus and Pactolus' banks,
Though at that time the river did not flow
Golden nor envied for its precious sands.
Around him thronged his usual company,
Satyrs and Bacchants, but Silenus then
Was missing. For the peasants of those parts
Had caught the old man, tottering along
Muddled with wine and years, and crowned his head
With country flowers and brought him to their king,
Midas, whom Orpheus and Eumolpus* once
Had taught the Bacchic rites. He recognized
His old companion of the mysteries,

And for his guest made merry in a feast
For ten great days on end and nights to match;
Then on the eleventh morning Lucifer
Marshalled the starry host to leave the sky,
And Midas came to Lydia, light at heart,
Bringing Silenus back to his young ward.

MIDAS

Bacchus, rejoicing in the safe return
Of old Silenus (once his guardian),
Granted the king to choose his heart's desire,
A choice that seemed a boon, but proved a bane.*
So Midas chose, a sorry choice: 'Ordain
That everything I touch shall turn to gold.'
The god indulged his wish, gave the reward,
Dire as it was, and mourned a choice so bad.

    The king departed, happy with his bane,
And tried its truth by touching this and that,
And, scarce believing, from a low oak branch
Broke a green twig; the twig was changed to gold.
He stooped and grasped a stone; at once the stone
Shone with a golden sheen. He touched a clod;
His magic touch made it a lump of gold.
He picked ripe heads of wheat and in his hand
He held a golden crop. He plucked an apple;
It seemed the gift of the Hesperides.*
And if he laid his fingers on the pillars
Of his high palace, lo! the pillars gleamed.
When he but rinsed his hands in running water,
The water might have cheated Danae.*
His heart could hardly hold his golden hopes
When everything was gold. As he rejoiced,
His serving-men arrayed a sumptuous feast
And there were splendid wheaten loaves. But then,
Ah, then! when Midas reached his hand and touched
Kind Ceres' gift, that gift grew hard and stiff;
And when with watering mouth he tried to bite
The tempting food, he bit but golden flakes;

When wine, when water filled his glass, behold
Between his lips there flowed a stream of gold!
  Aghast at his grotesque calamity,
So rich, so wretched, he would fain escape
His wealth and hates what was but now his hope.
No plenty can relieve his hunger; thirst
Burns in his throat; justly the loathsome gold
Tortures him and, with hands upraised, he cries,
'Grant pardon, Bacchus, father, I have sinned!
Have mercy, I beseech thee! Hear my prayer
And save me from the curse that gleams so fair!'
The gods are kind. Bacchus, the sin confessed,
Restored him and discharged the pact and pledge.
'And lest', he said, 'you stay bedaubed with gold—
Your foolish choice—betake you to that river
That girdles mighty Sardis* and ascend
The Lydian hills against the tumbling stream
Up to its source and, where with fullest flood
It issues foaming, plunge your head and body,
And in its waters wash your crime away.'
The king obeyed and plunged beneath the flow,
And in the foam, passing from man to river,
The golden power dissolved and tinged the stream;
And still today,* washed by that ancient vein,
The water-meadows gleam with seeds of gold.
  Then, loathing riches, Midas gave his heart
To fields and forests and the countryside
And Pan who dwells among the mountain caves.
But crass his wits* remained, in folly set
To bring their master trouble as before.
  The crags of Tmolus, steep and wide and high,
Gazing across the sea, at one side fall
To Sardis, at the other reach their end
At small Hypaepae. There Pan sang his songs,
Flaunting among the gentle nymphs, and played
Light airs upon his pipes, and dared to boast
Apollo's music second to his own,
Essaying with old Tmolus as the judge
Unequal contest. On his mountain top*
The judge was seated; from his ears he freed

The forest trees; only a wreath of oak
Fringed his green locks, with acorns dangling round
His hollow temples. Then, looking towards
The shepherd-god, he said, 'The judge attends.'
So Pan made music on his rustic reeds
And with his uncouth song entranced the king.
(Midas by chance was there.) To Phoebus next
Grave Tmolus turned and, as he turned, his fringe
Of trees turned too. Apollo's golden hair
Was garlanded with laurel of Parnassus;
His mantle, rich with Tyrian purple, swept
The ground he trod; in his left hand he bore
His lyre, inlaid with gems and ivory;
His right the plectrum held; his very pose
Proclaimed the artist. Then with expert touch
He plucked the strings and, won by strains so sweet,
Old Tmolus bade the reed bow to the lyre.

The sacred mountain's judgement and award
Pleased all who heard; yet one voice challenging,
Crass-witted Midas' voice, called it unjust.*
Apollo could not suffer ears so dull
To keep their human shape. He stretched them long,
Filled them with coarse grey hairs, and hinged their base
To move and twitch and flop; all else was man;
In that one part his punishment; he wears
Henceforth a little ambling ass's ears.
Disfigured and ashamed he sought to hide
His temples with a clinging purple turban.*
Even so the slave whose scissors used to trim
His flowing hair saw all, and longed to spread
The news, but neither dared betray the shame
Nor yet could keep it close. So off he went
And dug a hole, and whispered in the hole
What sort of ears his master had, and then
Threw back the earth again and buried deep
His voice's evidence, and when the hole
Was full and smooth he stole home silently.
But there a waving bed of whispering reeds
Began to grow and, as the year came full,
Stood ripe and tall and, by and by, betrayed

His husbandry. For in the soft south wind
They sway and speak the buried words and tell
The tale* of Midas and his ass's ears.

FIRST FOUNDATION AND DESTRUCTION OF TROY

His vengeance won, Apollo made his way*
From Tmolus through the bright clear air and reached,
On the same side of Helle's narrow strait,*
Laomedon's domains. An altar stands
Between two headlands, on the right Sigeum,
Rhaeteum on the left, an ancient shrine
Of Jove whose thunders speak to all the world.
And there he saw Laomedon at work,
Toiling to build the first new battlements
Of Troy, a huge slow formidable task,
Needing no small resources. With the god
Who wields the trident, father of the main,
Assuming mortal shape, he built* the walls
For Phrygia's monarch, striking at the start
A golden bargain for those battlements.
The work stood built: the king denied the debt,
With perjury to cap his perfidy.*
'You'll pay for this!' said Ocean's lord and sloped
All his vast waters to the shores of Troy,
Tight-fisted Troy, and filled the land to form
A seascape, swept away the farmers' wealth
And whelmed the countryside beneath the waves.
Nor did this punishment suffice; the king's
Daughter was claimed as well to satisfy
A monster of the deep. Chained to the rocks,
Hercules rescued her* and claimed his fee,
The promised horses,* and, the price of that
Great task denied him, seized the battlements,
Twice-perjured battlements, and conquered Troy.
Nor did his battle-comrade Telamon*
Leave without honour there—Hesione
Was the reward he won. For Peleus had
The glory of a goddess wife and pride
In her great father Nereus just as strong

As in his grandfather; for he, of course,
Was not alone a grandson of great Jove,*
But won alone a bride from heaven above.

PELEUS AND THETIS

Old Proteus* once had said to Thetis, 'Bear
A child, fair goddess of the waves. For you
Shall be the mother of a youth whose deeds
In his brave years of manhood shall surpass
His father's and he'll win a greater name.'
Therefore, for fear the world might ever have
A greater than himself, Jove shunned the bed
Of Thetis, fair sea-goddess, though his heart
Was fired with no cool flame, and in his place
As lover bade his grandson Peleus take
In his embrace the virgin of the waves.
    There is a curving bay* in Thessaly,
Shaped like a sickle; two long arms run out
And were the water deeper there would be
A harbour. Smooth across the shallow sand
The sea extends; the shore is firm; it holds
No footprints, slows no passage, slopes unlined
By seaweed. Myrtles grow near by, a grove
Of double-coloured berries. In their midst
There lies a grotto, formed maybe by art,
Maybe by nature, rather though by art,
Where Thetis used to come, naked, astride
Her bridled dolphin. There, as she lay lapped
In sleep, Peleus surprised her and, his fond
Entreaties all repulsed, assaulted her,
Winding his two strong arms around her neck.
And had she not resorted to her arts*
And changed her shape so often, he'd have gained
The end he dared. But first she was a bird—
That bird he held; and then a sturdy tree—
That tree he fastened on; her third shape was
A stripy tigress—Peleus, terrified,
Released his hold on her and let her go.
He prayed then to the sea-gods, offering wine

Poured on the water, smoke of incense, flesh
Of sheep, till Proteus from his briny deep
Said, 'Peleus, you shall gain the bride you seek
If, while she's sleeping in her rocky cave,
You catch her off her guard and truss her tight
With ropes that won't give way and, though she takes
A hundred spurious shapes, don't be deceived
But grapple it, whatever it is, until
She forms again the shape she had before.'
So Proteus spoke and sank into the sea,
His wavelets washing over his last words.*
     The sun was setting and his chariot
Sloped to the western waves, when the fair child
Of Nereus sought the grotto and resumed
Her usual couch. Peleus had barely touched
Her lovely limbs before from shape to shape
She changed, until she felt her body trussed,
Her arms pinioned apart. And then at last,
Sighing, 'With some god's* help', she said, 'you've won.'
And there revealed stood . . . Thetis. Self-confessed,
He held her, hopes triumphant, to his side
And filled with great Achilles his fair bride.

DAEDALION

His son, his wife brought Peleus blessedness
And all had prospered, could one clear the crime
Of Phocus'* murder. With his brother's blood
Upon his hands, forced from his father's house,
He found refuge in Trachis. Here the son
Of Lucifer, King Ceyx, reigned without
Bloodshed or force and in his royal face
His father's brightness shone, though at that time,
Unlike himself, he mourned in sorrow for
His brother's loss. Here Peleus, worn with cares
And travel's toil arrived and made his way
Into the city with his faithful few,
Leaving the sheep and cattle he had brought
Safe in a shady dell hard by the walls;
And, granted audience by the king, held out

His suppliant's olive-branch and told his name
And lineage, but kept his crime concealed
And hid with lies the reason for his flight.
The king's reply was gracious: 'In our state
Bounties lie open even to common folk
And ours is no inhospitable realm.
To these our traits you add strong motives too,
A name of glory and descent from Jove.
So waste no time in asking. What you seek,
All you shall have. Count this your own to share,
Such as you see. Would it were worthier!'
He wept; and Peleus and his comrades asked
The reason for such woe and he replied:
'Perhaps you think this bird that lives on prey,
The terror of the sky, has always had
Feathers. It was a man and—character
So constant—harsh and warlike then and prone
To violence, his name Daedalion.*
We two were brothers, children of the star
That wakes the dawn and leaves the heavens last.
My path was peace and peace was my pursuit,
And care for my dear wife. My brother's choice
Was cruel war. His prowess overthrew
Peoples and kings, as now in altered shape
It harasses the doves of Thisbe's* strand.
    He had a daughter, Chione, a girl
Most blessed with beauty's dower, her fourteen years
Ready for marriage, and her hand was sought
By countless suitors. Phoebus, as it chanced,
And Mercury, on their way back, the one
From Delphi, the other from Cyllene's crest,
Both saw her, both alike caught love's hot fire.
Phoebus delayed till night his hopes of love;
Mercury would not wait and with his wand
That soothes to slumber touched her on the lips;
Touch-tranced she lay and suffered his assault.
Night strewed the sky with stars; Apollo took
The guise of an old woman and obtained
His joys—forestalled. Her womb fulfilled its time
And to the wing-foot god a wily brat

Was born, Autolycus, adept at tricks
Of every kind, well used to make black white,
White black, a son who kept his father's skill.
To Phoebus there was born (for she had twins)
Philammon, famed alike for song and lyre.
What profit was it to have pleased two gods,
Produced two boys, to have a valiant father,
A shining grandfather? Is glory not
A curse as well? A curse indeed to many!
To her for sure! She dared to set herself
Above Diana, faulting her fair face.
The goddess, fierce in fury, cried "You'll like
My actions better!" and she bent her bow
And shot her arrow, and the shaft transfixed
That tongue that well deserved it. Then that tongue
Was dumb, speech failed the words she tried to say:
Her blood and life together ebbed away.

   Sadly I held her, feeling in my heart
Her father's grief, and gave my brother words
Of comfort, for he loved her—words he heard
As rocks the roaring waves—and bitterly
Bewailed his daughter's loss. Yes, when he saw
Her on the pyre, four times an impulse came
To rush into the flames; four times forced back,
He fled away in frenzy; like an ox,
Its bowed neck stung by hornets, so he charged
Where no way was. His speed seemed even then
Faster than man could run, and you'd believe
His feet had wings. So fleeing from us all,
With death-bent speed he gained Parnassus' crest.
Apollo, pitying, when Daedalion
Threw himself from a cliff made him a bird,
And held him hovering on sudden wings,
And gave him a hooked beak, gave curving claws,
With courage as of old and strength that more
Than matched his body's build. And now a hawk,
Benign to none, he vents his savagery
On every bird and, as in grief he goes,
Ensures that others grieve and share his woes.'

THE CATTLE OF PELEUS

Now while the son of Lucifer relates
His brother's miracle in bursts Onetor,
The royal herdsman, breathless in his haste,*
And 'Peleus, Peleus!' cries, 'I've brought the news—
Disaster!' Peleus bids him tell the worst,
And Ceyx trembles in suspense himself,
Fear in his face. 'I'd driven', the man said,
'My weary bullocks to the curving beach.
The sun stood at his zenith in mid course,
Seeing as much behind as lay ahead.
Some of the cattle knelt on the brown sand
And, lying, gazed across the wide flat sea;
Some wandered, ambling slowly to and fro;
Some swam or stood neck-deep amid the water.
Close to the sea a temple stood, not bright
With gold and marble, but a timber frame
Of beams and shaded by an ancient grove.
The shrine belonged to Nereus and his daughters
(They are the sea-gods there, a sailor said,
Spreading his nets to dry along the beach).
Adjoining it a marsh, a backwater
Left swampy by the tide, lay overgrown
With willows. Here a heavy crashing sound
Filled the whole place with fear—a giant beast!
A wolf! He came out smeared in swampy slime,
His great jaws flashing, flecked with blood and foam,
His eyes aflame. Hunger and fury both
Spurred him, but fury most. For when he killed
The cattle, he was not concerned to glut
His ghastly greed, but savaged the whole herd,
And in his battling blood-lust slew them all.
Some of ourselves too, trying to fend him off,
Were done to death, felled by his fatal fangs.
The beach and water's edge were red with blood,
The marsh too, all aroar with bellowings.
Before all's lost, together let us go!
To arms! To arms! All join against the foe!'
     The yokel finished. All his losses left

Peleus unmoved: remembering his crime,
He knew the Nereid whom he'd bereaved
Had sent these losses as a sacrifice
For murdered Phocus. Ceyx bade his men
Put on their mail and take their weaponry,
Ready himself to join them; but his wife,
Alcyone, roused by the noise and stir,
Ran out, her hair half-dressed, and tossed it back
And clinging round her husband's neck besought
Him, weeping, not to go himself, but save
Two lives in one.* Then Peleus: 'Lay aside,
Your majesty, those loyal fears of yours
That grace you well. Your promises fill me
With gratitude, but I have no desire
That this prodigious beast be brought to bay—
To the sea-goddess now I needs must pray!'
    There was a tower, a beacon high atop
The citadel, a landmark to rejoice
A weary ship. They climbed here and beheld,
With groans, the cattle strewn along the shore,
And the destroyer, wild and bloody-jawed,
His shaggy coat all red and caked with gore.
Stretching his hands towards the open sea,
Peleus addressed his prayers to Psamathe,
The wave-blue nymph, that she would end her wrath
And bring her succour. Her no prayer of his
Could turn, but Thetis* for her husband's sake
Pleaded and won her pardon. But the wolf,
Though called from his fierce slaughter, still kept on,
Wild with the nectar-taste of blood, until,
As he tore a heifer's neck and held it fast,
She changed him into marble. Everything
Save colour was preserved; the marble's hue
Proclaimed him wolf no longer and no more
A terror to be dreaded as before.
Yet in that country, even so, the Fates
Would not let banished Peleus find a home.
He roamed in exile to Magnesia,
And there Acastus, king of Thessaly,
Gave absolution for his guilt of blood.

CEYX AND ALCYONE

King Ceyx, shaken by his brother's fate
So monstrous and the uncanny things that followed,
Was fain to turn, as troubled men will turn,
For help and comfort to an oracle,
And planned a journey to the Clarian shrine,*
Since godless bandits blocked the mountain road
To holy Delphi. First he told his plan
To his devoted wife Alcyone.
Fear froze her to the marrow of her bones,
Her face turned pale as boxwood, and her cheeks
Were wet with flowing tears. Three times she strove
In vain to speak; three times her weeping eyes
Brimmed over; till at last, between her sobs,
In loving protest 'Oh, what fault of mine',
She cried, 'my dearest, has estranged your heart?
Your care for me came first—where is it now?
Can you abandon your Alcyone
Without a qualm? Is now this long far road
Your choice? Will absence make you love me more?
If it were overland your journey lay,
Grief would be mine, not fear—anxious and sad,
But not afraid. The *sea* makes me afraid
And Ocean's face of gloom. I saw just now
Wrecked broken timbers cast upon the shore;
I've often read dead names on empty tombs.
    Take no vain comfort in false confidence
That my great father* rules the winds of heaven,
Holding imprisoned all their stormy strength,
Soothing at will the anger of the seas.
When once the winds are loosed and seize the main,
Naught is forbidden them; the continents
And oceans cower forsaken; in the sky
They drive the clouds and with their wild collisions
Strike fiery lightnings crashing down the world.
The more I know them (for I know them well,
And in my father's house, when I was small,
I often saw them) my heart fears the more.
But if no prayer can alter your resolve,

And still your heart is set—too set—to go,
My dearest, take me with you. So together
We'll face the storms—I'll fear but what I feel—
Together what may come we both shall bear,
Together on the wide seas we shall fare.'
   Her weeping words distressed her star-born husband,
For in his heart love burned no less than hers;
Yet still his purpose held to cross the sea,
Nor would he share with his Alcyone
Perils unknown, and long he tried to soothe
Her anxious fears but urged his cause in vain,
Till this last word of comfort turned her heart:
'Long to our love seems every waiting hour,
But by my father's radiance I swear,
If only the Fates let me, I'll return
Before the moon twice fills her silver orb.'
This promise gave her hope, and he straightway
Ordered his ship from dock, and had her launched
And fitted out with gear and stores and tackle.
And at the sight Alcyone again
Shuddered as if forewarned of woes to come;
Her tears burst forth afresh, as in her arms
She held him, and at last with broken heart
She said farewell and fainted in a swoon.
   But the young crew, though Ceyx sought delay,
Rowing in double ranks, pulled back the oars
To their stout chests and clove with even rhythm
The widening waters. Raising her moist eyes,
She saw her husband standing in the stern,
Waving goodbye, and she waved back to him.
And as the shore receded and her eyes
Could see his face no longer, still her gaze
Followed the vessel, watching till at last
It sank below the horizon; still she watched
The sails at masthead floating, till they too
Vanished; and then with heavy heart she sought
Her empty room, and on her bed lay down,
Her lonely bed, and room and bed renewed
Alcyone's hot tears, telling her heart
Part of her life, part of herself, was gone.

The harbour cleared, a light breeze stirred the shrouds,
The oars were shipped, the yards at masthead set,
And all sail spread to catch the coming wind.
The ship had crossed but half the sea or less,
And land on either side lay far away,
When at nightfall the waves began to rise*
And whiten and the wind drove from the east
With stronger force. 'Quick now!' the captain cries,
'Lower the yards, take in all sail!'—he shouts
In vain, the blustering gale thwarts his commands;
No voice can reach above the roaring sea.
But the crew haste unbidden, making fast
The oars, closing the port-holes, furling sails,
Bailing and flinging sea back into sea,
Securing spars—all tumult and confusion.
Now wilder grows the storm, the warring winds
From every quarter* hurl their huge attack,
And in mad turmoil toss the raging seas.
    The captain, terrified himself, admits
He cannot tell how matters fare nor what
To order or forbid, so dire the weight
Of doom, its force so far beyond his skill.
All is uproar, men shouting, rigging clattering,
Wave crashing down on wave, and thunder rolling.
Sea piles on sea as if to reach the sky,
The hanging pall of clouds is wet with spray.
Here the waves take the colour of the sand,
Swept from the deep, here black as Styx they swirl,
There flat and white they hiss in sheets of foam.
So on wild turns of chance the ship is tossed;
Now lifted mountain-high she sees below
Great gorges and the yawning Underworld,
And now, in circling walls of water plunged
Hell-deep, descries the zenith far above.
Often with booming thuds her sides resound,
When huge waves strike, as iron rams of war
And engines pound a battered barbican;
And like ferocious lions, with gathered strength,
Charging the hunters' blades and levelled spears,
The rushing waves, lashed by the raging storm,

Charge and leap high above her bastions.
And now the wedges slip, the caulking pitch
Fails, the seams gape, in floods the fatal sea.
Rain from the bursting clouds in sheets cascades;
All heaven it seems is falling to the sea
And Ocean's towering waters scale the sky.
The cloudburst soaks the sails, the sky-fed streams
With the sea's floods are mingled. No star shines;
The darkness of the storm makes blacker still
The blindness of the night; yet through the gloom
The lightnings flash and flicker and their glare
The incandescent seas illuminates.

    And now a leaping wave bursts through the hatches,
And as a soldier, boldest of them all,
Essays to scale a city's battlements,
Time after time, and gains at last his hope,
And fired by dreams of glory stands alone,
One of a thousand, victor on the wall,
So when the waves nine times the ship's steep sides
Had battered, higher, vaster, mightier rushed
The tenth* and battled with the weary barque
Till down within her captive walls it plunged.
Now half the sea was in her; half, outside,
Maintained the escalade. All are distraught
In terror, as a city is distraught
Whose walls are mined without and seized within.
Skill fails and hearts are faint, and every wave
Advancing seems a charging shattering death.
Some are in tears, some dazed, some—in despair—
Envy a decent burial, some make vows,
Hands held to heaven (a heaven they cannot see),
Praying in vain for help; and thoughts of home
And children, parents, brothers come to mind,
As each remembers all he's left behind.
    Ceyx recalls his dear Alcyone:
Alcyone alone is on his lips,
Alone he longs for, yet his heart is glad
To know she's far away. He longs to look
Back to his native shore, turn his last gaze
Homeward, but knows not where home lies, so wild

The waters whirl, and the whole firmament
Is shrouded in the murk of inky clouds,
That double the drear darkness of the night.
The mast is shattered by a whirling blast,
The rudder too is shattered; one last wave,
Victorious, exulting in its spoils,
Looks down in triumph on the encircling seas,
And then—as if, from their foundations torn,
Pindus and Athos, mountains twain, were flung
Into the ocean—with a crash so huge,
Headlong it fell and by its weight and force
Overwhelmed the ship and sank her to the depths.
And with her, swallowed in the swirling gulfs,
Never to rise again, her hapless crew
Went to their doom, save for some few who clung
To spars and wreckage. Ceyx in his hand,
That once had held the sceptre, clutched a plank,
And prayed to his wife's father and his own
For help, in vain; but chiefly on his lips
And in his thoughts was his Alcyone.
And, as he swam, he prayed the waves would bear
His corpse before her eyes and her dear hands
Would tend his burial; and while the waves
Allow him breath he calls Alcyone,
And, as they close, still murmurs her sweet name.
And now a black and towering arch of waters
Breaks on his head and drowns him in its fall.
    That dawn the Morning Star shone faint and strange;
The heavens he might not leave, but veiled his grief
In a dense canopy of weeping clouds.
    Meanwhile the Wind-god's daughter, unaware
Of these disasters, counts the passing nights,
And hastens to make ready for her lord
The robes that he shall wear and, when he comes,
What she shall wear herself, warming her heart
With promises, all vain, of his return.
Incense she burnt to every god in heaven,
But worshipped before all at Juno's shrine,*
And kneeling at the altar prayed for him
Who was no more, that he be saved from harm,

That he return and love none more than her.
So many prayers she made, but of them all
This last petition could alone befall.

But the great goddess could endure no more
Entreaties for the dead and, to protect
Her altars* from the hands of mourning, said:
'Iris, my voice's trustiest messenger,
Hie quickly* to the drowsy hall of Sleep,
And bid him send a dream of Ceyx drowned
To break the tidings to Alcyone.'
Then Iris, in her thousand hues enrobed,
Traced through the sky her arching bow and reached
The cloud-hid palace of the drowsy king.

Near the Cimmerians'* land a cavern lies
Deep in the hollow of a mountainside,
The home and sanctuary of lazy Sleep,*
Where the sun's beams can never reach at morn
Or noon or eve, but cloudy vapours rise
In doubtful twilight; there no wakeful cock
Crows summons to the dawn, no guarding hound
The silence breaks, nor goose, a keener guard;*
No creature wild or tame is heard, no sound
Of human clamour and no rustling branch.
There silence dwells: only the lazy stream
Of Lethe 'neath the rock with whisper low
O'er pebbly shallows trickling lulls to sleep.
Before the cavern's mouth lush poppies grow
And countless herbs, from whose bland essences
A drowsy infusion dewy night distils
And sprinkles sleep across the darkening world.
No doors are there for fear a hinge should creak,
No janitor before the entrance stands,
But in the midst a high-raised couch is set
Of ebony, sable and downy-soft,
And covered with a dusky counterpane,
Whereon the god, relaxed in languor, lies.
Around him everywhere in various guise
Lie empty dreams, countless as ears of corn
At harvest time or sands cast on the shore
Or leaves that fall upon the forest floor.

There Iris entered, brushing the dreams aside,
And the bright sudden radiance of her robe
Lit up the hallowed place; slowly the god
His heavy eyelids raised, and sinking back
Time after time, his languid drooping head
Nodding upon his chest, at last he shook
Himself out of himself, and leaning up
He recognized her* and asked why she came,
And she replied: 'Sleep, quietest of the gods,
Sleep, peace of all the world, balm of the soul,
Who drivest care away, who givest ease
To weary limbs after the hard day's toil
And strength renewed to meet the morrow's tasks,
Bid now thy dreams, whose perfect mimicry
Matches the truth, in Ceyx's likeness formed,
Appear in Trachis to Alcyone
And feign the shipwreck and her dear love drowned.
So Juno orders.' Then, her task performed,
Iris departed, for she could no more
Endure the power of sleep,* as drowsiness
Stole seeping through her frame, and fled away
Back o'er the arching rainbow as she came.
  Then Father Sleep* chose from among his sons,
His thronging thousand sons, one who in skill
Excelled to imitate the human form;
Morpheus* his name, than whom none can present
More cunningly the features, gait and speech
Of men, their wonted clothes and turn of phrase.
He mirrors only men; another forms
The beasts and birds and the long sliding snakes.
The gods have named him* Icelos;* here below
The tribe of mortals call him Phobetor.*
A third, excelling in an art diverse,
Is Phantasos; he wears the cheating shapes
Of earth, rocks, water, trees—inanimate things.
To kings and chieftains* these at night display
Their phantom features; other dreams will roam
Among the people, haunting common folk.
All these dream-brothers the old god passed by
And chose Morpheus alone to undertake

Iris' commands; then in sweet drowsiness
On his high couch he sank his head to sleep.
    Soon through the dewy dark on noiseless wings
Flew Morpheus and with brief delay arrived
At Trachis town and, laying his wings aside,
Took Ceyx's form and face and, deathly pale
And naked, stood beside his poor wife's bed.
His beard was wet and from his sodden hair
The sea-drips flowed; then leaning over her,
Weeping, he said: 'Poor, poor Alcyone!
Do you know me, your Ceyx? Am I changed
In death? Look! Now you see, you recognize—
Ah! not your husband but your husband's ghost.
Your prayers availed me nothing. I am dead.
Feed not your heart with hope, hope false and vain.
A wild sou'wester in the Aegean sea,
Striking my ship, in its huge hurricane
Destroyed her. Over my lips, calling your name—
Calling in vain—the waters washed. These tidings
No dubious courier brings, no vague report:
Myself, here, shipwrecked, my own fate reveal.
Come, rise and weep! Put on your mourning! Weep!
Nor unlamented suffer me to join
The shadowy spirits of the Underworld.'
    So Morpheus spoke, spoke too in such a voice
As she must think her husband's (and his tears
She took for true), and used her Ceyx' gestures.
Asleep, she moaned and wept and stretched her arms
To hold him, but embraced the empty air.
'Oh wait for me!' she cried, 'Why haste away?
I will come too.' Roused by her voice's sound
And by her husband's ghost, now wide awake,
She looked (her anxious maids had brought a lamp)—
Was he still there where he just now had stood?—
But found him nowhere. Then she beat her brow
And rent her robe and struck her naked breast
And tore her hair, too wild to let it down;
And when her nurse asked why she grieved so sore,
'Alcyone's no more, no more!' she cried,
'She died with Ceyx, died when Ceyx died!

Give me no words of comfort—he is dead,
Shipwrecked and drowned. I saw him, knew him, tried
To hold him—as he vanished—in my arms.
He was a ghost, but yet distinct and clear,
Truly my husband's ghost, though to be sure
His face was changed, his shining grace was gone.
Naked and deathly pale, with dripping hair,
I saw him—woe is me! He stood just here
(She searched for footprints) in his misery.
This, this it was that my prophetic soul
Dreaded when I besought you not to leave me,
Not to set sail. At least, since you were bound
For death, I should have been aboard. How blest
Had I sailed with you, so had spent no hour
Without you, had in death not been apart!
Now far away* I've died, oh, far away
I'm tossed amid the billows; ocean's deeps
Are holding me, me now without myself.
My heart were cruel as the sea, if I
Strove to live on, fought to survive a grief
So great! But I'll not fight, nor ever more
Leave you, poor Ceyx. Now at least we'll be
Together; though no urn our ashes hold,
On one tomb letters carved shall link our love;
So shall our names, if not our bones, embrace!'
Grief checked her then, each word a sobbing choke,
As from her heart low moans of anguish broke.

    Morning had come; she went down to the shore
And sadly sought the place where she had stood
To see him go, and, while she lingered there,
Thinking 'Here he cast off, on the beach here
Kissed me goodbye', each spot a memory,
And gazing out to sea, she thought she saw,
Floating far out, what seemed to be a corpse.
At first she stood uncertain, till the waves
Washed it a little nearer, then for sure,
Though still not close, it was a corpse, but whose
She knew not, yet the omen—a man drowned—
Moved her to tears. 'Alas for you', she said,
'Poor soul, whoever you are, and for your wife,

If wife you have.' Then nearer, on the waves,
The body floated and the more she gazed,
The more distraught she grew, till close inshore
It came—dear God!—and she could recognize
Her husband! 'Oh, it's he', she shrieked and tore
Her hair, her robe and, trembling arms outstretched,
'Is this', she cried, 'my dearest love, is this—
So piteous—how you come home to me!'

    Hard by was a high mole built to exhaust
The sea's attack and break the battling waves.
On this she leapt—most wonderful—and then
She flew and through the air on new-found wings
Sped skimming o'er the waves, a hapless bird;
And, as she flew, her slender bill poured forth
Sad plaintive cries that seemed to speak of grief.
And when she reached the silent bloodless corpse
Her new wings clasped her loved one; her hard beak
Printed cold futile kisses on his lips.
Whether he felt them or the lapping waves
Raised Ceyx' head, folk doubted; yet for sure
He felt them, and at last for pity's sake
The gods* changed both to birds;* the same strange fate
They shared, and still their love endured, the bonds
Of wedlock bound them still, though they were birds.
They mate and rear their young and in the winter
For seven days of calm Alcyone
Broods on her nest, borne cradled on the waves.
Calm lies the sea. The Wind-god keeps his squalls
Imprisoned and forbids the storms to break,
And days are tranquil for his grandsons' sake.

AESACUS

An old man watched these birds once wing to wing
Over the open sea and praised their love,
Steadfast until the end. His neighbour said
(Or maybe the same man*) 'This bird as well
With trailing legs, you see, that skims the waves'
(He pointed to a long-necked diver) 'came
Of royal stock, and if you seek to trace

Down in unbroken line his forebears were
Ilus, Assaracus and Ganymede,
Jove's stolen lad, and old Laomedon
And Priam who was destined for defeat
In Troy's last days. That bird was Hector's brother
And, had he not in his first manhood found
A weird new fate, his name might well have been
No less than Hector's. Hecuba indeed
Gave Hector birth, while Alexiroe,
Daughter of horned Granicus,* secretly,
It's said, on Ida's shady mountainside
Bore Aesacus. He hated towns and dwelt
Remote from glittering palaces among
Deep-hidden hills in countryside that slept
Without ambition, rarely visiting
The throngs of Ilium. Yet he was not
A boor at heart nor unassailable
By love, and many a time through all the woods
Pursued Hesperie. He saw her by
Her father Cebren's* river bank, her hair
Loose on her shoulders drying in the sun.
The nymph, observed, took flight, as a frightened hind
Flees from a grizzled wolf, or a mallard caught
Far from the lake she's left flies from a hawk.
He followed in pursuit, she swift in fear,
He swift in love, when lurking in the grass
A snake,* look, struck her as she fled and fanged
Her foot and left its venom in her veins—
Her flight, her life cut short! Beside himself
He held her lifeless in his arms and cried
"I chased you! Oh, it breaks, it breaks my heart!
But this I never feared! Oh, never worth
So much to win you! Two of us, poor soul,
Have laid you low: the viper gave the wound,
And I the cause. The greater guilt have I:
For your death's solace I myself shall die."
     Then from a cliff-top that the booming waves
Had eaten out below he flung himself
Into the sea. In pity as he fell
Tethys received him gently, and as he swam

Clothed him with feathers; thus the golden chance
Of death so much desired was never given.
The lover, outraged to be forced to live
Against his will, to find his soul that longed
To leave its lamentable home restrained,
With new wings on his shoulders flew aloft
And once more launched himself into the waves.
His feathers broke his fall. In fury then
Poor Aesacus dived down into the deep
Trying endlessly to take the road to death.
Love made him lean; his jointed legs are long,
And long his neck, and long his head extends.
He loves the sea; that name of his he keeps,
A diver,* for he dives into its deeps.'

BOOK XII

THE EXPEDITION AGAINST TROY

PRIAM, his father, mourned for Aesacus,
Not knowing of the wings that saved his life,
And Hector with his brothers had performed
The funeral rites beside an empty tomb
That bore his name. At those sad obsequies
Paris was missing, he who afterwards
Brought with the wife he stole long years of war
Upon his country. In pursuit there sailed
The commonwealth of Greece, a thousand ships
Leagued and allied, and vengeance would have fallen
Forthwith, had stormy winds not made the sea
Unsailable and held the chafing fleet
At fish-famed Aulis in Boeotia's bay.
Here, in the fashion of their land, the Greeks
Made sacrifice to Jove. As kindled flames
Glowed on an ancient altar, they beheld
A sea-blue serpent crawling up a plane
That stood near by beside the ceremony.
High up the tree there was a nest with eight
Small fledgeling birds, and these the serpent seized,
Their mother with them, fluttering round her loss,
And swallowed greedily. All stood aghast;
But Thestor's son,* wise augur, who foreknew
The truth, cried 'We shall win! Rejoice, brave Greeks!
For Troy shall fall, but long our toils shall wait',
And spelt from those nine birds nine years of war.
The serpent, winding in the leafy boughs,
Was turned to stone;* stone fixed its snaky form.
    But storming still amid the Aonian main
Nereus opposed war's passage. Some believed
Neptune was sparing Troy because he'd built
Her battlements. Not so Calchas, for he
Knew and announced that by a virgin's blood
The Virgin's wrath* must be appeased. Then love
Yielded to public weal, the father to

The king: Iphigenia stood to give
Her chaste life-blood amid the weeping priests
Before the altar. Yielding then at last,
The goddess drew a mist before their eyes,
And in the turmoil of the ceremony,
The chants and prayers, in place of the princess
The tale is told Diana set a hind.
Appeased then by that seemly sacrifice,
Her divine anger and the ocean's rage
Alike subsided, and those thousand ships
Welcomed the wind abaft and reached at last
After much suffering the shores of Troy.
    At the world's centre lies a place between
The lands and seas and regions of the sky,
The limits of the threefold universe,
Whence all things everywhere, however far,
Are scanned and watched, and every voice and word
Reaches its listening ears. Here Rumour* dwells,
Her chosen home set on the highest peak,
Constructed with a thousand apertures
And countless entrances and never a door.*
It's open night and day and built throughout
Of echoing bronze; it all reverberates,
Repeating voices, doubling what it hears.
Inside, no peace, no silence anywhere,
And yet no noise, but muted murmurings
Like waves one hears of some far-distant sea,
Or like a last late rumbling thunder-roll,
When Jupiter has made the rain-clouds crash.
Crowds throng its halls, a lightweight populace
That comes and goes, and rumours everywhere,
Thousands, false mixed with true, roam to and fro,
And words flit by and phrases all confused.
Some pour their tattle into idle ears,
Some pass on what they've gathered, and as each
Gossip adds something new the story grows.
Here is Credulity, here reckless Error,
Groundless Delight, Whispers of unknown source,
Sudden Sedition, overwhelming Fears.
All that goes on in heaven or sea or land

Rumour observes and scours the whole wide world.
　Now she had brought the news that ships from Greece
Were on their way with valiant warriors:
Not unforeseen the hostile force appears.
The Trojans, to prevent a landing, guard
Their shores. Protesilaus* is the first
To fall, as fate ordained, by Hector's spear.
High is the price those battles cost the Greeks,
As Hector's prowess shines in brave men's deaths.
The Trojans too learn with no little blood
What Greek right arms can do.

ACHILLES AND CYCNUS

　　　　　　　　　　Sigeum's shores
Ran red and Cycnus, Neptune's son, had sent
A thousand men to death; and now Achilles
Charged in his chariot and with his spear
From Pelion* laid whole battalions low,
And seeking Cycnus in the fray or Hector,
Confronted Cycnus (leaving Hector till
The tenth long year), then shouting to his steeds
Whose snowy necks were straining at the yoke,
He drove his chariot against his foe
And cried, his strong arm brandishing his spear,
'Whoever you are, take comfort when you die,
That great Achilles killed you!' Those high words
His huge spear followed fast. Yet, though no fault
Deflected the sure shaft, that steely point
Achieved no good: it only bruised his breast
As if the blow were blunt. 'You goddess' son',
Cried Cycnus, '—Yes, I know you by repute—
Why are you so surprised that I've no wound?'
(Surprised he was) 'This helmet that you see
With chestnut horse-hair crest, this convex shield,
My left arm's load, they're not for my defence,
They're for adornment. That's why Mars too wears
His armour. Strip their guardian services
Away—I'll leave the field without a scratch.
It's something surely to be born the son,

Not of a Nereid, but him who rules
Nereus and Nereids and the whole wide sea.'
With that he threw his lance—to lodge fast in
Achilles' curving shield. It pierced the bronze
And the next nine bull's-hides, but at the tenth
Paused. The great hero wrenched it out and again
His strong hand hurled a quivering spear; again
Cycnus stood whole, unharmed; nor could the third
Scratch him, though wide-exposed he bared himself.
Achilles raged in fury like a bull
In the broad ring* that with his frightful horns
Charges the scarlet cloak that baits his wrath
And finds his wounds eluded. The iron point
Perhaps was loose and lost; but no, he found
It fixed fast to the shaft. 'Then is my hand
'So weak', he said, 'and is the strength it had
Withered this once? For sure it had its strength
When in the van I overthrew the walls
Of Lyrnesus and when with their own blood
I drenched the towns of Thebes and Tenedos,
Or when the slaughter of compatriots
Crimsoned Caicus' stream, and Telephus*
Felt twice my lance's work. On this field too
So many slain, whose heaps I made and see
Along the shore—my right hand had its strength
And keeps it still!' As if he disbelieved
The deeds he'd done he hurled his spear to strike
Menoetes, one of Lycia's rank and file,
And pierced his breastplate and his breast beneath.
His dying head beat on the stony ground
And out from the warm wound Achilles plucked
His spear again, and cried 'This is the hand,
This is the spear that triumphs. Against *him*
I'll use the same and pray he finds the same
Result!' and aimed at Cycnus once again.
The ash-shaft made no error, Cycnus no
Move to escape; it thudded on his left
Sh'oulder and bounced away as off a wall
Or rocky cliff—yet where it struck, a streak
Of blood! Achilles' heart rejoiced—in vain:

There was no wound: it was Menoetes' blood.
In fury then from his high chariot
Leaping headlong, he drew his sword to close
With his unfearing foe and saw his steel
Gouge shield and helmet, but that flint-hard body
Even blunted the blade! Enough! No more!
With shield and sword-hilt time and time again
He beat the face and forehead of his foe;
Pressed close as he retreated, harried him,
Rushed him, gave him no pause to get his wits.
Fear seizes Cycnus, darkness swims before
His eyes and as he staggers back he's stopped
By a boulder in mid-field. Achilles forced
Him backwards, swung him round with all his strength,
And dashed him to the ground. Then with hard knees
And shield clamped on his chest, he hauled upon
The helmet-strings, strained tight beneath his chin,
Choked his breath's passages and throttled him.
Conquered! He stooped to strip the spoils—and saw
The armour empty: Neptune had transformed
Cycnus to the white bird whose name he bore.
   These mighty toils, this battle brought a lull
Of many days; both sides laid down their arms
And took their rest. And while upon Troy's walls
A constant guard was kept, and constant guard
In the Greek lines, there came a festal day
When Cycnus' conqueror, Achilles, gave
Pallas* her sacrifice with a heifer's blood.
He placed the entrails on the glowing altar
And when the welcome aroma reached the gods
In heaven, the rites took their due share; the rest
Was set upon the tables for the feast.
The chiefs reclined on couches, took their fill
Of roasted meats, and lightened cares and thirst
With flowing wine. No harp played for their pleasure,
No songs, no boxwood flutes of many holes;
The night grew long with talking and their theme
Was valour. Tales were told of how they fought
And how their foes; they relished, turn by turn,
Recounting dangers shared and overborne.

What else indeed should be Achilles' theme?
What else their theme with great Achilles there?
Chiefly their talk was of his latest triumph,
Cycnus subdued. It seemed a miracle
That he possessed a body impervious
To any weapon, proof against all wounds,
Blunting an iron blade. And while the Greeks,
And great Achilles too, were marvelling
Old Nestor* said: 'In your lifetime one man
Alone could scorn the sword, no stroke could pierce,
Cycnus. But I myself saw years ago
Caeneus of Thessaly with a thousand wounds
Unharmed, Caeneus of Thessaly, who lived
Famed for his feats on Othrys; and what makes
It more miraculous, he had been born
A woman.' Such a freak of nature made
All present marvel, and they asked him for
The story; and Achilles said, 'My lord,
You are so full of years, so eloquent,
The wisdom of our age, come, let us hear
(We all have the same wish) who Caeneus was,
And why his change of sex, in what campaign,
What battle-line* you knew him, and by whom
He was defeated, if he met defeat.'
Then the old man: 'Despite the impediments
Of my slow years, though much seen in my youth
Escapes me now, I still remember more.
Among so many deeds of war and peace
None sticks more firmly in my memory;
And if great length of years enables one
To see a multitude of things, I've lived
Two centuries* and now am in my third.

CAENIS

Caenis,* the child of Elatus, was once
A famous beauty, loveliest of all
The girls of Thessaly, and jealous hopes
Fired many a suitor in the neighbouring towns
And your town too, Achilles (she was your

Fair fellow-citizen). Peleus, perhaps,
Might well have wooed her, but by then had wed
Your mother, or her hand was pledged to him.
And Caenis married no one. Strolling on
A lonely beach the Sea-god ravished her
(So the tale ran) and when great Neptune gained
His new love's joys, "No wish of yours", he said,
"Need fear refusal. Chose what wish you will."
(This too in the same tale.) So Caenis said
"This wrong you've done me needs an enormous wish—
Put pain like that beyond my power. Grant me
To cease to be a woman—everything
That gift will be to me." She spoke her last
Words in a deeper tone; they might well seem
A man's voice. So it was. For Ocean's god
Approved her wish, and added power to be
Proof against every wound and not to fall
To spear or sword. Rejoicing in the gift,
Caeneus fared forth to range Peneus' ways,
And there in men's pursuits he passed his days.

THE BATTLE OF THE LAPITHS AND CENTAURS

Pirithous* had wed Hippodame*
And called the cloud-born* centaurs to recline
At tables ranged within a tree-clad cave.
The lords of Thessaly were there and I
Was there myself. The festive palace rang
With the merry hubbub of the milling guests.
And now the wedding hymn was sung, the fires
Smoked in the royal hall, in came the bride
With wives and matrons walking at her side,
Supreme in beauty. Blessed indeed we called
Pirithous with such a bride—and brought,
Nearly, thereby their wedded bliss to naught!
For Eurytus, the fiercest of the fierce
Centaurs, was fired by wine and by the sight
Of that fair girl, and drink was in command,
Doubled by lust. Tables were overturned,
The banquet in confusion, and the bride,

Held by her hair, was seized and carried off.
Hippodame was seized by Eurytus;
The others seized what girl each would or could.
The scene was like a city sacked; the house
Echoed with women's screams. At once we all
Sprang to our feet and Theseus shouted first
"What madness, Eurytus, possesses you
To provoke Pirithous while I'm alive—
Two men, you fool, in one!"* To back his words
The great-souled prince, thrusting the throng aside,
Rescued the ravished girl from their wild rage.
No answer came; for no words could defend
Such deeds. The dastard charged her champion,
Pummelled his noble chest and punched his chin.
An antique wine-bowl chanced to stand near by,
Jagged with high relief; huge as it was,
Theseus still huger lifted it and hurled
It crashing on his foe. He vomited
Great gouts of blood with brains and wine from wound
And throat, and falling backwards beat his heels
Upon the soaking sand. His death incensed
His twiformed brothers and with one accord,
Each vying with the rest, "To arms, to arms!"
They shouted. Wine gave courage. In the first
Fighting goblets went flying and fragile jars
And bowls and dishes meant for banqueting,
Now turned to war and carnage. Amycus,
Ophion's son, first robbed the sanctuary,
Daring to seize its gifts, and first again
Snatched a great candlestick with clustered lights
And, lifting it at arm's length like a priest
Straining with sacrificial axe to cleave
A white bull's neck, he crashed it on the brow
Of Lapith Celadon and left his face
Smashed beyond recognition. Both his eyes
Leapt out, cheek bones were shattered, nose forced back
And wedged inside his mouth. Then Amycus
Was felled by Pelates who'd wrenched away
A maple table-leg; his chin was forced
Into his chest, and as he spat dark blood

And teeth a second wound sent him away
Down to the shades of Hades. Gryneus next,
With murder in his eyes, stood gazing at
The smoking altar. "Why don't we use this?"
He cried, and lifted up its giant bulk,
Aglow with fires, and hurled it at a group
Of Lapiths and crushed two of them, Orion
And Broteas. Orion was the son
Of Mycale, whose magic spells, men say,
Had many a time forced down the struggling moon.
"You'll pay for this, if I've a means to find
A weapon!" cried Exadius and found
Antlers, a votive gift on a tall pine.
He rammed the double prongs in Gryneus' eyes
And gouged his eyeballs. One stuck to the horn,
One rolling down his beard hung caked in blood.
    Then Rhoetus, snatching up a blazing brand
Of plum-wood from the altar, on the right
Slashes Charaxus' forehead sheltered by
His auburn hair. Caught by the ravening flame
The tresses blaze like sun-baked corn; the blood,
Scorched in the wound, hissed with a ghastly sound,
The sound of red-hot iron when a smith
Takes it in his curved tongs and plunges it
Into his water-tank and down it goes,
Hissing and sizzling, and the water's warm.
Wounded, he shook away the hungry flame
From his dishevelled hair, and pulling up
A slab, a threshold-stone, he shouldered it,
A wagon-load, whose very weight ensured
It reached no foe: yes, one of his own side,
Cometes, standing near, was crushed beneath
That granite block. Rhoetus could not contain
His joy. "Well done! May all your camp today",
He shouted, "prove your prowess in that way!"
And with the half-burnt brand he aimed again
At his head-wound, until with blow on blow
He crushed his cranium and the shattered skull
Collapsed and settled in a pool of brains.
    Victorious he turned on Corythus

And Dryas and Euagrus. One of them,
Young Corythus (his cheeks wore their first down),
Dropped, and Euagrus cried "To fell a boy—
What glory do you gain?" Not a word more
Would Rhoetus let him speak, but fiercely thrust
The ruddy flame into his open mouth,
Right down his throat; and savage Dryas too
He chased, whirling the brand above his head.
But not the same end this time. As he swaggered,
Proud of his trail of slaughter, Dryas thrust
Him through with a charred pointed stake where neck
And shoulder join. He groaned and strained to wrench
The stake from the hard bone and fled away,
Soaked in his own red blood. Orneus fled
And Lycabas and Medon, with a gash
In his right shoulder, Thaumas and Pisenor,
And Mermeros whose speed of foot till then
Surpassed them all, but now slowed by a wound;
And Melaneus and Phobas and Abas,
The boar-hunter, and Astylos, the seer
Whose warnings failed to keep his friends from war.
He'd said to Nessus too who feared a wound,
"No need to run: you'll be kept safe to serve
The bow of Hercules." But Lycidas,
Areos, Imbreus and Eurynomus—
Death overtook them. Dryas' right arm felled
All of them as they faced him. Facing him
Crenaeus too was wounded though he'd turned
His back in flight; for looking round he took
The weighty steel between his eyes, just where
Nose finds its way to forehead. In that din
Aphidas lay with every vein relaxed
In endless sleep, unwoken, undisturbed,
Sprawled on a shaggy bearskin from Mount Ossa,
His wine-filled cup in his unconscious hand,
Out of the fight—in vain! Observing him
Lying apart there, Phorbas fingered firm
His lance's thong: "You'd better mix", he cried,
"Your wine with Styx's water!" There and then
He hurled his lance and through Aphidas' neck,

As he lay sprawled face-up, the iron-tipped ash
Drove deep. Death came unfelt. Over the couch—
Into the cup—blood gushed from his full throat.
     I saw Petraeus trying to uproot
An acorn-laden oak and as his arms
Embraced it and he forced it to and fro,
Rocking its tottering trunk, Pirithous,
Hurling a lance that pierced Petraeus' ribs,
Pinned fast his writhing chest to the tough wood.
The prowess of Pirithous, men say,
Laid Lycas low, laid Chromis low, but each
Gave less distinction to the victor than
Dictys and Helops. Helops was transfixed
By a lance that struck his forehead from the right
And pierced to his left ear. Dictys, in flight
Before the onslaught of Ixion's son,
Slipped on a mountain precipice and fell
Headlong; his weight broke a huge mountain-ash
Whose splintered spike impaled him in his groin.
     For vengeance Aphareus was there and tried
To throw a rock wrenched from the mountainside.
But Theseus caught him as he threw and smashed
His giant elbow with a club of oak.
Enough! No time nor wish to do to death
That good-for-nothing! On Bienor's back
He leapt (a back not used to carry a soul
Except himself) and, knees gripping his flanks
And left hand holding fast his head of hair,
He swung the knotted club and smashed his mouth,
Screaming out threats, and broke his bony brow.
That club then felled Nedymnus and Lycopes,
Famed for his javelin, and Hippasos
Whose long beard draped his chest, and Ripheus too
Whose stature overtopped the forest trees,
And Thereus who would capture mountain bears
Of Thessaly and bring them home alive
And snarling. Theseus' triumphs in the fight
Were too much for Demoleon. He tried
With a huge heave to uproot an ancient pine,
A sturdy trunk, and, when his efforts failed,

He snapped it off and threw it at his foe.
But as the missile came Theseus drew back
Beyond its range, on Pallas's advice
(Or so he'd have us think). But still the trunk
Did not fall idle: from tall Crantor's neck
It severed his left shoulder and his breast.
Crantor, Achilles, was your father's squire;
Amyntor, leader of the Dolopes,
Worsted in war, had sent him as a gift,
To be a pledge of peace and loyalty.
When Peleus, at a distance, saw the lad
Cleft by that hideous wound, "Crantor", he cried,
"My favourite, at least receive from me
Your death-right gift!" and with his powerful arm
And all his passion's strength he hurled his spear
Full at Demoleon. It broke his ribs
And hung there quivering in the box of bones.
The centaur wrenched the shaft away without
The point (the shaft would hardly come); the point
Stuck in his lung. His very agony
Gave him wild strength. Despite his wound he reared
And pounded Peleus with his horse's hooves.
On helm and ringing shield Peleus received
The lashing hooves and, so defended, held
His lance-point levelled and with one thrust pierced
The centaur's shoulder and his two-formed chest.
Already at a longer range he'd slain
Phlegraeos and Hyles and, hand-to-hand,
Iphinous and Clanis; now to them
He added Dorylas who wore a cap
Of wolf-skin on his head with, for a lance,
A splendid pair of bull's horns red with blood.
I shouted to him (anger gave me strength)
"See how your horns yield to my steel!" and threw
My spear. Unable to escape, he raised his hand
To shield his threatened brow, and hand was nailed
To brow. A shout went up. He stood there stuck
And beaten by the bitter wound, and Peleus
(For he stood nearer) struck him with his sword
Full in his belly. Leaping fiercely forward,

He trailed his guts, trampled them as they trailed,
And trampling burst them, and the tangle tripped
His legs and, belly empty, he collapsed.
   Nor did his beauty ransom Cyllarus,
Fighting that day, if hybrids such as he
Be granted beauty. His beard was just beginning,
A golden beard, and golden tresses fell
Down on his shoulders reaching to his flanks.
High-mettled grace shone in his face; his neck,
Chest, shoulders, hands and every manly part
Seemed like a sculptor's much-praised masterpiece.
Unblemished too his equine shape, nor less
Fine than his man's. With horse's head and neck
He'd make fit mount for Castor, so high stood
His chest-muscles, so rideable his back.
Jet black he was, the whole of him, save that
His tail was white and legs were milk-white too.
Many a centauress would be his mate,
But one had gained his heart, Hylonome.
In the high woods there was none comelier
Of all the centaur-girls, and she alone
By love and love's sweet words and winning ways
Held Cyllarus, yes, and the care she took
To look her best (so far as that may be
With limbs like that). She combed her glossy hair,
And twined her curls in turn with rosemary
Or violets or roses, and sometimes
She wore a pure white lily. Twice a day
She bathed her face in the clear brook that fell
From Pagasae's high forest, twice she plunged
Her body in its flow, nor would she wear
On her left side and shoulder any skin
But what became her from best-chosen beasts.
Their love was equal; on the hills they roamed
Together, and together they would go
Back to their cave; and this time too they went
Into the Lapiths' palace side by side
And side by side were fighting in the fray.
A javelin (no knowing from whose hand)
Came from the left and wounded Cyllarus,

Landing below the place where chest joins neck—
Slight wound, but when the point was pulled away,
Cold grew his damaged heart and cold his limbs.
Hylonome embraced him as he died,
Caressed the wound and, putting lips to lips,
She tried to stay his spirit as it fled.
And when she saw him lifeless, she moaned words
That in that uproar failed to reach my ears;
And fell upon the spear that pierced her love,
And, dying, held her husband in her arms.

   There stands as well before my eyes the one
Who'd laced together six great lion-hides,
Phaeocomes, so shielding horse and man.
He hurled a log which two ox-teams could scarce
Have moved and crushed the skull of Tectaphos,
The son of Olenus. His skull's broad dome
Was shattered and through mouth, nose, eyes and ears
The soft brains oozed like whey when curds are strained
Or juice that trickles from a weighted press,
Squeezed through a strainer's fine-meshed apertures.
But I, as he prepared to strip the spoils,
(Your father knows) I plunged my sword deep in
The spoiler's groin. And Teleboas too
And Chthonius fell by my sword; the one
Had carried a forked pole, the other a spear.
That spear gave me a wound—you see the mark—
The ancient scar still shows. Yes, in those days
I ought to have been sent to capture Troy;
In those far days my prowess could have stayed,
If not subdued, great Hector; then, of course,
Hector, if he was born, was but a boy,
And now my long years fail me. Need I tell
How the half-horse Pyretus was outfought
By Periphas or how Ampyx had thrust
His lance that lacked its point into the face
Of four-footed Echeclus? Macareus
Felled Erigdupus with a crowbar through
His chest. And I recall a hunting-spear
From Nessus' hand was buried in the groin
Of Cymelus. Nor would you have supposed

Mopsus had but the power of prophecy;
By Mopsus' lance Hodites, double-formed,
Lay vanquished and in vain he tried to speak,
For tongue was pinned to chin and chin to throat.
    To Caeneus five had fallen: Antimachus,
Axe-armed Pyraemon, Bromus, Elymus
And Styphelus. I don't recall their wounds;
I noted names and number. Latreus next,
Giant in limbs and frame, came flying forth,
Armed with the spoils of Thracian Halesus
Whom he had slain. His years were then half-way
From youth to age, with still a young man's strength
And temples flecked with grey. A striking sight,
With shield and sword and Macedonian lance,*
He faced in turn both forces, clashed his arms,
And riding a tight ring cried haughtily
Across the empty air "You, Caenis, there!
Must I endure you? You, always a wench,
Always Caenis to me! Doesn't your birth
Remind you, don't you realize what act
Won your reward, what price you paid to seem
A spurious man? Just think what you were born,
Think what you bore! Away! Back to your wheel
And wool-box! Spin your thread. Leave war to men!"
Such were his taunts and, as he galloped by,
Caeneus let fly his spear and furrowed out
The centaur's flank where horse and man unite.
Mad with the pain, he thrust his long lance full
In Caeneus' unprotected face. Away
It bounced like hailstones dancing on a roof
Or little pebbles dropped upon a drum.
He closed, and in that rock-hard side he strove
To sink his sword: the sword found no way in.
"You'll not escape! If my sword-point's so blunt,
I'll slay you with the edge!" He held the sword
Aslant and reached to slash him round his loins.
The blow made a loud thud as if it struck
Marble. Against that carapace the blade
Broke into flying pieces. Long enough
Caeneus had posed unwounded there before

His wondering foe. "Come now", he cried, "I'll try
My steel on you!" and drove his deadly sword
Up to the hilt into the centaur's flank,
And turned and twisted the blind blade about
Inside his guts to wound and wound again.
   The frenzied centaurs now with a huge shout
Rush hurling, wielding all against that one
Their armoury. Their arms fall blunted; still
Unpierced by every blow, with no blood drawn,
Caeneus, the child of Elatus, stands firm.
A miracle! They stood there stunned. "Disgrace!"
Cried Monychus, "Disgrace! Our multitude
Worsted by one—hardly a man! Yet man
He is and we—such feeble efforts—we
Are what he was! What good's our giant size,
Our twofold strength? That our twin characters
Unite in us the bravest things that breathe?
No goddess gave us birth for sure. We're not
Ixion's sons whose stout heart hoped to win
Great Juno—half a man has laid us low!
Roll on him rocks and trees, whole mountainsides;
Hurl down the woods and crush his stubborn life,
Woods on his windpipe—weight in place of wounds!"
He happened on a tree blown down by wild
South winds and launched it at his sturdy foe.
That gave a lead; in no time Othrys' sides
Were stripped of trees and Pelion lost its shade.
Buried beneath the giant pile, Caeneus,
Tossing and heaving under the weight of trees,
Sustained on sturdy shoulders the vast mass
Of timber. Even so the burden towered
Higher than mouth and head and he could draw
No air to breathe. With failing strength, at times
He tried in vain to raise himself to reach
The air and roll the high-piled woods away;
At times he heaved, as if an earthquake shook
The heights of Ida that we look at there.
His end remains uncertain. Some declare
The woods' vast weight had forced him to the void
Of Tartarus. But Mopsus disagreed.

For from the middle of the mound he saw
A brown-winged bird fly up to the bright air.
I saw it too, the first time and the last.
As Mopsus watched him wheel in easy flight
Above his camp and heard his wings' huge whirr,
His eyes and thoughts pursued him, and he cried
"Hail, Caeneus, glory of the Lapith race,
Once a great hero, now a bird unique!"*
A prophet's words! And we believed. Our grief
Gave us fresh rage. That one of us should fall
To foes so many, rankled bitterly.
Nor did our sword-blades cease to wreak our grief
Till half were slain, half flight and night dispersed.'

NESTOR AND HERCULES

As Nestor told this tale of battles fought
Between the Lapiths and the half-man centaurs,
Tlepolemus took offence that Hercules
Had been passed by in silence and exclaimed:
'I am surprised, my lord, that you've forgotten
The feats of Hercules. Why, many a time
My father used to tell me how he quelled
The cloud-born centaurs.' Sadly Nestor then:
'Why force me to remember evil things,
And open griefs that time has healed, the wrongs
Your father did and how I hated him?
Heaven knows his deeds were past belief: the world
Was full of his fine feats: I only wish
I could dispute it. But we never praise
Deiphobus, never Polydamas,
Nor even Hector. Who would praise his foe?
That father of yours laid low in times gone by
Messene's walls, destroyed those blameless towns,
Elis and Pylos, ruined my own home
By fire and sword. Yes—to say nothing of
Others he murdered—there were twelve of us,
The sons of Neleus, fine young men to see:
All twelve the might of Hercules destroyed
Save me alone. No doubt one must accept

The others could be conquered, but the death
Of Periclymenus was strange indeed.
For Neptune, founder of King Neleus' line,
Had given him power to take what shape he pleased
And put it off again; and, when he'd tried
Every variety of form, he turned himself
Into that bird whose talons bear the bolts
Of thunder, favourite of heaven's king.
Then with an eagle's strength of wing, hooked beak
And curving claws he tore the famous face
Of Hercules. He, aiming with his bow
(Aim too unerring), as the bird soared high
Among the clouds and hovered, wounded him
Where wing joins side—slight wound but sinews failed,
Refusing motion and the means of flight.
Down to the earth he fell; his weak wings kept
No purchase on the air; his body's weight
Forced the light arrow, clinging to his wing,
Up through his left breast high into his throat.
So now, do you think I'm bound to cry abroad
Your Hercules' affairs, my Admiral,*
My glorious leader of the fleet of Rhodes?
Yet to avenge my brothers it's enough
To hush his feats in silence; between you
And me affection's founded firm and true.'

　　So Nestor told his fascinating tale,
And when the old king ended wine again
Went round the company, and then they rose
And what remained of night was given to sleep.

THE DEATH OF ACHILLES

But the god who with his trident rules the sea
Grieved with a father's sorrow for his son,
Changed to a swan like Phaethon's dear friend;*
And hating fierce Achilles nursed his rage,
Rage more than decent* and did not forget.
Now, when the war had lasted nigh ten years,
He addressed long-haired Apollo with these words:
'You, who are my first favourite of all

My brother's sons and built Troy's walls with me,
Walls built in vain, do you not groan to see
This citadel at any moment now
About to fall? Yes, does your heart not grieve
For all the thousands slain for her defence?
Not to name every one, is Hector's ghost,
He who was dragged round his dear Pergamum,
Not in your thoughts? Yet there's still left alive,
More cruel than war itself, the ruiner
Of all our handiwork, savage Achilles!
Let him face me: I'll make him feel what I
Can do with my forked trident! Yet, because
I may not meet my enemy face to face,*
Let fly your secret arrow suddenly
And take his life!' The Delian god agreed,
Gratifying alike his own desire*
And his great uncle's. In a veil of cloud
He reached the ranks of Troy and there amidst
The carnage he saw Paris casually
Shooting sporadic shots at unknown Greeks.
Revealing his divinity, 'Why waste
Weapons', he said, 'on blooding rank and file?
If you would serve your side, aim at Achilles,
And take your vengeance for your brothers' deaths!'
He pointed to Achilles laying low
The troops of Troy, and turned the bow on him
And guided the sure shaft with deadly aim.
This, after Hector, was a thing to make
Old Priam glad. And so Achilles fell,
Victor of mighty triumphs, vanquished by
The craven ravisher of that Greek wife:
If in a woman's fight he had to fall,
He'd have preferred the Amazon's double axe.

    And now that terror of the ranks of Troy,
The grace and guardian of the name of Greece,
Achilles, prince unconquerable in war,
Had burned upon the pyre. The selfsame god*
Had armed him and consumed him in the end.
Now he is ashes; of that prince so great
Some little thing is left, hardly enough

To fill an urn. Yet still his glory lives
To fill the whole wide world. By that true gauge
He's measured and by that his greatness matched;
He never knows the void of Tartarus.*
Why, from his shield, that you may know for sure
Who owned it, conflict comes, and for his arms
Men spring to arms. To claim them Diomede
Had never dared, nor Ajax, Oileus' son,*
Nor Atreus' sons,* the younger or his brother,
Greater in war and years, nor any other.
Two only had the confidence to win
Glory so great, the one Laertes' son,
The other Telamon's.* To escape the choice,
The burden and the blame, King Agamemnon
Ordered the captains of the Greeks to take
Their seats in the camp's centre, and transferred
To all the judgement of the case they heard.

BOOK XIII

AJAX AND ULYSSES AND THE ARMS OF ACHILLES

THE captains took their seats; the rank and file
Stood in a circle round. Then Ajax rose,
Lord of the sevenfold shield, now quick as ever
To anger,* and turned his smouldering gaze towards
The fleet that lay along Sigeum's shore,
And, pointing to them, cried 'Before these ships,*
By Jupiter, I plead my cause—and my
Opponent is Ulysses! Yet he had
No qualms in giving way to Hector's brands
Which I withstood, which I forced from this fleet!
It's safer then to fight with lies than face
A foe in arms. But I've no way with words,
Nor he with action; in the battle-line
Of bloody war I'm master, so is he
Master of language. Yet, I'm sure, no words,
My friends, need tell my exploits. Your own eyes
Have seen them. Let Ulysses speak of his,
Done without witness, only known to night!*
The prize is splendid, true; but honour's lost
With such a rival; there's no pride for Ajax
In winning anything Ulysses wants,
Great though this is. Ulysses even now
Gains from this contest, since, when he has lost,
He will be known to have matched himself with me.
 I, though my valour were in doubt, would be
In noble birth his better. My great father
Was Telamon, who took the walls of Troy
With valiant Hercules and reached the shores
Of Colchis on the ship from Thessaly.*
His father's Aeacus, who sits as judge
There in that silent world where Sisyphus*
Strains at his heavy stone; and Jove most high
Claims Aeacus and owns him as his son.
Ajax is therefore third in line from Jove.
But count this link as nothing in my cause,

Were it not common too to great Achilles.
He was my cousin: a cousin's arms I claim.
You, son of Sisyphus, his living likeness
In treachery and tricks, why graft the stock
Of Aeacus with a strange family's name?
　　And shall I be refused these arms for this,
That I took arms before him, needed no one
To expose me? Shall he seem the better man,
Who took them last, feigned madness to escape
Service, until a shrewder man than he,
(Though less to his own profit) Nauplius' son,*
Revealed his coward's tricks and forced him to
The arms he shirked and shunned? And shall he take
The best, because he wanted to take none?
And shall I lose my glorious cousin's gift,
Disgraced, because I faced the dangers first?
　　Would that his madness had been real indeed
Or else believed so, and he'd never joined
Our company against the walls of Troy,
To counsel crime! We'd not have had the guilt
Of leaving Philoctetes* to his fate
On Lemnos, hiding in the forest caves,
Moving, they say, the rocks with his laments,
And calling curses on Laertes' son,*
Curses, if gods exist, not called in vain.
Now he who took the oath of arms with us,
One of our captains, he to whom Hercules
Bequeathed his arrows, now, alas, laid low
By hunger and disease, must find from birds
His food and clothing, driven thus to employ
Those arrows meant to seal the fate of Troy.
Still, he's alive, because he did not keep
Ulysses company. Poor Palamedes
Likewise would rather have been left behind.
He'd be alive, or would at least have died
Without dishonour: he, whom that man there,
Too well remembering how disastrously
His madness was exposed, trapped with a charge,
Trumped up, that he'd betrayed the cause of Greece,
And showed the gold that he himself had buried

To prove him guilty. So, by death or exile,
He undermines our army. So it is
Ulysses fights and so he must be feared.
    In eloquence he may perhaps surpass
Even loyal Nestor,* yet he'll not convince me—
Try as he may—that he was free from guilt
When he abandoned him.* The tired old king,
Slowed by his horse's wound, cried out for help,
Cried to Ulysses—who betrayed his friend!
And Diomede knows well this charge is true:
He shouted to Ulysses, shouted his name,
And cursed his cowardly friend who ran away.
The gods' regard for men's affairs is just.
See, he needs help,* who would not help; yes, he
Who left his friend, should have been left in turn;
He'd set the rule himself. He cries to his friends;
I'm there and see him trembling, pale with fear,
Cowering from instant death. I shielded him,
My massive shield above him as he lay,
And saved (small praise in that) his feeble life.
If you still choose to challenge, let's go back*
To the same spot, bring back the enemy,
Your wound and usual terror; hide yourself
Behind my shield, and fight it out with me!
But, when I'd saved him, he, too weak with wounds
To stand, ran off and no wound* slowed his flight.
    Hector was there and brought his gods* with him
To battle. Brave men cowered, not you alone,
Ulysses; such the fear that he inspired.
I, as he triumphed in his bloody deeds,
I hurled a rock and laid him on his back;
And when he challenged single combat, I
Singly withstood him. You, my good Greeks, prayed
The lot* should fall on me; your prayers prevailed;
And, if you ask the fortune of that fight,
I was not worsted. See, the hosts of Troy,
How they brought fire and sword and Jove himself
Against our ships of Greece. Where then was glib
Ulysses? I, yes, I made my own breast
Bulwark and barrier for these thousand ships,

Your hopes of home, held safe to sail away:
For all those ships give me these arms today.
Though, if the truth be told, it's they, not I
Who claim the greater honour; our renown
Is linked, goes hand in hand; those glorious arms
Are claiming Ajax, not Ajax those arms.
Beside these feats that Ithacan may set
His Rhesus, faint-heart Dolon,* Helenus,
King Priam's son, the stolen Pallas,* all
Done in the dark, all due to Diomede.
If you award those arms for services
So vain, so valueless, divide them up
And give the greater share to Diomede.

  Yet what's the use of *these* to the Ithacan,
Who always operates unarmed, by stealth,
And traps his napping enemy with tricks?
Why, that bright helmet's gleam, its flashing gold,
Can but betray his ambushes, lay bare
His coverts. That poor cranium beneath
Achilles' helm could never bear the weight.
His faint-heart arm must find that famous spear
A grievous burden, and that shield, engraved
With scenes that show the whole wide world,* ill suits
That shy left hand that nature meant for theft.
Why seek a prize to crush and cripple you,
You scoundrel? If the Greeks are gulled enough
To give it you, you'll simply be a source
Of loot not fear; your speed to sprint away,
Sole prize you win against the world, will fail,
You chicken-heart, beneath that weight of gear.
What's more, *your* shield, so seldom used in war,
Is still intact; for mine, holed by the brunt
Of countless spears, a new one's needed now.

  No more: what need of words? Let us be seen
In action. Let that brave man's arms* be set
Amidst our foe; command they be brought back;
And with them, rescued, deck the rescuer.'

  Ajax was done; a rumble of applause
Went rolling through the ranks, until at last
Laertes' famous son stood forth, his gaze

Briefly upon the ground,* then raised his eyes
Towards the captains* and began his speech,
The speech for which they waited, and his words
Were lacking neither grace nor eloquence.

  'Good comrades, had my prayers and yours prevailed,
There'd be no heirship in dispute today
In this great contest. Your arms there, Achilles,
You'd have yourself; and we should still have you.
But since the Fates' unfairness has denied him
To me and you alike' (he wiped his eyes
As if he wept*) 'who'd better win, as heir
Of great Achilles, than the man who won
The aid of great Achilles for the Greeks?
Let it not help this man that he's a dolt,
Nor let it harm me, comrades, that my wit
Has always served you well; let no ill will
Attend my eloquence, such as it is,
Which speaks now for its master, as it spoke
Often for you: to each his own good gifts.

  One's lineage, one's ancestry, the feats
We've not performed ourselves, I hardly count
As ours.* Even so, since Ajax has announced
That he is Jove's great-grandson, my stock too
Is sprung from Jove, the same third link away.
My father is Laertes, his Arcesius,
And his was Jove, and in that ancestry
No criminal* condemned to banishment.
And on my mother's side add Mercury,
Nobility again, both sides divine.
Yet though I'm nobler by my mother's line,
My father guiltless of his brother's blood,
Not on these grounds I claim those arms laid there.
Weigh our true worth, provided that no worth
Is judged to Ajax in that Telamon
Was Peleus' brother, that no credit comes
From consanguinity; for this great prize
Set valour's honour first before your eyes.
Or if your quest is for the next of kin,
The nearest heir, well, Peleus is his father,
Pyrrhus* his son. What room for Ajax there?

Convey the arms to Phthia or to Scyros.
And Teucer is Achilles' cousin too,
No less than Ajax. Is *he* then to claim?
Or, claiming, would he win? In naked truth
We duel about deeds, and though my deeds
Are more than I have ready words to tell,
Their sum and sequence shall be ordered well.
    Achilles' Nereid mother who foreknew
The death that he would die,* disguised her son
In women's clothes, and all the world was tricked,
And Ajax too.* Among some girlish gear
I smuggled arms that must excite a man,
And as, in girl's dress still, he held the shield
And spear, I said "My lad, my goddess' son,
Why shrink from overthrowing giant Troy?
Troy, doomed to perish, keeps herself for you!"*
And clasped his hand and sent the gallant lad
To feats of gallantry. Therefore his feats
Are mine. The lance that mastered Telephus*
Was mine, and when he begged *I* made him well.
The fall of Thebes was mine; credit to me
Lesbos and Tenedos, Chryse and Cilla,
Apollo's towns, and Scyros too. My hand,
Be sure, sent crashing, levelled to the ground,
Lyrnessus' walls, and—not to mention more—
I gave you him whose prowess could destroy
Fierce Hector; thanks to me illustrious Hector
Lies low at last. Those arms I gave revealed
Achilles: in return these arms I claim:
My gift in life, my due now he is dead.
    When one man's sorrow* spread through all the Greeks
And Aulis' harbour held a thousand ships,
They waited long, but long the wind was still
Or contrary, and then the harsh oracle*
Bade Agamemnon sacrifice his child,
His innocent child, to merciless Diana.
Her father, furious with the gods themselves,
Refused—the king indeed, but father too—
Until I turned* his loving heart to thoughts
Of public policy—a plea, I grant

(And may the king forgive my granting it)
Most difficult before a biased judge.
Yet interests of state, his brother's honour,
His sceptre's trust and duty bade him weigh
Glory against that blood. The mother* next
I went to, not a woman words would win,
But to be gulled by guile. Had Ajax gone,
Our sails would still be left without their wind.

    Again, to Ilium's high citadel
I was dispatched, a bold ambassador.
I saw, I entered, Troy's great senate-house,
Still crowded with their warriors; undismayed,
I put the plea with which united Greece
Had trusted me. I pressed the charge against
Paris, and I demanded the return
Of Helen and his loot; and my words moved
King Priam and Antenor too. But Paris,
His brothers and his fellow-plunderers
(You, Menelaus, know) could hardly keep
Their sacrilegious hands away. We shared
The first of many dangers on that day.

    The tale would be too long of all the aid
I gave in action and advice throughout
The interminable war. The enemy,
After the first pitched battles, long stood fast
Within the city walls; there was no chance
Of open warfare; then at last we reached
The tenth long year and fought. In all that time
What were you doing? You, when all you know
Is bloody battlefields? What use were you?
But, if you ask what I did,* I ensnared
The enemy in ambushes, I ringed
The trenches round the battlements, I braced
Our allies' hearts to suffer patiently
The long war's boredom, I advised how best
To victual us and arm us, and I went
Wherever need required that I be sent.

    Then see, at Jove's command our king, beguiled
At night by dreams, gave orders to lay down*
The burden of the war that we'd begun.

He'd sanction for his orders, true; but Ajax,
He should have stopped it, should have called for Troy's
Destruction, should have—what he *can* do—fought.
Why didn't he stop them streaming back? And draw
His sword and give the straggling mob a lead?
Was that too much, when every word's a boast?
Yes, and he fled himself. I saw—with shame—
You turn your back and set your abject sails.
"What are you doing?" I cried, "Troy's in your hands,
My friends! What lunacy to loose your hold!
Ten years—and nothing to take home but shame!"
Grief gave me eloquence, and with these words
And more I turned them, led them back again
From the deserting ships. And Agamemnon
Called the allies* to council, still in fear,
And Ajax dared then stammer not a word.
Thersites* dared; he railed against the kings,
But not unscathed, the scoundrel, thanks to me.
I rose and roused my cowering countrymen,
My voice gave them their valour once again.
From that time on, whatever doughty deeds
May seem to be that man's, are mine, I say,
For I retrieved him when he ran away.
    Who of the Greeks enjoys your company
Or gives you words of praise? Yet Diomede
Thinks much of me, shares all he does with me,
Trusts in his friend Ulysses all the time.
It's something, of so many thousand Greeks,
To be the choice of Diomede. No lots
Were drawn to bid *me* go. Yet I went out,
Scorning the dangers of the enemy
And of the night, and slew the Trojan Dolon,
Running the same high risks as we; but first
I forced him to tell all and learnt full well
The plans of treacherous Troy. I knew the whole,
Had nothing more to spy, could have returned
To praise well-promised. Not content with that,
I turned to Rhesus' tents and in his own
Camp I dispatched him and his comrades too.
And so, victorious, all my prayers attained,

In Rhesus' captured chariot I rode
My happy triumph* homeward. Dolon claimed
Achilles' steeds for that night's price; if you
Refuse Achilles' arms to me, Ajax
Will be more generous!* What need to tell
How with my sword I did to death the ranks
Of Lycian Sarpedon; all the blood
I shed of Caenaros and Chromius,
Alastor and Alcander, Halius,
Noemon, Prytanis; and how I slew
Charops and Thoon and Chersidamas
And Ennomos, whom ruthless fate drove on;
And others less renowned whom my hand felled
Beneath their city's walls. And I have wounds
As well, wounds in proud places: see, and know
I speak no empty words'—he pulled apart
His tunic*—'This breast here has ever served
And suffered for your sake. But Ajax, why,
In all these years he's spent no blood at all
To serve his friends, his body has no wounds!*

   What does it matter if he says he fought
Both Troy and Jupiter to save the fleet?
It's true, he did (I'm not one to decry
Good actions out of malice); but he must
Not claim as his alone what's due to all.*
He must allow some honour too to you.
Patroclus,* safe in great Achilles' guise,
Forced back the Trojans from the fleet, when fire
Was bound to burn the ships, and Ajax too.
Again, he thinks that only he dared meet
The might of Hector; he forgets the king,
The captains and myself, that he was ninth*
To volunteer, and given precedence
By the lot's luck. Yet what was the result
Of your great duel, you soul of bravery?
Hector retired unscarred by any wound!*

  Alas, with what deep grief must I recall
The time when that brave bulwark of the Greeks,
Achilles, was laid low! Yet neither fear,
Nor tears, nor sorrow made me hesitate

To lift his body up as he lay there.
Upon these shoulders, these, I say, I bore*
The body of Achilles with his arms,
Those arms that now again I strive to bear.
Yes, I have strength well matched for such a weight,
And wit to judge the glory of your gift.
Think, when his sea-nymph mother had that high
Ambition for her son, was it for this—
That these celestial gifts, this work of art
So fine, should deck a rough and doltish soldier?*
Why, he knows nothing of the scenes embossed
Upon the shield, the ocean and the lands,
The constellations in the height of heaven,
The Pleiads and the Hyads and the Bear,
Banned from the sea, Orion's shining sword,
The cities set apart. He claims to win
Arms that his brain's too stupid to take in!

What of his accusation that I shirked
The war's hard duties, that I joined so late
The labours long begun? Does he not know
That he's maligning great Achilles too?
If to pretend's a crime, we both pretended;
If you blame lateness, I was earlier.
A loving wife held me, a loving mother
Achilles. Our first time we gave to them,
The rest to you. Even if I've no defence,
I shirk no charge I share with such a man.
But yet it was Ulysses' wit that caught
Achilles, never Ajax' that caught me.

We need not wonder that his stupid tongue
Pours such abuse on me; he smears you too*
With shameful words. If it was base of me
To blackguard Palamedes with my charge,
Was it then seemly when you sentenced him?
But Palamedes never could defend
A crime so great, so naked. Why, that charge
You did not hear, you saw: the bribe lay bare.

Nor should the blame be mine that Philoctetes
Is still on Lemnos, Vulcan's isle. (Defend
Yourselves! You gave consent.) I'll not deny

That I persuaded him* to quit the toil
Of travel and the war and try if rest
Would soothe his savage anguish. He obeyed—
And lives! Yes, my advice was both sincere
And proved successful—though sincerity
Suffices. Now the seers declare the doom
Of Troy demands his presence. Not a task
For me! Much better Ajax goes and calms
With his command of words that tortured man,
So angry and so ill, or brings him here
By one of his shrewd subtle stratagems.
No, Ida will stand leafless, Simois flow
Backwards, Achaea serve and succour Troy
Before, should my skill fail for your affairs,
Crass Ajax's cunning ever helps the Greeks.
Despite harsh Philoctetes' enmity
Towards the allies and the king and me,
Though he calls endless curses on my head,
Longs, in his pain, to get me in his power,
To drink my blood, to have the means to deal*
With me as I with him, yet I'll approach him,
And strive amain to bring him back with me.*
And in my grasp, if fortune favours me,
I'll hold his arrows, just as I once held
The Trojan prophet captive, just as I
Revealed the oracle* and the fate of Troy,
Just as I seized, deep in among our foes,
Their Pallas' image from her sanctuary.
And Ajax vies with me?* Without that image
The Fates in fact refused that Troy should fall.
Where was brave Ajax then? Where the big words
Of that great man? Why did Ulysses dare
To pass the sentries, trust to the dark night,
And brave their savage swords and penetrate
Not just the walls, but Troy's high citadel,
And seize the goddess from her shrine and go
Back with his holy captive through the foe?
Had I not done this, Ajax would have worn
That shield of his, those seven bulls' hides, in vain.
I gained the victory over Troy that night:

I conquered Troy's high places in that hour
When my feat put their conquest in your power.

   You scowl,* you whisper "What of Diomede?"
Enough of that! He has his share of praise.
You, also, when you held your shield to guard
The allies' ships, were not alone. You had
Your crowd around you; I had just the one;
And did that one not know that fighting men
Count less than wise men, that the prize is due
Not merely to high prowess, he'd himself
Be claiming it; so would the lesser Ajax,
And glorious Andraemon's son* and fierce
Eurypylus, so would Idomeneus,
And Meriones, whose fatherland's the same,
And Menelaus too. Yes, these brave men,
My equals all in battle, yield to me
In wit and wisdom. Your fine brawn in war
Serves well enough, but when it comes to brains
You miss my management. That strength of yours
Is mindless; my concern is for the morrow.
You have the power to fight; the time to fight
I choose with Agamemnon. Your real worth
Is nothing but your body, mine's my mind.
The captain of a ship counts more than crew,
A general more than just the rank and file.
So much my worth is more than yours: in me
Mind counts for more than muscle: mind is man.*

   My lords,* to me, your constant guardian,
Grant this great prize, and, for so many years
Of anxious service, weighing my deserts,
Give me this honour as my due reward.
My toil is finished. I've removed the Fates'
Impediment: by making possible
The doom of soaring Troy, I've sealed her doom.
I beg you now, by all the hopes we share,
By Troy's walls soon to totter, by the gods
That I abducted from the enemy,
If there are deeds that wise men still should do,
If there are dangers brave men still should dare,
If something still you need to seal Troy's fate,

Remember me! Or, if you'll not give me
The arms, give them to her!' He pointed to
Minerva's fateful statue standing there.
    The company of the captains was much moved;
Their verdict proved the power of eloquence;*
The man of words was given the brave man's arms.
He who in single combat had withstood
Hector, withstood so often fire and sword
And Jove, one thing—his rage—could not withstand.
His anguish conquered that unconquered soul.
He drew his sword and 'This', he cried, 'at least
Is mine. Or does Ulysses claim this too?
This must be used against myself! This, steeped
So often in Trojan slaughter, now shall be
Steeped in its master's blood, to prove it true
That none but Ajax Ajax can subdue.'
With that, deep in his breast that then at last
Suffered a wound, where he could find a way,
He plunged his fatal sword. No hand had strength
To draw the fast-fixed blade away; the *blood*
Expelled it,* and the ground, crimsoned with gore,
From the green turf that purple flower bore,
Which first had sprung from wounded Hyacinth.*
Upon its petals letters are inscribed,
Letters* for boy and man alike the same,
There for a wail of woe, here for a name.

THE FALL OF TROY

Victorious Ulysses now set sail
For Lemnos, land of Queen Hypsipyle
And glorious Thoas, island infamous
For husbands murdered* in the days of old.
He sailed to fetch the shafts of Hercules
And when he'd brought those arrows to the Greeks
And brought their master with them, at long last
The final stroke was given to that great war.
Troy fell and Priam too. His ill-starred wife
Lost, after all besides, her human shape;
Her weird new barking terrified the breeze
On foreign shores where the long Hellespont

Contracts in narrows.* Ilium was burning,
Its fires not yet died down; Jove's altar drank
Old Priam's scanty blood. Dragged by the hair,
Apollo's priestess* stretched her hands to heaven
In vain appeal. Embracing while they might
The statues of their country's gods, the wives
Of Troy crowded the burning shrines, until
The Greeks in triumph carried them away,
Their bitter prize. Astyanax* was hurled
Down from the turret whence he'd often watched
(His mother pointing) his great father fight
To save the ancestral city and himself.
And now the north wind urges them away,
Sails flap, the breeze blows fair, the signal's made
To use the wind. 'Farewell, farewell, to Troy!'
The Trojan women cry, 'We're stolen away!'
And kiss the soil and leave their smoking homes.
The last aboard, poor pitiable sight,
Was Hecuba. Among her children's tombs
They found her. As she embraced the sepulchres,
Kissing their bones goodbye, Ulysses' hands
Dragged her away. Even so, from one she saved
The ashes, Hector's ashes, and so saved
She bore them at her breast. On Hector's tomb
(Poor offering!) a white tress of her hair
She left, a last white tress and many a tear.

HECUBA, POLYXENA, AND POLYDORUS

There lie across the strait from Phrygia,
Where Ilium was, the provinces of Thrace,
Where Polymestor had his wealthy palace.
To him in secret Priam gave in charge
His young son Polydorus to be reared
Far from the strife of Troy; a prudent plan
Had he not sent a store of treasure too,
The goad of greed, the prize of perfidy.
When Troy's fair fortune fell, that wicked king
Took his sharp sword and slit his charge's throat,
And then, as though removal of the corpse

Removed the crime, he threw it from a cliff
Down to the waves below.
                     Upon the coast
Of Thrace King Agamemnon now had moored
His fleet until the waves should sink to rest
And winds blow friendlier. Here suddenly,
Large as in life, up from the fissured earth
Achilles sprang with threatening mien and fierce
As when he drew his treasonable sword
On Agamemnon. 'Greeks!' he cried, 'can you
Forget me when you go? Is gratitude
For my fine feats of arms interred with me?
It shall not be! My tomb must have its honour!
To appease Achilles' shade your sacrifice
Shall be Polyxena.' The allied host
Obeyed the bidding of his ruthless ghost.

    Torn from her mother's arms, the ill-starred girl
(Almost her mother's only comfort), brave
With more than woman's spirit, was led forth
Up to the sepulchre, the sacrifice
For that grim tomb. And when they stationed her
Before the cruel altar and she knew
The fearful rite was ready for herself,
True to herself she was, and when she saw
Achilles' son standing with knife in hand,
His eyes fixed on her face, 'Be quick!' she said,
'Take, use my noble blood. We need not wait.
Into my throat or bosom plunge your blade!'
(Bosom and throat she bared—Polyxena
For sure would never live in slavery!)
'By such a sacrifice as this no Power in heaven
Will be appeased! I only wish my fate
Were hidden from my mother. In my way
My mother stands and lessens my delight
In death; though not my death but her own life
She ought to mourn. Now stand aside, that I
May go in freedom to the shades of Styx—
A fair plea surely. Let no touch of man*
Handle my virgin body. Blood that's free
He will prefer, whoever he may be,

Whom you prepare to appease by killing me.
Even so, if my last words have power to move
Any of you (King Priam's daughter speaks,
Not some slave girl) restore my corpse to my
Mother unransomed. Let the tragic right
Of sepulture be priced in tears not gold;
Once, when she could, she paid in gold* as well.'
She finished, and the whole assembly shed
The tears she would not shed. The priest himself,
Weeping, against his will, drove his blade home,
Piercing the breast she offered. On the ground,
Her knees failing, she sank and held her look
Of fearless resolution to the last;
And she took trouble, even as she fell,
To wrap* what should be kept in privacy,
And guard the honour of her chastity.
    The Trojan women took her body up,
Counting the roll, the lamentable roll,
Of Priam's children and the blood so often
Given by that one house. They mourned for her,
The princess, and for her so lately queen,
Consort and royal mother, paragon
Of Asia's pride, now but a sorry share
Of spoils, a lot victorious Ulysses
Would have refused, had it not been that she
Was Hector's mother: Hector hardly found
A master for his mother! She embraced
The corpse of that brave soul and shed for her
Tears shed so often for her fatherland,
Her sons and husband; tears too on her wounds
She poured and smothered kisses on her face.
She beat her own woe-seasoned breast and swept
Her white locks in the clotted gore and wailed
In threnodies of grief these bitter words:
    'Dear child, last of my woes (for what is left?),
Dear darling lying there, I see your wound,
My wound as well. Look, so that I should lose
No child of mine unslaughtered, your wound too
You have. But you, I thought, because a woman,
Were safe from steel; yet you, a woman, fell

By steel. He who destroyed your many brothers,
He destroyed you, Achilles, doom of Troy
And my bereaver. But when Paris' arrows
And Phoebus' felled him, now for sure, I said,
We need not fear Achilles: now again
I had to fear him: in the sepulchre
His ashes raged against our race; entombed,
We felt him as our foe. For him I bore
My children! Mighty Ilium lies low.
In tragedy our nation's ruin reached
Its end; but end it has. For me alone
Troy lives; my woes stream on. Why, yesterday
I was supreme, with all the power of sons,
Daughters, husband and family; and now I'm dragged,
A pauper fugitive, torn from the tombs
Of those I love, given to Penelope.
And as I spin the task I'm set, she'll point
To me and tell the wives of Ithaca
"This woman here is Hector's glorious mother,
This woman's Priam's queen"; and you, my child,
You, when so many others have been lost,
Your mother's only solace, meet your doom
In sacrifice upon our foeman's tomb!
Death-offerings for our foe from my own womb!
    Why does my iron heart not break? Why now
Linger? For what does my calamitous
Old age preserve me? Why, you cruel gods,
Keep an old woman still alive, unless
To see fresh funerals? Who would believe
Priam could be called happy after Troy
Was overwhelmed? Happy he is in death!
His eyes don't see you done to death, my darling—
To life and reign he said the same farewell.
But you're a princess; you'll be dowered no doubt
With royal rites, your body laid to rest
In your ancestral sepulchre! Our house
Has no such luck! For your last dues you'll find
A mother's tears, a scoop* of foreign sand.
We have lost all. Yet there's still one hope why
I should endure to live some brief while yet—

His mother's favourite, now her only child,
Once youngest of my sons, given to the king
Of Thrace upon this shore, my Polydorus.
But why do I delay to wash your wounds,
Your dear face spattered with that ruthless blood?'
    With her old shaky steps and torn white hair
She walked down to the beach. 'Give me a jar',
She bade the Trojan women—ill-starred soul!—
'For water from the waves.' Upon the beach
Cast up she saw her Polydorus' corpse
And the huge wounds the Thracian knives had made.
The Trojan women screamed. She was struck dumb
In anguish; anguish—agony—engulfed
Her voice and springing tears, and like a rock
Of granite she stood rigid, her eyes fixed
Upon the ground she faced. And then she raised
Wild tragic eyes to heaven, then gazed upon
Her son's face lying there, and then his wounds,
His wounds especially, and armed herself
With anger towering high. And, as it flared,
As though she still were queen, her sentence stood
For vengeance, and the pictured punishment
Filled all her thoughts; and, as a lioness
Whose suckling whelp is stolen, wild with rage,
Tracks down her unseen foe, so Hecuba,
Rage linked with grief, oblivious of her years
But not her resolution, made her way
To Polymestor, author of that foul
Murder, and sought an audience, her wish
Being, she said, to show him hidden gold
She still had left and destined for her son.
The King of Thrace with his habitual
Passion for plunder kept the secret tryst,
And sly and smooth he spoke: 'Quick, Hecuba,
Give your son's gift to me. All shall be his,
What you give now and what you gave before,
By heaven I swear it.' As he spoke and swore
His lies, she eyed him savagely and rage,
Her seething rage, boiled over. Shouting to
The crowd of captive women, she attacked

The king and dug her fingers in his eyes,
His treacherous eyes, and gouged his eyeballs out
(Rage gave her strength) and, plunging in her hands,
Scooped out, all filthy with that felon's blood,
Not eyes (for they were gone) but eye-sockets.
     Incensed to see their king's calamity,
The Thracians started to attack the queen
With sticks and stones, but she snapped at the stones,
Snarling, and when her lips were set to frame
Words and she tried to speak, she barked. The place
Remains today, named from what happened there.*
Then still remembering her ancient ills,
She howled in sorrow through the land of Thrace.
That fate of hers stirred pity in the hearts
Of friend and foe, Trojans and Greeks alike,
And all the gods as well—all: Juno too,
Jove's wife and sister, did herself declare
The tragic end of Hecuba unfair.

MEMNON

Aurora, who had favoured Troy's arms too,
Had no time to lament the tragedy
Of Troy and Hecuba. A closer trouble,
A family grief, had wrung her heart, the loss
Of Memnon. Slaughtered by Achilles' spear,
She, his bright golden mother, saw him dead
Upon the plain of Troy. The rosy blush
That dyes the hour of dawn grew pale and clouds
Hid the bright heavens. But when his limbs were laid
On the last flames, she could not bear to look.
With hair unbound, just as she was, she knelt
(Nor did her pride disdain) before the knees
Of mighty Jove and pleaded through her tears:
'Least I may be of all the goddesses
The golden heavens hold (in all the world
My shrines are rarest), yet a deity
I am, and I have come not for a gift
Of fanes or altar-fires or holy days;
Though should you see how great the services

I, but a woman, give when I preserve
At each new dawn the boundaries of night,
You'd judge some guerdon due. But it's not now
Aurora's errand nor her care to claim
Honours well-earned. I come because my son,
Memnon, is lost, who for his uncle's sake*
In vain bore valiant arms and in his first
Youth (so you willed it) fell to brave Achilles.
Grant him, I pray, Ruler of Heaven most high,
Some honour, solace that he had to die,
And soothe a wounded mother's misery!'
Jove nodded his assent as Memnon's pyre
Fell to the leaping flames. Black rolling smoke
Darkened the daylight, as a stream breathes forth
The mist it breeds that lets no sunlight through.
Up flew black ashes, and they clustered thick
Into a single mass, which took a shape
And from the fire drew heat and breath of life.
Its lightness gave it wings and like a bird
At first, and presently a real bird,
Its great wings whirred and with it sister-birds
Whirred beyond counting, all from the same source.
Three times they circled round the pyre; three times
Their cries, united, echoed through the air.
On the fourth flight the flock split up; then two
Fierce legions, so divided, fought each other*
With claws and beaks in fury, till their wings
And battling breasts were weary; then they fell,
Death-offerings, on the ash whose kin they were,
Recalling that brave soul from whom they sprang.
He who begot them gave those sudden birds
Their name 'Memnonides';* and when the sun
Has coursed through the twelve signs, they fight again
To die in memory of Memnon slain.
While others wept that Hecuba should bark,
Aurora was intent on her own grief:
Now still her loving sorrow she renews
And with her tears the whole wide world bedews.*

THE PILGRIMAGE OF AENEAS

Even so the Fates did not allow Troy's hopes
To fall to ruins with her walls. The son
Of Venus on his shoulders bore away
Her holy images and, holy too,
His ancient father, venerable freight.
Of all his wealth that was the prize he chose
In love and loyalty, that and his son,
Ascanius. On board the escaping fleet
He set sail from Antandros, left behind
The guilty homes of Thrace, the land that dripped
With Polydorus' blood, and finding winds
That served him well and tides that favoured reached
Apollo's city* with his retinue.
There Anius, who served Apollo as priest
And men as monarch, made him welcome to
His court and temple, showed his city's sights,
The famous shrine and the two trees to which
Latona once had clung when she gave birth.*
Incense was given to flames and wine poured forth
On incense, bulls were slain and entrails burnt
According to the rite; then, entering
The palace, they partook of Bacchus' boon
And Ceres' gifts, couched on high coverlets.
Then good Anchises spoke: 'Your reverence,
Apollo's chosen priest, am I mistaken,
Or had you not, when I last saw these walls,
Four daughters and a son as I recall?'
Shaking his head beneath its snow-white bands,
In sorrow Anius replied: 'My lord,
Most noble hero, you make no mistake.
You saw me father of five children, now
(Such is the fickleness of fate) you see
Me almost childless. For what help to me
Is my son far away on Andros isle
(Named after him) where in his father's stead
He reigns? The god of Delos gave him power
Of prophecy and Bacchus gave my girls
Gifts greater than their prayers or their belief.

For at my daughters' touch all things were turned
To corn or wine or oil of Pallas' tree.
Rich was that role of theirs! When it was known
To Agamemnon, plunderer of Troy
(You'll understand we too have felt some part
Of your great storm), with force of arms he stole
My girls, protesting, from their father's arms
And bade them victual with that gift divine
The fleet of Greece. They fled, each as she could,
Two to Euboea, two to their brother's isle,
Andros. A force arrived and threatened war,
Were they not given up. Fear overcame
His love and he gave up his kith and kin
To punishment. And one could well forgive
Their frightened brother. In Andros' defence
Aeneas was not there to fight, nor Hector
Who made you last those ten long years of war.
Now fetters were made ready to secure
The captured sisters' arms: their arms still free
The captives raised to heaven, crying "Help!
Help, father Bacchus!" and the god who gave
Their gift brought help, if help it can be called
In some strange way to lose one's nature. How
They lost it, that I never learnt, nor could
I tell you now. The bitter end's well known.
With wings and feathers, birds your consort loves,
My daughters were transformed to snow-white doves.'*
    With these and other tales they filled the feast;
Then, the meal ended, they retired to sleep.
With day they rose and went to the oracle
Of Phoebus, who commanded them to seek
Their ancient mother* and ancestral shores.
As they set forth the king attended them
And gave them gifts, a sceptre for Anchises,
A quiver for his grandson and a robe,
A wine-bowl for Aeneas, which a friend,
Therses of Thebes, had given from his far home.
Therses had sent it; Alcon of Hyle
Had fashioned it, engraving a long tale.*
There was a city; one could point and count

Seven gates; these served to name it* and explain
What place it was. Before the city, scenes
Of grief, with funerals and flaming pyres
And tombs, and matrons with dishevelled hair
And naked breasts; and nymphs in tears were seen
Mourning their drought-dried springs. A tree stood bare
And leafless, goats were gnawing round parched rocks.
Look, he has fashioned in the heart of Thebes
Orion's daughters,* one cutting her throat—
No woman's wound—one with her shuttle's point
Stabbing herself, brave injury, as both
Die for their country's sake, and through the city
Are borne in funeral pomp to the great square
And there are burnt. Then, lest their line should die,
From those two virgins' embers twin youths* rise
Whom fame calls the Coroni, and they lead
The files that lay their natal ash to rest.
Thus on the antique bronze stood shining scenes,
And round the wine-bowl's rim acanthus leaves
High-raised in gold. The Trojans give in turn
No meaner gifts, presenting to the priest
A thurible, a salver and a crown,
A glorious crown of gold and precious stones.
    From Andros, mindful that from Teucer's stock
Troy drew its origin, they sailed to Crete.
But there they could not long endure the land's
Inclemency and left those hundred towns,
Eager to reach the shores of Italy.
Storms raged and tossed the crews and, when they reached
The treacherous harbour of the Strophades,*
The bird Aello* filled their hearts with fear.
And now their passage passed Dulichium
And Ithaca and Samos and the homes
Of Neritos where wily Ulysses reigned.
Ambracia they saw, for which the gods
Contended, and the likeness of the judge*
Then turned to stone, and Actium now famed
For great Apollo's sake;* Dodona too,
With its speaking oaks, and that Chaonian bay
Where Munichus'* three sons grew wings one day

To escape the wicked fire and flew away.
    They made next for the happy countryside
Of the Phaeacians* clothed in orchard-lands;
And thence Epirus and Buthrotos where
A Trojan prophet ruled a copied Troy.
Thence, learning from the faithful prophecies
Of Priam's son, wise Helenus, the whole
Future that lay in store, they made landfall
In Sicily. There three capes run to sea;
Pachynus turns towards the rainy south,
While Lilybaeum lies in soft west winds,
And, facing north, Pelorus looks upon
The sea-shy bears. Hither the Trojans came;
Rowing with favouring tides the fleet made land
At evenfall on Zancle's shelving sand.
Scylla infests the right-hand coast, the left
Restless Charybdis; one grasps passing ships
And sucks them down to spew them up again;
The other's ringed below her hell-black waist
With raging dogs. She has a girl's sweet face,
And if the tales the poets have passed down
Are not all false, she was a sweet girl once.
Many a suitor sought her hand, but she
Repulsed them all and went to the sea-nymphs
(She was the sea-nymphs' favourite) and told
How she'd eluded all the young men's love.
Then Galatea letting Scylla comb
Her hair, heaved a deep sigh and said, 'My dear,
Your suitors after all are men and not
Unkind: you can reject them, as you do,
Unscathed. But I whom sea-blue Doris bore,
Whose father's Nereus, who am safe besides
Among my school of sisters, I could not
Foil Cyclops' love except in bitter grief.'
Tears choked her as she told it. Scylla wiped
The tears with sleek white fingers, comforting
The goddess: 'Tell me, darling. Do not hide
(You know you trust me) how you were so hurt.'
    And Galatea answered with these words:

ACIS AND GALATEA

'Acis was son of river-nymph Symaethis
And Faunus was his father, a great joy
To both his parents, and a greater joy
To me; for me, and me alone, he loved.
He was sixteen, the down upon his cheek
Scarce yet a beard, and he was beautiful.
He was my love, but I was Cyclops' love,
Who wooed me endlessly and, if you ask
Whether my hate for him or love for Acis
Was stronger in my heart, I could not tell;
For both were equal. Oh, how powerful,
Kind Venus, is thy reign! That savage creature,
The forest's terror, whom no wayfarer
Set eyes upon unscathed, who scorned the gods*
Of great Olympus, now felt pangs of love,
Burnt with a mighty passion, and forgot
His flocks and caves. Now lovelorn Polyphemus
Cared for his looks, cared earnestly to please;
Now with a rake he combed his matted hair,
And with a sickle trimmed his shaggy beard,
And studied his fierce features in a pool
And practised to compose them. His wild urge
To kill, his fierceness and his lust for blood
Ceased and in safety ships might come and go.

    Meanwhile a famous seer had sailed to Etna,
Wise Telemus, whom no bird* could delude,
And warned the dreadful giant "That one eye
Upon your brow Ulysses soon shall take."*
He answered laughing "You delude yourself!
Of all the stupid prophets! Someone else
Has taken it* already." So he mocked
The warning truth; then tramped along the shore
With giant crushing strides or, tired anon,
Returned to the dark cave that was his home.

    There juts into the sea* a wedge-shaped point,
Washed by the ocean waves on either side.
Here Cyclops climbed and at the top sat down,
His sheep untended trailing after him.

Before him at his feet he laid his staff,
A pine, fit for the mainmast of a ship,
And took his pipe, made of a hundred reeds.*
His pastoral whistles rang among the cliffs
And over the waves; and I behind a rock,
Hidden and lying in my Acis' arms,*
Heard far away these words* and marked them well.
   "Fair Galatea, whiter than the snow,
Taller than alders, flowerier than the meads,
Brighter than crystal, livelier than a kid,
Sleeker than shells worn by the ceaseless waves,
Gladder than winter's sun and summer's shade,
Nobler than apples, sweeter than ripe grapes,
Fairer than lofty planes, clearer than ice,
Softer than down of swans or creamy cheese,
And, would you welcome me, more beautiful
Than fertile gardens watered by cool streams.
Yet, Galatea, fiercer than wild bulls,
Harder than ancient oak, falser than waves,
Tougher than willow wands or branching vines,
Wilder than torrents, firmer than these rocks,
Prouder than peacocks, crueller than fire,
Sharper than briars, deafer than the sea,
More savage than a bear guarding her cubs,
More pitiless than snakes beneath the heel,
And—what above all else I'd wrest from you—
Swifter in flight than ever hind that flees
The baying hounds, yes, swifter than the wind
And all the racing breezes of the sky.
(Though, if you knew, you would repent your flight,
Condemn your coyness, strive to hold me fast.)
   Deep in the mountain I have hanging caves
Of living rock where never summer suns
Are felt nor winter's cold. Apples I have
Loading the boughs, and I have golden grapes
And purple in my vineyards—all for you.
Your hands shall gather luscious strawberries
In woodland shade; in autumn you shall pick
Cherries and plums, not only dusky black,
But yellow fat and waxen in the sun,

And chestnuts shall be yours, if I am yours,
And every tree shall bear its fruit for you.

　　All this fine flock is mine, and many more
Roam in the dales or shelter in the woods
Or in my caves are folded; should you chance
To ask how many, that I could not tell:
A *poor* man counts his flocks. Nor need you trust
My praises; here before your eyes you see
Their legs can scarce support the bulging udders.
And I have younger stock, lambs in warm folds,
And kids of equal age in other folds,
And snowy milk always, some kept to drink
And some the rennet curdles into cheese.

　　No easy gifts or commonplace delights
Shall be your portion—does and goats and hares,
A pair of doves, a gull's nest from the cliff.
I found one day among the mountain peaks,
For you to play with, twins so much alike
You scarce could tell, cubs of a shaggy bear.
I found them and I said 'She shall have these;
I'll keep them for my mistress for her own.'
Now, Galatea, raise your glorious head
From the blue sea;* spurn not my gifts, but come!
For sure I know—I have just seen—myself
Reflected in a pool, and what I saw
Was truly pleasing. See how large I am!
No bigger body Jove himself can boast
Up in the sky—you always talk of Jove
Or someone reigning there. My ample hair
O'erhangs my grave stern face and like a grove
Darkens my shoulders; and you must not think
Me ugly, that my body is so thick
With prickly bristles. Trees without their leaves
Are ugly, and a horse is ugly too
Without a mane to veil its sorrel neck.
Feathers clothe birds and fleeces grace the sheep:
So beard and bristles best become a man.
Upon my brow I have one single eye,
But it is huge, like some vast shield. What then?
Does not the mighty sun see from the sky

All things on earth? Yet the sun's orb is one.
   Moreover in your sea my father reigns;
Him I give you—my father,* yours to be,
Would you but pity me and hear my prayer.
To you alone I yield. I, who despise
Jove and his heaven and his thunderbolt,
Sweet Nereid, you I fear, your anger flames
More dreadful than his bolt. Oh, I could bear
Your scorn more patiently did you but spurn
All others, but, if Cyclops you reject,
Why prefer Acis, Acis' arms to mine?
Acis may please himself and please, alas,
You, Galatea. Give me but the chance,
He'll find my strength no smaller than my size.
I'll gouge his living guts, I'll rend his limbs
And strew them in the fields and in the sea—
Your sea, so may he be one flesh* with you!
I burn! The fire you fight is fanned to flame;
All Etna's furnace in my breast I bear,
And you, my Galatea, never care!"
   Such was his vain lament; then up he rose
(I saw it all) as a fierce thwarted bull
Roams through the woodlands and familiar fields,
And, spying in his rage Acis and me,
All unaware and fearing no such fate,
Shouted "I see you; now I shall make sure
That loving fond embrace shall be your last."
Loud as an angry Cyclops ought to shout
He shouted; Etna shuddered at the din.
Then I in panic dived into the sea
Beside us; Acis had already turned
His hero's back and shouted as he fled
"Help, Galatea! Father, mother, help!
Admit me to your kingdom* for I die."
Cyclops pursued and hurled a massive rock,
Torn from the hill, and though its merest tip
Reached Acis, yet it crushed and smothered him.
But I (it was all the Fates permitted me)
Caused Acis to assume ancestral powers.
Beneath the rock came trickling crimson blood,

And soon the ruddy hue began to fade,
And turned the colour of a swollen stream
After the first rain falls, and in a while
It cleared. Then in the rock a crack split wide
And in the fissure rose a tall green reed,
And from the hollow opening came the sound
Of waters leaping forth, and suddenly—
Most wonderful!—there stood a youth* waist deep
With woven rushes round his new-sprung horns;
And he, though larger and his face wave-blue,
Was surely Acis—Acis there himself,
Changed to a river-god; and still the same
His waters keep that legendary name.'
    So Galatea ended and the group
Of Nereids dispersed and swam away
Across the placid waters of the bay.

SCYLLA AND GLAUCUS

Scylla turned back; she dared not trust herself
Far out at sea. Along the thirsty sands
She sauntered naked or, when she was tired,
Made for a little land-locked cove and in
Its sheltered waves enjoyed a cooling bathe.
Suddenly, breaking the surface of the sea,
Glaucus appeared, a new inhabitant
Of ocean's deeps since on Anthedon's* shore
He suffered a sea change. He saw the girl,
And stopped, his heart transfixed, then spoke to her,
Spoke anything he thought might stay her flight.
But Scylla fled (her terror gave her speed)
And reached a cliff-top rising from the shore,
A vast cliff by the strait,* that towered up
To one great peak and with its tree-clad height
Rose in a curve far out over the sea.
The place was safe; she stopped; she could not tell
If he were god or monster, and she gazed
In wonder at his colour and his hair
That clothed his shoulders and streamed down his back,
And thighs that formed a twisting fish's tail.

He knew her thoughts, and leaning on a ledge
Of rock that rose near by, 'Fair maid', he said,
'I am no monster nor a savage beast;
I am a sea-god. Over the open sea
Not Proteus,* no, nor Triton* nor Palaemon*
Has greater power than I. Yet I was once
A mortal, dedicated even then
To the open sea—there all my time and toil.
I used to haul the nets that hauled the fish,
Or sitting on a rock plied rod and line.
Beside a lush green lea there lies a beach,*
One side the sea, the other side the meadow,
A meadow never marred by grazing cows,
Nor cropped by shaggy goats or placid sheep.
No busy bee had worked the flowers there,
No gracious garland thence was ever given,
Nor hands had swung a scythe. I was the first
To sit upon that sward and dry my lines,
And on it range my row of fish to count
What I had caught, as chance had guided them
Into my nets or trust to my barbed hook.
It sounds a fairy-tale, but what have I
To gain by fairy-tales? My fish, my catch,
In contact with the grass, began to move
And turn from side to side and glide across
The ground as in the sea, and while I watched,
Waiting and wondering, they all made off,
The lot of them, back to the sea, their home,
Leaving their new-found master and the beach.
I was amazed and pondered long to find
The reason. Could some god have done it or
The juices of some plant? And yet what plant
Could have such power? I picked some stalks and chewed
What I had picked. The juice, the unknown juice,
Had hardly passed my throat when suddenly
I felt my heart-strings tremble and my soul
Consumed with yearning for that other world.
I could not wait. "Farewell", I cried, "farewell,
Land never more my home", and plunged beneath
The waves. The sea-gods welcomed me to join

Their company (so well was I esteemed)
And called on Tethys and Oceanus
To take away my mortal essences.
They purified me with a ninefold chant
That purged my sins; then bade me plunge my body
Beneath a hundred rivers. Instantly
Torrents cascaded down from near and far
And poured whole seas of waters on my head.
So far I can relate what I recall,
So far remember; but the rest is lost.
   When sense returned, I found myself in body
Another self, nor was my mind the same.
For the first time I saw this bronze-green beard,
These flowing locks that sweep along the swell,
These huge broad shoulders and my sea-blue arms,
My legs that curve to form a fish's tail.
But what avail my looks, what to have pleased
The ocean's gods? What good to be a god
Myself, unless such things can touch your heart?'
So much he said, and would have said more too,
But Scylla fled. Enraged at his repulse,
He made in fury for the magic halls
Of Circe,* daughter of the glorious Sun.

BOOK XIV

SCYLLA AND GLAUCUS (*continued*)

AND now the Euboean merman through the main,
The main that held his heart, had left behind
Etna heaped high upon the giant's throat,*
The Cyclops' fields that never knew the use
Of plough or harrow, nor owed any debt
To teams of oxen; Zancle too behind
And Rhegium's facing bastions, and the strait,
The ship-destroying strait, whose twin shores hem
The bounds of Italy and Sicily.
Then on he swam with mighty strokes across
The Tyrrhene Sea* and reached the herb-clad hills
And magic halls of Circe,* the Sun's child,
Crowded with phantom beasts.* He met her then
And, mutual greetings given, 'Goddess', he said,
'Have pity on a god, I beg of you.
For you alone can ease this love of mine,
If only I am worthy. No one knows
Better than I the power of herbs, for I
Was changed by herbs. And I would have you learn
My passion's cause: on the Italian coast,
Facing Messina's battlements, I saw
Scylla. I blush to tell my wooing words,
My promises, my prayers—she scorned them all.
But you, let now your magic lips, if spells
Have aught of sovereignty, pronounce a spell,
Or if your herbs have surer power, let herbs
Of proven virtue do their work and win.
I crave no cure, nor want my wounds made well;
Pain need not pass; but make her share my hell!'

   But Circe (never heart more sensitive
Than hers to love's assault, whether the trait
Was in herself or Venus might perhaps
In anger at her father's gossiping*
Have made her so) said: 'You would better woo
One who is willing, wants the same as you,

Is caught by love no less. You should be wooed
(How well you could have been!) and if you give
Some hope, believe me, wooed you well shall be!
Trust in those looks of yours; be bold and brave.
See, I, the daughter of the shining Sun,
A goddess who possess the magic powers
Of spell and herb, I, Circe, pray that I
Be yours. Spurn her who spurns you; welcome one
Who wants you. By one act requite us both!'
     But Glaucus answered: 'Sooner shall green leaves
Grow in the sea or seaweed on the hills
Than I shall change my love while Scylla lives.'
Rage filled the goddess' heart. She had no power
Nor wish to wound him (for she loved him well),
So turned her anger on the girl he chose.
In fury at his scorn, she ground together
Her ill-famed herbs, her herbs of ghastly juice,
And, as she ground them, sang her demon spells.
Then in a robe of deepest blue went forth
Out of her palace, through the fawning throng
Of beasts, to Rhegium that looks across
To Zancle's cliffs. Over the raging waves
She passed as if she stepped on solid ground,
And skimmed dry-shod the surface of the sea.
     There was a little bay,* bent like a bow,
A place of peace, where Scylla loved to laze,
Her refuge from the rage of sea and sky,
When in mid heaven the sun with strongest power
Shone from his zenith and the shade lay least.
Against her coming Circe had defiled
This quiet bay with her deforming drugs,
And after them had sprinkled essences
Of noxious roots; then with her witch's lips
Had muttered thrice nine times a baffling maze
Of magic incantations. Scylla came
And waded in waist-deep, when round her loins
She saw foul monstrous barking beasts. At first,
Not dreaming they were part of her, she fled
And thrust in fear the bullying brutes away.
But what she feared and fled, she fetched along,

And looking for her thighs, her legs, her feet,
Found gaping jaws instead like Hell's vile hound.*
Poised on a pack of beasts! No legs! Below
Her midriff dogs, ringed in a raging row!
   Glaucus, her lover, wept and fled the embrace
Of Circe who had used too cruelly
The power of her magic. Scylla stayed
There where she was and, when the first chance came
To vent her rage and hate on Circe, robbed
Ulysses* of his comrades. Later, too,
She would have sunk the Trojan galleons,
Had she not been transformed before they came
Into a reef whose rocks rise up today,
And sailors shun her still and steer away.

THE PILGRIMAGE OF AENEAS (continued)

Past Scylla's reef and ravening Charybdis
The Trojan galleons had won their way
And almost reached the shores of Italy,
When head winds drove them to the Libyan coast.
There Dido made Aeneas welcome to
Her home and heart, her heart too ill-inured
To bear the parting from her Trojan spouse.
Feigning a holy rite, she built a pyre
And fell upon his sword and, duped herself,
Duped all. Aeneas, fugitive again
Fled the new city on the sandy shore,
Back to the bounds of Eryx and the lands
Of loyal Acestes,* where he sacrificed
In honour of his father's tomb. The fleet
That Iris, Juno's envoy, nearly fired,
Cast off and left behind Hippotades'
Domain,* the smoking lands of sulphur fumes,
And the three Sirens' rocks; and then his ship,
Her pilot lost, sailed past Inarime
And Prochyte and Pithecusae placed
On a bare hill, named from its denizens.
For once the Father of the Gods, who loathed
The fraud and falsehood of the Cercopes

And all their crafty crimes, transformed the men
Into misshapen animals* that seemed
Both like and unlike humans, shrivelling
Their limbs, tilting and flattening their noses,
Ploughing their cheeks with wrinkles of old age.
Then, swathed all over in a tawny pelt,
He sent them to dwell here, but first removed
The means of speech and use of tongues designed
For shocking perjury, and left them but
Screeches and screams for protest and complaint.
    Leaving these places, on the right he passed
The city walls of Naples, on the left
Misenus'* tomb, brave trumpeter, and reached
The shore of Cumae, with its wilderness
Of marshes. Entering the grotto there
Of the long-living Sibyl, he besought
Leave to pass down to the Underworld and meet
His father's ghost. And she, her eyes long kept
Upon the ground, raised them, inspired at last
By heavenly ecstasy. 'Great is the gift
You seek', she said, 'Prince of great deeds, whose hand
The sword has proved, whose loyalty the fire.
Yet, Trojan, have no fear. You shall achieve
Your aim and with my guidance you shall know
The dwellings of Elysium and the last
Realm of the world and your dear father's ghost:
To righteousness no path's impassable.'
She showed him in the glade of Proserpine
A gleaming golden bough and bade him break
It from the trunk. Aeneas did her bidding
And saw the riches of Hell's frightful realm
And his own ancestors and the aged ghost
Of great-hearted Anchises; he learnt too
That region's rules and what new perils he
Must face afresh in war. Retracing thence
His weary steps he eased his journey's toil
In converse with his guide,* and as he paced
Through the dim twilight up the fearful path,
'Whether thou art a goddess at my side,
Or the gods' favourite', he said, 'to me

Less than divine thou'lt never be. For I
Owe all to thee, all truly, by whose will
I visited the world of death and come
Back from the world of death that I've now seen.
For services so great, when I have reached
The air above, to thee I shall erect
A temple and in thine honour incense burn.'
The Sibyl held him in her gaze and sighed:
'I am no goddess, nor must you believe
A mortal worthy to be honoured with
The smoke of incense. Know, lest you should err
In ignorance, I once had offered me
Eternal life, life without end, if I
Lost my virginity to Phoebus' love.
Hoping for that and meaning to corrupt
My heart with bribes, "Choose, Sibyl, what you will",
He said, "and you shall win your choice." And I,
Pointing towards a gathered heap of dust,
Asked in my futile folly to attain
Birthdays as many as those dusty grains.
It slipped my mind to ask those years should be
For ever young. Those years he granted me;
And youth for ever too, if I would yield.
I scorned Apollo's gift and still remain
Unmarried; but my years of happier times
Have turned their back and old and feeble age
Comes on with shaky steps which I must long
Endure. For now, you see, seven centuries
Have passed for me: to match those grains of dust
There still remain to see three hundred more
Harvests brought home, three hundred vintages.
The time shall come when length of days will shrivel
This frame of mine, and my age-wasted limbs
Shrink to a feather's weight;* none will believe
That I was loved and pleased a god. Perhaps
Phoebus himself won't know me or deny
He loved me. To such changes I shall pass.
No eye shall see me then: my voice alone
The Fates will leave, my voice by which I'm known.'
      Thus as they climbed the track the Sibyl told

Her tale, and, rising from the Underworld,
Aeneas came to Cumae. After due
Sacrifice he reached the coast that later bore
His nurse's name.* Here too had Macareus
Of Neritos found haven after long
And weary toils, comrade of travel-worn
Ulysses. Spying Achaemenides,*
Abandoned long before among the rocks
Of Etna, now found unexpectedly
Alive, he cried in disbelief, 'What chance
Or god has saved you? Why are you, a Greek,
On board a Trojan vessel? For what land
Is your ship bound?' And Achaemenides,
In rags no more, his clothes no longer pinned
With thorns, now quite his former self, replied:
'May I see Polyphemus yet again,
That maw aswill with human blood, if I
Value my home and Ithaca above
This vessel here, if I revere Aeneas
Less than my father. I can never be
Grateful enough, though I should give my all.
That I can speak and breathe and see the sky
And the bright sun, could I lack gratitude,
Could I forget? To him I owe my life
That did not end between the Cyclops' jaws,
And should I leave the light of life today,
A proper grave will hold me or at least
Not that belly! What were my feelings then
(Except that terror swept away all sense
And feeling) when, abandoned there, I saw
You sail away to sea? I longed to shout
But dreaded to betray myself; your ship
Ulysses' shouting* almost wrecked. I saw
The Cyclops wrench a huge rock from the hill
And hurl it out to sea. I saw again
His giant biceps like a catapult
Slinging enormous stones, and feared the waves
Or wind-whistle would overwhelm the ship,
Forgetting I was not aboard. But when
Flight rescued you from certain death, he prowled

Groaning all over Etna, groping through
The forest, stumbling eyeless* on the rocks,
Stretching his bloodstained arms towards the waves,
Cursing the race of Greeks: "O for some chance
To get Ulysses or some mate of his
To vent my rage, whose guts I might devour,
Whose living limbs my hands might rend, whose blood
Might sluice my throat and mangled body writhe
Between my teeth! How slight, how nothing then
The loss of sight they ravished!" This and more
In frenzy. Horror filled me as I watched
His face still soaked with slaughter, his huge hands,
Those savage hands, his empty sightless eye,
His beard and body caked with human blood.
Death was before my eyes! Yet death the least
Of horrors! Now he's got me, I was sure.
He's going to sink my guts in his! My mind
Pictured the moment when I'd seen two friends
Time after time dashed to the ground, and he,
Like a hairy lion bending over them,
Guzzled their flesh and guts and marrow-bones,
Still half-alive. I shuddered as I stood
Blood-drained in horror, watching as he chewed
The filthy feast and retched it back again,
Belching great bloody gobbets mixed with wine.
That was the fate I fancied was in store
For me, poor soul. For many days I hid,
Starting at every rustle, fearing death
And longing too to die, my hunger kept
At bay with acorns, leaves and grass. Alone,
Helpless and hopeless, left to pain and death,
After an age I saw this ship far out
And signalled to be saved, and running down
Stood pleading on the beach. My plea was heard:
A Trojan ship welcomed a Greek on board!
Now you, my dearest friend, tell me your own
Fortunes and what befell your company
And captain when you took your chance at sea.'

   He told* how Aeolus ruled the Tyrrhene main,
Aeolus, son of Hippotes, and held

The winds imprisoned. These, secured within
A bull's-hide bag, Ulysses had received,
A memorable gift.* Nine days, he said,
They sailed with a fair breeze and they had seen
The land they sought, but when the tenth day dawned
Envy and lust for booty overcame
His shipmates. Sure that gold was there, they loosed
The lace that held the winds, and back their ship
Was blown over the waters she'd just crossed,
Back to the Wind-King's harbour once again.
'From there', he said, 'we sailed to the old town
Of Lamus and the Laestrygonians.
Antiphates was chieftain; I was sent
To him with two companions; one with me
Fled—we just saved ourselves; the third of us
Fed with his flesh those fiendish cannibals.
Antiphates pursued us, mustering
His braves, and in a crowd they came and threw
Tree-trunks and rocks and sank our craft, our crews.
Yet one ship, with Ulysses and ourselves,
Escaped. Mourning so many comrades lost,
Complaining bitterly, we reached the isle
You see there in the distance (distant, yes,
Believe me, it's best seen!). Take my advice,
Most just of Trojans, Venus' son (the war
Is done, Aeneas, you're a foe no more):
Keep well away, I say, from Circe's shore.

THE ISLAND OF CIRCE

On Circe's shore we moored our one last ship
But then, remembering Antiphates
And savage Polyphemus, we refused
To leave the beach; but lots were drawn and I
Was chosen to approach those unknown halls.
The lot sent me with shrewd Eurylochus
And my true friend Polites, and Elpenor,
Too fond of wine,* and eighteen more of us
To Circe's walls. As soon as we arrived
And reached the portal, lions, bears and wolves,

Hundreds of them together, rushed at us
And filled our hearts with fear; but fear we found
Was false; they meant no single scratch of harm.
No, they were gentle and they wagged their tails
And fawned on us and followed us along,
Until the maids-in-waiting welcomed us
And led us through the marble vestibule
Into their mistress' presence. There she sat,
In a fine chamber, on a stately throne,
In purple robe and cloak of woven gold;
And in attendance nymphs and Nereids,
Whose nimble fingers never comb a fleece
Nor spin a skein, but sort and set in baskets
Grasses and flowers, heaped in disarray,
And herbs of many hues; and as they work
She guides and watches,* knowing well herself
The lore of every leaf, what blend is best,
And checks them closely as the plants are weighed.
She saw us then and, salutations made,
Her welcome seemed an answer to our prayers.
     At once she bade the servants mix a brew*
Of roasted barley, honey and strong wine
And creamy curds, and then, to be disguised
In the sweet taste, she poured her essences.
We took the bowls she handed (magic hands!).
Our throats were dry and thirsty; we drank deep;
And then the demon goddess lightly laid
Her wand upon our hair, and instantly
Bristles (the shame of it! but I will tell)
Began to sprout; I could no longer speak;
My words were grunts, I grovelled to the ground.
I felt my nose change to a tough wide snout,
My neck thicken and bulge. My hands that held
The bowl just now made footprints on the floor.
And with my friends who suffered the same fate
(Such power have magic potions) I was shut
Into a sty. Eurylochus alone,
We saw, missed a swine's shape, for he alone
Refused the offered bowl, and, had he not
Escaped it, I should still be numbered with

That bristly herd today, for from his lips
Ulysses never would have learnt our ruin
Nor ever come to Circe for revenge.
    He had been given by Mercury, who brings
The boon of peace, a flower which the gods
Call moly,* a white bloom with root of black.
Secure with this and heaven's guiding grace,
He entered Circe's halls and as she coaxed
Him to the treacherous cup and with her wand
Was trying to stroke his hair, he thrust her off
And drew his sword, and back she shrank in dread.
Then trust was pledged and hands were clasped; she took
Him to her bed, and he, for wedding gift,
Called for his comrades' shape to be restored.
So we were sprinkled with the saving juice
Of some strange herb and on our heads the wand
Was touched reversed, and words of countering power
Were chanted to unspell the chanted spells.
The more she sang her charms, the more erect
We rose; our bristles fell; our cloven feet
Forsook their clefts; our shoulders, elbows, arms
Came back again. Our captain was in tears,
And we, in tears ourselves, with open arms
Embraced our lord, and the first words we spoke,
Our very first, were words of gratitude.
    A year we lingered in that land, and much
In that long time I saw and much I heard;
And this tale too which I learnt privately
From one of the four acolytes* who serve
Those magic rites. She pointed out to me,
One day, while Circe dallied with my lord,
A statue of a youth, in snow-white marble,
Set in a shrine and gaily garlanded
With many a wreath, who bore upon his head
A woodpecker. I asked her who he was,
Why worshipped in that shrine, and why the bird
Upon his head, for I was curious.
"Listen", she said, "and learn from this tale too
My mistress' magic power and mark my words.

PICUS AND CANENS

King Picus, son of Saturn,* ruled the land
Of Latium, a king whose chief delight
Was chargers trained for battle. You observe
His features. Gaze upon his striking grace*
And from his likeness here admire the truth.
His spirit matched his looks—too young as yet
To have seen four times the games held each five years
At Grecian Elis.* Many a glance he drew
From wood-nymphs born among the Latin hills;
He was the darling of the fountain-sprites
And all the water-nymphs of Albula
And Anio and Almo's stream, so short,
And Farfar's shady depths and Dian's pool,*
Her forest pool, and every neighbouring lake.
But he despised them all, and one alone
He worshipped whom of old Venilia bore
To two-faced Janus* on the Palatine.
She, when her burgeoning years were ripe for marriage,
Was Picus' bride and loved him best of all.
Rare was her beauty, rarer still her voice,
Her lovely voice, so she was named Canens.*
Her singing used to move the woods and rocks,
Tame the wild beasts, slow the long rivers' course,
And stay the wandering birds upon the wing.
Once, as her soaring voice poured out its song,
Picus left home to hunt the boars that roamed
His countryside. He rode a prancing bay,
Carried a pair of spears, and wore a cloak
Of purple with a clasp of tawny gold.
To those same woods the daughter of the Sun
Had also come from that Circean isle
Named after her, to search the fertile hills
For her strange herbs. Unseen in the undergrowth
She saw the young king—saw, and gazed entranced.
The herbs fell from her hands. Like blazing fire
A thrill of ecstasy raced through her veins.
Then, gathering her smouldering wits, she meant
To bare her heart, but could not come to him,

He rode so fast, so close his retinue.
'You'll not escape', she cried, 'No! though the wind
Whirl you away, if I still know myself,
If still my spells their magic power retain,
Nor all the virtue of my herbs is vain.'
    She summoned up a spectre of a boar,
A phantom boar,* and made it race across
Before his eyes, and dart, or seem to dart,
Into a spinney where the trees stood close
And crowded so no horse could penetrate.
Off in a trice, unconscious of the trick,
Sped Picus to pursue his shadowy prey,
And, leaping nimbly from his foam-flecked horse,
Fumbled on foot to follow his false hope
And soon had wandered deep into the wood.
Then Circe turned to prayers and incantations,
And unknown chants to worship unknown gods,
Chants which she used to eclipse the moon's pale face
And veil her father's orb* in thirsty clouds.
Now too the heavens are darkened as she sings;
The earth breathes vapours; blind along the trails
The courtiers grope; the king has lost his guards;
The time and place are hers. 'Oh, by your eyes,
Those eyes of yours', she said, 'that captured mine,
And by your beauty, loveliest of kings,
That makes me here, a goddess, kneel to you,
Favour my passion, and accept as yours
My father, who sees all, the Sun above,
And harden not your heart to Circe's love.'
    But fiercely he repulsed her and her plea.
'Be who you may', he cried, 'I am not yours.
Another holds my heart and many a year
I pray shall hold it. Never will I wound
For any stranger's love my loyalty,
While the Fates keep my Canens safe for me!'
Time after time she pleaded—all in vain.
'You'll pay for this', she said, 'never again
Shall Canens have you home. Now you shall know
What one who's wronged, who loves, who's woman too—
And I that loving woman wronged—can do!'

Then eastwards twice and westwards twice she turned,
Thrice sang a spell, thrice touched him with her wand.
He fled and marvelled that he ran so fast—
So strangely fast—then saw he'd sprouted wings!
Outraged to find himself so suddenly
A weird new bird in his own woodland glade,
He pecked the rough-barked oaks with his hard beak
And wounded angrily the spreading boughs.
His wings assumed the purple of his cloak,
The golden brooch that pinned his robe became
A golden band of feathers round his throat,
And naught was left of Picus but his name.*
    Meanwhile his courtiers through the countryside
Were calling him and calling, but in vain.
Picus was nowhere to be found. Instead
They chanced on Circe (who by now had cleared
The air and let the wind and sun disperse
The mists) and charged her, rightly, with her guilt
And claimed their king and threatened force and aimed
Their angry spears. She sprinkled round about
Her evil drugs and poisonous essences,
And out of Erebus and Chaos called
Night and the gods of Night and poured a prayer
With long-drawn wailing cries to Hecate.
The woods (wonder of wonders!) leapt away,
A groan came from the ground, the bushes blanched,
The spattered sward was soaked with gouts of blood,
Stones brayed and bellowed, dogs began to bark,
Black snakes swarmed on the soil and ghostly shapes
Of silent spirits floated through the air.
Stunned by such magic sorcery, the group
Of courtiers stood aghast; and as they gazed,
She touched their faces with her poisoned wand,
And at its touch each took the magic form
Of some wild beast; none kept his proper shape.
    The setting sun had bathed Tartessus'* shore,
And Canens' watching eyes and heart in vain
Had waited for her husband. Through the woods
Her household and the townspeople had spread
With torches in their hands to meet their lord.

Nor was the nymph content to tear her hair
And weep and wail in woe (all that she did);
Out like a madwoman she rushed herself
And roamed the countryside of Latium.
Six nights, six days, as the sun's beams returned,
Beheld her wandering over hill and dale
With neither sleep nor food, as chance might lead.
Tiber was last to see her; tired and worn
With grief and journeying, she laid her head
By his long riverside, and there, in tears,
Breathed weak faint words in cadences of woe,
As dying swans may sing their funeral hymns;
Until at last, her fragile frame dissolved
In misery, she wasted all away
And slowly vanished into empty air.
Yet now that place still marks her memory;
The ancient Muses* for the nymph's fair fame
Called it, most fitly, Canens from her name."
   Many such tales I heard and many sights
I saw in a long year. Our idleness
Had made us slow and slack. Then the command
Came to set sail again and put to sea.
Circe had spoken of vast journeyings,
Perplexing courses, perils of the sea,
The cruel sea, to face. I was afraid,
And having here found haven here I stayed.'

THE TRIUMPH AND APOTHEOSIS OF AENEAS

Macareus had finished. Then Aeneas' nurse*
Was buried in a marble sepulchre
And on it this brief epitaph engraved:
'Here me, Caieta, saved from Grecian fire,
My loyal charge burnt on a fitting pyre.'
They loosed their moorings from the grassy strand
And leaving far behind that treacherous isle,
The ill-famed goddess' home, held course towards
The groves where Tiber in deep dappled shade
Sweeps to the ocean with his golden sand.
And there Aeneas won Latinus' throne

And daughter* too, but not without a war.
War with a fierce race followed; Turnus fought
In fury for his promised bride and all
Etruria* was locked with Latium,
Strife long and anxious, victory hard-won.
Both sides increased their strength by foreign aid,
And many reinforced the Rutuli,
Many the Trojan camp. And not in vain
Aeneas visited Evander's walls,*
Though vain the embassy of Venulus
To exiled Diomede.
                In Daunus' realm,
Apulia, Diomede had built a great
City and with his marriage won domains.
But when, as Turnus charged him, Venulus
Requested aid Aetolian Diomede
Made his excuse: he'd not commit to war
The countrymen of Daunus, nor had he
Men of his own to arm. 'And lest you think
This false, although the memory renews
My bitter tragic grief, I'll bring myself
To tell the tale. When lofty Ilium
Was burnt and Pergamum had fed the flame
Of Greece, and Ajax for a virgin's rape*
Brought from the Virgin on us all the lash
That he alone deserved, we were dispersed.
Raped by the winds across the hostile main,
We Greeks endured storms, lightning, darkness, wrath
Of sky and sea and, crowning tragedy,
The cliffs of Caphereus.* Not to prolong
The whole tale of our troubles, at that time
Greece could have moved Priam himself to tears.
But me Minerva, warrior goddess, saved
And rescued from the waves; but then again
Argos, my homeland, drove me out—her price
Now claimed by fostering Venus who recalled
That wound* of long ago. Such tragic toils
I endured on ocean's waves, such toils in war
On land, that often I counted fortunate
Those whom shared storms and ruthless Caphereus

Had drowned, and wished that I were one of them.
    My comrades' sufferings had been extreme
In war and on the sea. With failing hearts
They pleaded for an end to wandering.
But Acmon, hot by nature, chafing too
At our disasters, cried "What's left, you men,
That your endurance will refuse to bear?
What else, what more can Venus do—suppose
She means to? While we fear things worse, there's room
For wounds, but when the worst has happened, fear
Is underfoot: the sum of suffering
Finds us serene. Though she herself should hear
And hate (as she *does* hate) all those who serve
With Diomede, yet all of us despise
Her hate: her mighty power means naught to us."
So Acmon taunted Venus, goading her,
And rousing up afresh her former rage.
His words pleased few; the greater part of us,
His friends, reproved him. Trying to reply,
His voice, his throat grew thin, his hair became
Feathers and feathers clothed his new-formed neck
And breast and back, and larger plumage spread
Over his arms. His elbows made a curve
Of buoyant wings; webbed feet replaced his toes,
Hard horn his mouth—it finished in a beak.
Lycas and Idas, Nycteus and Rhexenor
Stared open-mouthed, and Abas too, and while
They stood and stared they took the selfsame shape.
Most of the crew* flew up and, flying round,
Circled the rowers on their flapping wings.
Should you enquire their shape, those sudden birds,
Swans they were not, but likest snowy swans.*
I, Daunus' son-in-law, can hardly hold
His arid acres, this domain of mine,
With but a handful of my countrymen.'
    So answered Diomede, and Venulus
Departed from the prince of Calydon,
The bays and pastures of Apulia.
There he had seen a grotto deep in shade
Of forest trees, hidden by slender reeds,

The home of half-goat Pan, though once the nymphs
Lived there. A local shepherd frightened them;
They fled away at first in sudden fear,
But soon, recovering, disdained the lout
Who had pursued them and began again
The nimble measure of their country dance.
The shepherd mocked them, mimicking the dance
With loutish leaps and shouts of coarse abuse
And rustic insults. Nothing silenced him
Till wood enswathed his throat. For he's a tree,
And from its juice you judge its character.
The oleaster's* bitter berries bear
The taint of that tart tongue; they keep today
The sourness of the things he used to say.

    The ambassadors returned and brought the news
That Greek help was refused. Without that force
The Rutuli held on the course of war;
Much blood was shed on either side. And see,
Turnus had sent his firebrands to consume
The pine-framed vessels; ships the waves had spared
Feared flames. And now the conflagration burnt
Caulking and pitch and all the food of fire,
Climbing the mast-head, spreading to the sails;
The benches smoked across the curving hulls.
And then the holy Mother of the Gods,*
Remembering that on Ida's peak those pines
Were felled, made clashing cymbals fill the air
And shrilling fifes, and, borne along the breeze
By her tame lion-team, 'In vain', she cried,
'Turnus, your godless hands are flinging fire.
I'll rescue them! Never shall I allow
Flames to consume my forest's life and limb.'
It thundered as she spoke and hard upon
The thunder crushing squalls of leaping hail
Came crashing down and all the brother winds,
Battling in sudden shock and strife, convulsed
The skies and surging seas. And one wind's strength
The fostering Mother called in aid to break
The hempen hawsers of the Trojan fleet,
And on their beam ends drove the ships to sea

And sank them. Timbers softened and the wood
Was changed to flesh; the curved prows turned to heads,
The oars to toes and swimming legs; the sides
Remained as sides; the keel that underlay
The centre of the ship became a spine,
The rigging soft sleek hair, the yards were arms,
The colour sea-blue still; and in the waves
They used to fear they play their girlish games,
Nymphs of the sea,* born on the granite hills,
Now natives of the soft sea-deeps, untouched
By memories of their birthplace. Even so,
Remembering the perils of the main
Endured so many times, they often place
Their hands to steady storm-tossed keels, unless
Greeks are on board. The tragedy of Troy
They've not forgotten and they hate the Greeks;*
And joy shone in their faces when they saw
The wreckage of Ulysses' ship,* and joy
Seeing the galleon of Alcinous
Stiffen and all its timbers turned to stone.*
   Hope was that when the fleet was given life
As sea-nymphs, dread of demon magic might
Restrain the Rutuli. The war went on:
Both sides had gods and, what's as good as gods,
Courage; their aim not realm for dowry now,
Nor royal marriage, nor Lavinia,
Princess, for bride; they fought for victory,
Too proud to halt the conflict, till at last
Venus saw victory attend her son,
And Turnus fell. And Ardea fell; a strong
City while he was safe, but when the sword
From overseas destroyed her and her homes
Lay smothered in hot ashes, from the heap
Of ruins rose a bird unknown before,
That flapped and beat the embers with its wings.
The cries, the leanness, pallor, everything
That suits a captured city, even the name
That bird* has kept: for Ardea's defeat
In lamentation her own pinions beat.
   And now Aeneas' valour had constrained

All heaven's gods and even Juno herself
To end their ancient anger. Safe and sound
Stood growing Iulus' fortunes; Venus' son,
That hero son of hers, was ripe for heaven.
Venus had canvassed heaven's gods and thrown
Her arms about her father's neck and said:
'Father, you've *never* been unkind to me:
Now be most kind, I beg, and grant my son,
Aeneas, your grandson, our own blue blood,
Divinity, even though not much, yet still
Grant some! Once is enough to have beheld
The unlovely realm of Hell, once to have gone
Across the stream of Styx!' The gods approved,
Nor did the consort-queen look stern and stiff,
But seemed placated as she gave assent.
Then said the Father: 'Both of you deserve
The boon of heaven, you who ask and he
For whom you ask. Receive, my child, your wish!'
With happy heart she gave her father thanks,
And, carried by her doves across the sky,
Reached the Laurentian coast, where through his thatch
Of reeds Numicius' river* winds his way
Down to the neighbouring shore. She bade the river
Wash from Aeneas all that death could waste
And waft it in his silent stream to sea.
Obeying Venus' bidding the horned god
Purged in his waters every mortal part
And washed it all away—the best remained.
So purified, his mother anointed him
With heavenly perfume and, upon his lips
Touching ambrosia and sweet nectar, made
Her son a god whom now the Romans name
Indiges,* with shrines and altars for his fame.

　　Next double-named* Ascanius ruled the land
Of Latium and Alba. Silvius
Succeeded him. His son, Latinus, took
The name and sceptre of his ancestor.
After Latinus glorious Alba reigned;
Then Epytus, and next came Capetus
And Capys (Capys first), and following them

The reign of Tiberinus, king from whom
Was named* the Tuscan river where he drowned.
Fierce Acrota and Remulus were his sons;
Then Remulus, of riper years, who mimicked
Lightning, was by a lightning-flash destroyed.
Acrota, better balanced than his brother,
Passed on the sceptre to brave Aventine,
Who on the hill where he had reigned was buried
And to that hill bestowed his royal name.
And now King Proca held the sovereignty
And ruled the people of the Palatine.

POMONA AND VERTUMNUS

Pomona lived in good King Proca's reign
And none of all the Latin woodland-nymphs
Was cleverer than she in garden lore
Nor keener in the care of orchard trees.
Thence came her name. For in her heart she loved
Not woods nor rivers, but a plot of ground
And boughs of smiling apples all around.
She had no spear, only a pruning-knife
To check too greedy growth and trim to shape
The spreading shoots, or slit the bark and set
A slip for sap to feed a foreign stock.
She never let them thirst; her trickling rills
Watered the twisting fibres of their roots.
This was her love, her passion. Venus' charms
Meant nothing; yet for fear of rustic force
She walled her orchard in to keep away
The sex she shunned. What tricks did they not try,
The quick young light-foot Satyrs, and the Pans
Who wreathe their horns with pine, and that old rake,
Silenus, ever younger than his years,
And he, the god whose scythe or lusty loins*
Scare thieves away—what did they all not try
To win her love? And one loved more than all,
Vertumnus, but he found no better luck.
　　Dressed up as a tough reaper, many a time
He brought a sack of wheat, and looked the part.
Often, a band of hay tied round his brow,

He might have come from tossing the cut grass,
Or, in his gnarled fist wielding a big stick,
You'd swear he'd just unyoked his weary ox.
He'd be a hedger, hook in hand—a man
To prune the vines. With ladder on his shoulder,
He'd come to pick the apples; with a sword
A soldier, with a rod a fisherman.
In short, in many a guise he often gained
Admittance and enjoyed her lovely looks.
Indeed one day, wearing a pretty bonnet
Above a fringe of grey, and leaning on
A stick, like some old crone, he went inside
Her garden and admired the fruit and praised
The gardener too: 'And you're more charming still',
And kissed her more than once (but no old woman
Kissed quite like that) and sitting on the grass
The bent old body gazed up at the branches
That bowed above her with their autumn load.
A fine elm faced them, gay with gleaming grapes.
Praising the two companions, vine and elm,
'But had the tree', he said, 'not wed the vine,
Its only value now would be its leaves.*
So too this clinging vine that rests at ease
Upon the elm, had it remained unwed,
Would straggle prostrate, sprawling on the ground.
But you, unmoved by this tree's lesson, shun
A husband, and will link your life with none.
      Would you were willing! You would have a throng
Of suitors, more than Helen or the queen*
For whom the Lapiths battled or the wife
Of bold Ulysses,* brave when foes' hearts failed.
Why, now, though you may shun and scorn their suit,
Hundreds desire you, men and demigods,
And gods of heaven and every power that haunts
The Alban hills.* But you, if you are wise,
And mean to marry well and heed the words
Of an old dame like me, who love you more
Than all of them, yes, more than you'd believe—
Reject a vulgar union and enfold
Vertumnus to your heart, to have and hold!

You have my warrant. Why, he knows himself
No better than I know him! And, besides,
He does not rove around the whole wide world;
His land, his life is here. Nor does he love,
As young men mostly love, each latest girl;
You will be first and last; to you alone
He'll dedicate his life. Consider too,
He's young and has a gift of natural grace,
And skill to change to any shape that suits;
Name any shape, name all, that shape he'll be.
Your tastes too are the same. Of all your crop
He takes the firstfruits* and enjoys your gifts.
But now it's not the apples from your trees
He longs for, nor the tender juicy plants
Your garden grows; he only longs for you.
Pity his passion! Think that through my lips
He pleads in person for his heart's desire.
And you should fear the vengeance of the gods,
Venus who hates a stony heart, the wrath,
The unforgetting wrath of Nemesis.
That you may fear them more (my years have made
Me wise in many things) I'll tell a tale
Famous in Cyprus, whence you well may find
Your will less stubborn and your heart more kind.
　　Iphis, a man of humble origin,
Had seen the Lady Anaxarete,*
A high-born girl of ancient Teucer's line;
Had seen her and was heart and soul in love.
And long he fought that folly, but at last,
When reason failed, respectful at her door,
He told his hapless passion to her nurse
And begged her, by her hopes for her dear charge,
Not to be hard on him. And many a time
He coaxed her maids, her many maids, to do
A kindly favour, and would often give
Them notes to take with loving messages.
Sometimes he hung* a garland at her gate,
Bedewed with tears, and on her doorstep laid
His body down, soft side on the hard stone,
And cursed the misery of bolts and bars.

But she, more savage than the surging seas
When the Kids* set, more adamant than iron
Forged in the fires of Noricum,* or rocks,
Deep-rooted living rocks, despised the man
And laughed at him, with haughty words and acts
Of cruelty, and foiled the lover's hope.
The torture of his long-drawn agony
Was more than he could bear. Before her door
These last few final words poor Iphis cried:
"You triumph, Anaxarete! At last
I'll not molest you: you need bear no more.
Prepare the glad parade; sing out the song
Of victory, and wreathe your brow with bay!
You triumph; I die gladly; come, rejoice,
You stony heart! Here's surely in my love
Something that you must welcome, must admire,
That makes you willing to admit my worth.
Never forget I did not leave my love
Before my life, two lights* together lost.
Nor will some rumoured tale report my death.
I shall myself be present, never doubt,
In person for your eyes to see and feast—
Your cruel eyes!—upon my lifeless corpse.
But O ye Gods of heaven, if you behold
The actions of mankind, remember me
(My failing tongue's last prayer) and make my tale
Be told long ages hence, so may the time
You shortened of my life prolong my fame."
      Then to the posts he'd often garlanded
He turned his brimming eyes and wasted arms
And tied a noose above the door and cried:
"Here is a circlet, cruel godless girl,
To give you joy!" and thrust his head within
The noose, and facing towards her to the last,
Hung there, a tragic burden, choked to death.
His twitching feet strike on the door, which seems
To groan for many griefs,* and flying wide
Betrays the deed. The servants scream and lift—
Too late—the body down and carry it
(His father being dead) to his mother's house.

She takes him in her arms and clasps the corpse,
Her son's cold corpse, and speaks the words of grief
A parent speaks and mourns as mothers mourn.
Then through the middle of the town she leads
The weeping funeral, and on the bier
The death-pale body for the pyre to burn.
   It chanced the house of Anaxarete
Looked on the street through which the sad cortège
Was winding and the sound of wailing reached
The heartless girl, whom some avenging god
Now drove. And moved, despite herself, she thought
"We'll see this tearful funeral", and climbed
The attic stair and threw the windows wide.
Scarce had she fixed her gaze on Iphis there,
Laid out upon the bier, when the warm blood
Fled from her limbs, her face was white, her eyes
Were stark and stiff. She tried to walk away—
Her feet stuck fast. She tried to avert her face—
That too she could not. Gradually the stone,
That all along had lurked* in her hard heart,
Spread and possessed her body, limb by limb.
And still at Salamis a statue stands
Of that proud lady, proof the tale is true,
And there's a shrine of Gazing Venus* too.
   Ponder this tale, my darling nymph. Put by
Your scorn and scruples; link yourself in love.
So may the frosts of spring not scorch your buds,
Nor rough winds shake the blossoms from your boughs.'
   Thus the god pleaded in the old dame's guise,
But all in vain. Then he resumed his own
Young shape and shed the trappings of old age,
And stood revealed to her as when the sun
Triumphs in glory through the clouds and rain
And bright with beams untrammelled shines again.
No need of force.* His beauty wins the day,
As she with answering love is borne away.

LEGENDS OF EARLY ROME; THE APOTHEOSIS
OF ROMULUS

Next wicked Amulius by force of arms
Ruled rich Ausonia, till old Numitor
By a grandson's bounty gained the throne he'd lost.*
And then on Pales' festal day the walls
Of Rome were founded.* Led by Tatius
The Sabine fathers battled* and Tarpeia*
Betrayed the passageway and lost her life
Beneath the pile of arms, due punishment.
Then Cures'* warriors, like silent wolves
Stealing in whispers on the sleeping town,
Made for the gates which Romulus had barred,
But one of them Juno herself unlocked,*
Keeping the hinges silent. Only Venus
Perceived the gate's great bars had dropped, and would
Have closed it but that gods are never allowed
To undo what gods have done. Beside the shrine
Of Janus lived Ausonia's Naiad-nymphs,
Their watery home an ice-cold welling spring.
The goddess begged their help, nor did the nymphs
Baulk at her just request, but conjured forth
The currents of their spring; but still the gate
Of open Janus was unblocked, the gush
Of water had not barred the passageway.
Now they set yellow sulphur underneath
Their sparkling spring and fired the hollow veins
With smoking bitumen. Forced by their power
And other pressures, heat pierced its way down
Right to the bottom of the spring, until
Water that dared a moment past to vie
With Alpine cold now matched the flame of fire.
Splashed by the boiling flow the twin gateposts
Steamed and the gate, so vainly promised to
The stern Sabines, was blocked by the strange stream
Till the defending force could spring to arms.
Then Romulus attacked. The soil of Rome
Was strewn with Sabine dead and Roman too,
And blood of father-in-law and son-in-law

Was blent in godless butchery. At last
It was agreed* that peace should halt the war
Without the final verdict of the sword,
And Tatius should share the sovereignty.
    Now Tatius was dead and Romulus
Over both peoples ruled impartially.
Then Mars, laying aside his casque, addressed
The Father of gods and men: 'The time has come,
Father, since now the Roman state stands firm
On great foundations, not dependent still
On one man's power, to award the promised prize
(Earned by my grandson, promised to us both),
That he be taken from earth and placed in heaven.
Once in the assembled council of the gods
You said to me (my memory has marked
A father's loving words), "There shall be one*
Whom you shall raise to the blue vault of heaven."
Grant now fulfilment of those words of yours.'
The Almighty nodded his consent and hid
The sky in black blind clouds and terrified
The world with lightning and great thunderclaps.
Those were the signs, Mars knew, that warranted
His seizure of his son, and, undismayed,
Leaning upon his spear he leapt into
His bloodstained chariot and cracked his whip
And lashed his team and, plunging through the sky,
Stood on the sylvan peak* of Palatine,
Where Romulus dispensed no tyrant's laws,
And carried him away. His mortal frame
Dissolved into the air, as leaden balls
Propelled from a broad sling melt in mid sky:*
Finer his features now and worthier
Of heaven's high-raised couch,* his lineaments
Those of Quirinus* in his robe of state.
    Hersilia, his consort, mourned his loss,
And royal Juno bade Iris descend
Her rainbow and exhort the widowed queen:
'Illustrious lady, peerless jewel of
The Latin and the Sabine race alike,
Most worthy consort once of that great man,

Now worthy of Quirinus, stay your tears!
And if your heart is set to see your spouse,
Come, let me guide your footsteps to the grove
That crowns Quirinus' hill with greenery
And shades the temple of the King of Rome.'
Iris obeyed and gliding down to earth
Along her many-coloured bow addressed
Hersilia in the words prescribed; and she
In awe and reverence would hardly raise
Her eyes. 'Goddess', she answered, 'who thou art
I cannot well surmise, but clear it is
Thou art a goddess. Guide, oh guide, me now!
Show me my husband's face, for if but once
The Fates are gracious and enable me
To see him, heaven shall indeed be mine.'
Quickly she reached the hill of Romulus
With Thaumas' daughter. There a star from heaven
Dropped gliding to the ground and by its glow
Set the queen's hair ablaze,* and with the star
Hersilia ascended to the sky.
The founder of Rome's city welcomed her
In arms she knew of old and changed alike
Her body and the name she used to bear.
Then, renamed Hora,* she was deified,
A goddess consort at Quirinus' side.

BOOK XV

NUMA AND THE FOUNDATION OF CROTONA

MEANWHILE the question is who will sustain
The burden of so great a charge, who can
Succeed so great a monarch. For the throne
Fame, truth's prophetic herald, nominates
Illustrious Numa. He, not satisfied
With mastery of the Sabine rituals,
Engaged his interest on larger themes
And studied nature's causes.* His pursuit
Led him to leave Cures, his native town,
And reach the city that was once the host
Of Hercules. He asked the founder's name
Of those Greek walls beside the Italian shore,*
And one of the old citizens, well versed
In lore of long ago, gave this reply:
'Jove's son, it's said, returning from the Ocean,
Rich with the booty of the herds of Spain,*
Made happy landfall on Lacinium's coast,
And, while his cattle grazed the tender grass,
Entered great Croton's hospitable home
And rested there, relaxing from his toils;
And, as he took his leave, "This place", he said,
"Shall be a city in your grandsons' time."
And true the promise proved. For there was born
In Argos to Alemon* a fine son
Named Myscelus, in all that time the most
In favour with the gods. The Club-Bearer
Leant over him as he lay sound asleep
And said: "Away! Go, leave your native land
And seek far-distant Aesar's stony stream."
And, should he not obey him, added threats
Many and terrible. Then sleep and god
Vanished together. Myscelus arose
And pondered silently what he'd just seen.
Long was the conflict in his mind. The god
Commanded him to go, the law forbade

His leaving: death the punishment decreed
For one who chose to change his fatherland.
   The gleaming sun had hidden his bright head
Beneath the Ocean, spangled night had raised
Her starry face. The same god seemed to appear,
Giving the same commands and adding threats,
More and severer, should he not obey.
He was afraid and made a start at once
To move his hearth and home to a foreign land.
Talk murmured through the town. He was accused
Of treason. When the prosecution's case
Was heard, no need of evidence, the crime
Patent and proved. Bedraggled* in his guilt,
Raising his face and hands heavenwards, "Great god",
He cried, "Thou whose twelve labours won thy claim
To heaven, I beseech thee, help me now!
My crime was thy command." In days of old
Pebbles were used, black pebbles to condemn
The guilty, white to clear the innocent.
Thus was the grim decision given then:
Each pebble in the cruel urn was black;
But when it poured the pebbles out to count,
The hue of each was changed from black to white.
So by the heavenly power of Hercules
The judgement shone out bright and Myscelus
Went free. He thanked his patron deity
And sailed with favouring winds the Ionian sea.
   Neretum, city of the Sallentines,
He passed and Sybaris and Sparta's town,
Tarentum, Siris' bay and Crimisa
And Iapygia's shores. His wandering course
Had hardly left those coasts before he found
The Aesar's destined estuary and, near
At hand, the mound wherein the hallowed bones
Of Croton lay entombed, and, as the god
Ordered, he built his city's battlements
And named it from the hero buried there.'
Such were the place's ancient origins;
Thus rose, as sure tradition* certifies,
The city set beneath Italian skies.

THE DOCTRINES OF PYTHAGORAS

A man lived here, a Samian by birth,
But he had fled from Samos and its masters*
And, hating tyranny, by his own choice
Became an exile.* Though the gods in heaven
Live far removed, he approached them in his mind,*
And things that nature kept from mortal sight
His inward eye explored. When meditation
And vigils of long study had surveyed
All things that are, he made his wisdom free
For all to share; and he would teach his class,
Hanging in silent wonder on his words,
The great world's origin,* the cause of things,
What nature is, what god, and whence the snow,
What makes the lightning, whether thunder comes
From Jove or from the winds when clouds burst wide,
Why the earth quakes, what ordinance controls
The courses of the stars, and the whole sum
Of nature's secrets. He was first to ban
As food for men the flesh of living things:
These are the doctrines he was first to teach,
Wise words, though wisdom powerless to persuade:
    'Abstain! Preserve your bodies unabused,
Mortals, with food of sin! There are the crops,*
Apples that bend the branches with their weight,
Grapes swelling on the vines; there are fresh herbs
And those the tempered flame makes soft and mellow;
Milk is ungrudged and honey from the thyme;
Earth lavishes her wealth, gives sustenance
Benign, spreads feasts unstained by blood and death.
Flesh is for beasts to appease the pangs of hunger,
Yet not for all; since horses, cattle, sheep
Graze on the grass, but animals untamed
And fierce, Armenian tigers, ravening lions,
Wolves too and bears, all feed on flesh and blood.
How vile a crime that flesh should swallow flesh,
Body should fatten greedy body; life
Should live upon the death of other lives!
With all the bounteous riches that the earth,
Earth best of mothers, yields, can nothing please

But savage relish munching piteous wounds,
A Cyclops' banquet?* Can you not placate
Without another's doom—a life destroyed—
The urgent craving of your bellies' greed?
  But in the Golden Age of long ago
The orchard fruits and harvest in the fields
Were blessed boon and no blood stained men's lips.
The birds in safety then might wing their way,
No trust betrayed hung fishes on the hook,
And fearless in mid-field the hare would roam.
With never trap or snare or guile or fear
Peace filled the world—until some futile brain*
Envied the lions' diet and gulped down
A feast of flesh to fill his greedy guts,
And paved the way for crime. A wild beast's death
Maybe first warmed and stained a blade with blood;
That should suffice; creatures that seek our death
It is no sin, we say, to do to death—
To do to death, but not to make a meal!
    Thence wickedness spread wider. First, it seems,
The pig deserved a victim's death, whose snout
Dug up the seeds and cut the season's hope;
The goat that gnawed the vines was sacrificed
On vengeful Bacchus' altars; these two paid
The price of guilt. But what guilt have the sheep,
The peaceful flock, born but to serve mankind,
Whose udders sweet milk fills, whose fleeces yield
Soft clothes, more excellent in life than death?
What guilt have oxen, faithful guileless beasts,
Harmless and simple, born to lives of toil?
How short of memory, how mean of soul,
How undeserving of the harvest's boon,
Is he who, having just unyoked the weight
Of the bright curving plough, can find the heart
To kill his plough-mate; who upon that neck,
Tired with long toil, whose strength year after year
Renewed the stubborn acres and brought home
So many harvests, crashes down the axe!
    Nor is that crime enough. Even the gods
They enrol to share their guilt and make believe

The Powers of heaven are gladdened by the blood
Of bullocks, patient slaughtered labourers.
A victim without blemish, beautiful
Beyond compare (his beauty is his bane),
Splendid with gold and garlands, stands before
The altar, hears the prayer, watches the priest
Sprinkle, he knows not why, between his horns
Upon his brow the meal his toil has grown;
Then the knife strikes, crimsoned with blood, the knife
He saw perhaps reflected* as it fell.
And while the life's still warm, they snatch his guts
And probe and pore to prove heaven's purposes.*
That flesh, so great man's greed for food forbidden,
You dare to eat, you race of mortal men!
Abstain! Be warned! I beg you! Understand
The ox whose meat you savour, whom you slew,
Worked, your own farmhand, in your fields for you.
    Now heaven inspires my tongue and I will follow
Heaven's inspiration faithfully and reveal
The truths of Delphi shown to me and all
The secrets of the sky, and I'll unlock
Sure oracles of intellect sublime.
Great matters, long concealed nor yet explored,
Shall be my solemn theme. My soul rejoices*
To journey on the highways of the stars,
To leave earth's dull domains, to ride the clouds,
And, poised on Atlas' mighty shoulders, see
Far far below mankind in error lost,
Devoid of reason; and, for cheer and comfort
Of men's faint hearts oppressed with fear of death,
Unroll these chapters of the scroll of fate.
    You race of men whom death's cold chill appals,*
Why dread the Styx, the dark, the empty names,
Sad stuff of poets, perils of a world
That never was? Your bodies, whether age
Shall waste at last or burning pyre consume,
Be sure, no ills can ever harm. Our souls
Are deathless; when they leave their former home,
Always new habitations welcome them,*
To live afresh. Myself (I well remember)

Was once Euphorbus in the Trojan war,
Panthous' son, whom Menelaus killed,*
A spear-thrust to the heart. I recognized
Not long ago the shield* my left arm bore,
A trophy hung in Juno's shrine at Argos.
Everything changes; nothing dies; the soul
Roams to and fro, now here, now there, and takes
What frame it will, passing from beast to man,
From our own form to beast and never dies.
As yielding wax is stamped with new designs
And changes shape and seems not still the same,
Yet is indeed the same, even so our souls
Are still the same for ever, but adopt
In their migrations ever-varying forms.
Therefore lest appetite and greed destroy
The bonds of love and duty, heed my message!
Abstain! Never by slaughter dispossess
Souls that are kin and nourish blood with blood!

    Now since the sea's great surges sweep me on,
All canvas spread, hear me! In all creation
Nothing endures, all is in endless flux,*
Each wandering shape a pilgrim passing by.
And time itself glides on in ceaseless flow,
A rolling stream—and streams can never stay,
Nor lightfoot hours. As wave is driven by wave
And each, pursued, pursues the wave ahead ,
So time flies on and follows, flies and follows,
Always, for ever new. What was before
Is left behind; what never was is now;
And every passing moment is renewed.

    You see how day extends as night is spent,
And this bright radiance succeeds the dark;
Nor, when the tired world lies in midnight peace,
Is the sky's sheen the same as in the hour
When on his milk-white steed the Morning Star
Rides forth, or when, bright harbinger of day,
Aurora gilds the globe to greet the sun.
The sun's round shield at morning when he climbs
From earth's abyss glows red, and when he sinks
To earth's abyss at evening red again,

And at his zenith gleaming bright, for there
The air is pure and earth's dross far away.
Nor can the queenly moon ever retain
Her shape unchanged, but always, as her orb
Waxes or wanes, tomorrow she must shine
Larger or smaller than she is today.

Again, you notice how the year in four
Seasons revolves, completing one by one
Fit illustration of our human life.
The young springtime, the tender suckling spring,
Is like a child; the swelling shoots so fresh,
So soft and fragile, fill the farmers' hearts
With hope and gladness. Flowers are everywhere;
Their colours dance across the fostering fields,
While the green leaves still lack their strength and pride.
Spring passes, and the year, grown sturdier,
Rolls on to summer like a strong young man;
No age so sturdy, none so rich, so warm.
Then autumn follows, youth's fine fervour spent,
Mellow and ripe, a temperate time between
Youth and old age, his temples flecked with grey.
And last, with faltering footsteps, rough and wild,
His hair, if any, white, old winter comes.

Our bodies too are always, endlessly
Changing; what we have been, or are today,
We shall not be tomorrow. Years ago
We hid, mere seeds and promise, in the womb;
Nature applied her artist's hands to free
Us from our swollen mother's narrow home,
And sent us forth into the open air.
Born to the shining day, the infant lies
Strengthless, but soon on all fours like the beasts
Begins to crawl, and then by slow degrees,
Weak-kneed and wobbling, clutching for support
Some helping upright, learns at last to stand.
Then swift and strong he traverses the span
Of youth, and when the years of middle life
Have given their service too, he glides away
Down the last sunset slope of sad old age—
Old age that saps and mines and overthrows

The strength of earlier years. Milo,* grown old,
Sheds tears to see how shrunk and flabby hang
Those arms on which the muscles used to swell,
Massive like Hercules; and, when her glass
Shows every time-worn wrinkle, Helen weeps
And wonders why she twice* was stolen for love.
Time, the devourer, and the jealous years
With long corruption ruin all the world
And waste all things in slow mortality.

　　The elements* themselves do not endure;
Examine how they change and learn from me.
The everlasting universe contains
Four generative substances;* of these
Two, earth and water, sink of their own weight;
Two, air and fire (fire purer still than air),
Weightless, unburdened, seek the heights above.
Though spaced apart, all issue from each other
And to each other fall. So earth, reduced,
Is rarefied to water; moisture, thinned,
Dissolves to air and wind; air, losing weight,
So light, so insubstantial, flashes up
To empyrean fire. Then they return
In reverse order as the skein unwinds.
Thus fire, condensed, passes to heavier air,
Air into water, water in its turn
Compressed, conglobed, solidifies to earth.

　　Nothing retains its form; new shapes from old
Nature, the great inventor, ceaselessly
Contrives. In all creation, be assured,
There is no death—no death, but only change
And innovation; what we men call birth
Is but a different new beginning; death
Is but to cease to be the same. Perhaps
This may have moved to that and that to this,
Yet still the sum of things remains the same.

　　Nothing can last,* I do believe, for long
In the same image. The ages of the world
From Golden passed to Iron. How many times
The fortunes of a place have been reversed!
I've seen myself how solid stable ground

Became the open sea; I've seen the ocean
Turn to dry land; and sea shells often lie
Far from the shore; and on a mountain top
Is found a rusty anchor centuries old.
A plain is made a valley by the force
Of falling waters; floods have washed away
Mountains to make a plain; a marsh dries out
In parching dunes; a thirsty wilderness
Lies flooded and becomes a swampy fen.
Here nature sends new springs to flow, and there
Staunches them. In deep quakings of the earth
Rivers burst out or, drying, sink from sight.
So Lycus, swallowed by the yawning earth,
Rises reborn, a changed face far away.
So Erasinus' stream, engulfed to glide
In secret eddies underground, returns
A lordly river in the Argive fields.
Caicus too, disliking, so they say,
The source and banks he knew as Mysus once,
Now flows a different way. And Amenanus
Sometimes sweeps down his dark Sicilian sands,
Sometimes is dry, his sources stopped and stayed.
Anigrus once ran clear and wholesome; now
No man would drink his waters, since the time,
If poets' tales are true, the centaurs* there
Washed out the arrow-poison from their wounds.
And Hypanis, who rises in the hills
Of Scythia and flowed so fresh and sweet,
Is he not tainted now with bitter salts?

 The sea encompassed once Antissa and Tyre
And gleaming Pharos: none are islands now.
Leucas, the early settlers used to tell,
Was once a promontory; now the waves
Surround it. Zancle too, they say, was joined
To Italy until the ocean tore
Their boundary apart and straits between
Severed the land. And should you ask for Buris
And Helice, once cities of Achaea,
They lie beneath the waves; sailors still show
The tilted towns and sunken battlements.

Not far from ancient Troezen is a mound,
High, steep and treeless, once a level plain,
Quite flat, but now a hill. The winds' wild strength
(A ghastly story), pent within blind caves,
Seeking some vent, striving in vain to enjoy
The freedom of the sky, finding nowhere
In their whole prison a fissure for their blasts,
Made the ground stretch and swell, as one inflates
A bladder or a goatskin; in that place
The swollen bulge still stands, a tumulus,
Time-hardened, rising high above the plain.
 So many instances, things known and heard,
Throng to my mind; yet I will add but few.
Why, even water gives and takes new forms.
At noon ice-cold the spring of Ammon flows,
But hot at dawn and dusk. The Athamans*
Kindle their wood in water when the moon
Wanes last and least. The Cicons have a river
That turns to stone the bowels of all who drink,
And moulds in marble all its waters touch.
Crathis and Sybaris, our own twin streams,
Tint hair like gold or amber. Stranger still
Are waters charged with power to change men's minds
As well as bodies. All the world has heard*
Of obscene Salmacis and the Ethiop lakes,
One draught of which brings madness or a sleep
Of magic length. Whoso at Clitor's well
Has quenched his thirst loathes wine and soberly
Likes only water; some strange power perhaps
Is in the well that fights the warmth of wine,
Or, as the folk there tell, Melampus once,
Who cured with herbs and charms the maddened brains
Of Proetus' daughters,* threw his purging drugs
Into the well and there the wine-bane stays.
But he who the Lyncestian stream imbibes
Goes rolling drunk as if his wine were neat.
There is a place in Arcady, once known
As Pheneos, a suspect place with strange
Ambiguous waters. When night falls, beware!
At night to drink is danger, yet by day

No harm at all. So lakes and rivers gain
Diversity of powers. Once long ago
Ortygia* was afloat, now it rests fast.
The Argo feared the two Symplegades,*
Spray-drenched colliding cliffs, which now stand fixed
And motionless and breast the battling gales.
Nor will fierce Etna's sulphurous furnaces*
For ever burn, nor have they burnt for ever.
For if the earth should be a living creature
With nostrils breathing flame in many lands,
She can, by movement, change her breathing-channels
And end or open each deep orifice.
Or if in earth's foundations driving winds,
Pent fast, hurl rock on rock and substances
That hold the seeds of fire burst into flame,
The winds will die and earth's foundations cool.
Or if fire leaps from blazing bitumen,
Or yellow sulphur burns with wisps of smoke,
Why, when the earth after long ages fails,
Exhausted, to provide the flames with food,
Then hungry nature lacking nourishment
Will faint and, starving, starve her furnaces.
The tale is told how in the northern steppes
Of far Pallene people plunge nine times
Into a marshy mere and then their skin
Grows downy feathers; that seems past belief,
Though report says that Scythian women too
With magic ointments practise the same feat.
　　Yet trust should follow tested truths. You see,
When time and heat dissolve and putrefy
A corpse, it turns to tiny forms of life.*
Bury a prize bull, slain for sacrifice,
And from the rotting flesh—a well-known fact—
Bees everywhere are born, flower-loving bees,
Which like their parent range the countryside,
Work with a will and hope for work's reward.
A charger in his grave will generate
Hornets. If you remove the bending claws
Of a beach-crab and sink the rest in sand,
A scorpion will crawl from the buried part,

Tail curved to strike. And grubs, as country folk
Observe, whose white cocoons are wrapped in leaves,
Emerge as butterflies that grace a grave.*
    Mud contains seed from which green frogs are born;
Born without feet, they soon gain legs to swim,
Hind legs longer for leaping, forelegs short.
A cub to which a bear has just given birth
Is but a lump, hardly alive, until
His mother licks and forms her little bear
To take the big bear's shape she has herself.
Note how the offspring of the honey-bee,
Sealed in their wax six-sided cells, hatch out
Mere limbless maggots, then in course of time
Acquire their legs, in course of time their wings.
Juno's fine bird* whose tail bright stars adorn,
Jove's weapon-bearer,* Cytherea's* doves,
And the whole tribe of birds, who would suppose,
Unless he knew, were born inside an egg?
Some would believe that when a dead man's spine
Rots in his tomb his marrow makes a snake.
    These creatures all derive their first beginnings
From others of their kind. But one alone,
A bird, renews and re-begets itself—
The Phoenix* of Assyria, which feeds
Not upon seeds or verdure but the oils
Of balsam and the tears of frankincense.*
This bird, when five long centuries of life
Have passed, with claws and beak unsullied, builds
A nest high on a lofty swaying palm;
And lines the nest with cassia and spikenard
And golden myrrh and shreds of cinnamon,
And settles there at ease and, so embowered
In spicy perfumes, ends his life's long span.
Then from his father's body is reborn
A little Phoenix, so they say, to live
The same long years. When time has built his strength
With power to raise the weight, he lifts the nest—
The nest his cradle and his father's tomb—
As love and duty prompt, from that tall palm
And carries it across the sky to reach

The Sun's great city,* and before the doors
Of the Sun's holy temple lays it down.

   If all these things seem strange and marvellous,
Well might we marvel at the hyena's change;
A female lately mated with a male
Becomes a male herself. The creature* too,
That feeds on wind and air, will match at once
Whatever hue it touches. Vine-wreathed Bacchus
Received from conquered India a gift
Of lynxes, beasts whose urine, so men say,
Changes to stones,* congealing in the air.
So coral* too at the first touch of air
Hardens, yet in the sea a tender plant.

   The day will wane, the Sun beneath the waves
Will plunge his panting steeds before my tale
Recounts the sum of things that take new forms.
Times are upset, we see, and nations rise
To strength and greatness, others fail and fall.
Troy once was great in wealth and men and gave
For ten long years her lifeblood; humbled now
She shows her ancient ruins, for her riches
Only the broken tombs of ancestors.
Sparta was famous, great Mycenae strong,
And strong the walls of Cecrops and Amphion.
Now Sparta lies a waste,* Mycenae's towers
Have tumbled down. What but a name is left
Of Oedipus' brave Thebes, or what endures
Of proud Pandion's Athens but a name?
Today from Trojan stock a city rises,
Rome, where the Tiber flows from the Apennines,
And with vast effort founds her destiny.
Her change is increase; she one day shall reign,
The boundless world's great empress; so foretell
Prophets and oracles; so, I recall,
When Troy's high glory fell, King Priam's son*
Consoled Aeneas, weeping in despair:

   "Prince, son of Venus, if your heart hold fast
My prophecies, Troy shall not wholly fall,
While you are safe; before you fire and sword
Shall yield a path and you shall bear away,

As you fare forth, a rescued Pergamum,*
Till you shall find in some far foreign field
A kindlier welcome for yourself and Troy
Than in your fatherland. Now I discern
A city destined for the Trojan race,
Greater than any city was of old,
Or is or shall be. Through the length of years
Princes shall build her power, until one born
Of your son's line shall make her sovereign,
The mistress of the world; and when on earth
His work is ended, the sky's palaces
Shall welcome him and heaven shall be his home.''*

   Such were the prophecies of Priam's son,
Clear in my memory, as Aeneas bore
His guardian gods away, and I rejoice
That walls once mine shall rise anew, that Troy
Has turned to gain the triumph of the Greeks.

   So—lest I range too far and my steeds lose
Their course—the earth and all therein, the sky
And all thereunder change and change again.
We too ourselves, who of this world are part,
Not only flesh and blood but pilgrim souls,
Can make our homes in creatures of the wild
Or of the farm. These creatures might have housed
Souls of our parents, brothers, other kin,
Or men at least, and we must keep them safe,
Respected, honoured, lest we gorge ourselves
On such a banquet as Thyestes* ate.
How vilely he's inured, how wickedly
He fits himself to kill his human kin,
He who can slit his calf's throat, hear its cries
Unmoved, who has the heart to kill his kid
That screams like a small child, or eat the bird
His hand has reared and fed! How far does this
Fall short of murder? Where else does it lead?
No! Let the oxen plough and owe their death
To length of days; let the sheep give their shield
Against the north wind's fury; let the goats
Bring their full udders for your hand to milk.
Away with traps and snares and lures and wiles!

Never again lime twigs to cheat the birds,
Nor feather ropes* to drive the frightened deer,
Nor hide the hook with dainties that deceive!
Destroy what harms; destroy, but never eat;
Choose wholesome fare and never feast on meat!'

THE DEATH OF NUMA

With these and other precepts taught and trained
Numa returned, it's said, to his own land;
Entreated by his people, he assumed
The reins and guidance of the Latin realm,
And, blest to have a nymph* for wife, blest too
With guidance of the Muses, taught them modes
Of sacrifice and led the savage race,
Long used to warfare, to the arts of peace.
Then old age bringing to a close at last
His life and reign, King Numa's death was mourned
By high and low alike of Latium.
His wife forsook the city and hid herself
Deep in the forests of Aricia's vale,
And there her moans of misery disturbed
Diana's shrine* that once Orestes built.*
How many times the nymphs of lake and grove
Warned her to cease and tried to comfort her!
How often, as she wept, Theseus' great son*
Urged her, 'Come, set some limit! You are not
The only one* whom fortune marks for sorrow.
Picture how others' sufferings are the same;
And bear your own more gently. Would that my
Case could not serve to comfort you! But mine
Also can help.

HIPPOLYTUS

You will, I think, have heard
About Hippolytus and how he met
His death thanks to his father's trustfulness
And the trickery of his wicked stepmother.
You'll be amazed, and proof I'll hardly give,

But I am he. Phaedra in days gone by
Tried to tempt me*—in vain—to violate
My father's bed, and made believe that I
Had wanted what *she* wanted, and in fear
Perhaps that I'd betray her or in rage
At her repulse, reversed the guilt and charged
Me; and my father, guiltless as I was,
Expelled me from the city and, as I left,
Called curses on my head. A fugitive,
I made for Troezen in my chariot
(King Pittheus' town) and I was driving by
The shore of Corinth's bay when the sea rose
And a fantastic mound of water swelled
And towered mountain-high, with a loud noise
Of bellowing, and then its crest split wide
And out there burst, as the wave broke, a huge
Horned bull,* that reared breast-high into the air,
Its great wide mouth and nostrils spouting brine.
Fear gripped my comrades, but my heart, absorbed
With thoughts of exile, stood undaunted. Then
My team of high-strung horses turned their heads
Seawards and, ears pricked, trembling, terrified,
Stampeded at the monstrous sight and swept
The chariot down the steep rock-path. In vain
I fought to hold them with the foam-flecked bit,
And leaning backwards strained at the strong reins.
Yet their mad strength would not have overcome
My own, had not a wheel, striking its hub
Against a stump, been smashed and wrenched away.
Out I was thrown, my limbs caught in the reins;
You'd see my living flesh being dragged along,
My muscles held fast by the stump, my limbs,
Some torn away, some stuck and left behind,
Bones breaking with a loud report. I breathed
My shattered soul away; no part was left
That you could recognize—all one huge wound.
Now can you, dare you, set your tragedy,
Nymph, against mine? Then too the lightless realm
I saw and in the waves of Phlegethon
I bathed my mangled body; nor without

The potent physic of Apollo's son*
Was life restored. When thanks to valiant herbs
And Paean's* help, in Dis' despite, I gained
My life again, then round me Cynthia threw
A thick dark cloud for fear the sight of me
Should swell the grudge against that gift of life,
And that I might be seen unscathed and safe
She added to my years, and left my face
Unrecognizable; and pondered long
Whether for my new home to give me Crete
Or Delos. Crete and Delos put aside,
She placed me here and bade me put away
The name that might recall that team of mine,
Declaring, "You who were Hippolytus
Shall now be Virbius."* Thenceforth my home
Is in this grove: one of the lesser gods,
Unseen beneath my Mistress' power divine,
I serve her ministry and tend her shrine.'

    Yet others' tragedies cannot avail
To staunch Egeria's sorrow. As she lies
At the hill's foot, she melts away in tears,
Till, pitying her grief and loyal love,
Dian dissolved the nymph into a pool,
A spring that flows for ever clear and cool.

CIPUS

The nymphs were lost in wonder and he too,
Hippolytus, had marvelled like the man,
Ploughing one day Etruscan fields, who saw
The fateful clod first of its own accord
Move, though no one had touched it, and assume
A human form and lose its earthy shape,
And open its new mouth in prophecies.
The people called him Tages.* He first taught
The Etruscans to discover things to come.—
Or like great Romulus who saw his spear,
Stuck fast upon the Palatine hilltop,
Suddenly growing leaves and standing on
New roots instead of steel, and now no spear

But a tree* of strong lithe timber that surprised
The onlookers with unexpected shade.—
Or like brave Cipus when he saw his horns*
Reflected in a stream—saw them in truth,
And thought himself deceived by the reflection,
But when he felt his forehead found in fact
He fingered what he saw, and blamed his eyes
No longer. Halting his triumphant march,
He raised his hands and eyes to heaven and cried
'Ye Gods, whatever this monstrosity
Portends, if joy, let joy be for my land,
Quirinus' state, if menaces, for me!'
And built a grassy altar of green turf,
And offered wine in chalices and sought
The guidance of the victim's twitching guts.
The Etruscan seer, inspecting them, observed
At once great undertakings beyond doubt,
Though not made manifest. But when he raised
His keen eyes from the entrails to the horns
On Cipus' head, 'Hail, King!' he said, 'to you,
To you and to your horns shall bow this place
And Latium's citadels. But lose no time!
The gates are open; enter with all haste!
So fate commands. The city welcomes you.
You shall be king and you shall gain a throne
Secure for evermore.' Cipus recoiled
And said, stern eyes averted from the walls,
'Far, far from me may heaven drive such thoughts!
Much fairer were it that I spend my days
In banishment than that the Capitol
Should see me king!' And straightway he convoked
The people and the solemn senators,
Though first with laurel leaves of peace concealed
His horns; then, standing on a mound raised by
His valiant soldiers, made the accustomed prayer
To the ancient gods and said, 'One man is here
Who will be king unless you drive him from
The city. Who he is, not by a name
I'll tell but by a sign. Upon his brow
The man has horns! If he should enter Rome,

The seer foretells, his laws will make you slaves.
He could have broken in—the gates are open—
But I withstood him, though there's no one linked
Closer to him than I. Bar the man from
Your city! Fetter him with heavy chains,
If that suits his deserts, or end your fear
Of that doom-charged dictator by his death!'
Then like the hollow roar of high-trunked pines
When the wild east wind whistles, or of waves
When rollers break upon some distant shore,
A sound came from the people; yet amid
The clamour of confusing words one cry
Rose clear 'Who is he?' and from brow to brow
They looked about to find the horns foretold.

　　Then Cipus spoke again, 'Him whom you seek,
You have', and from his brow removed the wreath,
Though the crowd tried to stop him, and revealed
The pair of horns conspicuous on his head.
All lowered their eyes and groaned, so loath to see
(Who could believe?) that forehead that had won
Such fame. They would not suffer him to stand
Unhonoured there, but placed upon his brow
A festal garland. Since he was debarred
From entering the walls, the senators
Gave him for honour's sake so many acres
As he could compass,* ploughing with a team
Of oxen from first light to close of day;
And on the gate's bronze pillars they engraved
Horns that record the magic pair he wore,
To stand throughout long ages evermore.

AESCULAPIUS

Now show, ye Muses,* ever-present Powers
Of poets (for you know and time's vast span
Does not mislead you*), whence the island lapped
By Tiber's deeps received Coronis' son*
To reinforce the deities of Rome.
　　In Latium a ghastly pestilence
Once* poisoned all the air, and pale and foul

The bodies lay, blood drained by the disease.
Exhausted by the scenes of death, they saw
Nothing could be achieved by doctors' skill,
Nothing by human toil, and turned to heaven.
They went to Delphi, centre of the world,
Apollo's* oracle, and prayed the god
To succour their distress, to vouchsafe health
And end their mighty city's tragedy.
The holy place, the laurel and the quiver
Worn by the deity, all shook and trembled,
And from the inmost shrine the tripod spoke,
Filling their hearts with fear: 'What here you seek,
You should have sought, good Romans, nearer home.
Seek nearer home next time. You do not need
Phoebus to staunch your woes, but Phoebus' son.
Summon my son! Good omens go with you!'
So, when the senate in its wisdom heard
The oracle's instructions, they enquired
What city was the seat of Phoebus' son,
And sent envoys by ship to seek the port
Of Epidaurus.* Making landfall there,
They entered the grave council of the Greeks
And made petition to be given the god
Whose present power would end the deaths that doomed
Rome's people: so the oracle declared.
Opinions were divided. Some believed
Help must not be refused, many advised
Their treasure should be kept, not sent abroad,
Their deity not given to others' care.
While they sat undecided, twilight drove
The last late light away. Across the globe
Darkness had drawn its shadowy canopy,
When in a dream the god of health and hope
Appeared beside the Roman envoy's bed,
Standing as in his temple, his right hand
Seeming to stroke his flowing beard, his left
Grasping a rustic staff, and in calm tones
These words he uttered: 'Fear not! I shall come
And leave my images. Only be sure
To note this snake that twines about my staff

And mark it well to fix it in your mind.
To this snake I shall change, but I shall be
Larger, a size to which celestial forms
Should fitly change.' And straightway voice and god
Vanished, and sleep with voice and god, and day
Followed the flight of sleep with loving light.
    The morrow's dawn had put the stars to flight.
Uncertain what to do, the elders met
At the god's sumptuous temple and with prayers
Begged him to show by heavenly signs the place
Where *he* wished to abide. Almost before
They'd ceased the golden god, in serpent form,
High-crested, uttered a forewarning hiss,
And at his coming statue, altars, doors,
The marble floor, the golden gables swayed,
And towering in the temple's midst he stood
Breast-high and gazed about with flashing eyes.
Fear struck the whole assembly, but the priest,
His holy locks white-braided, recognized
The deity. 'The god! Behold the god!' he cried,
'All ye here present! O most beautiful,
Be thine epiphany our benison
And bless all those who worship at thy shrine!'
All present in obedience venerate
The deity, repeating the priest's words;
The Romans too with heart and voice revere.
The god inclined his head and swayed his crest,
Assurance of his favour; hiss on hiss
He gave with flickering tongue, then glided down
The gleaming steps and turned his head to gaze
Back at the ancient altars as he went;
And to the temple where he used to dwell,
Familiar home, signalled a last farewell,
And then across the flower-strewn pavement wound
His giant coils and, through the city's streets,
Made for the harbour with its curving mole.
And there he halted and dismissed, it seemed,
With calm kind eyes his train of worshippers,
His loyal retinue, and took his place
On board the Roman ship. It felt the weight

Of godhead;* burdened by the deity
The hull rode low. Joy filled the Romans' hearts;
They sacrificed a bull upon the beach
And garlanding their ship they put to sea.
A light breeze drove the vessel. Towering high,
His huge height heavy on the curving poop,
The god gazed down across the azure main.
With moderate winds he crossed the Ionian sea,
And as the sixth dawn rose reached Italy.
    Then past Lacinium* he sailed, the cape
Ennobled by the goddess'* shrine, and past
The shores of Scylaceum. Leaving next
Iapygia, his rowers on the left
Steered from Amphrisia's rocks and on the right
Cocinthus' crags; thence past Romethium
And Caulon and Narycia, till through
Pelorus' strait and the Sicilian sea
He won his way and made for the domain
Of King Hippotades,* the copper mines
Of Temesa and then Leucosia
And balmy Paestum where the roses bloom.
Next skirting Capri and Minerva's cape,
Sorrentum's hillsides with their noble vines,
The city of Hercules* and Stabiae,
And pleasure's paradise Parthenope,*
He came to Cumae and the Sibyl's shrine.
Thence on to the hot springs,* the mastic trees
Liternum grows so well, Volturnus' stream
Sweeping along vast loads of silty sand,
Warm Sinuessa where the white doves flock,
Minturnae with its heavy air,* the tomb
Of Caieta, Antiphates'* domain,
Trachas among salt marshes and the isle
Where Circe lived and Antium's firm strand.
    There they made landfall for the sea was rough,
And lowered sail, and then the deity
Unwound his coils and gliding curve on curve
In vast volutions reached his father's shrine,
The temple set beside the tawny strand.
The sea at peace again, the god from Greece,

Leaving his father's altars, where as guest
His kin had made him welcome, crossed the beach
(His rasping scales carved furrows in the sand)
And climbing up the rudder laid his head
On the high poop at ease, until he reached
Castrum and Lavinium's holy sanctuary
And entered Tiber's mouth. From every side
The thronging people pour their multitudes
To meet him, men and women, even the nuns
Who guard the flame of Vesta brought from Troy,
And all salute the god with shouts of joy.
And, as the ship passed rapidly upstream,
From altars spaced in line on either side
The scent of crackling incense filled the air
And victims warmed the knife of sacrifice.
    Now it had reached the world's great capital,
Rome, and the serpent raised his length to lean
Against the masthead, looking all around
To find a fit and worthy residence.
The river here divides and forms two streams
(The place is called the Island), flowing round
On either side, and stretching equal arms
To hold in their embrace the land between.
Here from the Roman ship the serpent-son
Of Phoebus disembarked and took again
His heavenly form—the god who gives relief
And health—and ended so the city's grief.

THE APOTHEOSIS OF JULIUS CAESAR

Yet he, even so, had come from overseas
To join our shrines; but Caesar is a god
In his own city here. He was supreme
In war and peace; though not his great campaigns
Triumphantly concluded, nor his feats
Achieved at home, his glory gained so fast,
Made him a star, a comet new in heaven,
Rather his son. For nothing he achieved
Was greater than to sire this son of his.
To tame the Britons in their sea-girt isle,

To sail victorious up the seven-mouthed Nile
Where the papyrus blows, to annex for Rome
Numidia's rebel tribesmen and their king,
Juba, and Pontus, bloated with the fame
Of mighty Mithridates, to exult
In triumphs and deserve so many more—
Fine feats indeed, but how can they compare
With being father of so fine an heir,
Under whose sovereignty mankind is given
Such plenteous blessings by the Powers of heaven?
Lest therefore he be born of mortal seed,
His father must be made divine.* And this
Aeneas' golden mother had perceived,
Perceived also the tragic death prepared
For her high priest,* that armed conspiracy.
She paled in fear and said to all the gods,
As she met each, 'See what pernicious plots
Are piled against me! See the treachery
That seeks the only life that's left to me
Of Trojan Iulus' stock. Shall I alone
Be always torn with troubles all too real?
I, wounded* by the lance of Diomede,
Confounded when great Troy's defences failed,
Who saw my dear son forced to roam so far,
Tossed on the seas and visiting the abodes
Of the dark silent shades and waging war
With Turnus or, in fact, if truth be told,
With Juno. Why recall now ancient wrongs
That racked my family? This fear of mine
Forbids the memory of former griefs.
Look! Do you see? They whet their wicked knives!
Prevent them, I beseech you! Stop this crime,
Nor ever by the blood of her high priest
Extinguish Vesta's flame!' To no avail
Distracted Venus cried her loud alarms
All over heaven. The gods were moved; but none
Can break the ancient Sisters'* iron decrees.
Yet they gave portents* unmistakable
Of future sorrows. Battles in the clouds
With clash of arms and horns heard in the sky

And trumpets sounding fear foretold the crime.
The sun's face too, in grief, shed lurid light
Upon the troubled lands. Among the stars
Firebrands were often seen to flare and flame,
And from black rain-clouds drops of blood would fall.
The star of dawn shone dim, his features blotched
With black and crimson; blood-blotches obscured
The chariot of the moon. The Stygian owl
In countless places cried his dirge of doom,
In countless places ivories shed tears,
And voices chanting menaces were heard
In sacred groves. No victim could avail:
The liver's lobe was found cut through, the guts
Foretold vast turmoils looming. In the squares
And round men's houses and the holy shrines
Dogs barked all night and silent ghosts were seen
Walking abroad and earthquakes shook the streets.
Even so the gods' forewarnings failed to foil
The treason and defeat the march of fate.
Into the sacred edifice drawn swords
Were brought: for that foul crime, that bloody deed
In the whole city no fit place sufficed
Except the senate-house! Then Cytherea
With both hands beat her breast and strove to hide
That scion of Aeneas in a cloud,
As once* in days gone by Paris had been
Rescued from Menelaus, his fierce foe,
And as Aeneas had escaped the sword
Of Diomede. To her the Father spoke:*
'Child, do you mean, by your sole self, to move
Unconquerable fate? You are allowed
To enter the three Sisters' dwelling. There
A giant fabric forged of steel and bronze
Will meet your eyes, the archives of the world,*
That fear no crash of heaven, no lightning's wrath,
Nor any cataclysm, standing safe
To all eternity. And there you'll find
Engraved on everlasting adamant
The fortunes of your line. I read them there
Myself and stored them in my memory;

And I'll declare them that you may not still
Labour in ignorance of things to come.
     Dear Cytherea, he for whom you toil
Has now fulfilled his span, the years he owed
To earth are done. That he should reach the sky,
A god in heaven, worshipped as divine,
You shall achieve, you and his son, the heir
Of his great name, who all alone shall bear
The burden and, most valiant to avenge
His father's murder, count us on his side
In battle. By the favour of his power
Beleaguered Mutina shall sue for peace;
Pharsalia shall know his battle-line,
Philippi swim with blood a second time,*
Pompey* be mastered in Sicilian seas.
The Egyptian consort* of a prince of Rome,
Trusting in wedlock to her cost, shall fall—
Vain then her threats to make my Capitol
The thrall of her Canopus. Need I count
Barbarian lands and peoples by the shores
Of Ocean, east and west? His writ shall run
Wherever men can live, in every land;
The sea likewise shall bow to his command!
     When peace has been bestowed upon the world,
Turning his thoughts to civil rights, he'll show
Justice and equity in lawgiving,
And by his own example guide men's ways.
Then, looking forward to the years ahead
And grandchildren to come, he'll bid the son,*
Born to his hallowed wife, assume his name
And cares of state, and not till his old age
Has equalled Nestor's years shall he attain
The abodes of heaven and touch the stars, his kin.
But you meanwhile from Caesar's murdered corpse
Must seize the soul and make it a bright star,
So that great Julius, a god divine,
From his high throne in heaven may ever shine
Upon the Forum and our Capitol.'
     His words were hardly done, when Venus stood
Within the senate-house, unseen of all,

And snatched from Caesar's corpse the new-freed soul ·
Before it could dissolve into the air,
And bore it up to join the stars of heaven,
And, as she bore it, felt it glow and burn.
She launched it from her bosom. Up it flies
Above the moon, a tress of flaming fire
Streaming behind, and shines as a bright star.
Now, seeing the achievements of his son,
He grants them greater than his own, well pleased
To be surpassed. Although the son would wish
His father's feats preferred above his own,
Fame that is free and bows to no commands,
In his despite, prefers him and defies
This once his will. Even so did Atreus yield
To Agamemnon's claim of honour, so
Aegeus to Theseus, Peleus to Achilles;
Indeed, to choose an instance that must match
Them both, Saturn is less than Jove. Jove rules
The citadels of heaven and the realms
Of all the immense three-natured universe;
The earth Augustus governs, each of them
Father and Leader. Hear my prayer, ye Gods
Who led Aeneas safe through fire and sword,
Ye gods of our dear homeland, Romulus,
Our city's founding father, and great Mars,
The father of unconquered Romulus,
Chaste Vesta worshipped with the household gods
Of Caesar, and with Caesar's Vesta thou,
Our own Apollo, and great Jupiter,
High-throned upon Tarpeia's citadel,
And all ye other deities* to whom
In duty bound a poet must appeal:
Grant the day dawn far off, a time beyond
Our generation, when Augustus' soul,
Leaving the world he rules, to heaven repairs
And there, though taken from us, hears our prayers!

EPILOGUE

Now stands my task accomplished, such a work
As not the wrath of Jove,* nor fire nor sword
Nor the devouring ages can destroy.
Let, when it will, that day, that has no claim
But to my mortal body, end the span
Of my uncertain years. Yet I'll be borne,
The finer part of me, above the stars,
Immortal, and my name shall never die.
Wherever through the lands beneath her sway
The might of Rome extends, my words shall be
Upon the lips of men. If truth at all
Is stablished by poetic prophecy,
My fame shall live to all eternity.

EXPLANATORY NOTES

A FULL commentary on the *Metamorphoses* would require several volumes. These notes are intended only to help the reader follow the twists and turns of Ovid's narrative and to illustrate, of necessity selectively, his poetic aims and methods. I am indebted to Mr Melville for references to earlier translations and for a number of illuminating contributions, including the list of English hounds and the quotation from *Paradise Lost* in Book III.

The numeration follows the Latin text, which in the main is that of F. J. Miller, with the readings of other editors occasionally preferred.

BOOK I

1-4 PROEM. For the literary implications of this very brief proem see Introd. xiv–xv.

1 Dryden started 'Of bodies changed to other forms I sing', following Sandys's 'Of bodies changed to other shapes I sing'.

2 *wrought every change*: the text is disputed. Ovid may have written 'changed that [sc. my enterprise] too'—a condensed and allusive reference to the conventional theophany in which a god intervenes to head the poet off unsuitable themes, as in the influential proem to Callimachus' *Aetia* and in Virgil's Sixth Eclogue.

5-88 THE CREATION. The narrative begins with a description of the first and greatest of all transformations, the creation of the world out of chaos, a process culminating in the appearance of Man. Ovid draws with impartial eclecticism on a rich poetical and philosophical tradition going back to Hesiod, but Roman readers would be especially conscious of the magnificent handling of this theme by Lucretius (*De Rerum Natura* v. 416 ff.); cf. xv. 6 n.

61-2 *royal Petra and the Persian hills*: not really the Far East, but Ovid often uses place-names for their sound as much as their sense.

78, 80 *perhaps . . . perhaps*: it is characteristic of the learned poet both to show that he was aware of variant versions of the tradition and to leave the choice between them open. See Introd. xxviii–xxix. A third version is in store: below, i. 157 n.

89-162 THE AGES OF MANKIND. This view of the early history of man as one of progressive decline from primeval abundance and innocence was that favoured by the poets from Hesiod onwards. Lucretius followed the opposite tradition of the philosophers, of an ascent from savagery to civilization (*De Rerum Natura* v. 925 ff.); this, of course, did not prevent Ovid from drawing on his account.

106 *Jove's spreading tree*: the oak, associated with Jupiter, particularly in his cult at Dodona.

113 *Saturn* was of the second generation of the gods. His reign, the legendary Golden Age, ended when he was succeeded by his son Jove (Jupiter). Cf. next note.

157 *children's weltering blood*: the giants were born of Earth, fertilized by the blood of Uranus (Heaven), father of Saturn. The Gigantomachy was a favourite, indeed a hackneyed, theme in art and poetry: v. 319 n.

163–261 LYCAON. The first story in the poem well exemplifies Ovid's way with his material. Lycaon, in the character of arch-representative of human depravity (not an original feature of the legend), provides the transition to the Flood. The setting for his story is a Council of the Gods, a standard epic motif already satirized by Lucilius and now again (next note) by Ovid; and the narrator is Jupiter himself.

176 *heaven's Palatine*: the Palatine hill was gradually taken over by Augustus and his successors for Imperial residences, hence our 'palace'. Sandys ingeniously translates 'This glorious Roofe I would not doubt to call, / Had I but boldness lent me, Heaven's White-Hall'.

189 *By that dark stream*: the oath by Styx was binding even on the gods.

201 *the blood/Of Caesar*: the reference is to the assassination of Julius Caesar in 44 BC.

204 *Augustus*: the poet's flattery of Augustus, who was to banish him, now reads ironically.

256 *the Fates foretold a time*: correctly, as the story of Phaethon (ii. 210 ff.) will show—a sly reference forward by the poet. His readers would also be aware that the periodical destruction of the universe by fire was a tenet of the Stoics in particular.

262–415 THE FLOOD. DEUCALION AND PYRRHA. The tradition of a world-wide flood was rooted in Near Eastern and Greek legend. Ovid's bravura description fell under the displeasure of Seneca, who objected (*Natural Questions* iii. 27. 13) that the destruction of the world was not a proper subject for foolery. But Ovid's wit may have a purpose. These incongruities—chaos come again—can be read as underlining an unspoken comment on the enormous injustice of Jupiter's actions, typical of the divine caprice that plays a decisive part in so many episodes in the poem.

271 *Iris*, messenger of the gods, is also the rainbow; Juno is the wife of Jupiter. The ends of the rainbow were believed to gather up the water and feed it back to the clouds.

275 *His sea-blue brother*: Neptune is depicted in paintings with a blue garment.

363 *my father's magic*: his father was Prometheus ('forethought') who, according to the legend, created man out of earth and water.

390 *Epimetheus* ('afterthought') was the brother of Prometheus.

416–51 REBIRTH OF LIFE. Ovid's description of the first creation of life on earth (72–5) suggests in its brevity an instantaneous manifestation of divine will. His account of the second creation reflects philosophical speculation, in particular that of Lucretius (*De Rerum Natura* v. 795 ff.). The monstrous Python provides a neat transition to Apollo.

446 *The sacred games*: held at Delphi every four years since the early sixth century BC.

452–567 APOLLO AND DAPHNE.

452 *the first love*: see Introd. xviii.

454 *Delos* was the birthplace of Apollo and the most holy place of his worship. His birth is recounted in the tale of the Lycian peasants at vi. 317 ff.

469 *rouses . . . routs*: Ovid has 'fugat hoc, facit illud amorem'. Not all his many alliterations and assonances can be represented satisfactorily in English.

560 ff. *You shall attend . . . oak*: this is the grossest possible flattery. The laurel was prominent in the cult of Apollo, and here is the god himself giving pride of place to its associations with Augustus. The laurel trees referred to, symbol of triumph, stood on each side of the palace door, and over it hung the civic crown of oak leaves, the traditional award to a soldier who saved a comrade's life in battle, voted to Augustus as saviour of the Roman people.

568-749 10. This was a very ancient legend. In course of time Io became identified with Isis, the great goddess of the Egyptians, whose cult was very popular in Rome when Ovid wrote.

568-87 *There is a vale . . . when knowledge fails*: a particularly elaborate transition, incorporating several recurrent features: (1) a formal description or *ecphrasis* (ii. 1-18 n., iii. 407 n.); (2) a catalogue of rivers, brief in this case but still exploiting the sound of their names (ii. 217-26 n.); (3) the first of several appearances of the 'all save only X' device for introducing a new character or episode.

649 *letters*: another anachronism, allowing a bilingual play on words. Inachus reads IO and exclaims 'io', the Greek word for 'woe', which Ovid then renders in the next verse as *me miserum*. Compare the metamorphosis of Ajax's blood at xiii. 398.

670 *the bright shining Pleiad bore*: Mercury's mother was Maia, one of the seven stars in the constellation of the Pleiads.

676 *A herdsman now*: . . . and the ensuing scene is enacted in the manner of Theocritean and Virgilian pastoral; cf. above, i. 452 n.

700 ff. *and how*: the Latin differentiates, as English cannot, between the told and the untold parts of the tale, developed at almost exactly the same length, by changing into indirect speech at this point, with the main verbs of the narrative in the infinitive. Such syntactical variation is one form of the linguistic wit which pervades the poem and in which Ovid took much evident pleasure.

722 *her bird*: the peacock.

725 *a frightful Fury*: in the story as told by Aeschylus in *Prometheus Vinctus* Io is haunted by the ghost of Argus. In making a Fury the agent of Juno's anger Ovid was probably influenced by Virgil (see *Aeneid* vii. 323 ff.).

750-78 PHAETHON. This ancient and famous myth had many ramifications. Ovid certainly knew and drew upon Euripides' play *Phaethon*, but he used other sources and treated them freely as usual, to produce one of the longest and most elaborate episodes in the poem. In contrast to Io (i. 568-87 n.) Phaethon is introduced by a transition which is abruptly and arbitrarily motivated: the friendship of Epaphus and Phaethon appears to be Ovid's own invention.

778 *his own Ethiopians*: his mother's husband Merops was their king. Since Homer Ethiopia had been the land of the sunrise.

BOOK II

1–400 PHAETHON (*cont.*).

1–18 Ovid's readers were probably intended to think of the temple of Palatine Apollo, dedicated by Augustus in 28 BC and already celebrated by Propertius (ii. 31, iv. 6); compare the palace of Jupiter in Book I (i. 176 n.). The elaborate formal description (*ecphrasis*) of the doors is in a tradition of such descriptions of works of art going back to the Homeric Shield of Achilles (*Iliad* xviii. 483–608). We have here an insight into Ovid's use of his poetic models. He has borrowed from the description of the abduction of Europa by the Greek poet Moschus (second century BC) in his celebrated poem *Europa*: Moschus' marine cortège (*Europa* 115–24) is adapted for this opening position and the enchanting vignette of Europa herself (ibid. 125–30) is reserved for the end of the book. This again is typical of the learned poet.

8–11 *Aegaeon*: a giant with a hundred arms, son of Neptune. *Proteus*: a sea-creature who could change his shape at will, hence 'protean'; see the story of Erysichthon, viii. 730 ff. *Triton*: a son of Neptune, who blows his horn at Neptune's bidding to calm the sea; see the story of the Flood, i. 332 ff. *Doris*: wife of Nereus and mother of the fifty Nereids, one of whom was Galatea; see xiii. 738 ff.

18 *upon each door*: these wonderful doors call to mind those of the Baptistery at Florence or the Duomo at Milan.

27–30 *Spring . . . Winter*: the four seasons were a favourite, almost hackneyed, subject in art as well as in literature.

46 *that dark marsh*: the waters of the Styx.

Though to my eyes unknown: ironical in view of the sequel to this oath (below, ll. 260–1).

70 *the sky streams by*: the heavens and the fixed stars were thought to rotate against the motion of the sun.

78 *Wild beasts . . . and shapes of fear*: the signs of the Zodiac. The idea of their threatening the progress of the Sun seems to be Ovid's own.

115 *Lucifer*: the Morning Star, actually the planet Venus and identical with Hesperus, the Evening Star.

124 *the flashing sunbeams*: the radiate crown which he had previously removed from his own head. This is the classic attribute

of the Sun in art and literature; it was also worn by kings and emperors.

131 *three zones*: as described at i. 45 ff.

133 *my wheeltracks*: compare l. 167 'the well-worn highway'. The commentators receive this remarkable statement in silence. Did Ovid perhaps mean his readers by another witty anachronism to think of the ecliptic as marked on a celestial globe?

138–9 *Snake . . . Altar*: constellations, here by way of variation for north and south.

153–4 *Aethon, Eous, Pyrois and Phlegon*: the names might be translated 'Blaze', 'Dawn', 'Fire', and 'Flame'.

156 *Tethys*: the Sun rises from and sets into Oceanus, and it is Tethys' duty, as the wife of Oceanus, to dispatch and to receive him. Phaethon's mother Clymene was the daughter of Tethys and Oceanus.

172 *in forbidden seas*: the Great Bear never sinks below the horizon —but see below, ii. 528 n.

176 *The Wagoner*: the driver of Charles's Wain, another name for the Great Bear.

195 *There is a place*: this phrase (*est locus*) is a standard introductory formula for idyllic topography (see iii. 407 n.). Its use here strikes a note of irony.

197 *two signs*: the Scorpion's claws form the sign Libra, the Balance.

217–26 *Athos . . .*: this and the catalogue of springs and rivers at ll. 239–59 below offer the learned poet a welcome opportunity to show off both his topographical and mythical knowledge and his metrical dexterity, also to exploit the sound of exotic proper names—the most notorious example of this being the roll-call of Actaeon's hounds at iii. 206 ff. Such lists were a feature of the poetical tradition from Homer onwards.

219 *virgin*: Helicon was the seat of the nine Muses, virgin goddesses.

still / Unknown, unhonoured: these words render Ovid's recondite expression *nondum Oeagrius* 'not yet Oeagrian', i.e. not yet famous for its association with Orpheus, son of Oeagrus. See Introd. xxvii.

245 *a second time*: when Hephaestus (Vulcan) at the request of Hera (Juno) was to enlist fire to help Achilles in his fight against the river (Homer, *Iliad* xxi. 328 ff.).

255 *still hidden*: the source, or rather sources, of the Nile remained a mystery until the nineteenth century. The oblique reference to a current scientific problem is characteristic of learned poetry.

291 *thy brother*: Neptune.

297 *sustain the flaming sky*: an anachronism: the transformation of the giant Atlas into a mountain has yet to take place (see the story of Perseus and Andromeda, iv. 657 ff.). Compare below, ii. 409 n., 528 n., for the inconsistency; and see Introd. xxviii–xxix.

307 *to veil the lands with clouds*: as in the case of Io (i. 600 ff.). Jupiter's style is cramped.

367 *Cycnus*: the first of three Cycnuses in the poem: vii. 371 n., xii. 72–188 n.

369 *Closer than kin*: a delicate allusion to the tradition that the two were lovers.

401–535 CALLISTO. A story with both metamorphosis and *aition*, the origin of the constellations of the Great and Little Bears. The tale, familiar now in Cavalli's opera, resembles that of Io in its mixture of humour and pathos; Ovid retold it more briefly at *Fasti* ii. 153–92. Cf. below, ii. 409 n.

406 *His own Arcadia*: birthplace of Jupiter (Zeus Lycaeus).

409 *a country nymph / Of Nonacris*: i.e. Arcadian. Callisto is not named, no doubt because the story was so ancient and familiar; but her anonymity helps to gloze over an inconsistency in the chronology adopted by Ovid, for being a daughter of Lycaon she had no business to have survived the Flood. Cf. Introd. xxviii–xxix.

441 *Dictynna*: a name of Diana, meaning 'Diana of the nets'.

495 *her father*: Lycaon, who had been turned into a wolf (i. 232 ff.).

507 *neighbouring stars*: the Great Bear and the Little Bear.

509 *Tethys*: she was Juno's nurse and the mother of many gods.

528 *debar ... That sevenfold star*: the Great Bear has seven stars. This is another 'anachronism': it had already been forbidden the ocean at the time of Phaethon's last ride. Cf. above, ii. 409 n. and Introd. xxviii–xxix.

534 *at the time*: an example of Ovid's sometimes abrupt and forced transitions from episode to episode.

536–632 THE RAVEN AND THE CROW. An example of 'Chinese box' technique (Introd. xxvii): the story of how the raven was changed from white to black encloses the story of Apollo and

Coronis, which in turn encloses the crow's narrative of the birth of Erichthonius and of her own metamorphosis.

538 *save the Capitol*: the Gauls attacked Rome about 390 BC; when they were scaling secretly by night the escarpment of the Capitol, the geese kept in the temple of Juno gave the alarm and saved the City.

545 *Phoebus' bird*: the raven was sacred to Apollo.

553 *Without a mother*: Hephaestus (Vulcan), in making an attempt on the chastity of Athene (Minerva), discharged his semen on her leg; she wiped it off on to the ground, from which Erichthonius ('Very-earthy') was born. Already in Homer (*Iliad* ii. 547-8) the grosser features of the story are passed over in silence. Ovid's immediate model for the episode was Callimachus' miniature epic *Hecale* (Frag. 260. 18 ff. Pfeiffer). See next note.

559-60 *Pandrosos . . . Herse . . . Aglauros*: the names—'Bedewed', 'Dew', 'Clearwater'—reflect the original connection of the story with fertility. In Callimachus' account Erichthonius is called 'the dew of Hephaestus'.

561 *a snake*: snakes were especially associated with earth-cults, and Erichthonius was worshipped in this guise at Athens.

579 *the Virgin's heart*: Pallas (Athene) was a virgin goddess.

589-90 *made a bird for her foul sin*: one of a number of metamorphoses slipped in briefly and parenthetically. Ovid reserves the full treatment of the incest theme for the famous cases of Byblis and Myrrha in Books IX and X. The owl was sacred to Minerva (Athene) and appeared as her emblem on the Athenian coinage.

621-2 *the gods / May never wet their cheeks with tears*: Homer forgot this rule, if he knew it, in the scene where Hera boxes Artemis' ears with her own quiver (*Iliad* xxi. 489 ff.).

624 *As a cow groans*: this unusual comparison probably owes more to literary models than to sensibility. It is based on a famous description by Lucretius of a cow seeking the calf which has been taken away from her for sacrifice (*De Rerum Natura* ii. 352-64); the additional pathos achieved by making the cow an eyewitness may have been suggested by the passage of Callimachus adapted in Pythagoras' speech in Book XV (see xv. 135 n.).

629 *his son*: Aesculapius (Asclepius), the god of medicine, wor-

shipped all over Greece. His cult was introduced at Rome in 293 BC for the purpose of averting a pestilence: see xv. 622 ff.

630 *Chiron's cave*: Chiron was a centaur, half-man, half-horse, the wisest and justest of the centaurs; all the most distinguished of the Greek heroes were his pupils.

633–75 OCYRHOE.

638 *Ocyrhoe*: in Greek = 'swift-flowing'.

648 *twice . . . renew your destiny*: first when he was snatched from his dead mother's womb, and again when he was punished with death by Jupiter for restoring Hippolytus to life and then deified at the intercession of Apollo (see Ovid, *Fasti* vi. 737–62, *Metamorphoses* xv. 532 ff.).

651 *the serpent's blood*: he was accidentally shot by Hercules, whose arrows were tipped with the Hydra's venom.

654 *the three / Goddesses*: the Fates, Clotho, Lachesis, and Atropos.

675 *a new name*: Hippe, 'mare'.

676–710 MERCURY AND BATTUS. Mercury's theft of the cattle of Apollo was a well-known legend. Only Nicander and Ovid record the metamorphosis of Battus.

683 *love*: for Admetus: see Ovid, *Ars Amatoria* ii. 239–42, Callimachus, *Hymn to Apollo* 49. As Admetus was king of Thessaly, it is natural to ask what Apollo was doing in the Western Peloponnese. Ovid was evidently less interested in consistency than in manipulating his narrative so as to bring in Pylos and Battus and to involve Mercury.

688 *Battus*: 'Chatterbox'.

706 *called tell-tale*: the point of this *aition* is obscure. In Nicander's version (as transmitted by Antoninus Liberalis) the rock is 'always either hot or cold(?)', which is even less enlightening.

709–10 *Munychia* and *Lyceum* were suburbs of Athens; the latter was to be the site of Aristotle's school, hence the ambiguous 'cultivated' (*culti*).

711–834 THE ENVY OF AGLAUROS. The festival of Pallas Athene, at which the opening of this tale is set, was held at Athens every five years on the 22nd of Hecatombaeon (corresponding roughly with July). The temple to which the procession went was the Parthenon on the Acropolis.

716 *Like a swift kite*: a designedly unflattering comparison. Mercury

was a thief, as has just been demonstrated, and the patron god of thieves.

729 *Heat not its own*: cf. xiv. 826; pseudo-science taken on trust by Lucretius (*De Rerum Natura* vi. 177–9, 306–7) and eagerly repeated by later poets. The Balearic Islands were indeed famous for their slingers.

743 *Pleione's grandson*: Pleione and Atlas were the parents of Maia, the mother of Mercury.

752 *The warrior goddess*: Minerva.

755 *aegis*: a kind of shield worn by both Jupiter and Minerva, sometimes represented in art as a fringed garment. See iv. 799–803.

760 *Envy*: this is the first of four such set-piece descriptions inspired by Virgil's great picture of Rumour (*Aeneid* iv. 173 ff.); the others are Hunger (viii. 799 ff.), Sleep (xi. 592 ff.) and—in direct emulation of Virgil—Rumour (xii. 39 ff.).

766 *she might not pass*: because it would pollute her. In the same way, Ceres cannot visit her antitype, Hunger, but must send a messenger (viii. 785–6), and Phoebus is barred from the cave of Sleep (xi. 594–5).

786 *Launched from her downthrust spear*: Nestor's pole-vault in the boar-hunt (viii. 366–7) is good knockabout comedy; here it seems an undignified exit for this most dignified of goddesses, but clearly she cannot wait to quit the noxious proximity of her disgusting agent.

835–75 JUPITER AND EUROPA. This story was familiar in both art and literature—notably in Moschus' *Europa*, to which Ovid is clearly indebted—and could be handled selectively and allusively. It serves chiefly to pave the way to the next important cycle of myths centring on Thebes.

873–5 *Her right hand . . . breeze*: for Ovid's debt to Moschus here see above, ii. 1–18 n. This is the pose in which Europa is repeatedly represented in ancient art.

BOOK III

1–130 CADMUS. Foundation legends were a favoured subject of Hellenistic history and poetry, and Thebes ranked second only to Troy in Greek song and story.

13 *Boeotia*: the Greek name was thought to mean 'land of the cow'.

14 *went down*: from the shrine at Delphi on Mount Parnassus.

35 *The Tyrians*: Cadmus was Prince of Tyre, thus Thebes was in origin a Phoenician colony. The recent discovery of Mesopotamian cylinder-seals on the ancient citadel suggests that the legend, which some scholars have received with scepticism, may have had some basis in historical fact.

45 *The Snake*: this constellation lies between the Great and the Little Bears.

103 *the serpent's teeth*: Cadmus sowed some of the teeth, the rest Pallas gave to Aeetes, the father of Medea. See the story of Jason and Medea at vii. 9 ff.

111 *at a theatre*: in a Roman theatre the curtain was raised, not lowered, at the end of a play, so the figures painted on the curtain rose head first and their feet, standing on the bottom edge, came last.

126 *all save five*: from whom the leading families of the Theban aristocracy traced their descent.
Echion: 'Viperman'.

131–255 DIANA AND ACTAEON. The classic treatment of the theme of the mortal surprising the goddess at her bath was that of Callimachus in his Fifth Hymn (*The Baths of Pallas*). The present version was to inspire Titian more than once. The long list of Actaeon's hounds is in the tradition of such catalogues (ii. 217–26 n.). Ovid is (for him) comparatively restrained: the tradition certainly knew more than the thirty-three names that he gives; the late mythographer Hyginus lists eighty-five. The Greek names have a melody that escapes in translation; the English names, though they convey the meaning well enough, have a harsher music.*

* For comparison here is a list of the bitch pack in a recent year of the Blackmore Vale:

Arctic	Canvas	Fallacy	Lapwing	Picture	Sapling
Arrogant	Catkin	Farthing	Lavish	Pinnacle	Sapphire
Artful	Caution	Flippant	Legacy	Placard	Sara
Bangle	Chaffinch	Florin	Liberty	Placid	Satchel
Blemish	Cloudy	Garter	Lilac	Precious	Satire
Blissful	Compact	Gradual	Linnet	Sable	Saucy
Bondage	Cordial	Grammar	Lottie	Safety	Stella
Bonnet	Costly	Gravel	Loyal	Saffron	Tragic
Bonus	Cosy	Hamper	Magpie	Salad	Tuffet
Bounty	Countess	Handy	Marble	Salvia	Widgeon
Bowbell	Crafty	Harmless	Pamper	Sample	Winsome
Burnish	Credit	Harmony	Passion	Sanction	
Bustle	Crocus	Landgirl	Penniless	Sandal	
Buxom	Crystal	Lantern	Picnic	Sandra	

The dog pack amounted to another twenty-eight names.

132   *The child of Mars and Venus*: Harmonia.

136–7   *nor count him fortunate / Before he dies*: a trite enough senti-
ment, but borne out by the sequel (cf. iv. 564 ff.). The cliché here
carries an ironical play on words, for 'A man's last day', *ultima
dies hominis*, was to be for Cadmus his last day *as* a man, his
first as a snake (iv. 576 ff.).

142   *to lose one's way*: it is tempting to speculate that this comment
was added in exile with the poet's own case in mind. He com-
pares himself explicitly to Actaeon at *Tristia* ii. 103 ff., and more
than once insists in the poems of exile that the offence for which
he was condemned was an *error* (indiscretion) and not a *scelus*
(crime)—the precise words used here.

173   *Titania*: her brother Phoebus is called *Titan* at ii. 118. Their
mother Latona (Leto) was daughter of the Titan Coeus.

256–315   SEMELE AND THE BIRTH OF BACCHUS. The transition
to this story is a variant of that noted at i. 568–87 n.: 'Jove's
wife alone . . . '. Semele is the subject of one of the most attrac-
tive of all Handel's operas.

258   *Tyrian concubine*: Europa, daughter of Agenor.

307   *his second armament*: this appears to be Ovid's own invention,
but the idea that 'the gods had a word for it' is Homeric
(*Odyssey* x. 305, the herb which 'the gods call *moly*'). Compare
xi. 640–1.

315   *kept him hidden away*: to be produced by the poet in all the
power of his godhead when required: l. 528 'Bacchus is there'.

316–38   TIRESIAS. By an abrupt transition in epic style ('While
down on earth . . . ') Ovid introduces the well-known story of
Tiresias' miraculous sex-changes, told briefly by way of a second
transition to the next, much more important, episode.

339–510   NARCISSUS AND ECHO. It seems likely that Ovid was
the first to combine the stories of Narcissus and Echo, to their
mutual enrichment. Cf. Introd. xxiii–xxiv. He would no doubt
have been amused to see the second metamorphosis inflicted on
his hero by Sigmund Freud.*

---

* The use made of this story by Milton (who evidently knew the *Metamor-
phoses* well) is fascinating. Eve is speaking to Adam; it is her first speech:

> That day I oft remember, when from sleep
> I first awaked and found myself reposed,
> Under a shade, on flowers, much wondering where
> And what I was, whence thither brought, and how.

348 *vain*: and a striking paradox. No oracular utterance was more famous or more frequently alluded to than the Delphic Apollo's 'know thyself'. Narcissus' life turns out to be an experience in paradox, which Ovid exploits to the limits of his linguistic ingenuity.

386 *'Join me here!'*: a virtually untranslatable play on words: *coeamus* = 'let us meet' and 'let us make love'.

400-1 *So in the woods ... just a sound*: it is very doubtful whether these lines are by Ovid.

407 *There was a pool*: this description is a classic instance of the so-called *locus amoenus*, the formal *ecphrasis* (see ii. 1-18 n.) of an idyllically beautiful place. As often in the *Metamorphoses*, the beauty is only skin-deep and the idyllic atmosphere decep-tive: see ii. 195 n. and compare the description of Diana's grotto at ll. 155 ff. above and the sequel. Here there is a heavy under-current of symbolism: the pool mirrors Narcissus in more senses than one.

472 *one death will die*: the culmination of a series of clichés from the standard repertory of love-poetry which Ovid turns to para-doxical effect in this richly ironic scene.

511-733 PENTHEUS AND BACCHUS. Bacchus (Dionysus) was a nature god, symbol of the forces which liberate man from the

> Not distant far from thence a murmuring sound
> Of waters issued from a cave, and spread
> Into a liquid plain, then stood unmoved
> Pure as the expanse of heaven. I thither went,
> With unexperienced thought, and laid me down
> On the green bank, to look into the clear
> Smooth lake, that seemed to me another sky.
> As I bent down to look, just opposite
> A shape within the watery gleam appeared,
> Bending to look on me: I started back,
> It started back; but pleased I soon returned,
> Pleased it returned as soon with answering looks
> Of sympathy and love. There had I fixed
> Mine eyes till now, and pined with vain desire,
> Had not a voice thus warned me: 'What thou seest,
> What there thou seest, fair creature, is thyself;
> With thee it came and goes. But follow me,
> And I will bring thee where no shadow stays
> Thy coming, and thy soft embraces; he
> Whose image thou art, him thou shalt enjoy
> Inseparably thine ...'

> (*Paradise Lost*, iv. 449-73)

artificial restraints of civilized behaviour, and source of the sometimes anarchic inspiration of poets—hence the hostility of Pentheus, representative of reason, law, and order. Ovid was to make play in the *Tristia* (v. 3. 35–46) with the fate of Pentheus in his polemic against Augustus. His main source in this episode is Euripides' great dramatization of this conflict of values, the *Bacchae*.

520 *Liber*: 'Free'; see previous note.

542 *not Bacchic wands*: the thyrsus was a staff entwined with vine and ivy leaves. Pentheus is to find that it can be quite as formidable as a spear (l. 712).

547 *Weaklings*: *molles* 'soft'; the word, repeated in the catalogue of Bacchus' luxurious trappings (l. 555 'tender garlands'), has connotations of homosexuality. Compare l. 607 'a boy, / As pretty as a girl'.

559 *Acrisius*: a forward cross-reference, though when Acrisius does appear it is merely to provide a transition (iv. 607 ff.).

580 *Tell me your name*: the standard epic request to a chance-met stranger. Acoetes' reply recalls the long, circumstantial, and mendacious yarns spun by Odysseus to Athene (*Odyssey* xiii. 256 ff.) and Eumaeus (xiv. 192 ff.). The details of landing and watering are characteristic of epic narrative.

582 *Acoetes*: Ovid now, in the manner of the learned poet, changes and conflates sources. The main Pentheus-narrative lacks a metamorphosis; this episode, freely adapted and expanded from the Homeric Hymn to Dionysus, provides one. Acoetes himself, however, is taken from the tragedy *Pentheus* of the Roman poet Pacuvius (second century BC); in Euripides' *Bacchae* it is Dionysus himself, incognito, who is imprisoned and miraculously released. Ovid does not identify Acoetes with the god, but clearly expects his readers to do so: see ll. 658–9 'there's no god / Closer than he' and iii. 658–9 n.

593 *helmsmanship*: in the Homeric Hymn it is the (anonymous) helmsman who realizes that their passenger is divine and who is exempted from the general punishment. The identification with Acoetes may be Ovid's idea.

637 *That is my home*: Naxos was only one, and not the best-attested, of Bacchus' birthplaces; it is associated with him principally through the legend of his rescue of Ariadne after her betrayal and abandonment by Theseus. The story is told by Ovid at *Ars Amatoria* i. 527 ff.

658-9 *Closer*: a play on two senses of *praesens*, 'ready at hand', i.e. effective, powerful (compare Psalm 46: 1 'God is our hope and strength: a very present help in trouble'), and literally 'present'.

683 *All round the ship*: unusually, nature as well as shape has been metamorphosed. Seafarers have always enjoyed the companionable escort of dolphins; and it was a dolphin that rescued Arion when he too was threatened with murder at sea, for which it was made into a constellation (see Ovid, *Fasti* ii. 83-118).

720 *Actaeon's ghost*: both are torn to pieces for seeing a forbidden sight, but Pentheus' offence is deliberate. The arch cross-reference is typical of Ovid.

721 *tore away*: in their frenzy the Bacchantes were supposed to tear wild animals apart with their bare hands (*sparagmos*).

725 *at the sight*: the Latin is ambiguous: *uisis*='what she (thought she) saw'. Actaeon really was a wild animal, Pentheus only seemed to his maddened pursuers to be one. It is from Bacchus that the poet's power to create illusion derives.

732 *That lesson learnt*: it ought to have been the Theban *men* who took the fate of Pentheus to heart, but Ovid is chiefly concerned with the transition to the next book and the next story.

BOOK IV

1-415 THE DAUGHTERS OF MINYAS. The daughters of Minyas impiously reject the cult of Bacchus. To pass the time as they work, they tell the stories which take up the first half of Book IV: one of Ovid's 'framing' devices.

1-54 THE MINYIADES REJECT BACCHUS.

11 *his many noble names*: a god was invoked in all his possible guises. Lyaeus 'Bringer of release'; Bromius 'Thunderer'; Nyseus, from Nysa in India, one of Bacchus' birthplaces; Lenaeus, from the Attic festival of the Lenaea; Thyoneus 'Stormer'; Nyctilius 'Worshipped by night'; Iacchus, Euhan, Eleleus, back-formations from the orgiastic cries *iacche, euoi, eleleu*.

16 *And all the countless titles*: the customary formula, to avoid giving offence by unintentional omissions.

For you . . . : the poet now modulates directly into the form of a cult-hymn. Hexameter hymns were actually used in Greek cults; as a literary form they are represented by the Homeric Hymns, so-called, and the Hymns of Callimachus.

20 *a lovely girl's*: cf. iii. 547 n.

22 *Lycurgus*: King of Thrace, mentioned in Homer (*Iliad* 6. 130 ff.) as opposing Dionysus.

26 *that old drunkard*: Silenus.

33 *untimely spinning*: the traditional employment of the frugal and virtuous housewife, now an affront to the god.

47 *her daughter*: Semiramis, changed into a dove.

53 *far from widely known*: an understatement. The story appears for the first time in Ovid, and all subsequent treatments—most notably Shakespeare's in *A Midsummer Night's Dream*—go back to him. He tells the story with a delicate touch and a straight face.

55–168 PYRAMUS AND THISBE. Ovid appears to have taken this and the other stories told by the Minyiades from an otherwise unattested collection of tales of Near Eastern origin. In mentioning other stories only to reject them (the rhetorical device called *praeteritio*) he demonstrates his learning and reminds his readers that there is an art of selection as well as of narration. Cf. below, iv. 276 n.

58 *that city*: Babylon. Its brick walls were one of the Seven Wonders of the ancient world, described by Herodotus (i. 178) and others.

88 *Ninus' tomb*: this well-known landmark seems to have been in Nineveh, which Ninus founded. His relationship with Semiramis was the subject of the so-called 'Ninus romance', generally dated to about 100 BC (see B. E. Perry, *The Ancient Romances* (1967), 153–67). The choice of rendezvous carries a note of foreboding.

122 *As when a pipe . . .*: this is not the only place in the poem where blood jets from a wound with implausible force (vi. 259), but the illustration—emphasized by its contemporary (anachronistic) subject-matter—is macabre in the extreme. As will be seen, Ovid sometimes went out of his way to cultivate gruesome effects; the battle in the next book offers many examples.

169–284 THE SUN IN LOVE.

189 *The choicest tale to go the rounds of heaven*: it had been told by the first and greatest of all story-tellers, Homer (*Odyssey* viii. 266 ff.), and by Ovid himself in the *Ars Amatoria* (ii. 561 ff.). The sisters share the poet's preoccupation with the relative

familiarity of their (his) material: cf. above, iv. 53 n., 55–168 n., below, iv. 276 n.

204 *Rhodos*: daughter of Neptune and Amphitrite, mother by the Sun of the Heliades (ii. 340).

205 *Circe's lovely mother*: Perse, daughter of Oceanus.

209 *the perfumed lands*: the East, here Persia, though Arabia was the land of spices *par excellence*.

213–14 *Belus*: legendary founder of Babylon. *Achaemenids*: Persians. Achaemenes was the founder of the Persian royal house, a real historical character. Real and fictitious dynasties are all the same to Ovid.

239 *buried her*: the traditional punishment of a Vestal Virgin detected in unchastity.

249 *destiny denied*: see ii. 648 n.

251 *touch the sky*: by rising heavenwards in smoke; the words (*tanges . . . aethera*) also mean 'you shall win immortality'.

270 *towards the sun she turns*: the Latin words render the Greek name of the flower, heliotrope.

273 *not one of them*: a reminder of the framing episode within which these stories are told and of the obdurate impiety of the sisters.

275 *upright*: the vertical loom was the normal pattern in antiquity; see vi. 55 ff.

276 *I'll not relate*: another learned *praeteritio*; cf. above, iv. 55–168 n.

277 *Daphnis*: a shepherd beloved by the nymphs, familiar to Ovid's readers from Theocritus' *Idylls* and Virgil's *Eclogues*. See Introd. xxviii–xxix.

280 *Sithon*: otherwise totally unknown. Sex-changes figure elsewhere in the poem: Tiresias (iii. 323 ff.), Iphis (ix. 666 ff.), Caeneus (xii. 169 ff.)—and, of course, the forthcoming story by Alcithoe (see esp. ll. 378–9).

282 *Celmis*: one of the Idaean Dactyls (see *Oxford Classical Dictionary*, s.v.), wizards or dwarfish smiths, identified in the later tradition with the Curetes (see next note). Both his service to Jupiter and the reason for his petrification are obscure.

Curetes, sprung from a sharp shower: the Sky-god fertilizes Mother Earth in the form of rain; even Lucretius (*De Rerum Natura* i. 250–1) exploits this primeval image. Cf. the earth-born Erichthonius (ii. 553 n.). The Curetes protected the infant

Zeus (Jupiter) from his father Kronos by dancing round him and drowning his cries by clashing their weapons.

283 *Crocus* ... *Smilax*: this version is also attested by the Elder Pliny (*Natural History* xvi. 154). In the version referred to at *Fasti* v. 227 Crocus was accidentally killed by Mercury and the flower sprang from his blood. Neither was exactly hackneyed.

285–388 SALMACIS AND HERMAPHRODITUS. Salmacis was the name of a spring at Halicarnassus in Asia Minor that was supposed to render men who bathed in it effeminate. Hermaphroditus was an androgynous deity. This story kills two birds with one stone, explaining the origin of Hermaphroditus as the result of a metamorphosis and providing an *aition* for the reputation of the spring. As with Narcissus and Echo (iii. 339–510 n.), a story with which this has a good deal in common, the combination was almost certainly due to Ovid. It is one of the most sensuous episodes in the poem, rich in description and simile.

289 *Ida*: the Phrygian, not the Cretan, mountain.

320 *Fair boy* ... : Salmacis' speech is modelled on the famous words of Odysseus to Nausicaa when he is shipwrecked (*Odyssey* vi. 149 ff.). However, whereas Odysseus is humble and respectful ('awestruck I behold you'), Salmacis concludes with an invitation to bed.

332 *to rescue her eclipse*: though the causes of eclipses were familiar to the educated (cf. above, ll. 202–3), they were popularly considered ill-omened. Loud noises were thought to deter the evil influences that were at work (cf. vii. 207–8): 'The sound of brass instruments is particularly terrifying to devils' (J. G. Frazer, *The Scapegoat* (*The Golden Bough*, Part VI), 3rd edn. (1913), 147). In 1888 A. H. Sayce described an experience in Egypt: 'While we were at dinner we were disturbed by a prodigious noise outside the tent; the moon was eclipsed, and the natives of the neighbouring village were vigorously beating their saucepans in order to frighten away the demon who they believed was devouring the moon' (*Reminiscences* (1923), 256).

373 *found gods to hear*: what gods? and why did they grant the prayer? As arbitrary is Hermaphroditus' wish and his parents' assent to it. But having willed the ends—the metamorphosis and the *aition*—the poet must will the means. Even for Ovid, who does not much regard plausibility except when it suits his poetic purpose—'let me lie so as to convince my hearers' had

written Callimachus (*Hymn* i. 65)—this is somewhat cavalier. However, conscious irony may be at work. Alcithoe's ready faith in the present power of gods to resolve a dilemma such as this contrasts with her failure to recognize the god who has manifested himself in her own city. To the sisters the myth is more real than what is taking place—if they cared to look— before their eyes (ll. 272–3).

389–415 THE DAUGHTERS OF MINYAS TRANSFORMED.

415 *take their name*: 'bat' in Latin is *uespertilio*, from *uesper* 'evening'; in 'flit by night' Ovid also alludes to its Greek name, *nykteris*, from *nyx* 'night'. In Nicander's much more elaborate version of the story the sisters are changed into a bat, an owl, and another, unidentified, bird.

416–562 ATHAMAS AND INO. Ovid considerably embellishes this story with motifs suggested by Virgil: the angry outburst of Juno (*Aeneid* i. 37 ff., vii. 293 ff.), the visit to the Underworld (vi. 295 ff.), and the Fury Tisiphone (vii. 323 ff.).

418 *the sisters*: Autonoe, mother of Actaeon; Agave, mother of Pentheus; Semele, mother of Bacchus.

421 *Her foster-child*: iii. 313.

440 *That city*: the conventional Underworld topography is handled vaguely and selectively. A City of the Dead appears to be Ovid's own invention, corresponding to the earlier picture of Olympus as a super-Rome (i. 168 ff.); indeed the opening line of the description of Hades evokes the earlier passage: '*est uia* <u>decliuis</u> *funesta nubila taxo*', cf. '*est uia* <u>sublimis</u> *caelo manifesta sereno*'.

446 *And some enduring their due punishment*: this verse, which is poorly attested in the manuscript tradition, is almost certainly not Ovid's.

447 *forced herself to go*: Olympian deities have no business in Hell; Virgil's Juno descended only as far as earth and summoned Allecto to her there (*Aeneid* vii. 323–4). Cf. ii. 766 n. and below, iv. 480 n.

450 *the threshold groaned*: as Charon's boat groans beneath the weight of flesh-and-blood passengers (*Aeneid* vi. 413); but the superhuman weight of the gods was a commonplace from Homer onwards.

451 *The Sisters*: the Furies (Greek Erinyes), Allecto, Megaera, and Tisiphone. Their function was to avenge and punish.

456 *The Dungeon of the Damned*: Sandys's translation.

457 ff. *There giant Tityus . . .*: no description of the Underworld was complete without a reference to these famous criminals and their punishments, though the composition of the list varied. Ovid's readers would remember especially Homer (*Odyssey* xi. 576 ff.), Lucretius (*De Rerum Natura* iii. 980 ff.), and Virgil (*Aeneid* vi. 580 ff.); there was also a well-known painting by Polygnotus at Delphi. *Tityus* tried to rape Latona (Leto). *Tantalus* stole the food of the gods and was punished by everlasting hunger and thirst. *Sisyphus* (a byword for unscrupulous cunning; in some genealogies the father of Odysseus) betrayed one of Jupiter's amours and was condemned to roll a stone uphill for ever. *Ixion* tried to rape Juno (who accordingly looks at him with particular loathing) and was tied to an eternally revolving wheel. The *Danaids* were the fifty daughters of Danaus, married to their cousins, the fifty sons of Aegyptus. On their wedding night all but one, Hypermestra, murdered their husbands; they were punished by being made to draw water in leaking jars or sieves.

466 *Of all the brothers*: Sisyphus and Athamas were sons of Aeolus; another brother, Salmoneus, figures in Virgil's list (*Aeneid* vi. 585–6); but Sisyphus' offence is one which Juno might well condone.

474 *Tisiphone*: 'Avenger of blood', chosen for this mission as senior Fury rather than the more ostensibly suitable Megaera 'Envy'. Allecto had been pre-empted by Virgil.

480 *Thaumas' child*: Iris. Ovid seems to go out of his way to draw attention to the breach of divine and literary convention (see above, iv. 447 n.).

501 *Cerberus . . . Hydra*: both were children of the snake-monster Echidna, the name by which Ovid here and elsewhere confusingly refers to the Hydra.

531 *her grandchild*: Venus was Harmonia's mother (iii. 132).

538 *my name*: Aphrodite, from *aphros* 'foam'.

563–614 THE TRANSFORMATION OF CADMUS. This episode rounds off the cycle of stories which began at the end of Book II with the rape of Europa.

575 *I pray that I / May be a snake*: this fate had been foretold to Cadmus (iii. 98), but his request seems to be made in a spirit of irony or exasperation: if the best way of finally escaping from divine persecution is to be a snake, well then . . . In fact he and Harmonia are now at last granted peace and security; possibly Ovid intends a hint of one of the alternative versions of the story,

in which the pair were translated to the Islands of the Blessed. This is one of the relatively rare 'happy endings' in the poem; comparable are Baucis and Philemon (viii. 711–24), Iphis (ix. 795–6), Pygmalion (x. 290–4), and Ceyx and Alcyone (xi. 742–8).

608 *Acrisius*: Pentheus had appealed to his example in his defiance of Bacchus (iii. 559–60), but we hear no more of him after he has served his turn by introducing Perseus. Abas was distantly related to Bacchus through his mother Hypermestra. Cadmus and Harmonia joyfully acknowledge their grandson, Bacchus; Acrisius repudiates both the god and his own grandson, Perseus. This is enough of a connection to provide the transition which Ovid requires.

611 *in that gold shower*: an oracle had declared that she would bear a son who would kill her father. Acrisius therefore imprisoned her in a brazen tower, but Jupiter visited her in the form of a shower of gold and she became the mother of Perseus. Ovid 'cuts' straight to the hero in mid adventure; the intermediate part of the story and the final fulfilment of the oracle (see *Oxford Classical Dictionary*, s.v. Perseus (1)) he omits—hardly as too familiar to be worth recounting, since the Andromeda episode itself, on which he is to expatiate, had been exploited over and over again in Greek and Roman drama.

614–803 PERSEUS AND ANDROMEDA.

615 *the snake-haired monster*: the Gorgon Medusa; how he obtained her head and she her snakes will be told in a flashback presently (ll. 772 ff.).

616 *rustling pinions*: the winged shoes, obtained from the nymphs with the rest of his outfit—the wallet and the cap of invisibility—with the help of Mercury, to whom after his victory over the sea-monster he duly (but with no explanation from the poet) builds an altar (l. 754).

625 *the icy Bears . . . the Crab*: the extreme north and south.

643 *the oracle*: apparently an invention of Ovid's. The 'son of Jove' is Hercules. In the traditional version of this Labour Atlas was a giant, not a mountain; cf. ii. 297 n. and below, iv. 772 n.

666 *his curving sword*: the *harpe*, associated with Mercury as well as Perseus (i. 717).

669 *for her mother's tongue*: Cassiope had boasted of her own beauty and incurred the jealousy of the Nereids, who persuaded their father Neptune to deluge the country with a disastrous flood. The oracle of Jupiter Ammon declared that there could be no relief

from the flood unless Andromeda was chained to a rock and offered to a sea-monster. The geographer Pomponius Mela, writing a generation or so after Ovid, recalls (i. 64) that the monster's bones were shown to tourists at Joppa; cf. viii. 15–16 n.

714 *Jove's bird*: the eagle.

754–5 *the warrior queen . . . Pallas*: cf. v. 46–7, 250–1. Ovid's readers were no doubt expected to know that she had already advised him how to deal with the Graiae (below, iv. 775 n.) and assisted him in the encounter with Medusa.

772 *Of icy Atlas*: who, however, at this point in the story was not yet a mountain; cf. above, iv. 643 n.

775 *Phorcys' daughters*: the Graiae, sisters and guardians of Medusa, with one eye between them. In some accounts they are three.

779 *the Gorgons*: there were three of them, cf. below, l. 791.

786 *Pegasus . . . his brother*: the winged horse and his (human) brother Chrysaor.

791 *asked why*: the book ends with two *aitia*, the first (in this form) apparently Ovid's own invention (though the liaison with Neptune is attested by Hesiod (*Theogony* 278)), the second anachronistic (below, iv. 803 n.).

798 *Ocean's lord*: Neptune.

803 *breastplate*: the Gorgon's head was the centre-piece of the Aegis (ii. 755 n.), but at this point of the story it was still in Perseus' possession.

BOOK V

1–249 PERSEUS' FIGHT IN THE PALACE OF CEPHEUS. This is the first of two exaggeratedly gory 'epic' battles in the poem (see on the Lapiths and the centaurs xii. 189–535 n.). It and the quarrel which occasions it appear to be due to Ovid's own invention; in no other earlier version is Phineus Andromeda's betrothed as well as her uncle. The situation is analogous to that of Aeneas, Turnus, and Lavinia in the Aeneid (see esp. v. 10 n. below); the effect verges on parody of epic. On Phineus see also vii. 3 n.

10 *My stolen bride*: the words *praereptae coniugis* echo a phrase *coniuge praerepta* from one of Turnus' speeches in the Aeneid (ix. 138).

11–12 *Jove's gold counterfeit*: iv. 611 n.

36 *the altar*: one of the domestic altars of the palace.

44   *to bear him witness*: like Virgil's Latinus when his efforts to avert war are fruitless (*Aeneid* vii. 593 ff.).

61   *his lover*: this pair recall Nisus and Euryalus in *Aeneid* ix; cf. Cyllarus and Hylonome at xii. 393 ff.

103   *Embraced the altar*: like Virgil's Priam (*Aeneid* ii. 550).

104–6   *On the altar . . . amidst the altar fires*: Ovid's variation on a conceit that descended from Homer (*Iliad* x. 457) through Ennius (*Annales* 501–2 Warmington) and Virgil (*Aeneid* x. 395–6) and that was imitated after him by Seneca (*Thyestes* 729), Lucan (ii. 181–2), and Silius Italicus (six instances). For yet another variation see vi. 560 n.

126   *Abas*: one of several characters of this name, not related to each other or to Perseus' grandfather (iv. 607).

164–5   *Two herds of cattle lowing*: *duōrum . . . mūgitibus armentōrum*; sound and rhythm (the slow and heavy spondaic ending) reinforce the sense; for an even more striking example see vii. 114 n.

177   *Yet Perseus saw*: somewhat belatedly, but Ovid must have his battle.

215   *Sideways*: he dare not face Perseus.

239   *Proetus had usurped . . .*: this part of the story is known only from Ovid.

242   *Polydectes*: king of Seriphus, who had rescued Danae and Perseus when they had been set adrift by Acrisius. He sent Perseus to win the Gorgon's head to leave himself free to seduce Danae.

250–678   MINERVA MEETS THE MUSES ON HELICON. Minerva, hitherto mentioned only in passing in the Perseus narrative, now provides the transition to a new group of stories, told by an unnamed Muse, one narrative enclosing the other, 'Chinese box' style: cf. Introd. xxvii.

252   *Gyaros and Cythnos*: like Seriphus, part of the Cyclades group.

259   *his mother's blood*: see iv. 786 n. The spring Hippocrene burst from his hoofprint (see next note). Another transitional device.

264   *issuing from his hoof's . . . stroke*: the Latin (*factas pedis ictibus*) also means 'made for rhythmic verse': Hippocrene was a source of poetic inspiration.

274   *Pyreneus*: known only from this passage.

278   *Parnassus*: Apollo was leader of the Muses, Musagetes.

282–3   *Have entered humbler homes*: a sly reference forward in the poem to the story of Baucis and Philemon (viii. 618 ff.).

288 *By taking wing*: airborne Muses are otherwise unknown.

294–678 THE PIERIDES. The contest with the Pierides frames the rest of the episodes in the book. The Muses themselves are frequently referred to as *Pierides*, daughters of Pierus: it is tempting to see here a reminiscence, preserved in myth, of an ancient victory of a Greek over a Macedonian cult of similar type: cf. below, ll. 311–14. Ovid found the story in Nicander; cf. below, v. 669 n.

294–340 THE PIERID'S SONG.

295 *a greeting voice*: as now, talking birds were taught to say 'hallo' (*chaire, aue*).

299 *magpies*: this is the usual identification of *picae*, but jays are perhaps more likely.

303 *Paeonian*: the Paeones were a people of northern Macedonia.

310 *Thespian goddesses*: Thespiae was a town near the foot of Helicon.

312 *Aganippe*: Helicon's other poetic spring.

319 *the great war in heaven*: the war of the giants against the gods (i. 151 ff.). The giants were a type of impiety; by representing them as the heroes of the war and dwelling on the rout and ignominious disguises of the gods the singer was asking for trouble (cf. vi. 103 n.), even though it was all 'true' (below, v. 326 n.). Ovid allows her only thirteen verses, all but the last five in indirect speech (cf. i. 700 ff. n.), as against Calliope's 321. Cf. Introd. xxvii–xxviii.

321 *Typhon*: also Typhoeus; see below, ll. 346 ff.

326 *In spurious shapes*: this is well attested in the literary and mythographical tradition, though the disguises vary. Behind the suggested connections with theriomorphic Egyptian deities lurks Alexandrian scholarship.

328 *with curling horns*: an *aition*; the shrine of Zeus (Jupiter) Ammon was at Siwa in Cyrene (Libya). In the classical period of Greece the oracle there had a reputation comparable to that of Delphi and Dodona.

329 *a raven*: cf. ii. 545 n.

     a goat: goats were sacrificed to Bacchus, who was god of tragedy (*tragoedia*='goat-song').

331 *a fish*: Dercetis (iv. 45) or Derceto was changed by Aphrodite (Venus) into a fish; as a goddess she was portrayed with a fish's tail.

331 *an ibis*: connected in cult with Thoth, identified with Mercury.

339 *Calliope*: 'Fair-voiced'; named by Hesiod (*Theogony* 79) as chief Muse and associated particularly with elevated poetry.

341–571 THE MUSE'S SONG: (1) THE RAPE OF PROSERPINE. This story is also told by Ovid in the *Fasti* (iv. 417–620); some significant differences in the treatments are noted below. The legend of Ceres (Demeter) and her daughter Proserpine (Persephone; also Kore, the Virgin) is an extremely ancient nature-myth. Proserpine represents the regenerative power of the seed-corn, which must be buried every year and lie in the darkness of the earth for the winter months, to be reborn each spring. Pluto was a god of wealth as well as death. Calliope begins with a short hymn to Ceres and introduces the story with a reference to the punishment of Typhon. This pious and pointed exordium immediately puts the previous singer in her place.

343 *first gave laws*: one of her titles was Thesmophoros, 'Lawgiver'; cf. Callimachus, *Hymn to Ceres* 18: 'tell how she gave welcome laws to the cities'.

350–1 *Pelorus . . . Pachynus . . . Lilybaeum*: the three capes of Sicily, Faro on the north-east, Passaro on the south-east, Marsala on the west. Cf. xiii. 725–7.

358 *terrify the trembling shades*: as had indeed happened once before (ii. 260–1). Pluto's patrol looks like a 'doublet' of Jupiter's at ii. 401 ff.

367 *shoot your speedy arrows*: as he had done once before, at Phoebus (i. 473). In the *Fasti* Pluto falls in love without Cupid's assistance. The episode is clearly suggested by the scene between Venus and Cupid in Virgil, *Aeneid* i. 663 ff.; the opening line of Venus' speech here echoes that in Virgil.

368 *the last lot*: when the three sons of Saturn (Kronos) drew lots for parts of the world, Jupiter drew the first, Neptune the second (cf. iv. 533), Pluto the third. Cf. below, l. 529.

379 *her uncle*: her father was Pluto's brother Jupiter.

383 *the pliant horn*: cf. Syrinx's 'bow of horn' (i. 697). Horn was indeed used in the construction of bows, but poets used *cornu* = 'bow' for literary reasons, on the model of Greek *keras*.

385 *Henna*: a city in the centre of Sicily with a famous shrine of Ceres. Ovid's descriptions here and in the *Fasti* would recall to Roman readers a famous passage of Cicero's indictment of Verres (*Verrines* ii. 4. 107). This one is a classic formal *ecphrasis* (ii.

1–18 n.) of a *locus amoenus*; as with Narcissus' pool (iii. 407 n.) it belies its promise.

389 *like awnings*: *ut uelo*; as at iii. 158–9 nature imitates art, perhaps here with a specific suggestion of a Roman amphitheatre, with the surrounding trees as the supporting masts of the *uelum*.

406 *Palica*: a town in Sicily near a sulphurous lake. The topographical details and the reference to the origins of Syracuse are typical learned embroidery.

409 *Arethusa . . . Cyane*: springs near Syracuse. Cicero (*Verrines* ii. 4. 107) and Diodorus Siculus (v. 4. 2) record that a spring arose where Pluto re-entered the Underworld; Ovid's version (existing spring and metamorphosis) appears to be his own invention. Cyane is to some extent a 'doublet' of Arethusa (see below, v. 487 n.); metamorphosis into springs is a recurrent theme (vi. 312 Niobe; vii. 371 Hyrie; xiii. 885 ff. Acis; xv. 547 ff. Egeria), but the total resolution of a water-nymph into water is both bizarre and unexampled.

417 *Anapus*: another Sicilian river which flows into Cyane; this no doubt suggested the idea of their love, otherwise unattested, and hence the motive for Cyane's disinterested (and disastrous) intervention.

461 *a starry-spotted newt*: *stellio*='newt', *stella*='star'. We learn from Nicander that his name was Ascalabus and his mother's Misme; presumably Ovid wanted to avoid confusion with Ascalaphus (below, v. 537 n.).

487 *that fair nymph*: in the Homeric Hymn to Ceres (63 ff.) and in the *Fasti* (iv. 581 ff.) the Sun is the informant. To cast Arethusa in the role, complementing Cyane, is ingeniously and finely imagined.

499 *Ortygia*: see below, v. 572–641 n.

507–8 *And yet . . . Hell*: in the original

> sed regina tamen, sed opaci maxima mundi,
> sed tamen inferni pollens matrona tyranni

—'two unforgettable lines' (Wilkinson, *Ovid Recalled*, p. 202). It is worth remembering that Ovid was capable of grandeur when the occasion called for it.

513 *let loose*: in grief and supplication.

537 *seven*: an unexpected number. In the *Fasti* (iv. 607) she eats three, one for each month of winter (cf. below, ll. 565–7). In the Homeric Hymn to Ceres (371 ff.) she is tricked into eating by

     Pluto. The Underworld garden is also peculiar to Ovid, and Ascalaphus is first heard of here.

539 *Orphne*: 'Darkness'.

544 *Phlegethon*: 'Fiery', one of the rivers of Hades.

555 *Sirens*: half-women, half-birds, a favourite subject in ancient art; famous in literature from Odysseus' encounter with them (Homer, *Odyssey* xii. 165 ff.).

572–641 THE MUSE'S SONG: (2) ARETHUSA. Ceres now has leisure and inclination to take up Arethusa's offer. Springs of this name were common in the Greek world; the best-known was this one on Ortygia ('The Quaily'), an island off Syracuse. The story of Arethusa's flight from Alpheus was clearly famous, as is shown by Pindar's allusive apostrophe to Ortygia at the beginning of his First Nemean Ode: 'Sacred breathing-place of Alpheus, Ortygia, child of famous Syracuse, home of Artemis . . .'. Cf. v. 619 n.

577 *Achaea*: here for the Peloponnese; Alpheus rises in southern Arcadia and flows into the Ionian Sea, thence, according to the legend, across the sea to mingle his waters with Arethusa (but see v. 638 n.).

587 *I found a stream*: another treacherous *locus amoenus* (above, v. 385 n.).

607–8 *Orchomenus . . . Erymanthus*: taken literally this catalogue of Arcadian towns and mountains implies a run of some 120 miles up hill and down dale. Ovid, as often (cf. on Actaeon's hounds, iii. 131–255 n.), is concerned principally with the verbal music of the names.

619 *Diana*: the natural helper for a huntress. However, in some versions of the story it is Diana herself (Artemis) who is loved by Alpheus, and Ortygia was sacred to her; hence Ortygia was one of her names (i. 694), transferred to her birthplace Delos (xv. 337).

638 *to join his stream with me*: *ut se mihi misceat*, with the same play on the primary and transferred senses of *misceo* as in Polyphemus' horrid witticism at xiii. 866. In the familiar form of the story as we meet it in Pindar (loc. cit. above, v. 572–641 n.) and Virgil (*Aeneid* iii. 694 ff.) he followed her and achieved his purpose. In Ovid's account it seems to be implied that she made her get-away.

642–78 THE MUSE'S SONG: (3) TRIPTOLEMUS; THE PIERIDES' PUNISHMENT.

646 *Triptolemus*: a 'culture-hero', the mythical inventor of agriculture. In the Homeric Hymn and elsewhere (e.g. Ovid, *Amores* iii.

10. 29) Ceres first destroys (above, ll. 477 ff.) and then restores cultivation. Ovid's reconciliation of the mythographical discrepancy is economical and allusive 'Partly in virgin land and part in fields/Long fallow'.

650 *Lyncus*: first known from this passage.

652 *Athens*: more precisely Eleusis, the home of the Mysteries and the most famous centre of the cult of Demeter (Ceres).

656 *gentle nourishment*: the invention of agriculture was regarded as a crucial step in the advance of civilization; for its association with Athens cf. Lucretius, *De Rerum Natura* vi. 1 ff.: 'It was glorious Athens who first shared out to suffering mortals corn-bearing crops.'

669 *Those nine girls*: in the Latin *Emathides*, from Emathia=Thessaly. The name occurs only here and in Nicander's version.

BOOK VI

1–145 ARACHNE. Minerva (Athene) now assumes an active role: as the Muses had punished the Pierides for their presumption, so she determines to punish Arachne for a similar offence. This is the first of a series of tales of divine vengeance.

5 *Arachne*: the word means 'spider' in Greek; it is connected etymologically with Latin *aranea*, 'web' or 'spider'.

8 *Idmon*: 'Knowing'.

24 *denied it*: all such gifts come from 'God', so Arachne's denial and her self-sufficiency are blasphemous. This must be the justification for Minerva's apparently unjust and arbitrary revenge.

70 *in Cecrops' citadel*: arx here stands for 'city'; Ovid knew that the Areopagus is not on the Acropolis.

71 *that old dispute*: between Minerva and Neptune, to determine who should be the city's patron deity; it is frequently alluded to from Herodotus (viii. 55) onwards. The scene was portrayed on the west gable of the Parthenon by Phidias. Minerva's choice of subject is in itself an implicit warning of the folly of challenging her. The lesson is underlined by the four subsidiary vignettes.

87 *Rhodope . . . Haemon*: brother and sister; they compounded their incest by calling each other Zeus (Jupiter) and Hera (Juno).

90 *the Pygmy matron*: Oenoe; no other source mentions a contest between her and Juno. The enmity between the cranes and the pygmies was famous from Homer onwards (*Iliad* iii. 3 ff.).

93 *Antigone*: a Trojan heroine who boasted of her beauty; again it is only in Ovid that we hear of a 'contest'.

98 *Cinyras*: the story is known only from this passage.

101 *The branch of peace*: in the circumstances an ironical touch.

103 *Arachne shows* . . .: in contrast to Minerva's calm, stately, and symmetrical composition, Arachne provocatively offers a hectic anthology of divine delinquency (l. 131 'crimes of heaven') at the expense of deluded women. Cf. v. 319 n. The scores are as follows: Jupiter 9, Neptune 6, Apollo 4, Bacchus and Saturn 1 each. Ovid, of course, improves the occasion by a display of recondite mythological learning.

104 *you'd think*: a common appreciative formula, ancient art being esteemed as it was representational; in this case 'you' would have been wrong, since it was Jupiter in disguise.

108 *Asterie*: this particular episode is otherwise unattested.

113 *in a flame*: this is unique to Ovid; elsewhere the disguise is the familiar eagle. Aegina's son by Jupiter was Aeacus, king of the island which he called after his mother (vii. 474).

114 *Mnemosyne*: mother by Jupiter of the Muses; the disguise is otherwise unattested.

Proserpine: incest into the bargain, for she was his daughter. The offspring of this union was the 'chthonic' Dionysus Zagreus (Callimachus, Frag. 43. 117 Pfeiffer).

117 *the Aloidae*: the giants Otus and Ephialtes; their mother was Iphimedia. This variant is attested only here. Better known is the version in which Neptune impersonated Enipeus to seduce Tyro (Homer, *Odyssey* xi. 235 ff.).

Bisaltes' child: Theophane. She bore the ram with the Golden Fleece.

118 *The corn's most gracious mother*: Ceres; as Demeter Erinys she took the shape of a mare.

119 *The snake-tressed mother*: Medusa; see iv. 615 n., 791 n. The bird-disguise is otherwise unattested.

122 *a herdsman's guise*: when he was in love with Admetus; see ii. 683 n.

123 *a lion's skin* . . . *hawk's plumage*: nothing is known of these stories.

125 *Erigone*: presumbly Bacchus took on the form of a bunch of grapes. Erigone was an important figure in Attic legend (x. 448–51 n.), but this episode is otherwise unknown.

126 *Begot*: on Philyra.

139 *Hecate*: daughter of Asterie (above, vi. 108 n.), an Underworld goddess sometimes identified with Diana (Artemis), and associated with ghosts and witchcraft. How Minerva happened to have these drugs by her (for the metamorphosis itself arises from an unforeseen impulse of pity) or why she should need them anyway Ovid does not explain.

146–317 NIOBE. This story was familiar from Homer onwards (*Iliad* xxiv. 599 ff.), both in literature and art, but Ovid's is the only full poetical treatment extant.

152 *her husband's skill*: Amphion and Zethus were the twin sons of Jupiter and Antiope (above, l. 111). The walls of Thebes built themselves to the music of Amphion's lyre (below, ll. 178–9).

157 *Manto*: apparently introduced into the story by Ovid. Her warning echoes that of her father Tiresias to Pentheus (iii. 514 ff.) and so helps to motivate Niobe's defiance and accentuate her insolence.

172 *Tantalus*: ironical: Tantalus had abused his privilege of intimacy with the gods and had been duly punished (iv. 457 ff. n.).

174 *My mother*: Dione; in Homer (*Iliad* v. 370–1) mother of Aphrodite (Venus) and often later identified with her.

   Atlas: more irony, as will appear, for he had been turned to stone (iv. 631 ff.).

176 *Jupiter the other*: as father of Tantalus.

177–9 *The Phrygian . . . by him and me*: in the Latin the repeated personal pronouns (*me . . . me . . . mei . . . me*) are in the style of a hymn (cf. iv. 16 n.). Niobe praises herself as if she really were a goddess.

187 *to give her children birth*: the story had been told in the Homeric Hymn to Apollo and more fully by Callimachus in his hymn to Delos (IV).

190 *I the sea*: cf. below, ll. 333–4. Delos was a floating island until it was rewarded for receiving Latona by being fixed to the seabed.

191 *two children*: Apollo (Phoebus) and Diana, by Jupiter—hence Juno's persecution (below, ll. 337 ff.).

204 *Cynthus*: Mount Cynthus on Delos was their birthplace.

213 *her paternity*: Tantalus' downfall was often ascribed to his garrulity.

259 *The blood expelled the arrow*: cf. iv. 122 n.

271 *Amphion*: his fate varies from one account to another; suicide is peculiar to Ovid. This detail 'serves to emphasize the unique pride of the queen' (W. S. Anderson).

311 *Upon a mountain peak*: Mount Sipylus in Phrygia. 'Niobe from close up is a rock and a stream, and nothing like a woman either grieving or otherwise; but if you go further off you seem to see a woman downcast and in tears' (Pausanias, *Guide to Greece* i. 21. 3, tr. Peter Levi). The whirlwind seems to be Ovid's invention; in other accounts she more tamely returns home to be transfigured.

317–81 THE LYCIAN PEASANTS. This story—an obscure one, as Ovid implies—offers a good example of the way in which his material came to him. It was included in a local history, the *Lyciaca* of Menecrates of Xanthus (fourth century BC), whence it was picked up by Nicander, from whom Ovid adapted it. Cf. Introd. xxiii.

319 *low-born louts*: whereas epic was concerned with gods and heroes; Ovid is, however, really pluming himself on his erudition in unearthing the story. The technique, with an 'interior' narrator providing the *aition* of a cult, is reminiscent of the *Fasti*.

335 *Pallas' tree*: the olive.

339 *the Chimaera*: see ix. 647 ff.

349 *Has right to water*: a legal and philosophical commonplace.

359 *It chanced . . .*: because the poet has seen to it that it did—a beautifully sly touch.

365 *Kicked the soft mud about*: their crime anticipates the punishment that is to fit it.

376 *squalid . . . squabbling*: these are the words happily chosen by A. E. Watts to render Ovid's brilliant onomatopoeia, 'quamuis sunt *sub aqua, sub aqua* maledicere temptant'.

382–400 MARSYAS. The ultimate in gruesome wit. More than one critic has tried to justify the treatment on artistic grounds, just as more than one pundit has assured the world that Titian's picture of the subject offers an uplifting experience to the beholder.

394 *All were in tears*: the wording is designed to recall the mourning for Gallus in Virgil's Tenth Eclogue (ll. 13 ff.), which in turn is indebted to Theocritus' Daphnis (*Idyll* i. 71 ff.). Marsyas was both an artist and an inhabitant of the world of pastoral.

Olympus: Marsyas' pupil and lover.

401–11 PELOPS. This familiar legend is introduced very briefly for
the sake of the reconstitution of Pelops, ranked by courtesy as a
metamorphosis. It assists the transition to the next cycle of
stories, centred on Athens, and prefigures a theme in the follow-
ing story (below, ll. 644 ff.).

407 *his father*: Tantalus; having killed and butchered Pelops he
cooked and served the joints to the gods to test their omniscience.
The missing shoulder was eaten by Ceres, in her distraction over
Proserpine.

412–674 TEREUS, PROCNE, AND PHILOMELA. This story was
known from Homer onwards (*Odyssey* xix. 518 ff.) in more than
one version; as often, Ovid gave it more or less definitive literary
form. The technique of the catalogue of mourners, with the sole
absentee providing the transition to the next story, is repeated
from i. 577 ff.

415 *Not yet*: a hint that the story will be told in Book VIII. Cf. below,
vi. 418 n.

416 *famed/For bronzes*: at this point in mythological chronology the
renown of Corinthian bronzework was some nine or ten centuries
in the future.

418 *Where Pittheus later reigned*: another reference forward: cf. viii.
623 n.

427 *From Mars*: first attested here. Thrace was the home of Mars
(Ares) (Homer, *Odyssey* viii. 361).

428 *Juno was not there*: reminiscence with inversion of the ill-omened
wedding of Dido and Aeneas (Virgil, *Aeneid* iv. 166), at which
Juno was present.

433–4 *That bird*: 'bird' in Greek and Latin also means 'omen'.

454 *warm for wenching*: Herodotus (v. 5), Menander (Fragg. 794, 795
Sandbach), and others note that the Thracians were polygamous.
Their besetting sins in the eyes of the Greeks were drunkenness
and violence.

517 *Jove's bird of prey*: the eagle.

560 *tried to reach/Its mistress' feet*: a peculiarly grotesque version of
the commonplace illustrated at v. 104–6 n. The snake-simile was
probably suggested by Lucretius (*De Rerum Natura* iii. 657 ff.).

582 *the tragic tale*: Ovid's word is *carmen*, here='spell'; writing
borders on the magical. Sophocles made Philomela weave a
picture of her experiences, the version used by Chaucer and

illustrated by Burne-Jones. Rape as a theme for tapestry had previously been exploited by Arachne (above, ll. 103 ff.).

609 *Then Procne . . .*: throughout what follows runs a thread of indebtedness to the great figure of Euripides' Medea; Ovid himself had written a tragedy about her, now lost.

668-9 *the woods . . . the roof*: generally Greek poets made Procne the nightingale, Philomela the swallow; in Roman poets it is usually the other way about. See Introd. xxviii–xxix.

675-721 BOREAS AND ORITHYIA. This story—a favourite subject for Attic vase-painters—constitutes a 'frame' for the next group of episodes. One sister, Orithyia, provides through her sons a transition to the Argonauts and Medea (herself already fore-shadowed: above, vi. 609 n.); Procris, barely mentioned here, will be the heroine of the long tragic episode that ends the next book.

683 *Orithyia*: 'Mountain-Rager'.

693-9 *I, when I meet . . . terrify the world*: allusions to contemporary scientific explanations of the causes of thunder and lightning and of earthquakes—the effect in the mouth of Boreas is humorous.

707 *His . . . tawny wings*: how he managed to fly at the same time Ovid leaves his readers to conjecture.

721 *that first ship*: in the popular tradition—but not in the *Metamorphoses* (i. 293 ff., vi. 444–5, 511). See Introd. xxviii–xxix.

BOOK VII

1-158 MEDEA AND JASON. Medea, the barbaric witch from the shores of the Black Sea, clearly fascinated Ovid: her letter to Jason is no. xii in his *Heroides* and he had also written a tragedy named after her, now lost. The long and subtle soliloquy with which the story starts reads very much like a dramatic monologue. This is the first such soliloquy in the poem; others follow as Ovid studies the psychology of love in people who are the victims of their own passions, in particular women faced with the decision whether or not to commit a crime. The story of Medea's love for Jason had been told by Apollonius of Rhodes in Book III of his *Argonautica*, and his treatment influenced Virgil's handling of Dido's love for Aeneas in the *Aeneid*.

3 *Phineus*: not the Phineus turned to stone by the Gorgon's head (v. 230 ff.) but a blind seer encountered by the Argonauts on their way; he was tormented by the Harpies, monstrous birds with women's faces.

6 *Phasis*: a legendary river, variously identified, flowing from the Caucasus into the eastern end of the Black Sea.

7 *the king*: Aeetes, king of Colchis.

Golden Fleece: Ovid takes his readers' acquaintance with the story for granted. Phrixus and Helle were the children of Athamas by his first wife Nephele ('Cloud'), who rescued them from death at the hands of their stepmother Ino. In their flight on the back of the golden-fleeced ram Helle fell into the sea named after her, the Hellespont, and was drowned; Phrixus came to Colchis and sacrificed the ram in gratitude for his escape. The ram became the constellation Aries. Jason's mission was to bring back the Fleece; the Argo was manned by the pick of the Greek heroes.

21 *The worse I follow*: *uideo meliora proboque,/deteriora sequor*; a famous formulation of an old paradox.

32–3 *A tigress . . . iron and stone*: the motif goes back to Homer (*Iliad* xvi. 34 ff., *Odyssey* xxiii. 103), but Ovid's readers would immediately recall Dido's reproach of Aeneas (*Aeneid* iv. 366–7). Medea is 'placed' in the company of heroines who risked and lost all for love. Cf. viii. 120 ff., ix. 613 ff. for further variations.

34 *Yet why not watch . . .*: the irony is characteristic of the declamatory style of this monologue.

38 *Shall I betray . . .*: recalls the predicament of Dido.

55 *The mightiest god*: Love, no longer 'some deity', *nescioquis deus* (l. 12).

62–3 *cliffs that clash*: the Symplegades (cf. xv. 337–9), confused in the tradition with the Homeric Planktai, the Wandering Rocks (*Odyssey* xii. 59 ff.). In fact the Argo on its return voyage avoided both this hazard and Scylla and Charybdis.

65 *Scylla*: her story and her metamorphosis are as yet in the future (xiv. 59 ff.).

69–70 *that fair name . . . your infamy*: another trait borrowed from Virgil's Dido (*Aeneid* iv. 171 f.).

74 *Hecate*: vi. 139 n.

96 *Her father's father*: Aeetes was the son of Helios (the Sun).

101 *field of Mars*: this sounds like an anachronism, but is in fact taken from Apollonius (*Argonautica* iii. 495, 1270).

105 *bulls*: they were the work of Hephaestus (Vulcan).

114 *filled the waiting field*: *fūmificisque locūm mūgitibus im-plēuērūnt*; sound and rhythm (spondaic ending) enhance the description. Cf. v. 164–5 n.

117 *with daring hand*: in fact it was a walk-over for Jason; Vulcan had not apparently programmed the bulls to do anything but breathe fire and bellow. Jason was generally portrayed as one of the least heroic of heroes, but if Ovid's handling of the ordeals is perfunctory beside Apollonius', it is because what really interested him was Medea and her conflicting states of mind.

122 *the serpent's teeth*: the teeth of the dragon slain by Cadmus, divided by Athene between Cadmus and Aeetes (Apollonius, *Argonautica* iii. 1184). What follows is a virtual 'doublet' of the scene at iii. 106 ff.

137–8 *she reinforced*: *carmen/auxiliare*; *auxiliaris* 'auxiliary' belongs properly to the military vocabulary: Medea calls up her magical reinforcements.

139 *hurled a heavy rock*: the point of this ruse (low cunning rather than magic) was that they should not see who threw the stone (Apollonius, *Argonautica* iii. 1057 'surreptitiously'). Medea (l. 212) attributes its success to her arts.

151 *golden*: because the Golden Fleece was hung on it.

159–296 MEDEA AND AESON. The homeward voyage of the Argo, which occupies the whole of the fourth book of Apollonius, is dismissed by Ovid in one verse. Medea now takes the centre of the stage in her character as sorceress. The rejuvenation of Aeson may do duty as a metamorphosis.

207–8 *The clanging bronze*: iv. 332 n.

219 *there the chariot stood*: provided by her grandfather the Sun (below, l. 398). She has just boasted (ll. 208–9) that she can control even him.

223 *regions that she knew of old*: where the magic herbs were to be found. Most of the places mentioned in this aerial tour are in Thessaly, always for the ancients the land of witchcraft.

233 *the Euboean merman*: the story of Glaucus is to be told at xiii. 904 ff.; the grass is 'not yet renowned' because Ovid has not yet told the story (cf. ii. 219 n.). Anthedon is on the north coast of Boeotia, hence 'Euboean' as facing Euboea.

295–6 *his own/Nurses*: identity obscure; not the nymphs of iii. 314–15, who were immortal anyway.

297-403 MEDEA AND PELIAS: HER FLIGHT.

297 *to continue with her witch's tricks*: Pelias had usurped the throne from his brother Aeson and sent Jason after the Golden Fleece to get him out of the way. Ovid ignores this motive for revenge and makes Medea act from pure malevolence.

324 *Ebro*: in the west of Spain, bordering on Ocean. Medea again waits for three nights (cf. above, ll. 179–80), here merely to blind the deluded women with science.

351 *she fled*: in Euripides' classic account the aerial chariot first appears to carry her off after the murder of her children, alluded to by Ovid only in passing (below, ll. 396–7). This tour, like its shorter predecessor, is Ovid's own invention; it enables him to display his acquaintance with a number of stories not selected for more elaborate treatment.

353 *Cerambus*: this form of his story only here; in Nicander's version he was changed as a punishment into a beetle (Greek *cerambyx*).

358 *the long dragon*: apparently a metamorphosis that had yet to happen (xi. 56 ff.), but the geography is studiously vague: Pitane is not in Lesbos but opposite to it.

359 *Ida*: in the Troad; the story is otherwise unknown.

362 *Maera*: otherwise (in this connection) unknown; a 'doublet' of Hecuba (xiii. 567 ff.).

364 *Hercules*: on his way back from Troy (see xi. 212 ff.) he put in at Cos and was repulsed by Eurypylus, whom he killed. The metamorphosis of the Coan women is mentioned nowhere else.

365 *Phoebus' favourite*: Rhodes was traditionally the Island of the Sun.

the vile Telchines: legendary metalworkers and wizards. The name was applied to his critics by Callimachus as typifying spite and envy (Frag. 1. 1 ff. Pfeiffer); Ovid is the first to attribute the evil eye to them.

368 *Carthaea*: on the island of Ceos or Cea. Ovid found the story of Ctesylla in Nicander.

371 *Hyrie . . . Cycnus*: this story too was in Nicander, but the metamorphosis of Hyrie appears to be Ovid's own invention. The lake is in Aetolia, near Pleuron (cf. below, l. 382).

383 *Combe*; 385 *changed . . . into birds*; 388 *Cephisus*: all otherwise unknown.

390 *Eumelus*: he struck and killed his son for an act of disrespect to Apollo, to whom he was especially devoted. The story was in

Boios' *Ornithogonia*. There is a bilingual word-play in the Latin: *in aere natum* alludes to the name of the bird (*aeropus*) into which Apollo in pity changed the boy.

393 *from mushrooms*: the tradition is otherwise unknown.

394-403 *But when . . .*: a summary of the catastrophe of Euripides' *Medea*.

395 *on either side*: of the Isthmus. The burning of the palace is not in Euripides; Ovid may have borrowed from his own *Medea*.

401 *on new wings*: three more bird-metamorphoses for good measure. Periphas and Phene were changed by Zeus (Jupiter) into an eagle and a vulture respectively. The 'granddaughter of Polypemon' was Alcyone, thrown into the sea by her father for unchastity and changed into a kingfisher. Ovid prefers to elaborate the much more affecting story of another Alcyone (xi. 410 ff.).

404-52 THESEUS. This famous hero figures less in his own right than as a peg for a further series of stories. He sustains this background role until ix. 96, after which nothing more is heard of him.

418-19 *on hard bare rocks . . . aconites*: a bilingual pun: *cautes* 'rock' =Greek *acone* '(whet)stone'; *a-conitum*=Greek 'dustless, soil-less'. Cf. Pliny, *Natural History* xxvii. 10.

433 *hymns of praise*: the hymnic recital of Theseus' exploits recalls the Labours of Hercules, one of which has just been mentioned (above, ll. 410 ff.); both were honoured as destroyers of monsters and benefactors of mankind. The pacification of the earth may rank as a kind of metamorphosis; cf. the panegyric of Caesar, xv. 746 ff.

434 *of Crete*: in the literary mythological tradition the bull of Marathon was identified with the bull previously captured by Hercules (ix. 186).

435 *Cromyon*: infested by a huge boar which Theseus killed.

437 *the Club-Bearer*: Periphetes.

438 *Procrustes*: his guests were lopped or stretched to fit the bed, hence 'procrustean'.

439 *Cercyon*: he challenged travellers to wrestle with him, killing them when they lost.

444 *Sciron*: he threw his victims over a cliff on to the rocks below. The metamorphosis of his bones is first attested here.

453–664 MINOS, AEACUS, THE PLAGUE AT AEGINA, THE
MYRMIDONS. Cephalus now appears as, in succession, audi-
ence and narrator of the two episodes which close the book. He
has no special connection with Aeacus in the mythological tradi-
tion: Ovid juxtaposes them because their stories complement and
contrast with each other.

456 *Minos:* his role is analogous to that of Theseus, as peg for
another, 'inner', cycle of stories.

457 *strong in ships:* 'Minos was the first ruler to build a fleet and to
take command of the sea' (Thucydides i. 4).

458 *the murder of his son:* there were several versions of this in the
tradition; Ovid does not particularize.

460 *roamed the Aegean sea:* the visit to Aegina is Ovid's invention to
provide a transition to the story of the Myrmidons; he takes the
opportunity to include another of his catalogues, geographical
accuracy taking second place to euphony.

465 *Arne:* the story is otherwise unknown; apart from the metamor-
phosis it is essentially identical with that of the Roman arch-
traitress Tarpeia, told by Propertius (iv. 4) and (more allusively)
by Ovid himself (*Fasti* i. 259 ff.). Arne's crime foreshadows and
perhaps (since her motive is not love but greed) palliates that of
Scylla in the next book.

474 *Aegina:* cf. vi. 113 n.

479 *Aeacus:* after his death he became one of the Judges of the Under-
world, with Minos and Rhadamanthus (ix. 441–2, xiii. 25–6), so
that this meeting of the two kings is invested with a certain
piquancy.

498 *His country's tree:* cf. vi. 80–1.

500 *Pallas:* Aegeus' brother. These sons are invented by Ovid for the
occasion.

523 *a fearsome plague:* this theme was evidently grafted on to the
original story by Ovid in deliberate emulation of Lucretius (*De
Rerum Natura* vi. 1138 ff.) and Virgil (*Georgics* iii. 478 ff.). The
prototype of what became almost a genre in its own right was
Thucydides' account of the Athenian plague (ii. 47–52); famous
modern examples are Defoe's *Journal of the Plague Year* and
Camus's *La Peste.* Cf., on his storm, xi. 480 ff. n.

524 *her rival:* Aegina, mother of Aeacus by Jupiter.

600 *the signs:* marks on the organs, especially the liver, which the
diviners (*haruspices*) were trained to interpret.

611 *drifted round*: the souls of those who had not been regularly buried and mourned were thought to wander homeless in the afterlife.

629 *swayed and rustled*: it had inherited the oracular powers of its parent tree.

654 *Myrmidons*: Greek *myrmex* = 'ant'.

665–865 CEPHALUS AND PROCRIS. Ovid had previously told part of this story at *Ars Amatoria* iii. 687 ff. He appears to have refined the myth as he found it, probably in Nicander (cf. below, vii. 687–8 n.); the metamorphoses which are the pretext for including it were no doubt his own invention. It is one of the most moving and consistently tragic episodes in the poem. The final scene is depicted in a masterly painting by Veronese.

667 *still claimed the king*: a simple and unscrupulous ploy to eliminate Aeacus, who must have known the story already, from the audience.

687–8 *for shame withheld/The price he paid*: if the text translated here is correct, Ovid is slyly hinting at certain lubricious details suppressed by Cephalus but preserved in other versions of the story. See Antoninus Liberalis xli. 6, Hyginus, *Fabulae* 189. 7–8.

694 *May be the more familiar*: addressed over Phocus' head to the reader, to remind him of vi. 681 ff.

703 *Dawn*: 'She was one of the most predatory of goddesses; besides Tithonus and Cephalus she also carried off Orion (*Od.* 5. 121) and Cleitus (*Od.* 15. 250)' (M. L. West on Hesiod, *Theogony* 986–91).

757 *You ask . . . gift?*: Cephalus steers his hearer away from the embarrassing circumstances which he prefers to forget (vii. 687–8 n.). This story within a story is a fresh variation on the 'Chinese box' technique: Introd. xxvii.

759 *The riddle*: 'What animal walks on four legs in the morning, two at noon, and three in the evening?' Answer: Man. Passers-by who failed to answer were killed by being thrown over a cliff; enraged by Oedipus' success the Sphinx threw herself over. He was rewarded by being made king of Thebes. Ovid could of course rely on his readers' knowledge of all this.

765 *A savage beast*: a giant fox.

788 *the loop*: *amentum*, a throwing-strap which imparted extra impetus.

792 *Some god*: according to the mythographers, Jupiter. This is in fact a (somewhat drastic) solution to another riddle: What happens

when an irresistible force meets an immovable object? Answer:
The referee awards a draw.

804 *when the sun's first beams/Coloured the hilltops*: precisely and
ominously when he got into trouble before, and when disaster
was to strike (below, ll. 835-7). *Aura* (see next note) is *Aurora*
abbreviated.

810 *zephyr*: in the Latin *aura* 'breeze', a feminine noun which can
also be heard as a girl's name, *Aura*. This resists translation.
Experience shows that the modern reader's ear accepts 'Zephyr'
(though Latin *Zephyrus* is masculine) as a possible girl's name.

BOOK VIII

1-151 SCYLLA AND MINOS. The story of Scylla combines more
than one element. The traditional theme of the traitress within
the gates had been adumbrated in Medea and, more explicitly,
in Arne (vii. 465 n.). The main emphasis is on the motif of
forbidden/unnatural/thwarted passion, prominent in the Tereus-
Procne and Medea episodes and to be further developed in the
following books. Scylla's two deliberative soliloquies again recall
Medea, and dominate the episode. The narrative element is rela-
tively unimportant; it is the heroine's state of mind that interests
the poet.

8 *Alcathous*: legendary founder of Megara.

15-16 *Latona's son . . . in the stones*: this was still a tourist attraction
in the second century AD: 'When Apollo was helping [Alcathous]
build the wall, he laid his harp on a stone, and if you hit this
stone with a pebble it twangs like a struck harp-string' (Pausanias
i. 42. 1).

49 *she*: Europa, his mother by Jupiter: below, ll. 122 ff.

108 *she cried*: her speech is a *tour de force*, for which Ovid has laid
under contribution the outbursts of Euripides' Medea, Catullus'
Ariadne, and Virgil's Dido. Cf. Introd. xxv. For other such
excesses in emulation cf. vii. 523 n., xi. 480 ff. n.

120 *Syrtes*: notorious quicksands off the coast of Africa. For these
invidious comparisons cf. vii. 32-3 n.

121 *Charybdis*: but not (the other) Scylla, which might here be
confusing.

131 *that adulteress*: Pasiphae, mother of the Minotaur. The story had
been told by Ovid, in flippant vein, at *Ars Amatoria* i. 289 ff.

141 *I'll follow*: in other versions Minos drags Scylla behind his ship.

150 *Shearer . . . shorn: ciris* from Greek *keiro* and *tonso* from Latin *tondeo* both='cut, shear'. No convincing identification has been proposed for this bird; Golding (strangely) chose the lark.

152–82 THE MINOTAUR.

171 *the third choice mastered him*: the tribute consisted of seven youths and seven maidens; Theseus voluntarily included himself in the third contingent, killed the Minotaur, and carried off Ariadne, who had equipped him with the thread by which he found his way through the maze. The story of his desertion of Ariadne and her rescue by Bacchus had been told by Ovid at *Ars Amatoria* i. 527 ff.

182 *Between the Kneeler . . .*: i.e. between Engonasin, sometimes identified as Hercules, and Ophiuchus.

183–259 DAEDALUS AND ICARUS; PERDIX. An admirable adaptation of a story admirably told by Ovid at *Ars Amatoria* ii. 21 ff. There is a famous painting of the subject by Bruegel.

184 *exile*: the reason emerges later, ll. 236 ff.

230 *The blue sea*: the Icarian Sea, between the Cyclades and southwestern Asia Minor. Cf. next note.

235 *that island*: Icaria, west of Samos. Two *aitia* do duty for a metamorphosis; but the phrase 'altered nature's laws' (*naturam . . . nouat*) at l. 189 above is pointed.

250 *Pallas' sacred citadel*: the Athenian Acropolis.

255 *his former name*: Perdix, Greek for partridge.

260–444 MELEAGER AND THE CALYDONIAN BOAR. Theseus now returns to introduce the next long episode, which occcupies the central portion of the book. The story of Meleager and the Calydonian Boar ranked in importance with that of the Argonauts and was a favourite in art and literature. Ovid's prime source was Euripides' lost *Meleager*. The hunt offers another opportunity for an epicizing *tour de force*, complete with catalogue of heroes (viii. 300 n.); technically it is interesting for the ingenuity with which battlefield motifs are transferred to the chase. It is a somewhat knockabout affair, distinguished by the extreme incompetence of most of those engaged, and contrasting strongly with the following tragic scene in which Althaea faces her agonizing dilemma.

261 *Cocalus*: king of Sicily. The usual story is that he treacherously murdered Minos; Ovid seems to refer obscurely to a different version.

269 *his aid*: it turns out to be singularly ineffective (ll. 408–10).

273 *Oeneus*: father of Meleager—but cf. viii. 437 n.

277 *Only Diana's altars*: on the face of it the harvest was no business of hers, but the motivation is as old as Homer (*Iliad* ix. 533 ff.). In this context it is a reminder of the injustice of the world of the *Metamorphoses* and the role of divine caprice.

300 *A chosen band*: Ovid's love of catalogues has been noted more than once. Catalogues of heroes were a particularly characteristic feature of epic from Homer (*Iliad* ii. 484 ff.) to Virgil (*Aeneid* vii. 641 ff.) and beyond.

301 *the twins*: Castor and Pollux; cf. below, viii. 372 n.

304 *Thestius' two sons*: Althaea's brothers, Meleager's uncles.

305 *no woman then*: see xii. 181 ff.

308 *Actor's pair*: his twin sons Cteatus and Eurytus. Attentive students of Homer would remember that they once outplayed Nestor in a very early example of gamesmanship (*Iliad* xxiii. 638 ff.).

309 *Achilles' father*: Peleus.

310 *Pheres' son*: Admetus.

313 *Still in his prime*: in introducing the young Nestor into the story (it is nowhere else recorded that he was among those present) Ovid sends up the Iliadic Nestor, eternally reminiscing about what a devil of a fellow he was in his prime—for his contribution to the proceedings is *not* impressive.

314 *those Hippocoon/Had sent*: one was Enaesimus (below, l. 362).

316 *the son/Of Ampycus*: the seer Mopsus (cf. xii. 456).

   As yet unruined: see ix. 403 ff.

317 *A Tegean girl*: (Arcadian) Atalanta, not named and to be distinguished from the (Boeotian) Atalanta of x. 560 ff.

320 *Hung rattling*: a quite specific Homeric allusion; when Apollo came down bringing plague among the Greeks 'the arrows on his shoulder resounded as he moved in wrath' (*Iliad* i. 46). A hint of destruction that she is to cause?

353–4 *Diana stole the steel*: a particularly sneaky instance of a common practice on Homeric battlefields.

372 *Not stars of heaven as yet*: the constellation Gemini (the Twins); the Dioscuri were also associated with St Elmo's Fire. The story of their transformation is briefly told by Ovid at *Fasti* v. 693 ff.

437 *son of Mars*: the revelation that Oeneus was only his legal father (cf. l. 414 where he is called *Oenides*) is appropriate at this moment of his detonation into heroic wrath.

445–546 ALTHAEA AND MELEAGER. The story of the brand on which Meleager's life depended was ancient, possibly a folk-tale. Ovid's treatment reflects his rhetorical education: conflict between the feelings of a mother and a sister is just the sort of thing the declaimers revelled in. The tone, however, is tragic: one is reminded of Orestes' choice, neglect to avenge a father's murder or matricide; and some features of Althaea's speech may fairly be called Euripidean.

452 *the Sisters*: the three Fates.

483 *My vengeance is my guilt*: *ulciscor facioque nefas*, just the sort of pointed contradiction (oxymoron) that the declaimers loved.

487 *Better that both should mourn*: typical declamatory logic.

528 *Euenus*: the local river.

533 ff. *Not if a god . . .*: an epic cliché from Homer (*Iliad* ii. 488 ff.) onwards, signalling a change of tone from high tragedy to burlesque exaggeration.

543–4 *all/Save Gorge and the wife of Hercules*: this had been recorded by Nicander, Ovid's source for the metamorphosis. Of Gorge we hear no more; Deianira has a part to play in the next book.

546 *into the air*: as guinea-fowl, Greek *meleagris*.

547–617 ACHELOUS AND THE NYMPHS. Theseus reappears to provide the transition (heavily contrived: viii. 570 n.) to Achelous, whose house is the setting for the two narratives which conclude the book. Achelous in turn provides the transition to Hercules. He was a very senior river indeed, oldest of the sons of Oceanus by Tethys, and he is made to hold forth in a correspondingly pompous style.

564 *The residence*: the cave, with its view out to sea, recalls the grottoes, such as that at Sperlonga, which adorned many Roman coastal villas. There are also echoes of Virgil's description of the underwater home of Cyrene (*Georgics* iv. 374).

567 *Ixion's son*: Pirithous.

570 *Acarnanian*: it was not really on Theseus' way home.

589 *Echinades*: *echinos* is 'hedgehog' in Greek; this and Perimele's metamorphosis are known only from Ovid.

612–13 *who scorned/The gods*: like his father (iv. 457 ff. n.) before him and like Erysichthon later in this book. Assisted by Theseus, he tried to carry off Proserpine (Persephone) from the Underworld.

615 *if they chop and change/The shapes of things*: he little realizes that the poem in which he is a character was the product of just such an intervention (i. 2 n.).

618–728 PHILEMON AND BAUCIS. This charming story, like so many others in the poem, is the product of an Ovidian transformation. On to a folk-tale originating apparently in Asia Minor he has grafted a literary motif inherited through Callimachus from Homer: the reception of a great personage in a humble dwelling. This typically Hellenistic theme was a favourite with Greek and Roman poets: it recurs in Ovid himself (*Fasti* iv. 507 ff., Celeus; v. 499 ff., Hyrieus), Virgil (*Aeneid* viii. 364 ff.), the anonymous *Moretum*, Lucan (v. 504 ff.), Silius (vii. 166 ff.); and satirically in Petronius (135 ff.) and Juvenal (xi. 78 ff.).

623 *where once his father reigned*: Pittheus was by then (cf. vi. 418) king of Troezen; his grandfather Tantalus was king of Lydian Sipylus.

626 *in mortal guise*: as at i. 212 ff. Zeus and Hermes (or gods for which they were the nearest Greek equivalents) were jointly worshipped in this region: cf. Acts 14: 11–12 'And when the people saw what Paul had done, they lifted up their voices, saying in the speech of Lycaonia, "The gods are come down to us in the likeness of men." And they called Barnabas, Jupiter; and Paul, Mercurius, because he was the chief speaker.'

647–8 *cabbage . . . pork*: a contemporary detail; these were the traditional staples of the Italian peasant's diet. The whole menu implies a virtuous and frugal enjoyment of the earth's bounty: this establishment is a survival from the Age of Gold.

718–19 *dear love . . .*: the sibilants of the Latin suggest the rustling of the miraculously burgeoning leaves: '*o coniunX' diXere Simul, Simul abdita teXit/ora fruteX.*

724 *To them who worship gave is worship given*: this renders *cura deum di sunt et qui coluere coluntur* (not *sint . . . colantur*), the only reading which gives sense and point and which editors never by any chance print.

726 *Theseus especially*: a device for introducing the next, contrasting, story; but also a nudge to the reader (Introd. xxviii).

728–878 ERYSICHTHON AND HIS DAUGHTER. A tale of piety rewarded is now complemented by one of impiety punished. Callimachus had told the story of Erysichthon in his Sixth Hymn to Demeter (Ceres) in a spirit of high comedy, with the misguided hero portrayed as a skeleton in the family cupboard, embarrassing them in the eyes of the neighbours. Ovid's Erysichthon is a monster, instigated by pure savagery, and the comedy has become black. The episode is narrated in a high epic style of vast exaggeration, mitigated momentarily by the charming interlude of Mestra on the seashore.

731 *Proteus*: ii. 8–11 n., xi. 221 n.; mention of him here recalls Menelaus' encounter with him in the Odyssey (iv. 351 ff.).

738 *Erysichthon's daughter*: Mestra, not named by Ovid. She is not mentioned by Callimachus; Lycophron refers to her as 'the crafty pantomorph vixen who by her daily gains assuaged her father's raging hunger' (*Alexandra* 1394–5).

786 *May never meet*: cf. ii. 766 n.

799 *Hunger*: cf. ii. 760 n.

855 ff. *Good sir . . .*: a parody of the ceremonious accostings of epic. The bewilderment of the speaker, who cannot believe his eyes, is neatly conveyed by the time he takes to come to the point.

866–7 *my skill*: a *double entendre*: the skill ostensibly meant is fishing, that really meant is changing shape.

871 *changeability*: *transformia (corpora)*, a very rare word, occurring only here and at *Fasti* i. 373, probably a coinage of Ovid's.

879–84 ACHELOUS (*cont.*).

882 *my horns*: they were a usual attribute of river-gods; cf. Acis after his metamorphosis (xiii. 894).

BOOK IX

1–100 ACHELOUS (*cont.*) AND HERCULES. Achelous provides continuity by telling the first of a new cycle of tales concerning Hercules. Hercules (Heracles) was the most celebrated of all Greek and (by adoption) Roman heroes. He was particularly dear to the Stoics, disparaged therefore by Lucretius (*De Rerum Natura* v. 22 ff.), and honoured by Virgil and Horace as a type of virtue rewarded by apotheosis. The tone of Ovid's treatment, as often in the poem, is not altogether easy to define.

5 *the whole tale*: Achelous' account of his defeat by Hercules is endearingly ludicrous; for a country squire (*agrestis*, l. 96), he is remarkably articulate.

8 *You may perhaps have heard*: she was not named at viii. 543-4 (see note).

14 *her father-in-law*: cf. below, ll. 285 ff.

35 *threw it over me*: this was common practice, to give a grip.

62-3 *out'man'ned . . . I slid from him*: *inferior uirtute . . . elabor . . . uiro*; Achelous has so far fought in the shape of a man, but his manhood (*uirtus*) was not good enough, so he tries another shape. Escaping from manliness the god becomes a beast.

67 *child's play*: as a baby Hercules had strangled the two snakes sent by angry Juno.

80-1 A *savage bull*: just as unfortunate a choice (ix. 186).

88 *Good Plenty*: the horn of plenty, *cornu copiae*, a favourite motif in art through the ages. There is a totally different and more familiar version of the *aition* at *Fasti* v. 111 ff.

101-58 HERCULES, NESSUS, AND DEIANIRA. Ovid had previously used this subject in the *Heroides* (ix. Deianira to Hercules); his principal source, not slavishly followed, was Sophocles' *Trachiniae*.

103 *his native city*: Tiryns.

124 *your father*: Ixion (iv. 457 ff. n., xii. 211 n.).

130 *The Hydra's poison*: with which Hercules had envenomed his arrows.

137 *rumour*: the natural inference from this is that the report was false, whereas in Sophocles Hercules' intention to marry Iole is brutally plain. Ovid appears to be concerned not to detract from the glory of the apotheosis, but the death of Lichas (ll. 211 ff.) was too integral a part of the story to be glossed over.

140 *Iole*: daughter of Eurytus, king of Oechalia.

159-280 THE DEATH AND APOTHEOSIS OF HERCULES.

165 *Oeta*: Cenaeum is at the north-western tip of Euboea, Oeta on the mainland near Trachis; Ovid passes over as irrelevant to his purpose the return of Hercules to Trachis and the suicide of Deianira.

182-97 *Was it for this . . .*: he passes his chief exploits in review. Along with the canonical list of the Twelve Labours imposed on him by Eurystheus (203) at Juno's orders are included a selection of subsidiary feats: Busiris, Antaeus, the centaurs, and Atlas.

183 *Busiris*: a king of Egypt who sacrificed and ate strangers.

184 *Antaeus*: a giant who was invincible so long as he was in contact with his mother Earth.

. *Geryon*: a monstrous three-headed herdsman of the far west of Spain.

186 *The great bull*: of Crete; cf. vii. 434 n.

187–8 *Elis*: where King Augeas had his stables; Hercules cleansed them by diverting the rivers Alpheus and Peneus through them.

Parthenius: in Arcadia, where he captured Artemis' (Diana's) deer with golden horns.

Stymphalus: also in Arcadia, infested by birds which he scared away and shot.

189 *Thermodon*: a river on the Black Sea. He defeated Hippolyta, queen of the Amazons, and took her golden belt.

190 *the apples*: of the Hesperides, guarded by Atlas (iv. 646–8).

191 *The centaurs*: an incidental embroilment. Cf. xv. 283.

192 *the boar*: of Erymanthus.

194 *the Thracian's horses*: the man-eating mares of Diomedes, king of Thrace.

198 *sustained the sky*: for Atlas, while he fetched the golden apples.

203–4 *And men can still believe/In gods!*: Hercules believes himself abandoned at last by his divine father. This and other parallels with Christ have often been noted by students of myth.

211 *Lichas*: Hercules' herald, who brought the fatal robe from Deianira.

220 *as in icy winds . . .* : a simile which recalls Lucretius; contrast ii. 729 n.

229 *'Lichas'*: other sources speak of a group of islands, the Lichades. Ovid is the first to treat Lichas' death as a metamorphosis rather than an *aition*.

232–3 *Poeas' son*: Philoctetes; see xiii. 45 n.

a second time: Hercules had already conquered Troy, as we shall later be reminded (xi. 215), angered by Laomedon's perfidy. See also xiii. 45 n.

237 *As at a feast . . .* : this is modelled on the conclusion to Horace's 'Regulus' Ode (iii. 5), where Regulus moves off to voluntary death by torture 'for all the world as if he were leaving the tedious business of some clients, the suit at last adjudged, for a journey to the fields of Venafrum or to Spartan-built Tarentum'.

243 *addressed them*: it is hardly possible to take this speech seriously. The reference to Jupiter's universal fatherhood, after some of the adventures related earlier in the poem, strikes an unmistakably

ironical note, as does the by-play with Juno.

269 *his finer parts*: *parte sui meliore*, the same turn of phrase used by Ovid of his own apotheosis through his poetry (xv. 875).

270 *majesty and awe*: *augusta . . . grauitate*, with an unmistakable reference to the identification of the Princeps with Hercules, recurrent in the Augustan poets.

280-323 THE BIRTH OF HERCULES. Hercules' death is followed immediately by his birth, and his metamorphosis into a god by that of Galanthis into a weasel. The hero's parting role in the poem is thus to provide an anticlimactic transition to the short episodes which preface the story of Byblis. In Nicander's version the story was told to explain the joint cult of Heracles and Galinthias as the result of his gratitude for her intervention.

283 *Ilithyia*: the Greek equivalent of Lucina (l. 294).

300 *She barred the birth*: a common superstition: 'To sit in the presence of pregnant women . . . with the fingers interlaced comb-wise, is to be guilty of sorcery' (Pliny, *Natural History* xxviii. 59).

322-3 *Out of her mouth*: this was a very ancient belief; the *aition* is first found here.

323 *in and out*: weasels, polecats, or martens seem to have occupied the role of the domestic cat in classical Greece.

324-93 DRYOPE. Ovid's version of this charming story, a typical blend of comedy and pathos, is radically different from that of Nicander, and there is some uncertainty about the intended denouement (see below, ix. 365 n.).

332 *He who rules/Delphi and Delos*: Apollo.

334 *There is a lake*: see iii. 407 n.

347 *Lotis*: a 'doublet' of Daphne (i. 452 ff.) and Syrinx (i. 689 ff.). The story as told by Ovid at *Fasti* i. 415 ff. has no metamorphosis.

365 *The lotus*: this is the text of the manuscripts, but the story lacks point unless the word *loton* has ousted the name of some other tree. In Nicander's (very different) version Dryope was turned into a poplar.

394-453 IOLAUS AND THE SONS OF CALLIRHOE. A transitional passage into which Ovid packs much miscellaneous mythological learning in typically allusive fashion.

399 *Iolaus*: cf. viii. 310. He had been Hercules' squire-charioteer.

401 *her husband*: Hercules; *hebe* is Greek for 'youth'.

403 *Themis*: as befits an oracular goddess, she is cryptic (cf. her reply to Deucalion and Pyrrha (i. 381 ff.)). She refers to the events of the famous expedition of the Seven against Thebes, familiar from Aeschylus' tragedy of that name and from the lost *Thebaid* of Antimachus.

404 *Capaneus*: he was struck by lightning.

405 *brothers*: Eteocles and Polynices, sons of Oedipus, who were disputing the kingdom.

407 *the prophet*: Amphiaraus; he was precipitated alive down to Hades, hence 'saw his own ghost' (*suos manes*).

408 *his son*: Alcmaeon. His mother Eriphyle was bribed by Polynices with a gold necklace to persuade Amphiaraus to take part in expedition, though he was fated to die at Thebes. In vengeance Alcmaeon killed her.

412 *Phegeus*: father of his first wife, from whom he got the necklace by a trick to give to his second wife, Callirhoe.

413-14 *those years*: the years taken from Iolaus are to be added to the ages of Callirhoe's small sons.

416 *his stepdaughter*: Hebe; Ovid follows the less usual tradition in which she was not Jupiter's daughter.

424 *Erichthonius*: son of Vulcan and the odd man out; the others are mortal lovers of goddesses.

424-5 W*orried about the future*: of Rome, to be founded by the descendants of Aeneas, her son by Anchises.

430 *To conquer fate*: this recalls the scene in the Iliad in which Zeus debates whether to save Sarpedon from death at the hands of Patroclus and is rebuked by Hera, who remarks that if Sarpedon is spared all the other gods will claim exemption for their own favourites (*Iliad* xvi. 440 ff.).

454-668 BYBLIS. This is another story of a woman steeling herself to commit a crime, with more of those passionate soliloquies in which Ovid excelled and for which his declamatory training had equipped him. The theme of unnatural love continues with Orpheus into the next book. The incestuous love of a sister for her brother had been the subject of *Heroides* xi (Canace to Macareus). The story of Byblis was predictably a favourite with Alexandrian poets, including Nicander.

454 *The tale of Byblis shows*: it is rare for Ovid thus overtly to

declare the moral of his stories; here his tongue is firmly in his cheek.

466 *My lord*: *dominus*, a term of endearment in Latin.

507 *the fabled sons/Of Aeolus*: Homer makes Odysseus record his impressions of this happy ménage (*Odyssey* x. 1 ff.).

508 *Why so pat/These precedents*: a reminder of the poet's learning; in fact Ovid's treatment in the *Heroides* of the loves of Canace and Macareus, who were the children of Aeolus, followed a different tradition from Homer's.

551 *Let old men know the law*: a theme which Ovid had handled as a boy in one of his practice declamations (Seneca, *Controversiae* ii. 2. 10); cf. also Catullus 5.

601 *not have risked/Myself in writing*: ironical; she had followed Ovid's own advice to the lover to plead his cause first by a letter (*Ars Amatoria* i. 437 ff.).

613 ff. *He's no tigress' son . . .*: see vii. 32–3 n.

634 *a city*: Caunus, in south-western Caria.

645–6 *Bubasis*, a town; *Cragus*, a mountain; *Limyre* and *Xanthos*, rivers; all in Lycia.

664 *became a spring*: the usual version was that she hanged herself (so Ovid, *Ars Amatoria* i. 283–4).

666–7 *might well/Have been the talk*: one of Ovid's more ostentatiously casual transitions.

669–797 IPHIS AND IANTHE. To contrast with the tragic and melodramatic tale of Byblis' guilty passion, Ovid ends the book with a story whose themes—baffled innocence and resolution through wish-fulfilment—look forward to Pygmalion in Book X. Ovid apparently found the story in Nicander; if so, the real interest, Iphis' hopeless love for Ianthe, was added by him (cf. ix. 687 ff. n.).

679 *she must die*: exposure of unwanted children was commoner among the Greeks than the Romans.

687 ff. *Isis with her train . . .*: in Nicander the rescuing deity is Leto, and the story was connected with a (doubtless obscene) premarital custom. The cult of Isis flourished at Rome in Ovid's day, and he had addressed a prayer to her on behalf of Corinna (*Amores* ii. 13. 7 ff.) which is echoed verbatim at ll. 773–4, implying that women were under her special protection. A good idea of the veneration in which she was held and of the multiplicity of her names, attributes, and functions emerges from the great invocation and epiphany of the goddess in Book XI of Apuleius' *Golden Ass*

(*Metamorphoses*). The names and attributes of her attendant gods add exotic colour. *Anubis* was represented as a human being with the head of a dog; *Apis* was worshipped as a bull; *Bubastis* (daughter of Isis and Osiris) was represented as a cat or a woman with a cat's head. The various sacred animals of Egypt always fascinated the Greeks and Romans; cf. v. 326 n. Harpocrates, son of Isis, was represented as a child with his finger to his lips. *Osiris*, husband of Isis, was killed by his brother Seth, torn into pieces, and scattered throughout Egypt. Isis searched desperately, found the pieces, and revived him. The words 'the endless search' refer to the annual festival of the god's resurrection.

708 *after its grandfather*: a common, though not universal, Greek custom.

735 Would I *were not a girl*: *uellem nulla forem*, meaning also 'would I did not exist'.

736 *the daughter of the Sun*: Pasiphae; see viii. 131 n.

773-4 O Isis . . .: see ix. 687 ff. n. The names are chosen for their Egyptian flavour rather than for any specific associations with Isis.

790 *her strength*: Iphis is derived from Greek *is* 'power'.

BOOK X

1-739 ORPHEUS. A transition by contrast—happy/unhappy marriage—abruptly brings Orpheus, the mythical founder of the poetic tradition, on to the stage, which he occupies until xi. 66. A cycle of stories told by him is prefaced and followed by episodes of which he is the suffering hero.

1-105 ORPHEUS AND EURYDICE. This famous story of how Orpheus descended to the Underworld to bring back his dead wife and lost her a second time had been memorably told by Virgil in the Georgics (iv. 453 ff.) a generation earlier. Ovid tells the story at similar length but in a very different way. The operas of Monteverdi, Gluck, and Offenbach are a reminder of the possibilities for widely differing treatment inherent in this moving legend.

12-13 *Taenarus*: a gloomy cavern on Cape Matapan (southern Peloponnese), believed to be the entrance to Hades.

to make trial: *ne non temptaret et umbras*: Ovid's words carry a suggestion of *hybris*.

16 *Lord of the shades*: Pluto; see next note.

28 *if that ancient tale/Of ravishment is true*: at first sight another
sly cross-reference by the poet (v. 341 ff.)—but possibly slyer than
appears, for he had put the story into the mouth of Calliope, who
was Orpheus' mother (below, x. 148 n.). What could have been
more natural than that she should have taught her *Preislied* to
her son?

41–4 *And Tantalus...*: See iv. 457 ff. n.

65–71 *like him ...*: Ovid slips in parenthetically two otherwise un-
attested metamorphoses.

77 *Haemus*: see ii. 219 n.

78–9 *That close the year*: Pisces is the twelfth sign of the Zodiac,
marking the end of winter (below, ll. 164–5).

84 *The love for tender boys*: this tradition is attested by the Alex-
andrian poet Phanocles. Ovid himself was not attracted to boys
(*Ars Amatoria* ii. 684), but Ganymede was too familiar and too
apposite to his theme to omit (below, ll. 155 ff.). Sandys found
the lines too shocking to translate.

90 *Every tree was there*: that Orpheus could charm trees and animals
(xi. 1) was part of the legend. Lists of trees felled for heroic
funeral pyres were a stock motif of Latin epic; Ovid produces a
virtuoso variation in the shape of yet another of his catalogues.

90–1 *durmast . . . oaks with lofty leaves*: *Chaonis arbor*, the large
Eurasian oak, Q. petraea; *frondibus aesculus altis*, the Italian oak,
the tallest species.

91 *The Sun's sad daughters*: ii. 340 ff.

92 *virgin laurel*: i. 557 ff.

95 *social*: *genialis*; it was the shade tree of the ancient world *par
excellence*, under which men gathered to drink and converse.

105 *doffed/His human shape*: *exuit hac hominem*; the words can also
means 'emasculated himself', as Attis did (Catullus 63). For a
similar ambiguity cf. ix. 735 n. The pine-tree was associated with
his cult, but only Ovid mentions this metamorphosis. Cf. iv.
283 n.

106–42 CYPARISSUS. The story of Cyparissus makes its first appear-
ance here. It is a *tour de force* of literary combination. Ovid is
anticipating Orpheus' theme 'boys beloved of gods' (152–3), and
Cyparissus himself is an inverse anticipation of Hyacinthus (and
indeed Adonis), slaying not slain by accident. The pet stag is
modelled on Silvia's in Virgil, shot by Ascanius (*Aeneid* vii.
483 ff.), the mistaken javelin-cast recalls the death of Procris (vii.

840 ff.), and the motif of the mourning cypress inverts that of the triumphant laurel (i. 560 ff.).

109 *Carthaea*: vii. 368 n.

133 *So ill-proportioned*: Introd. xxviii.

143–219 THE SONG OF ORPHEUS: GANYMEDE AND HYACINTH.

148 *From Jove . . .*: a standard form of invocation, mockingly chosen to contrast with the subject-matter. Orpheus' mother was Calliope.

150 *the giants*: i. 151 ff., v. 319 n. The Phlegrean Fields, near Vesuvius, were the scene of their defeat.

155 *Ganymede*: (the usual English form of) Ganymedes, son of Tros. The legend of his abduction by Jupiter's eagle or (as here) by Jupiter in the shape of an eagle was endlessly exploited in literature and art. Ovid accordingly treats it briefly to introduce Hyacinthus.

162 *Hyacinth*: a pre-Greek (as the -*nth*- element shows) hero or god whose cult was taken over by Apollo and whose status was degraded by the literary tradition to that of Apollo's catamite.

165 *the Ram . . . the watery Fish*: above, x. 78–9 n.

167 *my father*: Apollo; contrast ii. 219 n. and cf. viii. 437 n. The archetypal case of a hero with a divine and a human father was Hercules.

169 *unwalled*: it was the pride of the Spartans that their bravery made walls unnecessary.

182 *Unthinking*: *imprudens*, the same word as was used (l. 130) of Cyparissus; cf. above, x. 106–42 n.

207 *the bravest hero born*: an authorial reference forward to the story of Ajax (xiii. 1 ff.).

212 *a flower*: variously identified; not the modern hyacinth.

219 *his feast*: the Hyacinthia; Amyclae near Sparta was the chief centre of the cult, which was widespread in Dorian Greece.

220–42 THE CERASTAE AND THE PROPOETIDES. Again employing transition by contrast (Sparta honours Hyacinthus—Cyprus abominates the Propoetides) Ovid moves to a sequence of stories set in Cyprus. The Cerastae and Propoetides are otherwise unknown; they serve as foil and introduction to Pygmalion.

220 *Amathus*: a town in Cyprus with an ancient temple of Aphrodite (Venus); cf. below, l. 531.

234 *what can it be . . .*: what, indeed, given that they owe their presence in the poem to their metamorphosis? Cf. below, x. 698 n.

240 *made them the first*: inventions and inventors, good and bad (cf. above, x. 84 n.), were a literary commonplace. Venus takes her place as the inventor of prostitution, Ovid giving a characteristic twist to the notorious fact that Cyprus was a famous centre of sacred harlotry.

243-97 PYGMALION. This story is a remarkable example of Ovid's ability to transform his material. In the myth as he found it Pygmalion was a king of Cyprus who cohabited with a statue of Venus. The myth no doubt reflects an ancient enactment of a ritual marriage (*hieros gamos*) between a priest-king and the goddess. Ovid's version is admirable in its own right as a charming story of wish-fulfilment; it is also (in the favourable sense) highly suggestive, as is shown by the numerous modern variations on the theme. Pygmalion's love is not called Galatea until much later.

252 *Such art his art concealed*: an epigrammatic variation on one of Ovid's favourite ideas, the power of art to equal or indeed outdo nature. (For the reverse idea see iii. 157 ff.) The ancients were firmly convinced of the virtues of representational art.

263 *the daughters of the Sun*: see ii. 364-6.

298-518 MYRRHA. Orpheus redeems his promise 'to sing/Of . . . girls bewitched/By lawless fires' (ll. 153-4) with a story which complements that of Byblis in the preceding book. The transition is again by (implicit) contrast: Pygmalion's love for his 'daughter' (his creation) ends in a divinely sanctioned marriage, Myrrha's love for her father in tragedy. The story would have been well known to Roman readers in Cinna's *Zmyrna*, praised by Catullus (95); its fragments are too scanty to allow its influence on Ovid to be assessed.

300 *Away, daughters! . . .*: ix. 454 n.

306 *this land/Of Thrace*: heavily ironical in view of both vi. 458-60 and Orpheus' own preferences (x. 83-5).

309 *Panchaia*: a legendary land of spices.

314 *the three dread Sisters*: the Furies. In other versions her love was a punishment for slighting Venus or another god.

331 *Yet there exist . . .*: a hint of the learned ethnographical tradition, but Myrrha's gloss is purely romantic.

382 *her faithful nurse*: her role in extorting Myrrha's confession re-

calls that of Phaedra's nurse in Euripides' *Hippolytus*. As Ovid tells the story the moral dilemma—the choice between death and dishonour—is hers rather than the heroine's.

429 *have your—*: *potiere tuo*; in the Latin the sense is complete, since *tuus* can = 'your own (loved one)'.

447–8 *the Wagoner*: ii. 176 n.

448–51 *The golden moon/Fled from the sky . . .*: as the Sun hid his face from the banquet of Thyestes (xv. 462 n.); Ovid slyly recalls to his readers' minds something that has not yet happened. The moon (Phoebe) was a symbol of chastity, Icarus (or Icarius) and Erigone of the mutual devotion of father and daughter. She hanged herself when he was killed and they were placed among the stars as Virgo and Arcturus.

464 *She's yours*: *ista tua est*, ambiguously; cf. above, x. 429 n.

473 *Brought in a lamp*: this recognition of a mysterious lover is a motif of folk-tale, familiar from the story of Cupid and Psyche.

480 *Saba*: in south-western Arabia. Its riches were proverbial: Ps. 72: 10 'the kings of Arabia and Saba shall bring gifts'.

487 *let me neither die nor live*: this prayer appears to have been in Ovid's source, which was possibly Nicander. Cf. above, ll. 233–4 and note.

489 *found gods to hear*: variously identified in other sources; cf. iv. 373 n.

519–59 VENUS AND ADONIS. The lament for Adonis, a 'dying god' (cf. Hyacinthus) of Eastern origin, was a familiar theme of Greek poetry. A love-interest entered with the Alexandrians: see Theocritus, *Idyll* xv (*Adoniazusae*) and Bion, *Epitaphios*. The story as Ovid tells it was almost certainly in large part his own creation.

560–707 ATALANTA. This was a famous story. It is barely relevant to Venus' warning, for the protagonists end up as *tamed* lions. However, it is really Orpheus-Ovid who takes leave to include it as another example of 'girls bewitched by lawless fires', for Atalanta's love induces her to disregard an oracle—though it is admittedly Hippomenes' neglect of Venus and consequent ill-timed lust that precipitates her punishment. The princess whose hand must be won in a race is a type of folk-tale (compare Hippodamia and Pelops); as Ovid presents her, Atalanta takes her place, agonized soliloquy and all, with his other suffering heroines. The motivation of the story as he tells it is more subtle than as he probably found it. The apples symbolize the power of Venus, who indeed applies additional pressure to Atalanta at the crucial moment (ll. 676–8); and Atalanta herself neither wants (l. 630) nor tries (ll. 659–62) to win. The trick survives as part of the original mechanism of the story, but the interest has been shifted to Atalanta's psychology. Contrast the simplicity of Theocritus: 'She saw [the apples], she was ravished, she plunged headlong into love' (iii. 42).

564 *she had consulted*: this (somewhat arbitrary) motivation seems to be due to Ovid.

578 *now unrobed*: she is shown naked on vase-paintings of the story. Greek men in classical times exercised and competed naked, to the scandal of the Romans; only in Sparta were girls supposed to have followed suit.

590, 593 *The ribbons*: this is a free paraphrase: the details of her running gear are hopelessly obscure. She seems to have worn some kind of binding at ankle and knee which fluttered seductively as she ran.

595–6 *vestibule*: *atria*, a Roman word for a Roman thing. For the contemporary tone of the simile cf. v. 389 n.—but this is supposed to be Orpheus reporting Venus!

605 *Onchestus*: a city in Boeotia.

620 *Blood stains my bed . . .*: the Latin is ambiguous and ironical—it is ostensibly *failure in the attempt* to wed Atalanta that is fatal, but the singer knows that in this case success will be equally disastrous.

648 *And golden branches*: the wording recalls Virgil's Golden Bough (*Aeneid* vi. 209). In the usual version the apples came from the Garden of the Hesperides (ix. 190 n.).

650–1 *I stood . . . unseen . . . and taught*: an epic trait.

654 *across the surface of the sea . . .*: like Virgil's Camilla (*Aeneid* vii. 808 ff.), herself a tragic figure.

686 *Echion*: iii. 126 n.

696 *wooden statues*: an antiquarian touch. Such images, as they were superseded by marble in a more modern taste, acquired venerability as relics of ancient piety.

698 *seemed light*: it is better to be a dead human being than a live lion (in the service of the Mother of the Gods). A considered judgement, irony, or simple nonchalance on the part of the poet?

708-39 VENUS AND ADONIS (cont.).

726 *Memorials of my sorrow*: the Adonia was an annual festival when statues of Venus and Adonis were carried in procession. There is a vivid description in Theocritus' Fifteenth Idyll, the *Adoniazusae*. The cult was established in Rome in Ovid's day (*Ars Amatoria* i. 75).

729 *to fragrant mint*: the metamorphosis of the nymph Minthe is mentioned otherwise only by the Greek geographer Strabo (viii. 3. 14).

733 *as on a pond . . .*: a free version of the Latin text, which is uncertain.

737 *pomegranates*: associated with Persephone (Proserpine) and a symbol of fertility; cf. v. 536 and above, l. 729 and note.

738 *its name*: anemone, 'wind-flower', from Greek *anemos*; the etymology is unattested before Ovid.

BOOK XI

1-99 THE DEATH OF ORPHEUS.

1-2 While *Orpheus sang his minstrel's songs*: *carmine dum tali . . . uates* picks up the wording of x. 143 *tale nemus uates* to resume the story of Orpheus himself.

7 *The man who scorns us*: cf. x. 84 n. Virgil (*Georgics* iv. 516) delicately scouts the Alexandrian tradition: 'no love, no thought of marriage moved his mind'.

9 *tipped/With leaves*: iii. 542 n.

25 *in the amphitheatre*: cf. v. 389 n. These wild-beast hunts began the programme; the precision of 'the morning sand' draws attention to the contemporary nature of the illustration.

38 *tore apart the oxen*: iii. 721 n.

45 *For Orpheus*: in the Latin the poet apostrophizes him: the five-times repeated *te* echoes and recalls Virgil's description of Orpheus' lament for Eurydice (*Georgics* iv. 465-6). See next note.

47-8 *Tonsured in grief . . . swollen with their tears*: in Virgil the mountains mourn for Eurydice (*Georgics* iv. 461-3); Ovid predictably goes one better. *Coma* 'hair' is common of foliage; for the second conceit cf. Inachus at i. 584.

50 *Hebrus*: cf. ii. 219 n.

56 ff. *a fierce snake . . .*: this episode is attested only here. It replaces the *aition* which readers who knew their Phanocles (x. 84 n.)

would have expected, especially as it is *not* mentioned by Virgil: that ever since the head and lyre were washed up on Lesbos the island had been pre-eminent in lyric poetry.

63 *he found Eurydice*: this happy ending is Ovid's invention.

67 *did not permit this crime to pass/Unpunished, unavenged*: this episode is otherwise unattested. It is poetic justice that the Maenads should be changed into trees, once a captive audience for Orpheus' songs; and reversion to the tree-theme helps to enclose and round off the episode (cf. above, xi. 1–2 n.).

93 *Eumolpus*: pupil of Orpheus and founder of the Eleusinian Mysteries. According to Theopompus, a Hellenistic historian, Midas questioned Silenus about nature and history; his role as an archetypal fool is in strong contrast to this background.

100–93 MIDAS. In the earlier tradition Midas is a rather vague figure, though his asses' ears were evidently proverbial as early as Aristophanes (*Plutus* 287). As so often, Ovid has given the story its definitive shape.

102 *proved a bane*: the age-old theme of the Binding Promise and the Foolish Wish; cf. Phaethon (ii. 44 ff.), Semele (iii. 287 ff.), and the Sibyl (xiv. 130 ff.).

114 *gift of the Hesperides*: ix. 190 n.

117 *Danae*: iv. 611 n.

137 *Sardis*: seat of the kings of Lydia.

144 *And still today . . .*: the gold of the region and its rivers was proverbial; the *aition* is probably Ovid's.

148 *But crass his wits*: Introd. xxvii.

157 *On his mountain top . . .*: as, for instance, Achelous is both god and river (viii. 549 ff.), so Tmolus is both god and mountain. Ovid's extravagant development of this not uncommon figure of speech (metonymy) is heavily indebted to Virgil's description of Atlas (*Aeneid* iv. 246 ff.), but is playful and decorative where Virgil's is symbolic and functional.

173 *called it unjust*: Midas is not merely unmusical but ignorant of the rudiments of criticism (Introd. xxvii). His punishment is to be made the living embodiment of the Greek proverb describing the unmusical as *onos lyras*, a donkey (listening to) the lyre.

181 *turban: tiara*, an Oriental cap which tied under the chin.

193 *tell/The tale*: this part of the story is alluded to by the Greek epigrammatist Dioscorides (? late third century BC), *Greek Anthology* v. 56. It is a motif of folk-tale.

194–220 FIRST FOUNDATION AND DESTRUCTION OF TROY.
For the ancients, in so far as a distinction was made between history and myth, the Trojan War tended to mark the dividing line. This, with its aftermath, occupies the next three books. The next episode, from Troy's 'prehistory', announces the theme; its immediate role is to introduce Peleus, important also as the father of Achilles, who provides the transition to the story of Ceyx and Alcyone.

194 *Apollo made his way*: for this casual causation compare Bacchus, above, ll. 85 ff.

195 *Helle's narrow strait*: vii. 7 n.

202–4 *With the god / Who wields the trident . . ./ . . . he built*: in Homer (*Iliad* xxi. 441 ff.) the task was laid on them by Zeus (Jupiter).

206 *perjury . . . perfidy*: Ovid's readers would remember the familiar passages of Horace (*Odes* iii. 3. 21 ff.) and Virgil (*Georgics* i. 501–2, *Aeneid* iv. 541–2) in which the fall of Troy and the tribulations of the Trojans and their descendants are traced back to Laomedon's treachery.

213 *Hercules rescued her*: cf. ix. 262 ff. Ovid makes no attempt to reconcile the chronology. Cf. Introd. xxviii–xxix.

214 *The promised horses*: divine beasts, given by Zeus to Tros, grandfather of Laomedon, for his help in the abduction of Ganymede (x. 155 ff.). Laomedon tried to fob him off with mortal substitutes.

216 *Telamon*: brother of Peleus and father of the greater Ajax.

219 *a grandson of great Jove*: through Aeacus (cf. vii. 479 n.).

221–65 PELEUS AND THETIS.

221 *Proteus*: cf. ii. 8–11 n., viii. 731 n. Ovid here manipulates the mythological data with some freedom. In the traditional legend the oracle is given by Themis (cf. iv. 643 n.), and it is Chiron the centaur who advises Peleus on his tactics (Pindar, *Nemeans* iv. 60 ff.). The advice itself is pointedly modelled on that given in Virgil by Cyrene to Aristaeus on how to ensnare Proteus himself (*Georgics* iv. 405 ff.), whose powers have been described at viii. 732 ff.

229 *There is a curving bay . . .*: a maritime version of the *locus amoenus* (iii. 407 n.); for the grotto 'formed maybe by art./ Maybe by nature' cf. iii. 158 ff. and viii. 564 n. As usual it is the scene for very un-idyllic goings-on.

242 *her arts*: ascribed to her from Pindar (*Nemeans* iv. 60 ff.) onwards.

256 *His wavelets . . . his last words*: cf. above, xi. 157 n.

263 *some god*: Proteus' part in all this—after all, why should he take
it upon himself to reply for 'the sea-gods'?—as Ovid engineers
it (xi. 221 n.) is distinctly two-faced. A reminder of the instability
of the ever-changing world of the *Metamorphoses*? It is also
worth noting that perfidy and perjury (cf. above, xi. 206 n.)
attend the conception of the greatest of the *Greek* heroes,
Achilles.

266–409 DAEDALION. THE CATTLE OF PELEUS.

267 *Phocus*: Peleus' half-brother by the Nereid Psamathe (below,
l. 398).

295 *Daedalion*: the story first occurs here.

300 *Thisbe*: a city of Boeotia, described by Homer as 'many-doved'
(*Iliad* ii. 502).

347 *breathless in his haste*: Ovid used (and varied) Nicander for this
episode, but the leisurely and circumstantial narrative now un-
folded reads like a parody of the standard Messenger's Speech of
Greek tragedy. Ovid may also have drawn on a lost play, for his
treatment here is very different from Nicander's. He can hardly
have been unaware of the ludicrous effect of this speech.

388 *but save/Two lives in one*: animasque duas ut seruet in una; a
repeated theme in Latin love-poetry. Here it, and Alcyone's
loving concern, foreshadow the story to which these events are
a prelude. Cf. xi. 700–1 n.

400 *Thetis*: now returned, as in Homer, to her divine family in the
sea.

410–748 CEYX AND ALCYONE. This is one of the longest stories
in the poem and perhaps the most moving. In the oldest version
of the legend the transformation of the pair was punishment for
their impiety in calling themselves Zeus (Jupiter) and Hera
(Juno); cf. vi. 87 n. How much Ovid's strikingly different
emphasis owes to Nicander's handling of the story we cannot tell.
The elaborate structure, in which the departure and return of
Ceyx are separated by the contrasting descriptions of the storm
and the cave of Sleep, is clearly of Ovid's devising. On the other
Alcyone see vii. 401 n.

413 *the Clarian shrine*: the temple and oracle of Apollo at Claros in
Ionia were second in importance only to Delphi.

431 *my great father*: Aeolus.

480 ff. *the waves began to rise . . .*: since Homer (*Odyssey* v. 291 ff.) a

storm at sea had been a standard set piece of heroic epic. The components of such descriptions were already somewhat stereotyped when Virgil produced the storm that served as the model for all future generations of Latin epic poets (Aeneid i. 84 ff.). Ovid naturally exploits the traditional exaggerations (see, e.g., ll. 497 ff.) for all he is worth in a demonstration of his, so to say, epic virility. In the Aeneid the storm makes sense as part of the divine counterplot against the rise of Rome; in the Metamorphoses it is a blind unmotivated convulsion of nature dealing impersonal destruction to innocent individuals. On the technical level it also prepares for the concluding aition.

490 From every quarter: a traditional impossibility, which Seneca exploits as a poet (Agamemnon 474 ff.) and mocks as a scientist (Natural Questions v. 16. 2).

530 The tenth: it was believed that every tenth wave was especially large.

578 at Juno's shrine: as goddess of marriage.

584 to protect/Her altars: Alcyone, though she does not know it, is in mourning and therefore until the funeral rites are duly performed her touch pollutes the altar. Juno's indifference to Alcyone's grief and her coldly formal response reflects the isolation of the pair in a hostile world.

586 Hie quickly: Ovid combines Iris' Virgilian role as Juno's messenger (Aeneid v. 606 ff.) with Juno's (Hera's) own visit to Sleep in Homer to ask him to beguile Zeus (Iliad xiv. 225 ff.).

592 the Cimmerians: this legendary people 'enveloped in mist and cloud' (cf. ll. 595–6 'cloudy vapours rise/In doubtful twilight') dwelt by Ocean (Homer, Odyssey xi. 15), and it is in the same vicinity that Homer locates 'the country of dreams' (Odyssey xxiv. 11–12).

593 Sleep: cf. ii. 760 n. Unlike Ovid's other allegorical figures, Sleep was a favourite subject in art. His unforgettable description inspired a famous passage in Spenser's Faerie Queen (I. i. 39–41) and is exploited dramatically in Handel's Semele.

599 a keener guard: the word used is sagax, proper of dogs. Ovid's readers were meant to recall the story of the geese who saved the Capitol from the Gauls in 390 BC.

622 recognized her: a touch of irony. A god can always detect another god (Homer, Odyssey v. 77 ff.), but Iris, as we have been reminded, has come equipped with all her unique and unmistakable attributes.

630–1 *she could no more / Endure the power of sleep*: cf. ii. 766 n.

633 *Father Sleep*: cf. below, l. 646 'the old god'. Sleep was usually portrayed by artists as young, but an older bearded version occurs on sarcophagi of Imperial date.

635 *Morpheus*: from Greek *morphe* 'shape'. His identification with Sleep himself ('in the arms of Morpheus', etc.) is quite modern.

640 *The gods have named him*: iii. 307 n.

     Icelos: 'like'; *Phobetor*: 'frightener'.

644 *To kings and chieftains . . .* : Ovid's gods are nothing if not class-conscious: cf. i. 171–4.

700–1 *Now far away . . .* : the verbal ingenuity with which Ovid expresses the paradox that Alcyone 'really' died along with Ceyx (see above, xi. 388 n.) resists translation.

741 *The gods*: not specified; cf. iv. 373 n. The resolution of their suffering is as arbitrary and impersonal as its infliction.

742 *birds*: kingfishers (often found along the shore of the Mediterranean). Ovid's charming picture of their sea-borne nests and the 'halcyon days' faithfully reflects ancient scientific teaching; the *aition* is his own.

748–95 AESACUS. This story makes its first appearance here. It relaxes the emotional tension at the end of the book—for Aesacus reads like a low-key complement of Alcyone—and provides a transition to Priam and the Trojan War in the next book.

751 *Or maybe the same man*: Ovid gently mocks the learned poet's obsession with sources: Introd. xxviii.

763, 769 *Granicus, Cebren*: rivers of the Troad.

775 *lurking in the grass / A snake*: her death is a 'doublet' of Eurydice's (x. 8 ff.).

795 *A diver*: *mergus* from *mergo* 'dive'. Ovid's ornithology is faulted by the experts, but that is not what interested him.

BOOK XII

1–72 THE EXPEDITION AGAINST TROY.

19 *Thestor's son*: Calchas.

23 *Was turned to stone*: the episode, including the metamorphosis, is taken from Homer, *Iliad* ii. 308 ff.

28 *The Virgin's wrath*: Artemis (Diana) had been offended by Agamemnon. The sacrifice of Iphigenia was familiar in both art

and literature; Ovid would have known the great chorus of Aeschylus' *Agamemnon* (228 ff.) and Lucretius' passionate denunciation (*De Rerum Natura* i. 84 ff.). By accepting the version in which an animal was substituted for the girl (itself a sort of metamorphosis) he is able to treat the story unemotionally in a passage of fast-moving 'bridging' narrative.

43 *Rumour*: see ii. 760 n. Whereas Virgil (*Aeneid* iv. 173 ff.) had described *Fama* herself and her activities, Ovid depicts a global centre for the dissemination of hearsay. Envy, Hunger, and Sleep each play a part in their respective episodes; this passage is a largely gratuitous *tour de force*, Ovid's exuberant fancy kicking over the traces.

45 *never a door*: as in the cave of Sleep (xi. 608–9), though for different reasons. So at l. 48 below, 'Inside, no peace', *nulla quies intus*, picks up xi. 602 'There silence dwells', *muta quies habitat*. Such variation is of the essence of Latin poetic rhetoric.

68 *Protesilaus*: 'first of the host'. The story had been used by Ovid in *Heroides* xiii, Laodamia to Protesilaus.

72–188 ACHILLES AND CYCNUS. This is the third Cycnus to be changed into a swan (ii. 367 ff., vii. 371 ff.) and he receives the most elaborate treatment. In the 'Trojan' books Ovid works for the most part in the margins, as it were, of Homer and Virgil, avoiding direct confrontation. Cycnus, though his story was well known, does not figure in the *Iliad*. He is made the pretext for an exaggeratedly epicizing description of heroic single combat, with variations arising from his invulnerability; his death also serves to motivate the death of Achilles and hence the next important episode thereafter.

74 *his spear / From Pelion*: this ashen spear is in Homer Achilles' trade mark.

102 *In the broad ring*: cf. xi. 25 n. Ovid is the only ancient writer to mention the 'red rag' familiar in modern parlance.

112 *Telephus*: healed, in accordance with an oracle, by rust from the spear that dealt the wound.

151 *Pallas*: Neptune would have been a more politic choice (below, ll. 580 ff.); there was no special reason to thank or propitiate Minerva.

169 *Nestor*: he now reappears (viii. 313 n.) in his familiar Homeric role of arch-reminiscer. Ovid uses his long monologue to play a trick with chronology; when the main narrative resumes the war is in its tenth year (below, l. 584).

180 *What battle-line*: Achilles gets more than he bargained for. Caeneus, who will not appear until near its end (l. 459), is merely the excuse for the story of the battle.

188 *Two centuries*: in Homer Nestor had seen out 'two generations' of men; Greek *genea* = Latin *saeculum*, which can mean both 'generation' and 'century'.

189–535 CAENIS. THE BATTLE OF THE LAPITHS AND CENTAURS. This famous fight is alluded to only in passing by the Homeric Nestor (*Iliad* i. 263 ff.). The Ovidian Nestor makes it the occasion for another grotesque parody of heroic warfare. The battle of Perseus and Phineus (see v. 1–249 n.) might seem to have exhausted this theme; Ovid is stimulated to fresh excesses by the opportunities offered by the use of unconventional weapons and the half-animal nature of the centaurs. It was a very popular theme in Greek classical art: there is a piquant contrast between the idealizing treatment of (for instance) the Parthenon metopes and Ovid's baroque fantasy.

189 *Caenis*: *kainos* = 'new'. Caeneus' change of sex, not mentioned by Homer, goes back at least to Hesiod (fr. 87); Virgil (A*eneid* vi. 448–9) has him revert to womanhood in the Underworld.

210 *Pirithous*: see viii. 567 n., 612–13 n. *Hippodame*: otherwise Hippodamia.

211 *cloud-born*: begotten by Ixion (iv. 457 ff. n.) on an imitation Juno fashioned by Jupiter out of cloud. Cf. below, ll. 504 ff.

229 *Two men . . . in one*: cf. viii. 405–6, xi. 388 n.

466 *Macedonian lance*: the *sarisa*, the armament of the Macedonian infantry phalanx; *not* a cavalry weapon.

531 *now a bird unique*: hardly the phoenix (xv. 392 ff.). This metamorphosis is otherwise unattested.

536–79 NESTOR AND HERCULES. The Homeric Nestor mentions Hercules' slaughter of his brothers without especial feeling (*Iliad* xi. 689 ff.). Ovid, using Hercules' fight with the centaurs (ix. 191 n.) to assist the transition, presents him as still a prey to grief and indignation—an interesting flight of imagination. His denunciation of Hercules' career of destruction in the Peloponnese (ll. 549 ff.) is in the spirit of Lucretius' ironical disparagement of the alleged 'benefits' conferred by him on mankind (*De Rerum Natura* v. 22 ff.).

574 *Admiral*: this detail is from the Homeric Catalogue of the Ships (*Iliad* ii. 653 ff.).

580–628 THE DEATH OF ACHILLES. The part played by Neptune (Poseidon) in the death of Achilles is peculiar to Ovid. In the *Iliad* he had helped Achilles against the Scamander (xxi. 284 ff.); now he identifies with Troy, which he helped to build.

581 *Phaethon's dear friend*: ii. 367 ff.

583 *Rage more than decent*: plus quam ciuiliter, contrasting with the gentlemanly conduct of Nestor towards Tlepolemus.

595 *I may not meet my enemy face to face*: because the mythological and literary tradition forbade. Achilles had to be killed by an arrow shot by Paris and directed by Apollo.

597 *his own desire*: Apollo was always on the Trojan side.

614 *The selfsame god*: Hephaestus (Vulcan), who forged his arms at the request of his mother Thetis.

619 *He never knows the void of Tartarus*: Ovid follows the (un-Homeric) version in which Achilles was translated to Elysium or the Islands of the Blessed.

622 *Oileus' son*: the lesser Ajax.

623 *Atreus' sons*: Agamemnon and Menelaus.

624–5 *Laertes' son . . . Telamon's*: Odysseus (Ulysses) and the greater Ajax.

BOOK XIII

1–398 AJAX AND ULYSSES AND THE ARMS OF ACHILLES. Speeches and debates form an important element in ancient epic. Ovid in this great disputation draws on (and freely adapts: xiii. 81 n., 211 n., 216–17 n., 230 n., 279 n.) Homer; the episode itself fell outside the scope of the *Iliad*, though it is referred to in passing in the *Odyssey* (xi. 543 ff.). It was a popular subject, used for instance by Aeschylus, whose play was imitated by Accius; and there survive a pair of speeches for Ajax and Odysseus by the fourth-century Sophist Antisthenes. It was naturally exploited by the rhetorical schools (xiii. 121 n.). Ovid's characterization reflects the general depreciation of Odysseus (Ulysses) in the post-Homeric tradition, though his concluding comment is ambiguous (xiii. 382–3 n.).

3 *quick as ever / To anger*: he is like a bull at a gate. His appeal is to the sympathies of the rank and file, who have no votes. Ulysses is careful throughout to conciliate the important heroes, especially Agamemnon, with whom the decision rests.

6 *Before these ships*: Ajax recalls his great defence of the Greek

fleet against Hector (Homer, *Iliad* xv. 674 ff.). Quintilian quotes this outburst to illustrate how a speaker can make use of a place 'for praise or blame' (*Institutio Oratoria* v. 10. 41).

15 *only known to night*: see below, ll. 98 ff. Ulysses' answer to this repeated provocation is adroit: ll. 239 ff., 337 ff.

24 *the ship from Thessaly*: Argo.

26 *Sisyphus*: iv. 457 ff. n.

39 *Nauplius' son*: Palamedes, who exposed Ulysses when he feigned madness to avoid military service. Ulysses later 'framed' him and had him executed (below, ll. 58 ff.). The story is not in Homer.

45 *Philoctetes*: a famous archer, bitten by a snake on the island of Lemnos and marooned there on Ulysses' advice because of the smell of his festering wound. In the tenth year of the war, an oracle having declared that Troy could not be taken without the arrows of Hercules, which Philoctetes had inherited, Ulysses went to Lemnos and induced him to join the Greeks (cf. xiii. 333 n.).

48 *Laertes' son*: Ulysses.

63 *Even loyal Nestor*: only a reader fresh from Book XII will appreciate how much scope the poet thus allows Ulysses.

64 *When he abandoned him* . . .: Homer, *Iliad* viii. 97 ff.

71 *See, he needs help* . . . : Homer, *Iliad* xi. 428 ff.

77 *let's go back*: cf. xiii. 121 n.

81 *no wound*: this contradicts Homer.

82 *brought his gods*: Hector was encouraged by Apollo under the orders of Zeus (Homer, *Iliad* xv. 220 ff.). All this is put together from various episodes in *Iliad* vii, xiv, and xv.

88 *The lot*: the volunteers drew lots to decide which should face Hector.

98 *Rhesus . . . Dolon*: Rhesus, king of Thrace, was one of the Trojan allies. Odysseus and Diomede attacked his camp on the night of his arrival and captured his wonderful horses (cf. xiii. 252 n.). Dolon was a Trojan spy whom they forced to reveal the Trojan dispositions. These exploits form the subject of the so-called Doloneia in *Iliad* x.

99 *Helenus . . . the stolen Pallas*: cf. below, ll. 335 ff. Not in Homer, but familiar from other (now lost) poems in the epic Cycle; cf. Virgil, *Aeneid* ii. 163 ff. So long as 'Minerva's fateful statue' (below, l. 381) remained in Troy the city was inviolable.

110 *scenes that show the whole wide world*: Iliad xviii. 478 ff. This rather ponderous sarcasm, like other parts of his speech, rebounds on Ajax: below, ll. 287 ff.

121 *Let that brave man's arms . . .*: this flourish, we learn from Seneca (*Controversiae* ii. 2. 8), Ovid borrowed from his teacher Porcius Latro. It is in character that Ajax should end with this vigorous challenge and that the troops should like the idea of the two generals slugging it out hand to hand in public; it cuts no ice with the other generals.

125 *his gaze/Briefly upon the ground*: this is taken from Antenor's report to Helen of the embassy of Ulysses and Menelaus (*Iliad* iii. 216); see below, ll. 196 ff.

126 *Towards the captains*: Ulysses loses no opportunity of identifying himself with the influential part of his audience and isolating Ajax. He begins with a ploy of a kind familiar to all practised committee-men—something Ajax is far too indignant to think of—a graceful tribute to the dead Achilles, in which his hearers are joined ('my prayers and yours').

132–3 *As if he wept*: 'At this pathetic description of the decease of Mr Bardell, who had been knocked on the head with a quart-pot in a public-house cellar, the learned serjeant's voice faltered, and he proceeded with emotion' (Dickens, *The Pickwick Papers*). Cf. xiii. 264 n., 350 n.

141 *I hardly count/As ours*: a famous statement of meritocratic principle. This was a thoroughly 'modern' sentiment which gained ground steadily from the time of Cicero onwards, expressed most eloquently in the Eighth Satire of Juvenal. Ulysses paradoxically goes on to claim—it is indeed the leitmotiv of his speech—that all the feats of other men that have been decisive in the fall of Troy are 'really' his. Cf. ll. 171 ff., 236 f., 348 f., 373 f.

145 *No criminal*: Telamon, jointly guilty of the murder of Phocus (xi. 266 ff.).

155 *Pyrrhus*: otherwise Neoptolemus, son of Achilles and Deidamia (see next note).

163 *who foreknew/The death that he would die*: it was fated that he should fall after killing Hector (Homer, *Iliad* xviii. 94 ff.). While in hiding on Scyros he proved his manhood on Deidamia, daughter of King Lycomedes (Ovid, *Ars Amatoria* i. 681 ff.): their son was Pyrrhus.

164 *And Ajax too*: a stroke of Ovid's invention to allow Ulysses to castigate Ajax's stupidity. The episode is not in Homer.

168 *keeps herself for you*: Troy would not fall unless Achilles came on the expedition.

171 *Telephus*: xii. 112 n.

181 *one man's sorrow*: the affront offered to Menelaus by Paris' abduction of Helen.

184 *the harsh oracle*: xii. 28 n.

187 *I turned . . .*: he conciliates Agamemnon by palliating and sharing the odium of this terrible decision; cf. below, xiii. 216–17 n., 230 n.

193 *The mother*: Clytemnestra. She was hoodwinked by the story that Iphigenia was to be married to Achilles.

211 *what I did . . .*: an acute stroke of Ovid's invention. The *Iliad* knows nothing of Odysseus in these capacities—indeed the advice to entrench the camp is ascribed to Nestor (vii. 337 ff.)—but they are precisely what would make an impression on the other leaders.

216–17 *at Jove's command . . . gave orders to lay down*: in the *Iliad* (ii. 73–5) this disastrous inspiration is Agamemnon's own. See next note.

230 *Agamemnon / Called the allies*: in the *Iliad* (ii. 188 ff.) it is Odysseus, on Agamemnon's authority, who calls the assembly. This tactful shading of events is obviously aimed at conciliating the king.

233 *Thersites*: an ugly and noisy trouble-maker who abused Agamemnon in the assembly and was thumped by Odysseus for his insolence amid general hilarity (*Iliad* ii. 212 ff.). A service to the dignity of the king and of their order generally.

252 *My happy triumph*: Ovid makes no play with the tradition, not in Homer but known to Virgil (*Aeneid* i. 472–3), that Troy could not be taken once these horses had eaten the grass or drunk the water of Troy.

254 *Will be more generous*: refers to the offer at ll. 101–2.

264 *pulled apart / His tunic*: another standard ploy.

267 *no wounds*: Ajax indeed is unwounded in the *Iliad*; the later tradition made him invulnerable, and the wording of l. 392 may possibly be a hint that Ovid was well aware of the fact.

271 *what's due to all*: Ulysses continues his tactics of isolating Ajax.

274 *Patroclus*: the friend (in the post-Homeric tradition lover) of Achilles, who fought in his armour (*Iliad* xvi. 130 ff.) and whose death at the hands of Hector aroused Achilles from his sulks.

277 *ninth*: this is the common meaning of *nonus*, but it can also mean 'one of nine'. Since in the *Iliad* the Ajaxes were third and fourth to volunteer the ambiguity is presumably deliberate, a verbal blow beneath the belt.

279 *unscarred by any wound*: in the *Iliad* he is wounded in the neck by Ajax's spear and then felled by a rock (vii. 262, 270-1). The fight is then stopped by the heralds and they part after an exchange of gifts.

284-5 *I bore . . .*: an effective answer to the jibes of ll. 107 ff. Ovid follows Sophocles here (*Philoctetes* 373); in Arctinus' *Aethiopis* it was Ajax who retrieved the body while Odysseus kept off the enemy.

290 *a rough and doltish soldier*: *rudis et sine pectore miles*; Ulysses continues to hit below the belt.

307-8 *smears you too*: again Ajax is isolated.

315 *That I persuaded him . . .*: wonderfully specious pleading.

332 *to have the means to deal . . .*: text uncertain and meaning doubtful.

333 *to bring him back with me*: as indeed he does in the version familiar from Greek tragedy. In the earlier epic tradition the mission was undertaken by Diomede.

336 *the oracle*: that Troy could not be taken without the help of Philoctetes.

338 *And Ajax vies with me?*: he picks up and retorts on him Ajax's opening words.

350 *You scowl . . .*: another standard orator's trick.

357 *Andraemon's son*: Thoas. He and the others named here are the volunteers to fight Hector.

369 *mind is man*: Dryden has

> Mind is the man: I claim my whole descent
> From the mind's vigour, and the immortal parts.

370 *My lords*: the peroration is directed exclusively to the other leaders, who respond accordingly (l. 382).

382-3 *proved the power of eloquence . . .*: Ajax's speech is by no means ineffective, but Ulysses outpoints him from start to finish. This concluding comment is studiedly ambiguous, leaving the reader to decide the justice of the award in accordance with his own sympathies. Is this a victory for intelligence over brute force or of political know-how and the gift of the gab over inarticulate courage? Close study of Ulysses' tactics suggests that the Unjust

Argument has won, but Ovid's main purpose is to demonstrate his ability to plead brilliantly on both sides of a question and the verdict is bound to be open.

394 *the* blood/*Expelled it*: iv. 122 n.

396 *Hyacinth*: see x. 207 n., 212 n. The grafting of Ajax on to the Hyacinth tradition may be Ovid's own invention.

397 *Letters*: AIAI='alas, woe'.

399–428 THE FALL OF TROY. Ovid offers the merest sketch of these events, familiar as they were from the epic Cycle, from drama and from Virgil, as a background to selected tragic episodes.

400 *husbands murdered*: for their neglect of her worship Aphrodite (Venus) afflicted the women of Lemnos with an evil smell. When their husbands sought consolation elsewhere the women murdered them. See Ovid, *Heroides* vi (Hypsipyle to Jason).

404–7 *Troy fell . . . Contracts in narrows*: these four verses are probably not Ovid's; they anticipate and summarize, in a way quite uncharacteristic of him, the full story of Hecuba's metamorphosis (below, ll. 565 ff.).

410 *Apollo's priestess*: Cassandra, raped by the lesser Ajax.

415 *Astyanax*: son of Hector and Andromache.

429–575 HECUBA, POLYXENA, AND POLYDORUS. Ovid here bases himself for the most part on Euripides' tragedy *Hecuba*. In Euripides Polyxena's death takes place, according to the laws of classical drama, off-stage and is reported by a herald. In his treatment of the scene, as indeed throughout the episode, Ovid handles his material freely for rhetorical and pathetic effect.

466 *no touch of man . . .*: Ovid imparts an erotic flavour to Euripides' 'let no one touch me' (*Hecuba* 548).

473 *she paid in gold*: when the body of Hector was ransomed from Achilles.

479 *To wrap . . .*: a gesture which achieved classic status when it was copied by the dying Julius Caesar (Suetonius, *Divus Julius* 82. 2). Cf. Euripides, *Hecuba* 568 ff., Ovid, *Fasti* ii. 833–4 (Lucretia).

526 *a scoop*: *haustus*, a handful; a mere sprinkling of dust was enough for ritual burial, and that is all she will get.

569–70 *named from what happened there*: Cynossema, 'Dogsbarrow'.

576–622 MEMNON. This story is introduced by a transition of a familiar type, 'all except so-and-so . . .' (cf., e.g., Inachus, i. 568–87 n.). Formally Memnon, a Trojan hero turned into a bird, can be seen as a complement to Cycnus (xii. 70 ff.), rounding off the Trojan section of the poem (though chronologically out of sequence), as he introduced it. He was a famous figure in myth, with bird-associations; his metamorphosis first occurs here, and only here in this peculiar form.

596 *his uncle's sake*: his father Tithonus was Priam's brother.

613 *fought each other*: like gladiators. The image and the vocabulary throughout the description are appropriate to Roman funeral games. Cf. next note.

618 *Memnonides*: ruffs. Memnon was king of the Ethiopians and therefore black. Ovid does not mention this well-known fact in so many words; but these dark-plumaged birds are born of *black* ash and *black* smoke—the epithets are doubly appropriate, to him and to the mourning context.

623 *with her tears . . . bedews*: an *aition*; *rorat* hints at an etymology of her name.

623-729 THE PILGRIMAGE OF AENEAS. After the fall of Troy, Aeneas, son of Venus and Anchises, led a select band of Trojans to found a new Troy in the West. That story is the subject of Virgil's *Aeneid*. From now until xiv. 608 the adventures of Aeneas are kept present to the reader's mind as framework and background; direct confrontation with Virgil is skilfully avoided.

631 *Apollo's city*: Delos.

635 *gave birth*: see vi. 187 n., 191 n., 335-6.

674 *doves*: a metamorphosis obscurely referred to by Lycophron, *Alexandra* 580.

678 *to seek/Their ancient mother*: an unmistakable allusion to Virgil, *Aeneid* iii. 96. Italy is meant; according to one legend Dardanus, ancestor of the Trojans, came from Latium.

684 *engraving a long tale*: cf. ii. 1-18 n. For a drinking-vessel as the subject of such a description cf. Theocritus, *Idyll* i. 27 ff., Virgil, *Eclogues* iii. 35 ff. Ovid goes out of his way to underline the Hellenistic flavour of the passage by calling the artist Alcon, which was the name of a real designer. Art snobbery was in full vigour in the classical world, and the specification of provenance is also typical.

686 *to name it*: Thebes.

692 *Orion's daughters*: they sacrificed themselves to save the country from a plague. The story, which is otherwise attested only by Nicander, has thematic similarities both with the daughters of Anius and with Polyxena.

698 *twin youths*: this denouement was not in Nicander, where the girls were turned to stars and worshipped as the Coronides.

709 *the Strophades*: a small group of islands in the south-east of the Ionian Sea.

710 *Aello*: one of the Harpies (vii. 3 n.).

715 *the judge*: Cragaleus, turned to stone by Apollo for awarding the disputed territory to Hercules; the story was in Nicander.

now famed / For great Apollo's sake: he had a famous shrine on the promontory opposite Ambracia. It was part of the Augustan legend that the victory of Octavian at Actium in 31 BC was won under Apollo's auspices (e.g. Virgil, *Aeneid* viii. 704 ff., Propertius iv. 6).

717 *Munichus*: king of the Molossians. When his house was attacked and set on fire by robbers, Jupiter as a reward for their piety changed him and his family into birds. This story too was in Nicander.

719 *the Phaeacians*: in Corfu.

730-49 SCYLLA. The monster Scylla, scourge of passing mariners, was famous from Homer's description (*Odyssey* xii. 85 ff.); the story of how she came by that guise is first told here. Ovid adroitly first whets and then defers satisfaction of the reader's curiosity, roused by l. 734 'a sweet girl once'. Scylla's immediate role is to provide a transition from Aeneas to the story of Galatea.

750-899 ACIS AND GALATEA. The love of the Cyclops Polyphemus for the nymph Galatea was the subject of two of Theocritus' *Idylls* (vi, xi). The love of Galatea and Acis is first found here. Ovid keeps the pastoral setting but reinvests the Cyclops, who in Theocritus is merely a rustic oaf, with the horrendous attributes of the Homeric monster, a gigantic one-eyed creature who lived in a cave under Mount Etna (*Odyssey* ix. 105 ff.). This is burlesque of a high poetic order, as good as anything in the *Metamorphoses*, and unique in its kind. The serio-comic charm of the original is wonderfully conveyed in Handel's oratorio *Acis and Galatea*, written to a libretto by Gay and others.

761 *who scorned the gods*: cf. below, ll. 843-4. A Homeric trait (*Odyssey* ix. 272 ff.).

771 *bird*: i.e. omen.

773 *Ulysses soon shall take*: by blinding him while he slept.

775 *Has taken it*: a hardly translatable play on *rapere*='snatch',

hence 'captivate'. In English it is hearts rather than eyes that are 'stolen'.

778 *There juts into the sea*: this scene, with Cyclops serenading and Galatea listening from the sea, as in Theocritus (xi. 17–18), was much favoured by artists; Ovid necessarily modifies it in the interests of his erotic triangle.

784 *a hundred reeds*: 'Cut me a hundred reeds of decent growth,/To make a pipe for my capacious mouth' (Handel's libretto). The usual number was seven. This is hyper-pastoral (below, xiii. 788 n.).

786–7 *lying in my Acis' arms*: a touch of sexual cruelty—this is a case of Beauty and the Beast (Polyphemus as Ovid portrays him anticipates King Kong).

788 *these words*: a brilliant and wildly exaggerated expansion of ideas lifted from Theocritus and Virgil's *Eclogues*. On the grammatical *tour de force* in these verses see Introd. xxiv–xxv.

838 *From the blue sea*: cf. above, xiii. 778 n.

854 *my father*: Neptune.

866 *be one flesh*: Ovid plays on the literal and transferred senses of *miscere* 'mix'; cf. v. 638 n.

881 *your kingdom*: the river. His mother was the daughter of the river Symaethus.

893–4 *there stood a youth*: this has the quality of a pantomime transformation. Acis appears with all the conventional attributes of a river-god as depicted in ancient art. Is he still Galatea's lover? Ovid leaves matters ambiguous.

900–68 SCYLLA (*cont.*) AND GLAUCUS. Scylla, like Galatea, is wooed by (as she sees him) a monster; rejecting him she is herself transformed into a monster. Glaucus was a familiar figure in the literary tradition; his love for Scylla was treated by Hellenistic poets, but Ovid's sources cannot be identified or the degree of his independence of them established.

905 *Anthedon*: vii. 233 n.

910 *the strait*: of Messina, between Italy and Sicily.

918–19 *Proteus*: ii. 9. *Triton*: i. 333 ff. *Palaemon*: iv. 542.

924 *there lies a beach*: another *locus amoenus* (iii. 407 n.), which once again is not quite what it seems.

968 *Circe*: in the Latin her name is the last word of the book, beckoning the reader on.

BOOK XIV

1–74 SCYLLA AND GLAUCUS (*cont.*).

1 *the giant's throat*: Typhon or Typhoeus: iii. 303, v. 319 n., 346 ff.

8 *The Tyrrhene Sea*: on the west side of the Italian peninsula.

10 *Circe*: sister of Aeetes, thus Medea's aunt. Her terrible enchantments were famous from Homer (*Odyssey* x. 133 ff.) onwards. Like Homer and Virgil, Ovid places her on an island (l. 244); the historical Cercei is a promontory some 60 miles south of Ostia. The combination with Glaucus is probably Ovid's invention.

   phantom beasts: see below, ll. 276 ff.

27 *her father's gossiping*: iv. 171 f.

51 *There was a little bay*: another *locus ?amoenus*: iii. 407 n.

65 *Hell's vile hound*: Cerberus.

71 *robbed/Ulysses*: Homer, *Odyssey* xii. 245–6. He had enjoyed Circe's hospitality and shared her bed.

75–247 THE PILGRIMAGE OF AENEAS (*cont.*). With the mention of the Trojan fleet (l. 72) the summary narrative of Aeneas' adventures is resumed from xiii. 729, providing a framework for the stories which are Ovid's real concern.

83 *Acestes*: a king of Sicily, of Trojan descent.

86 *Hippotades'/Domain*: the volcanic Aeolian Islands.

93 *misshapen animals*: monkeys; *kerkos* in Greek = 'tail'.

103 *Misenus*: drowned for presuming to compete with the Tritons (Virgil, *Aeneid* vi. 162 ff.).

121 *In converse with his guide*: Ovid now departs from Virgil to introduce the Sibyl's story, which again turns on the Foolish Wish theme (xi. 102 n.).

149 *to a feather's weight*: Petronius, *Satyricon* 48. 8 (Trimalchio speaking) 'I once saw the Sibyl of Cumae in person. She was hanging in a bottle, and when the boys asked her, "Sibyl, what do you want?" she said, "I want to die" ' (tr. W. Arrowsmith).*

157 *that later bore/His nurse's name*: see below, ll. 441 ff. Virgil had named the place as Caieta (*Aeneid* vi. 900) *before* explaining how it came to be so called (vii. 1 ff.); cf. below, xiv. 616 n.

161 *Achaemenides*: the story of his rescue by Aeneas had been told

---

* This quotation, in the original Latin and Greek, was chosen by T. S. Eliot to preface *The Waste Land*.

by Virgil (*Aeneid* iii. 588 ff.); the reunion with Macareus is Ovid's own invention. Within the Virgilian frame Ovid inserts a second Homeric frame; variety is ingeniously achieved by allotting the events of *Odyssey* ix and x to Achaemenides and Macareus respectively.

180 *Ulysses' shouting*: Homer, *Odyssey* ix. 475 ff.

189 *eyeless*: Odysseus had put out his eye while he lay in a drunken stupor; cf. xiii. 772 ff.

223 *He told*: first (ll. 223–32) summarily in indirect, then more expansively in direct speech; cf. i. 700 ff. n.

225 A *memorable gift*: the phrase *memorabile munus* reads ironically —a hint perhaps that there is a limit to the demands a poet may make on his readers' credulity?

248–319 THE ISLAND OF CIRCE. Ovid retells the metamorphosis of Odysseus' crew by Circe (Homer, *Odyssey* x. 233 ff.) as experienced by one of them. Inset in the Homeric episode is the story of Picus, a wholly Italian figure (cf. below, xiv. 320 n., 434 n.).

252 *Too fond of wine*: Homer does not say or imply that he was a drunkard, only that he was drunk. Elpenor (*Odyssey* x. 552 ff., xi. 51 ff., xii. 8 ff.) has always puzzled critics; is there a hint of impatience in Ovid's words?

268 *She guides and watches*: this Circe is a parody of a Roman matron superintending the work of her maids.

273 *a brew*: this strange concoction was Homer's version of 'brandy for heroes'.

292 *the gods/Call moly*: iii. 307 n.

311 *the four acolytes*: a Homeric detail (*Odyssey* x. 349) grafted on to the much grander establishment depicted by Ovid.

320–440 PICUS AND CANENS. This story is somewhat obscurely summarized by Virgil in his description of Latinus' palace-temple (*Aeneid* vii. 187–91), with no mention of Canens, who is presumably Ovid's addition. It has obvious similarities with the Circe–Scylla episode, but we are now firmly on Italian soil: see xiv. 320 n., 434 n.

320 *son of Saturn*: hence autochthonous; Saturn (Kronos), expelled from Olympus by Jupiter (Zeus), settled in and civilized Latium, to which he gave its name (Virgil, *Aeneid* vii. 48–9, viii. 319 ff.).

322 *his striking grace*: Virgil represents him seated and regally arrayed, Ovid as a beautiful youth.

325 *At Grecian Elis*: i.e. at Olympia.

331 *Dian's pool*: xv. 489 n.

334 *Janus*: *ianus*='passage, archway', personified as the facing-both-ways Janus, god of beginnings and transitions.

338 *Canens*: 'singing', from *cano*.

358–9 *A phantom boar*: shades of the decoy Aeneases created by Apollo (Homer, *Iliad* v. 449 ff.) to deceive Diomede and by Juno (Virgil, *Aeneid* x. 636 ff.) to distract Turnus.

368 *veil her father's orb*: the Sun; she has no more filial scruples than Medea (vii. 219 n.).

396 *his name*: *picus*='woodpecker'.

416 *Tartessus*: the legendary name for Baetis (Guadalquivir), a river of south-west Spain, here standing for the far West.

434 *The ancient Muses*: *ueteres . . . Camenae.* The Camenae were Italian water-deities; they were early identified with the Greek Muses, but their name has in reality nothing to do with *cano* or *carmen*, though the etymology was traditional (Varro, *De Lingua Latina* vii. 27). Aition and the *locus canens* itself appear to spring from Ovid's imagination.

441–622 THE TRIUMPH AND APOTHEOSIS OF AENEAS.

441 *Aeneas' nurse*: this picks up l. 157 and resumes the summary of Aeneas' adventures. Caieta (Gaeta) is some 70 miles south-east of Rome.

449 *daughter*: Lavinia.

452 *Etruria*: the Etruscans under Tarchon joined Aeneas.

456 *Evander's walls*: the site of what was to be Rome. Ovid alludes briefly to a long and important episode in the *Aeneid* (viii. 97–369, 454–607). The unsuccessful embassy of the Latins to Diomede (*Aeneid* viii. 9–17, xi. 225–95) provides the setting for a metamorphosis treated very briefly by Virgil (*Aeneid* xi. 271–4), expansively by Ovid.

468 *a virgin's rape*: Cassandra (xiii. 410 n.). She was dragged by force from the temple of Athene (Minerva).

472 *Caphereus*: the easternmost point of Euboea, a notorious maritime hazard.

477 *That wound*: dealt to her by Diomede before Troy (Homer, *Iliad* v. 334 ff.).

506 *Most of the crew*: why, when only a minority had sided with Acmon?

509 *likest snowy swans*: this detail echoes Lycophron, *Alexandra* 599 'like in form to bright-eyed swans'. Other sources identify them as *erodioi* (?shearwaters) or resembling coots.

525 *The oleaster*: Ovid's source for this story was probably Nicander; its inclusion was perhaps suggested by geographical associations, for a similar tale set in this part of Italy had been told by Nicander, specifically naming Peucetians and Messapians, as in Ovid's text of l. 513.

536 *Mother of the Gods*: Cybele.

557 *Nymphs of the sea*: in Virgil's very different treatment of the episode (*Aeneid* ix. 69–122) the metamorphosis occupies four and a half lines.

562 *they hate the Greeks*: Ovid adapts, and in the manner of the learned poet reverses, a detail in his sources; Diomede's metamorphosed crew feared and avoided *non*-Greeks.

563 *Ulysses' ship*: wrecked by Zeus (Jupiter) (Homer, *Odyssey* xii. 403 ff.).

565 *its timbers turned to stone*: the ship that Alcinous lent Odysseus to take him to Ithaca was on its return petrified by Poseidon (Neptune) in the mouth of the harbour (Homer, *Odyssey* xiii. 159–64).

579 *That bird*: *ardea*='heron'; this metamorphosis is otherwise unattested.

599 *Numicius' river*: a small stream some 10 miles south of the Tiber, where Aeneas met his death.

608 *Indiges*: a name of uncertain meaning and etymology applied to native gods. Aeneas was identified with *Iuppiter Indiges*, the local Jove.

609 *double-named*: he was also called Iulus.

616 *from whom/Was named*: for the name of Tiber Virgil prefers *Thybris* but also admits *Tiberis* and *Tiberinus*; Ovid in his Latin has hitherto used *Thybris* (above, ll. 426, 448) and may be unobtrusively taxing Virgil with inconsistency. Needless to say, this king-list was totally fictitious, though already traditional by Ovid's day.

623–771 POMONA AND VERTUMNUS. These were native deities of growth and fertility, Pomona associated with garden fruit (*poma*: ll. 626–7), Vertumnus with the changing seasons (*uerto* 'turn', 'change'). As elsewhere, it seems to have been Ovid who first brought them together. The transition to the episode is as abrupt and arbitrary as any in the poem. Ovid's treatment of

Vertumnus is clearly indebted to that of Propertius (iv. 2 *passim*).

640 *lusty loins*: ithyphallic statues of Priapus were placed in gardens and orchards.

664 *would be its leaves*: i.e. not much; the elm was favoured for training vines precisely because (unlike, e.g., the plane) its foliage was not too thick. Its 'unwedded' value (the metaphor is common in Latin) is therefore small.

670 *the queen*: Hippodamia; xii. 210 ff.

671 *the wife/Of bold Ulysses*: Penelope, courted by many suitors in his absence. Text and sense of what follows are uncertain.

674 *The Alban hills*: some 10 miles south-east of Rome, in Ovid's day studded with the splendid country houses of the aristocracy.

688 *takes the firstfruits*: they are offered to him as god of the seasons.

699 *Iphis . . . Anaxarete*: this story, inserted as a warning like that of Hippomenes and Atalanta (x. 560 ff.), was in various forms popular with Hellenistic writers.

708–10 *Sometimes he hung . . .*: the lover's doorstep vigil, a stock theme of epigram, elegy, comedy, and satire.

711 *the Kids*: their rising and setting was associated with storms.

712 *Noricum*: a province in the eastern Alps, south of the Danube, famous for its iron.

725 *two lights*: lux='the light of day'; *mea lux* 'my light', a common endearment.

739 *seems/To groan for many griefs*: text and sense uncertain.

757–8 *the stone,/That all along had lurked . . .*: a secondary (verbal) metamorphosis, of a metaphor (cf. vii. 32–3 n.) into a physical reality. Cf. above, l. 693 'Venus who hates a stony heart' (*pectora dura*).

759–60 *Gazing Venus*: Venus Prospiciens; this *aition* was evidently in Ovid's Greek source; cf. Plutarch, *Amatorius* 20.

770 *No need of force*: for once—but Ovid's text makes it clear that it would have been forthcoming at need (*uimque parat*). Now and again the poet lets his characters off light.

772–851 LEGENDS OF EARLY ROME; THE APOTHEOSIS OF ROMULUS.

774 *gained the throne he'd lost*: Numitor was deposed by his younger brother Amulius, who murdered his other children and made a Vestal Virgin of his daughter Rea Silvia. He was restored and

Amulius slain by Romulus, one of her twin sons by Mars. This familiar story is told at length by, e.g., Livy (i. 3. 10-5. 7).

775 *were founded*: by Romulus (Livy i. 7. 1-3). Pales was an ancient goddess of flocks and herds; her festival was on 21 April (Ovid, *Fasti* iv. 807-62).

776 *battled*: in the war precipitated by the rape of the Sabine women (Livy i. 9 ff.).

Tarpeia: her price for the betrayal of the citadel, of which her father was commander, was what the Sabine soldiers wore on their left arms; instead of their gold bracelets they threw their shields on her. The story is told by Livy (i. 11. 5-9) and Propertius (iv. 4). She gave her name to the rock from which traitors were hurled to their death.

778 *Cures*: a Sabine city.

782 *Juno herself unlocked*: according to Virgil and indeed to Ovid himself (above, l. 582) her hostility to Rome had ended with the defeat of the Latins. This version of the story is that favoured by Propertius and Ovid in the *Fasti* (i. 263 ff.); in Livy the Sabines capture the citadel.

804 *It was agreed*: Ovid does not mention the dramatic mediation of the Sabine women (Livy i. 13).

814 *'There shall be one . . .'*: a quotation from Ennius' *Annales*.

822 *the sylvan peak*: the Augustan poets were fond of dwelling on the rural simplicity of early Rome. Cf. above, xiv. 674 n.

826 *melt in mid sky*: ii. 729 n.

827 *heaven's high-raised couch*: *puluinaria* were special couches on which effigies of the gods were displayed.

828 *Quirinus*: a Sabine god worshipped on the Quirinal hill, later as here identified with Romulus.

847-8 *Set the queen's hair ablaze*: a stock portent; Ovid's readers would inevitably think of the sign vouchsafed to Ascanius (Virgil, *Aeneid* ii. 679 ff.).

850-1 *Then, renamed Hora . . .*: this and the details of the apotheosis of Romulus Ovid took from Ennius' *Annales*. Here she is *Hŏra*, evidently the original quantity; in Ennius she is *Hōra*, presumably by assimilation to Greek *hōra* 'time, season'.

BOOK XV

1-59 NUMA AND THE FOUNDATION OF CROTONA. The last book of the poem moves in a thematic circle: at its end the deified

Julius is succeeded by the wise and virtuous Octavian (Augustus) as at its beginning the deified Romulus is succeeded by Numa. (On the importance of the idea of apotheosis in Book XV see Introd. xv–xvii.) Apart from this prefiguring function, Numa serves chiefly to introduce Pythagoras. The tradition connecting the two had come under fire long before Ovid's day on obvious chronological grounds (Numa *fl. c.*700 BC, Pythagoras *c.*500) and is expressly dismissed by Livy (i. 18. 2).

6 *nature's causes: quae sit rerum natura*; Ovid draws liberally on Lucretius' *De Rerum Natura* in Pythagoras' speech.

9 *beside the Italian shore*: Crotona lies a little to the north of the promontory of Lacinium in the extreme south of Italy.

12 *the herds of Spain*: Geryon's cattle: ix. 184 n.

19 *Alemon*: 'Wanderer'.

38 *Bedraggled*: it was usual for the accused to excite pity by appearing in court unshaven and dishevelled.

58 *sure tradition*: Ovid's source is unknown.

60–478 THE DOCTRINES OF PYTHAGORAS. For an account of Pythagoras' life and teaching see W. K. C. Guthrie, *A History of Greek Philosophy*, i (1962), 146–340. He is the only fully historical character in the poem; for Julius Caesar and Augustus are presented as superhuman types (see below, ll. 855–60). For the significance of his speech see Introd. xv–xvii. The speed and fluency of the writing match the theme.

61 *its masters*: Polycrates and his brothers.

an exile: like Ovid himself. It is hardly likely that this long and important speech is one of the possible afterthoughts added at Tomis (iii. 142 n.), but it is certainly ironical that, enshrining as it does Ovid's most deeply held beliefs, it should be put in the mouth of an exile.

63–5 *approached them in his mind*: this inevitably recalls Lucretius' celebration of Epicurus, who 'traversed the universe with mind and spirit' (*De Rerum Natura* i. 74). As Lucretius had called his hero, without naming him, *Graius homo*, a Greek man, so Ovid identifies Pythagoras only as *uir Samius*, a Samian man (hero).

67–72 *The great world's origin . . .*: these revelations are Epicurean (Lucretian) rather than Pythagorean.

76 ff. *There are the crops . . .*: this harks back to the Golden Age (i. 89 ff.); at 96 ff. the reference is made explicit.

93 *A Cyclops' banquet*: cf. xiv. 194 ff.

103 *some futile brain*: *non utilis auctor*, an antitype of Pythagoras himself (l. 72 'He was first to ban . . .').

135 *reflected*: sc. in the sacrificial water-vessel over which their heads were held. This detail, repeated at *Fasti* i. 327, is adapted from Callimachus, Frag. 75. 10–11 Pfeiffer 'the oxen were ready to tear their hearts seeing in the water the keen blade'.

137 *to prove heaven's purposes*: extispicy, divination by inspection of entrails, was an Etruscan science: below, ll. 558–9.

147 ff. *My soul rejoices . . .*: Lucretian language and sentiments combined from several passages of the *De Rerum Natura*.

153 *whom death's cold chill appals*: the Epicurean contention that death was not to be feared depended on proofs that the soul is mortal. Ovid makes Pythagoras use Lucretian language and arguments to prove the opposite.

159 *new habitations welcome them*: the Pythagorean doctrine of metempsychosis, transmigration of souls, allusively but emphatically scouted by Lucretius, *De Rerum Natura* i. 116 ff.

162 *whom Menelaus killed*: Homer, *Iliad* xvii. 43 ff.

163 *the shield*: Pausanias ii. 17. 3 'In the front chamber of the temple [the Heraeum of Argos] . . . is the dedication of a shield which Menelaus once took from Euphorbus at Troy.'

178 *all is in endless flux*: *cuncta fluunt*=Heraclitus' *panta rhei*.

229 *Milo*: a famous wrestler, often victor in the Olympic and Pythian games and a contemporary and disciple of Pythagoras. Ovid might have read this anecdote in Cicero's treatise on old age (*De Senectute* 27).

233 *twice*: Helen was carried off first by Theseus, then by Paris.

237 *The elements*: cf. i. 21 ff.

239 *generative substances*: *genitalia corpora*, used by Lucretius to mean 'atoms'; he had expressly rejected the theory of four elements (*De Rerum Natura* i. 714 ff.).

259 ff. *Nothing can last . . .*: the longest and most elaborate catalogue in the poem, a list of marvels—true, half-true, and wholly fictitious—culled from the copious resources of Hellenistic scholarship. Callimachus had shown the way with his 'Collection of Wonders from all over the World' (Frag. 407 Pfeiffer). Here too the similar catalogue in Lucretius (*De Rerum Natura* vi) was clearly in Ovid's mind.

283 *the centaurs*: ix. 191 n.

311 *The Athamans*: a tribe of Epirus; Pliny, *Natural History* ii. 228: 'The Fountain of Jupiter at Dodona, though it is cold and puts out torches dipped in it, sets them alight again if they are brought near to it when they are out.'

319 *All the world has heard*: those at least who have read the *Metamorphoses*.

326 *Proetus' daughters*: the story was famous from Hesiod onwards, and Virgil (*Eclogues* vi. 48) and Ovid here only allude to it in passing.

337 *Ortygia*: Delos; v. 619 n.

338 *Symplegades*: vii. 62–3 n.

340 *Etna's sulphurous furnaces . . .*: compare v. 346 ff. for the conventional mythical explanation.

363 ff. *tiny forms of life . . .*: the observation is true, but the examples which support it belong to folklore and poetry, though seriously held by ancient authorities. Virgil gives exact directions for *bugonia* (*Georgics* iv. 281 ff.) and Nicander had asserted that 'Horses breed wasps and bulls engender bees' (*Theriaca* 741). That scorpions can in certain circumstances originate from crabs is asserted by Pliny (*Natural History* ix. 99).

374 *that grace a grave*: because they undergo a kind of resurrection. The soul was often depicted on tombs as a butterfly; the motif is used on a charming neo-classical monument in the church at Wimpole Hall.

385 *Juno's fine bird*: the peacock (i. 722–3).

386 *Jove's weapon-bearer*: the eagle (xii. 560–1).

Cytherea: Venus.

393 *The Phoenix*: famous from Herodotus (ii. 73) onwards and equally suitable for use by pagans and Christians as a type of resurrection and immortality.

394 *tears of frankincense*: cf. x. 500–2.

406 *The Sun's great city*: the Egyptian Heliopolis.

411 *The creature*: the chameleon.

415 *stones*: lyncurium, a kind of amber.

416 *coral*: another sly cross-reference (iv. 744 ff.).

428 *Now Sparta lies a waste . . .*: this list recalls a famous passage in Sulpicius' letter to Cicero (*Ad Familiares* IV. v. 4) 'There behind me was Aegina, in front of me Megara, to the right Piraeus, to

the left Corinth; once flourishing towns, now lying low in ruins before one's eyes' (tr. D. R. Shackleton Bailey).

438 *King Priam's son*: Helenus, to whom this prophecy is attributed by Virgil (*Aeneid* iii. 374 ff.), but Pythagoras cannot have 'remembered' (as Euphorbus) that occasion, which took place not at Troy but at Buthrotum. The Iliadic prophecy of Aeneas' future is spoken by Poseidon (xx. 293 ff.).

442 *Pergamum*: sc. the household gods of the City, the Penates, housed in the citadel; cf. xiii. 624–5 and below l. 450.

449 *heaven shall be his home*: an anticipation, at nearly the mid point of the book, of the eventual apotheosis of Augustus (below, ll. 868–70).

462 *Thyestes*: he unwittingly ate his two sons, served up to him at dinner by his brother Atreus.

475 *ropes*: they were threaded with brightly coloured feathers and used to scare the game into the nets.

479–551 THE DEATH OF NUMA. HIPPOLYTUS-VIRBIUS.

482 *a nymph*: Egeria.

489 *Diana's shrine*: the famous sanctuary of Diana Nemorensis, Diana of the Wood, whose priest was 'the slayer, who must himself be slain'—the starting-point of Frazer's *Golden Bough*.

that once Orestes built: the story of Orestes' escape with his sister Iphigenia and the cult-image of Tauric Artemis was familiar from Euripides' play *Iphigenia in Tauris*; the legend that he set up the image at Aricia is typical of the connections made by the learned tradition between Greek and Italian cults and customs.

492 *Theseus' great son*: Hippolytus, identified with the native deity Virbius, who shared the sanctuary. His story too was familiar from Euripides' two tragedies, the extant *Hippolytus* and the lost *H. Kalyptomenos*. Ovid himself drew on it in the *Heroides* (iv. Phaedra to Hippolytus) and the *Fasti* (vi. 737 ff.).

492–3 *You are not/The only one . . .*: a cliché of the ancient rhetoric of consolation.

501 *Tried to tempt me*: the motif occurs in other stories in Greek mythology and outside it, as in the biblical episode of Joseph and Potiphar's wife.

511 *Horned bull*: sent by Poseidon (Neptune) in answer to Theseus' prayer.

533 *Apollo's son*: Asclepius (Aesculapius): ii. 629 n.

535 *Paean*: Apollo.

544 *Hippolytus . . . Virbius*: the context suggests punning etymologies: *Hippo-lytus* 'loosed (undone) by horses'; *Vir-bi(u)s* 'twice a hero' or 'hero-alive' (cf. 492 *Theseius heros*).

552–621 CIPUS. This curious story may be included by way of a compliment to Julius Caesar on account of Cipus' refusal of the kingship: *rex* was to the Roman ear a word of ill omen. The name Cipus may have some connection with *cip(p)us* 'boundary-stone'.

558 *Tages*: the story had been told by Cicero, *De Divinatione* ii. 50.

563 *a tree*: still shown in Ovid's day.

566 *horns*: a symbol of power; cf. viii. 882 n.

617–18 *so many acres/As he could compass*: a traditional reward.

622–744 AESCULAPIUS. The penultimate episode in the poem, leading to and prefiguring the culminating apotheosis of Julius Caesar. Like Julius' ancestor Aeneas, Aesculapius was a demigod; as Julius saved Rome from civil war, he came to save her from disease (l. 744 *salutifer Vrbi*). Ovid also tells the story more briefly in the *Fasti* (i. 291 ff.).

622 *Now show, ye Muses . . .*: the invocation follows both Homeric (*Iliad* ii. 484 ff.) and Virgilian (*Aeneid* vii. 641 ff., x. 163 ff.) models. Placed here it punctuates strongly, looking forward and lending emphasis and weight to the conclusion of the poem.

623 *Does not mislead you*: it has not escaped them that six centuries of Roman history, on the traditional chronology, separate Julius Caesar from Numa. That was material for the *Fasti*; Ovid bridges the gap with a single episode set at approximately the half-way mark (xv. 626 n.).

624 *Coronis' son*: ii. 542 ff.

626 *Once*: in 293 BC; the cult was introduced in the following year.

631 *Apollo*: this embassy to Delphi is unique to Ovid's version. Apollo was, of course, himself a god of healing and the source of his son's powers; and he was especially venerated by Augustus. Cf. below, l. 865 'our own Apollo', *Phoebe domestice*.

643 *Epidaurus*: the cult seems to have originated in Thessaly, but Epidaurus was from an early period its chief centre.

693–4 *felt the weight/Of godhead*: iv. 450 n.

701 ff. *Then past Lacinium . . .*: as Virgil had done in his catalogue of the Italian allies (*Aeneid* vii. 647 ff.), so Ovid uses the sounds

and associations of these sometimes obscure proper names to confer status and dignity on the god's adopted country.

702 *the goddess*: Juno.

707 *Hippotades*: Aeolus, god of the winds.

711 *The city of Hercules*: Herculaneum.

712 *Parthenope*: Naples.

713 *the hot springs*: at Baiae, in Ovid's day a famous resort.

716 *its heavy air*: it was marshy and malarial.

717 *Antiphates*: king of the Laestrygonians (xiv. 249).

745–870 THE APOTHEOSIS OF JULIUS CAESAR.

761 *must be made divine*: this sounds cynical, and Ovid may be ironizing, but the point was a perfectly serious one. Hellenistic ideas of soteriology and divine kingship were deliberately and effectively exploited by Caesar for his political ends.

763 *her high priest*: he was Pontifex Maximus, in supreme charge of Roman state religion.

769 *wounded*: xiv. 477 n.

781 *Sisters*: the Fates.

782 *portents*: already briefly referred to at i. 200–3, now fully listed after Virgil's classic treatment in the *Georgics* (i. 464 ff.).

805 *As once . . .*: Homer, *Iliad* iii. 380–2, v. 311 ff.

807 *the Father spoke*: this speech is modelled on Jupiter's speech of reassurance to Venus early in the *Aeneid* (i. 254 ff.), which, however, has a functional role quite lacking in Ovid's imitation.

810 *the archives of the world*: Ovid uses the technical word, *tabularia*. This celestial Record Office is of course his own invention, of a piece with 'heaven's Palatine' (i. 176 n.).

824 *a second time*: from Virgil onwards (*Georgics* i. 489 ff.) the poets persisted in writing as if the battlefields of Pharsalus (in Thessaly) and Philippi (in Macedonia) were one and the same.

825 *Pompey*: Sextus, youngest son of Magnus.

826 *The Egyptian consort*: Cleopatra, who with Antony fled from Augustus at Actium in 31 BC.

836 *the son*: Tiberius, born to Livia by her previous husband and adopted by Augustus (as indeed Octavian had been adopted by Julius).

867 *all ye other deities*: a customary safeguarding formula; cf. iv. 16 n.

EPILOGUE

871–9 EPILOGUE. Of surviving Latin epics only the *Metamorphoses* and Statius' *Thebaid* end with a formal coda. On the importance of these lines see Introd. xvi–xvii.

871 *the wrath of Jove*: the lightning; cf. above, l. 811. In the poems of exile Ovid constantly uses the image of Jupiter's thunderbolt when referring to his own punishment; and it is tempting to guess that these words may have been added at Tomis (iii. 142 n.).

GLOSSARY AND INDEX OF NAMES

THIS list includes all names of any importance. The references are to the pages on which they occur. As a guide to pronunciation, the stress is indicated by an accent; and in some instances two syllables are divided by a hyphen or the number of syllables is specified. Many names end in 'eus'; unless shown otherwise, this is one long syllable which rhymes with 'deuce', e.g. Orpheus. A final vowel, unless otherwise marked, is to be pronounced as a separate syllable, whether it follows another vowel or a consonant, e.g. Pasiphae and Penelope.

MAEÓNIA, an ancient name of Lydia, 68

MARS, god of war, son of Jove and Juno, 52, 55, 67, 79, 134, 276, 350, 378

MÁRSYAS, a Phrygian satyr and river; he challenged Apollo, 133

MEDÉA, daughter of Aeetes, king of Colchis, in love with Jason, an enchantress, 144–56

MEDÚSA, one of the Gorgons, 97, 106, 108, 124

MÉGARA, a city on the coast between Athens and Corinth, 171

MELEÁGER, prince of Calydon, son of Oeneus and Althaea, 179–88

MÉMNON, son of Tithonus and Aurora; the birds sprung from his ashes were the Memnonides, 312–13

MENELÁ-US, brother of Agamemnon, husband of Helen; king of Sparta, 300, 357, 376

MÉRCURY (Gr. Hermes), son of Jove and Maia; messenger of the gods, 21–2, 44–5, 46–9, 83, 109, 190, 258, 298, 334

MÉROPS, king of Ethiopia, husband of Clymene; putative father of Phaethon, 24–30

MÍDAS, king of Phrygia, 252–5

MILÉTUS, father of Caunus and Byblis, founder of the city that bears his name, 213

MINÉRVA (Gr. Pallas Athene), daughter of Jove, goddess of wisdom and technical skill, a virgin goddess, the patron goddess of Athens, 40, 45–8, 54, 75, 97–8, 100, 106–10, 121–2, 131, 133, 156, 179, 191, 285, 304, 315, 373

MÍNOS, son of Jove and Europa, king of Crete, husband of Pasiphae, 158, 171–6, 212–13

MÍNOTAUR, a monster, half-bull, half-man, 175–6

MÍNYAS, DAUGHTERS OF, changed to bats, 74, 86

MÓLY, a magic plant, 334

MÓPSUS, a soothsayer of the Lapiths, son of Ampycus, 181–2, 288–90

MÓRPHEUS, son of Sleep, 268–9

MÚLCIBER, a name for Vulcan (See Vulcan)

MÚSES, nine goddesses, patronesses of the arts, 106–9, 119, 121, 229, 370

MYCÉNAE, a city in Argolis, home of Agamemnon, 134, 364

MÝRMIDONS, men created from ants, 163–4

MÝRRHA, incestuous daughter of Cinyras, 234–41

MÝSCELUS, son of Alemon of Argos, founder of Crotona, 352–3

MÝSIA, a country in Asia Minor, 31, 360

NAÍADS, water-nymphs, female deities of springs and rivers, 20–1, 34, 66, 75, 83, 131, 135, 189, 201, 219, 225, 241, 250, 335, 342, 349

NARCÍSSUS, son of the river-god Cephisus and the Naiad Liriope, 61–6

NÁXOS, the largest island of the Cyclades, 70

NÉLEUS, son of Neptune and the nymph Tyro; king of Pylos, 45, 134, 290–1

NÉMESIS, a Greek goddess, who personifies the righteous anger of the gods and punishes the pride of mortals, 63, 346

NÉPTUNE, god of the sea, brother of Jupiter and Pluto, 9, 11, 32, 41, 90, 98, 123–4, 189, 197, 244, 255, 274, 291

NÉRE-IDS, sea-nymphs, daughters of Nereus, 10, 99, 261, 277, 299, 317, 321–2, 333

NÉREUS, a sea-god, husband of Doris; his fifty daughters included Thetis and Galatea, 32, 257, 260, 274, 277, 317

NÉSSUS, a centaur, 202–3

NÉSTOR, king of Pylos, famous for his wisdom, eloquence, and age, 180, 182, 279, 290–1, 296

NILE, the great river of Egypt, 13, 22, 32, 104, 109, 223, 375

NÍOBE, wife of Amphion, king of Thebes, mother of seven sons and seven daughters, 125–30

NÍSUS, king of Megara, father of Scylla, 171–5

NÓNACRIS, a city and mountain in Arcadia, 21, 36

NÚMA, the second king of Rome, 352, 366

NYCTÍMENE, daughter of Epopeus, changed into an owl, 42

OCEAN (OCÉANUS), the all-encircling sea, a deity, husband of Tethys, 1, 39, 98, 152, 214, 280, 324, 352, 377

OCÝRHO-E, daughter of Chiron, changed into a mare, 43–4

OÉNEUS, king of Calydon, husband of Althaea, father of Meleager, 179, 186

OÉTA, a mountain range in southern Thessaly, 10, 31, 204–6

OLÝMPUS, a mountain in Thessaly, supposed to be the home of the gods, 5, 7, 26, 31, 151, 214, 318

ÓRCHAMUS, king of Babylonia, father of Leucothoe, 80

ORITHÝIA, sister of Procris, wife of Boreas, 142–3, 165

ÓRPHEUS, musician and poet of Thrace, son of Apollo and Calliope, husband of Eurydice, 225–8, 249–52

ÓSSA, a mountain in Thessaly, 5, 31, 151, 283

ÓTHRYS, a mountain in Thessaly, 31, 151, 155, 279, 289

PACTÓLUS, a river in Lydia, famous for its gold, 121, 251

PALAMÉDES, son of Nauplius, a leader of the Greeks in the Trojan War, 295, 303

PÁLATINE, one of the seven hills of Rome (three syllables), 344, 368

PÁLLAS, a name of the Greek goddess Athene, whose Roman name was Minerva; in the poem Pallas and Minerva are used interchangeably. *See Minerva*

PAN, the god of woods and shepherds, 22, 253–4, 341, 344

PANDÍON, king of Athens, father of Procne and Philomela, son of Erichthonius, 134, 142, 364

PÁNDROSOS, a daughter of Cecrops, 41, 46

PÁPHOS, a city of Cyprus, 234, 242, 292

PÁRIS, son of Priam and Hecuba, brother of Hector, 274, 300, 376

The Oxford World's Classics Website

www.worldsclassics.co.uk

- Information about new titles
- Explore the full range of Oxford World's Classics
- Links to other literary sites and the main OUP webpage
- Imaginative competitions, with bookish prizes
- Peruse *Compass*, the Oxford World's Classics magazine
- Articles by editors
- Extracts from Introductions
- A forum for discussion and feedback on the series
- Special information for teachers and lecturers

www.worldsclassics.co.uk

American Literature

British and Irish Literature

Children's Literature

Classics and Ancient Literature

Colonial Literature

Eastern Literature

European Literature

History

Medieval Literature

Oxford English Drama

Poetry

Philosophy

Politics

Religion

The Oxford Shakespeare

A complete list of Oxford Paperbacks, including Oxford World's Classics, OPUS, Past Masters, Oxford Authors, Oxford Shakespeare, Oxford Drama, and Oxford Paperback Reference, is available in the UK from the Academic Division Publicity Department, Oxford University Press, Great Clarendon Street, Oxford OX2 6DP.

In the USA, complete lists are available from the Paperbacks Marketing Manager, Oxford University Press, 198 Madison Avenue, New York, NY 10016.

Oxford Paperbacks are available from all good bookshops. In case of difficulty, customers in the UK can order direct from Oxford University Press Bookshop, Freepost, 116 High Street, Oxford OX1 4BR, enclosing full payment. Please add 10 per cent of published price for postage and packing.